the me I **want** to be

Resources by John Ortberg

An Ordinary Day with Jesus
(curriculum series, with Ruth Haley Barton)

Everybody's Normal Till You Get to Know Them
(book, audio)

God Is Closer Than You Think
(book, audio, curriculum with Stephen and Amanda Sorenson)

If You Want to Walk on Water, You've Got to Get Out of the Boat
(book, audio, curriculum with Stephen and Amanda Sorenson)

Know Doubt
(book, formerly entitled *Faith and Doubt*)

The Life You've Always Wanted
(book, audio, curriculum with Stephen and Amanda Sorenson)

Living the God Life

Love Beyond Reason

Old Testament Challenge
(curriculum series, with Kevin and Sherry Harney)

When the Game Is Over, It All Goes Back in the Box
(book, audio, curriculum with Stephen and Amanda Sorenson)

the me I **want** to be

» becoming God's best version of you

john ortberg

ZONDERVAN®

ZONDERVAN.com/
AUTHORTRACKER
follow your favorite authors

ZONDERVAN

The Me I Want to Be
Copyright © 2010 by John Ortberg

This title is also available as a Zondervan ebook.
Visit www.zondervan.com/ebooks.

This title is also available in a Zondervan audio edition.
Visit www.zondervan.fm.

Requests for information should be addressed to:

Zondervan, Grand Rapids, Michigan 49530

Library of Congress Cataloging-in-Publication Data

Ortberg, John.
        The me I want to be : becoming God's best version of you / John Ortberg.
            p. cm.
        ISBN 978-0-310-27592-3 (hardcover, jacketed)
            1. Self-actualization (Psychology) — Religious aspects – Christianity. 2. Christian
    life. I. Title.
        BV4598.2O68 2009
        248.4 — dc22   2009040163

All Scripture quotations, unless otherwise indicated, are taken from the Holy Bible, *Today's New International Version™*, *TNIV®*. Copyright © 2001, 2005 by Biblica, Inc.™ Used by permission of Zondervan. All rights reserved worldwide.

Other translations used are the *New International Version* (NIV), the *New American Standard Bible* (NASB), the King James Version (KJV), the *New Revised Standard Version* (NRSV), the *New Living Translation* (NLT), the *Modern Language Bible* (MLB), the Living Bible (TLB), and *The Message*.

Any internet addresses (websites, blogs, etc.) and telephone numbers printed in this book are offered as a resource. These are not intended in any way to be or imply an endorsement by Zondervan, nor does Zondervan vouch for the content of these sites and numbers for the life of this book.

Cover and Interior Design: Lindsay Lang Sherbondy with Heartland Community Church Interior Design Management: Ben Fetterley

Printed in the United States of America

09 10 11 12 13 14 15 16 • 20 19 18 17 16 15 14 13 12 11 10 9 8 7 6 5 4 3 2 1

contents

acknowledgments

Love is eternal. What we achieve and possess may fade, but not love.

Books are gifts when they are acts of love. To what extent this book will be a gift only God knows, but I know that it would not have come into existence without much love from people who matter a great deal to me.

It started with a conversation on a golf course, when a few friends talked about a dream of creating a kind of movement for spiritual growth, and I talked about a book I hoped to write, and we wondered if what we hoped to do might intersect. What you hold is what we hope will be the first milepost on a long journey.

I am deeply grateful to Mark Bankford for his ceaseless encouragement and partnering and optimism and prayer. Sherri Bankord has offered wisdom and feedback; Eric Parks has been a fountain of energy and ideas; Nate May and Kevin Small have added enthusiasm and dreams; Elizabeth Maring and the entire Monvee team have been like working with family. Heartland Community Church in Rockford, Illinois, gave me chances to teach on much of this material and get voluminous feedback that sharpened it enormously.

To Menlo Park Presbyterian Church, I am grateful beyond words for love and shepherding and the freedom to write.

Laura (formerly Ortberg) Turner read through the entire manuscript and made hugely helpful suggestions about content, references, and presentation. I am glad you're a "J." Rick Blackmon has made amazingly generous contributions of his time and thoughts on the writing and beyond. Chuck Bergstrom gave both feedback and laughter. Ron Johnson gave wonderful insights on the structure and thoughts of the manuscript, and he cheered me on when I needed it most. My sister, Barbara Harrison, gave me a boost at just the right time.

I am grateful to Lindsay Lang and her team for creating visual illustrations that help illumine content with clarity and flair.

Trudi Barnes was helpful in a thousand ways. John Sloan and David Greene gave twice as much editorial panache as any writer could reasonably expect, and Jim Ruark did his usual excellent job of bringing clarity and life. John Topliff went above and beyond in helping create a unique partnership between a whole team of us involved in this project.

Neil Plantinga was kind enough to offer a long conversation about sin and spirit; I am lucky to get to talk to him. Dallas Willard gave more wisdom than any human being has a right to, as well as more love than I have a right to; his life is one of the reasons I believe.

And to my wife, Nancy—I have never needed you more deeply or loved you more fully than in this season.

PART ONE
finding my identity
»

Chapter 1

Learn Why God Made You

One evening my wife, Nancy, pulled me into our bedroom and said she wanted to talk. She closed the door so that none of the kids could hear, and she took out a list.

I was not happy to see a list. She claims it was an index card, not a list. But it had words written on it, so to me that's a list.

"You know," she said, "when our marriage is at its best, I feel we share responsibilities. We divide our work well and our kids see us do that and I feel valued, and I think that's important for our family. But for some time, because you feel so many demands on your life, this value has been slipping.

"When our marriage is working well, I also feel like we both know each other's lives. You know details about my life and I know details about yours. And I feel like that's been slipping too. Lately I know what's going on with you, but you don't ask me much about what's going on with me." She went on.

"When our marriage is at its best, you also bring a kind of lightness and joy to it." Then she reminded me of a story.

We were on our second date, in the lobby of the Disneyland Hotel waiting to get something to eat, and she had to use the restroom. When she came out, there were scores of people in the lobby, and I was in a goofy mood, so I said loudly enough for them all to hear, "Woman, I can't believe you kept me waiting for *two hours.*"

Her immediate response was, "Well, I wouldn't have to if you didn't insist on having your mother live with us so I have to wait on her hand and foot every day." She yelled that, right across the lobby, on only our *second* date, and my first thought was, *I like this woman.*

Nancy told me that story and said, "You know, when our marriage is at its best, you can listen and laugh and be spontaneous. You haven't been doing that for a while. I love that guy and I miss that guy."

I knew what she was talking about.

"I miss that guy too," I told her. "I'd love to feel free like that. But I feel like I'm carrying so many burdens. I have personnel issues and financial challenges at work. I have writing projects and travel commitments. I feel like I'm carrying this weight all the time. I get what you're saying, but I need you to know, I'm doing the best I can."

"No, you're not," she responded immediately.

That was not the response I had anticipated. Everybody is supposed to nod their head sympathetically when you say, "I'm doing the best I can." But Nancy loves truth (and me) too much to do that. So she rang my bell.

"No, you're *not.* You've talked about how it would be good to see a counselor, or an executive coach, or maybe a spiritual director. You've talked about building friendships, but I haven't seen you take steps toward any of that. No, you're not."

As soon as she said that I knew she was right.

But I didn't say that to her immediately because my spiritual gift is pouting, which I exercised beautifully over the next few days. As I did, a question emerged in my mind: *What is it that you really want?*

I began to realize that what I really want isn't any particular outcome on any particular project. Those are all just means to an end. What I really want is to be fully alive inside. What I really want is the inner freedom to live in love and joy.

I want to be that man she described.

I'm a grown man, I thought. *I do not know how many years of life are before me. I cannot wait anymore.* When I was going to school, I was preoccupied with good grades or getting cute girls to like me. As the years went by, I became preoccupied with work and my circumstances because I thought they would make me feel alive. *I can't wait anymore to be that man*, I thought.

I realized this then, and I know it now: I want that life more than I want anything else. Not because I think I'm supposed to, not because it says somewhere that you should. I want it.

There is a me I want to be.

Life is not about any particular achievement or experience. The most important task of your life is not what you do, but who you become.

There is a me you want to be.

Ironically, becoming this person will never happen if my primary focus is on me, just as no one becomes happy if their main goal is to be happy. God made you to flourish, but flourishing never happens by looking out for "number one." It is tied to a grander and nobler vision. The world badly needs wise and flourishing human beings, and we are called to bring God's wisdom and glory to the world. The truth is, those who flourish always bring blessing to others — and they can do so in the most unexpected and humble circumstances.

» One Flourishing Life

Not long ago I boarded an airport shuttle bus to get to the rental car lot. Driving a shuttle bus is usually a thankless job, for the driver is often regarded as the low man on the totem pole. People on the bus are often grumpy from travel and in a hurry to get to their car. No one says much except the name of their rental car company. But not on this bus.

The man who drove the bus was an absolute delight. He was scanning the curbside, looking for anybody who needed a ride. "You know," he told us, "I'm always looking because sometimes people are running late. You can tell it in their eyes. I'm always looking because I never want to miss one. Hey, here's another one! . . ."

The driver pulled over to pick up a latecomer, and he was so excited about what he was doing that *we* got excited. We were actually cheering him on when he was picking people up. It was like watching Jesus drive a shuttle bus. The man would grab people's luggage before they could lift it, then he would jump back on the bus and say, "Well we're off. I know you're all eager to get there as quickly as possible, so I'm going to get you there as soon as I can."

Jaded commuters put down their papers. He created such a little community of joy on that bus that people wanted to ride around in the terminal a second time just to hang out with the guy. We would say to people who got on after us, "Watch this guy!" He wasn't just our shuttle bus driver—he was our leader; he was our friend. And for a few moments, community flourished. On a shuttle bus for a rental car company—and one person moved toward the best version of himself.

What happened to that shuttle bus driver can happen in you. Sometimes it does. Every once in a while you do something that surprises you and catch a glimpse of the person you were made to be. You say something inspirational at a meeting. You help a homeless man no one else notices. You are patient with a rambunctious three-year-old. You lose yourself in a piece of music. You fall in love. You express compassion. You stand up to a bully. You freely make a sacrificial gift. You fix an engine. You forgive an old hurt. You say something you would normally never say, or you keep from saying something you would normally blurt out.

As you do, you glimpse for a moment why God made you. Only God knows your full potential, and he is guiding you toward that best version of yourself all the time. He has many tools and is never in a hurry. That can be frustrating for us, but even in our frustration, God is at work to produce patience in us. He never gets discouraged by how long it takes, and he delights every time you grow. Only God can see the "best version of you," and he is more concerned with you reaching your full potential than you are.

> For we are God's handiwork, created in Christ Jesus to do good
> works, which God prepared in advance for us to do.

You are not *your* handiwork; your life is not your project. Your life is *God's* project. God thought you up, and he knows what you were intended to be. He has many good works for you to do, but they are not the kind of "to do" lists we give spouses or employees. They are signposts to your true self.

Your "spiritual life" is not limited to certain devotional activities that you engage in. It is receiving power from the Spirit of God to become the person God had in mind when he created you—his handiwork.

» Where Growth Leads

God made you to flourish—to receive life from outside yourself, creating vitality within yourself and producing blessing beyond yourself. Flourishing is God's gift and plan, and when you flourish you are in harmony with God, other people, creation, and yourself. Flourishing is not measured by outward signs such as income, possessions, or attractiveness. It means becoming the person *he* had in mind in creating you.

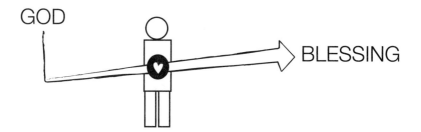

Flourishing means moving toward God's best version of you.

> "The righteous will flourish like a palm tree.... they will flourish in the courts of our God." (Psalm 92:12–13)

As God helps you grow, you will change, but you will always be you. An acorn can grow into an oak tree, but it cannot become a rose bush. It can be a healthy oak or it can be a stunted oak — but it won't be a shrub. You will always be you — a growing, healthy you or a languishing you — but God did not create you to be anybody else. He pre-wired your temperament. He determined your natural gifts and talents. He made you to feel certain passions and desires. He planned your body and mind. Your uniqueness is God-designed.

Some people think that if they seek to grow spiritually they will have to become someone else. But God won't discard your raw material. He redirects it. Before Paul met Jesus, he was a brilliant, passionate zealot who persecuted people. Afterward, he was a brilliant, passionate zealot who sacrificed himself for people.

Some friends of ours had a daughter named Shauna who was a classic strong-willed child. When she was four years old, she kept trying to go AWOL on her tricycle. Her mom could not rein her in and finally said, "Look, Shauna, there's a tree right here, and there's a driveway right there. You can ride your tricycle on the sidewalk in between the driveway and the tree, but you can't go past that. If you go past that, you will get a spanking. I have to be inside; I've got stuff to do. But I'm going to be watching you. Don't go past either one of those boundaries, or you're going to get a spanking."

Shauna backed up to her mom, pointed to her spanking zone, and said, "Well, you might as well spank me now, because I got places to go."

Would it surprise you to learn that when Shauna grew up, she had formidable leadership capacities and an indomitable drive? She always will have them.

God doesn't make anything and then decide to throw it away. He creates, and then, if there is a problem, he rescues. Redemption always involves the redemption of creation. The psalmist says, "Know that the LORD Himself is God. It is He who made us, and not we ourselves."

Here is the good news: When you flourish, you become more you. You become more that person God had in mind when he thought you up. You don't just become holier. You become you-ier. You will change; God wants you to become a "new creation." But "new" doesn't mean completely different; instead, it's like an old piece of furniture that gets restored to its intended beauty.

I used to have a chair my grandfather helped build seventy years ago. I loved it, but its arms were broken, the wood was chipped, and the upholstery was worn through. I finally gave up on it and sold it for fifty cents at a garage sale. The person who bought it knew about restoration, and a few months later I received a picture of it—repaired, refinished, revarnished, and reupholstered. I wish this was one of those stories where the restorer surprises the clueless owner by giving him back his now-glorious chair. But all I have is this alluring picture. Still, I keep the picture taped inside my desk drawer to remind me that "if anyone is in Christ, the new creation has come. The old is gone! The new is here!"

> ✱ Redemption always involves the redemption of creation.

God wants to redeem you, not exchange you. If you're a bookish, contemplative type, waiting for God to change you into the kind of person who wears lampshades on your head at parties, good luck on that. Maybe you are a raging extrovert, tired of putting your foot in your mouth all the time. Don't you wish you could become more like those of us who are introverted: wise, calm, and restrained? It's never going to happen.

Too bad—we all wish it could.

It is humbling that I cannot be anything I want. I don't get to create myself. I accept myself as God's gift to me and accept becoming that person as God's task set before me. Inside your soul there is a battle between a flourishing self—the person you were created to be—and a languishing self. This book is all about that battle as it moves from deep inside you to a world waiting for God's redemption.

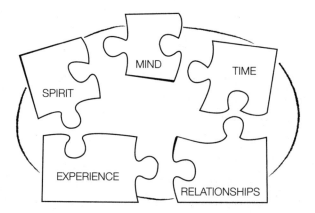

The journey begins with your *spirit*, which becomes empowered by God's Spirit. Every human being has had the sense of receiving ideas or energy from a source beyond ourselves. We speak of being *in-spired*, a Spirit-word that literally means something has been breathed into us. This means that flourishing—being connected with the Spirit of God—is available all the time. When your spirit flourishes, you are most fully alive. You have a purpose for living. You are drawn to put on virtue and put off sin.

Then there is your *mind*. The mental life of your flourishing self is marked by joy and peace. You are curious and love to learn. You do this in your own unique way by reading, talking with people, listening, building, or leading. You ask questions. You are not easily bored. When negative emotions arise, you take them as cues to act.

Your languishing self, on the other hand, feels uneasy and discontent inside. You find yourself drawn to bad habits—watching too much TV, drinking too much alcohol, misusing sex, or excess spending—because they anesthetize pain. In the languishing self, thoughts drift toward fear or anger. Learning does not feel worth the effort. You think about yourself a good deal.

Along with your spirit and mind, when you flourish, your *time* begins to be transformed as well. You have confidence that whatever life throws at you will not overthrow you. When the day dawns, you awake with a sense of expectancy. You have a vibrant sense that *things matter.* You begin to receive each moment as a God-filled gift.

You realize you are never too young to flourish. Mozart was composing brilliant music when he was five. The apostle Paul told Timothy, "Don't let anyone look down on you because you are young." You are also never too old to flourish. Grandma Moses was sixty-nine when she took up painting, and Marc Chagall spent hours a day at his art in his nineties. A few years ago my dad hit seventy, and at seventy years old he started walking three miles a day. (Five years later, we have no idea where to find him.)

Your flourishing self pours blessings into your *relationships.* You find other people to be a source of wonder. They often bring you energy. When you are with them, you listen deeply. You are struck by their dreams. You bless. You are able to disclose your own thoughts and feelings in a way that invites openness in others. You quickly admit your errors, and you freely forgive.

Relationally, your languishing self is often troubled. You are undisciplined in what you say, sometimes reverting to sarcasm, sometimes to gossip, sometimes to flattery. You isolate. You dominate. You attack. You withdraw.

But as God grows you, he wants to use you in his plan to redeem his world, and you find him changing your *experiences.* Your flourishing self works out of a richness and a desire to contribute. You live with a sense of calling. How much money you make does not matter as much as doing what you love and what creates value. You become resilient in suffering. You get better. You grow.

What could you want more than to become the person God created you to be?

» The World God Wants to See

Here is a great secret of the Bible: Your longing to become all you were meant to be is a tiny echo of God's longing to begin the new creation. The rabbis spoke of this as *tikkun olam* — to fix the world. The more concerned you are about your own fulfillment, the less fulfilled you will be. When your life is devoted to yourself, it is as small as a grain of wheat. When your life is given to God, however, it is as if that grain is planted in rich soil, growing into part of a much bigger project.

The picture used at the end of the Bible is that of a wedding, a glimpse of what God has been up to all this time: "I saw the Holy City, the new Jerusalem, coming down out of heaven from God, prepared as a bride beautifully dressed for her husband." One day there will be glorious harmony between God and all that he has made. God wants no one left out. As you flourish, you help in God's re-creation of the world he wants to see.

My niece Courtney got married not long ago, and at the wedding reception they had a dance for married couples in which they would eliminate couples from the dance floor based on the length of their marriage. At the beginning we were all on the floor. Courtney and Patrick were the first to leave, then all the couples married less than one year left, then those married less than five years, and so on. Nancy and I made it to the twenty-five-year cut, and by that time the crowd had thinned out considerably.

Finally, there was only one couple left on the dance floor, and they had been married fifty-three years. Everybody watched them — a tall, courtly, silver-haired man who stood a foot taller than his wife — but they watched only each other. They danced with joy, not in the skill of their dancing, but in the love they radiated for each other. What a contrast between the newlyweds, fresh in the health and beauty of their marriage, and the beauty of another kind of love that shone from the last couple on the floor! Perhaps part of why we appreciate such beauty is that it speaks to us of an inner flourishing not visible to the eye.

When the dancing ended, the master of ceremonies turned to Courtney and Patrick and said to them, "Take a good look at that couple on that dance floor. Your task now is to live and love together in such a way that fifty-three years from now that's you. That dance is your dance. Now it begins."

At that moment we all were struck by the mystery of the brevity of life. When that bride of fifty-three years looked at her husband, she didn't just see an aging grandfather. She saw the young, tanned tennis champion she married five decades earlier. He did not see only a grandmother in her seventies. He saw the lovely, effervescent belle he had loved since she was a teenager. I know, because they are my parents, Courtney's grandparents. And I thought of how, to my mom and dad, their wedding probably seems like yesterday. Time is that way.

Life is that way.

I projected my thoughts to about fifty-three years from now, when Courtney and Patrick will have been married as long as that couple. In fifty-three years my mother and my father will be gone. Nancy will be gone. And I will be 105 years old.

I don't want to miss the dance. I get hung up on so many things in life, worrying about what I will never do or achieve or have. But I don't want to miss the dance. I want to love my wife, care for my kids, and give life to my friends. I want to do the work God made me to do. I want to love God and the world he made. I want to do my part to help it flourish, for my spiritual maturity is not measured by following rules. "The me God made me to be" is measured by my capacity to love. When we live in love, we flourish. That is the dance.

The time to love is now. When we love, we enter into the mystery of eternity. Nothing offered in love is ever lost, for this mortal life is not the whole story. This life is to the next a kind of school, a kind of preparation for the me you were meant to be. That person will go into eternity. What matters most is not what you accomplish; it is who you become.

"The Spirit and the bride say, 'Come!' And let all who hear say, 'Come!' " It is the last, best invitation in the Bible.

Don't miss the wedding, God says. *Save the last dance for me.*

in the flow

"How is your spiritual life going?"

I used to answer this question by looking at the state of my devotional activities: Did I pray and read the Bible enough today? The problem is that by this measure the Pharisees always win. People can be very disciplined, but remain proud and spiteful. How do we measure spiritual growth so that the Pharisees don't win?

I asked a wise man, "How do you assess the well-being of your soul?"

He immediately said, "I ask myself two questions":

≈ Am I growing more easily discouraged these days?
≈ Am I growing more easily irritated these days?

At the core of a flourishing soul are the love of God and the peace of God. If peace is growing in me, I am less easily discouraged. If love is growing, I am less easily irritated. It was a brilliantly helpful diagnostic to assess the health of my soul.

How would you answer those two questions?

For more personalized help, turn to page 51 and find out about an online spiritual growth tool called Monvee.

Chapter 2

The Me I Don't Want to Be

Henri Nouwen, a priest and teacher who moved in the exalted circles of Harvard and Yale and Notre Dame, came to believe that those settings did not—for him—call forth the person God intended him to be. So this famous writer spent the last decade of his life caring for physically and mentally challenged residents of a small community called L'Arche.

There Henri made friends with a resident named Trevor, who had many mental and emotional challenges. One time when Trevor was sent to a hospital for evaluation, Henri called to arrange a visit. When the authorities found out the famous Henri Nouwen was coming, they asked him if he would meet with some doctors, chaplains, and clergy. He agreed, and when he arrived, there was a lovely luncheon laid out in the Golden Room—but Trevor was not there.

"Where is Trevor?" Henri asked.

"He cannot come to the lunch," they told him. "Patients and staff are not allowed to have lunch together, and no patient has ever had lunch in the Golden Room."

"But the whole purpose of my visit was to have lunch with Trevor,"

Henri said. "If Trevor is not allowed to attend the lunch, then I will not attend either."

A way was found for Trevor to attend the lunch.

The Golden Room was filled with people who were quite excited that the great Henri Nouwen was in their midst. Some angled to be close to him. They thought of how wonderful it would be to tell their friends, "As I was saying to Henri Nouwen the other day...." Some pretended to have read books they had not read and know ideas they did not know. Others were upset that the rule separating patients and staff had been broken.

Trevor, oblivious to all this, sat next to Henri, who was engaged in conversation with the person on his other side. Consequently, Henri did not notice that Trevor had risen to his feet.

"A toast," Trevor said. "I will now offer a toast."

The room grew quiet. *What in the world is this guy going to do?* everyone wondered.

Then Trevor began to sing.

If you're happy and you know it, raise your glass.
If you're happy and you know it, raise your glass.
If you're happy and you know it, if you're happy and you know it,
If you're happy and you know it, raise your glass.

At first people were not sure how to respond, but Trevor was beaming. His face and voice told everyone how glad and proud he was to be there with his friend Henri. Somehow Trevor, in his brokenness and joy, gave a gift no one else in the room could give. People began to sing — softly at first, but then with more enthusiasm — until doctors and priests and PhDs were almost shouting, "If you're happy and you know it...."

All under the direction of Trevor.

No one was preening anymore. No one worried about the rules. No one tried to separate the PhDs from the ADDs. For a few moments, a room full of people moved toward the best version of themselves because a wounded healer named Henri Nouwen lived among the challenged, and because a challenged man named Trevor was living out the best version of himself.

We do not just drift into becoming the best version of ourselves. It can be missed by a genius, and it can be found by Trevor. If I want to become that person I want to be, I will have to come to grips with the counterfeits who elbow in to take his place — the rivals who can keep me from becoming the me I am meant to be.

» The Me I Pretend to Be

God designed you to be you. When your life is over, he will not ask you why you weren't Moses or David or Esther or Henri Nouwen or Trevor. If you don't pursue that life we are talking about, he will ask you why you weren't *you*. God designed us to *delight* in our actual lives. When I am growing toward the me I want to be, I am being freed from the me I pretend to be. I no longer try to convince people I am important while secretly fearing I am not.

A few years ago I had lunch with a man I don't know well. We spent two hours together, and he used the whole time for name-dropping — one name after another of important people he knew, successful people he had impressed, corporate executives he had influenced. What is amazing is not simply that he went on so long, but that he was so clueless. By the end of the lunch I felt drained and depressed. How could someone be so blind, so unaware?

Then I had a horrible thought: *If this man could be that blind, what about other people? What about me? Do I have that same problem and that same blindness?* I decided I had better ask a close friend, so I did the next week during lunchtime.

This woman and I decided that we both had that problem. So we tried an experiment. The next week both of us were attending a gathering with a group of people we regarded as important, and we decided to refrain from saying anything to make us look intelligent or accomplished. I was amazed at how little I had to say.

Sometimes the me I pretend to be leaks out in small acts of vanity. A freshly minted lieutenant wanted to impress the first private to enter his new office, and he pretended to be on the phone with a general so that the private would know he was somebody. "Yes sir, General, you can count on me," he said as he banged the receiver down. Then he asked the private what he wanted. "I'm just here to connect your phone, sir."

Pretending to be someone we're not is hard work, which is why we feel tired after a first date or a job interview or among others we feel we have to project an image for. We are drawn to transparency and long to go where we can just "be ourselves." It is a relief to not have to pretend to pray more than we really do, or know more about the Bible than we really know, or act more humble than we really are.

Inside us is a person without pretense or guile. We never have to pretend with God, and genuine brokenness pleases God more than pretend spirituality. If I am ever going to become the me I want to be, I have to start by being honest about the me I am.

» The Me I Think I *Should* Be

Comparison kills spiritual growth. A mother with three preschool-age children hears her pastor talk about loving God so much that he is up very early every morning to spend an hour of quiet with him. She would love an hour of quiet at any time, but her children simply will not cooperate. What she takes away is that she ought to be doing the same thing, and so she does spirituality by comparison, living under a cloud of guilt. It never occurs to her that the love she expresses to her children might "count" as a spiritual activity. It never occurs to her that perhaps she is serving God more faithfully than the very pastor who may be neglecting his wife and children in the morning so he can have that hour of quiet.

A gregarious, spontaneous husband is married to a woman who loves to be alone. Solitude comes easily for her; she would have to become more extroverted just to be a hermit. He feels he is a failure at prayer because he cannot be alone the way she can. It never occurs to him that his ability to love people "counts," that the way he loves people is shaping his soul and delighting God.

> Henri Nouwen wrote, "Spiritual greatness has nothing to do with being greater than others. It has everything to do with being as great as each of us can be."

Each one of us has a me that we think we *should* be, which is at odds with the me that God *made* us to be. Sometimes letting go of that self may be a relief. Sometimes it will feel like death.

I grew up with a need to think of myself as a leader, as stronger, more popular, more confident than I really was. I ran for class president because grown-up leaders would always say, "Even when I was in high school I was class president." I would think up good slogans and campaign hard—but I always lost. The truth is that I was more introverted, more bookish, and less of the "class president" type than I wanted anyone to think.

As I grew up, my need to be a leader kept me trying to be someone I wasn't. It made me more defensive, pressured, unhappy, and inauthentic in ways I didn't even know. To make matters worse, the person I married is one of those people who ran for school office—and always won. She didn't even have a good slogan: "Don't be fancy, vote for Nancy." (No, I'm not making that up. She actually *won* with that.)

Finally, around the age of forty, I went through six months of deep, internal emptiness and depression like none I had ever experienced. Nancy was involved in work exploding with growth, and I felt as if the trajectory of my life and work was destined to keep arcing downward. It led to a moment I will never forget.

I sat in the basement of our home and said to God, "I give up my need to be a leader." Out of me came a volcano of emotion—wrenching sobs. I felt all my dreams had died. All I knew was that holding onto my need to lead was wrecking my life. So I prayed, "I'll let it go. It's been my dream for so long, I don't know what's left. If I can't become this leader I thought I was supposed to be, I don't know what to do. But I'll try to do the best I can to let it go."

What I was really dying to was a false self, an illusion of misplaced pride, ego, and neediness—the me I thought I was *supposed* to be.

Should is an important word for spiritual growth, but God's plan is not for you to obey him because you *should* even though you don't want to. He made you to *want* his plan for you.

On the other side of death is freedom, and no one is more free than a dead man. Jesus had much to say about death to self, and on the journey to the me you want to be, you will have some dying to do. But that kind of death is always death to a lesser self, a false self, so that a better and nobler self can come to life.

» The Me Other People Want Me to Be

Everyone in your life wants you to change. Your boss wants you to be more productive. Your health club wants you to be more fit. Your credit card company wants you to be in more debt. Networks want you to watch more television, and restaurants want you to eat more food. Your dentist wants you to visit more often. Everybody has an agenda for you. This is the me other people want you to be.

If I spend my life trying to become *that* me, I will never be free. Loving people means being willing to disappoint them sometimes. Jesus loved everyone, but that means at some point he disappointed everyone. Seeking to become the me that other people want me to be is a hollow way to live. Nobody else can tell you exactly how to change because nobody but God knows.

When Nelson Mandela was imprisoned on Robbins Island for his opposition to South Africa's apartheid, he was issued a pair of shorts — not long trousers — because his captors wanted his identity to be that of a *boy* instead of a man. People in power over him wanted him to be a docile accepter of a racist society. Angry people who suffered with him wanted him to be a vengeful hater of their oppressors.

Mandela was neither. During twenty-seven years in prison, he suffered and learned and grew. He called his prison "the University." He became both increasingly committed to justice and opposed to hate, and by the end of his captivity, even his guards were won over by his life. The final official charged to watch him used to cook Mandela gourmet meals. When he went from Prisoner Mandela to President Mandela, he sought to lead the country to peace through the Truth and Reconciliation Commission, established on the biblical principle that "the truth shall make you free."

God didn't make you to be Nelson Mandela. He made you to be you — and no human being in your life gets the final word on who God made you to be.

Even you can't tell yourself how to change, because you didn't create you. To love someone is to desire and work toward their becoming the best version of themselves. The one person in all the universe who can do this perfectly for you is God. He has no other agenda. He has no unmet needs he is hoping you can help him with. And he *knows* what the best version of you looks like. He delighted in the idea of it, and he is already working on it. The apostle Paul said, "We know that in all things God works for the good of those who love him."

Which means God is at work every moment to help you become his best version of you.

» The Me I'm Afraid God Wants

A recent study by the Barna Group found that the number one challenge to helping people grow spiritually is that most people equate spiritual maturity with trying hard to follow the rules in the Bible. No wonder people also said they find themselves unmotivated to pursue spiritual growth. If I think God's aim is to produce rule-followers, spiritual growth will always be an obligation rather than a desire of my heart.

"Rule-keeping does not naturally evolve into living by faith," Paul wrote, "but only perpetuates itself in more and more rule-keeping." In other words, it only results in a rule-keeping, desire-smothering, Bible-reading, emotion-controlling, self-righteous person who is not like *me*. In the end, I cannot follow God if I don't trust that he really has my best interests at heart.

The letter kills, but the Spirit gives life. There is an enormous difference between following rules and following Jesus, because I can follow rules without cultivating the right heart.

A friend of mine recently graduated from one of the service academies where they are very serious about the "clean your room" rule. Sometimes my friend got ink marks on the wall that would not come out, so he would chip the plaster off. The inspectors would give demerits for ink marks, but they figured missing chunks of plaster was a construction problem. The "rules" ended up encouraging the slow demolition of the room.

Jesus did not say, "I have come that you might follow the rules." He said, "I have come that you might have life, and have it with abundance." When we cease to understand spiritual growth as moving toward God's best version of ourselves, the question, *how is your spiritual life going?* frightens us. A nagging sense of guilt and a deficit of grace prompt us to say, "Not too well. Not as good as I should be doing." People often use external behaviors and devotional practices to measure their spiritual health. They measure their spiritual life by how early they are getting up to read the Bible, or how long their quiet times are, or how often they attend church services. But that is not what spiritual formation is about.

» The Me That Fails to Be

We have been overrun by what a friend of mine calls TLAs (three-letter acronyms), and the most memorable one I've ever heard of comes from the field of medicine: FTT.

My wife first introduced me to those initials. Trained to be a nurse, Nancy still loves diagnosing people. She is constantly telling me her private diagnoses of people — even total strangers — based on their skin color. If she gets a long look at your face and the light is good, she can pretty much tell you how long you have to live. But of all the diagnoses I ever heard her discuss, FTT is the one that sticks in my mind. It gets entered into the chart of an infant who, often for unknown reasons, is unable to gain weight or grow.

what is spiritual formation?

There is an outer you — your body — that is being shaped all the time by the way you eat, drink, sleep, exercise, and live. You may do this well or poorly, intentionally or not, but it *will* happen. Then there is an inner you — your thoughts, desires, will, and character. This is being shaped all the time by what you see, read, hear, think, and do. We can call this inner you the spirit.

Spiritual formation is the process by which your inner self and character are shaped.

People sometimes speak as if spiritual formation is an optional activity that some religious people may pursue and others bypass. They think it is reserved for monks, mystics, and missionaries. But that's not true.

Everyone has a spirit. *Everyone's* inner life is being formed — for better or worse.

We flourish when our spirits are rooted in and shaped by the Spirit of God — and God wants to do that in a way that uniquely fits us.

Failure to thrive.

Sometimes, doctors guess, failure to thrive happens when a parent or caregiver is depressed and the depression seems to get passed down. Sometimes something seems to be off in an infant's metabolism for reasons no one can understand, so FTT is one of those mysterious phrases that sounds like an explanation but explains nothing.

Psychologists have begun to speak of what is perhaps the largest mental health problem in our day. It is not depression or anxiety, at least not at clinical levels. It is languishing — a failure to thrive.

Languishing is the condition of someone who may be able to function but has lost a sense of hope and meaning. Languishing is not the presence of mental illness; it is the absence of mental and emotional vitality. In ancient lists of deadly sins it was called *acedia*—weariness of soul and inability to delight in life. We speak of dead marriages and dead-end jobs, and to languish is to feel inner deadness. Languishing is the opposite of flourishing, and it was the fear of Henry David Thoreau that "when I came to die, [I would] discover that I had not lived."

Often people have dreams for their life when they are young, but over time they simply give up. Writer and artist Gordan MacKenzie tells of visiting children in kindergarten and asking them, "Who is an artist?" Every hand shoots up. This decreases to half the class by third grade. By the time the students are twelve years old, only a few hands go up. Over time many find that becoming the me they were meant to be is too hard or that it takes too long. When we give up on our growth and life's purpose, we languish.

But there is a person inside of you waiting to come alive.

» The Me I Am Meant to Be

God showed the prophet Ezekiel a vision of languishing: a valley full of dry bones. It was the image of a failure to thrive. God asked Ezekiel, "Can these bones live?" and Ezekiel answered, "You alone know." God did know, and he made them come alive.

I know a man named Tim who was an addict, lost his family, lost everything, found God, gave up his addiction, and got his life back again. I know a man named Peter who was a tormented slave to sexual impulses, and God got ahold of him and that changed. I know of a woman who hated confrontation so badly she once drove on an extended road trip with her best friend for three days in silence to avoid confrontation. Today she confronts recreationally.

God wants you to grow! He created the very idea of growth. The Talmud says that every blade of grass has an angel bending over it, whispering, "Grow, grow." Paul said that in Christ the whole redeemed community "grows and builds itself up in love."

Your flourishing is never just about you. It is a "so that" kind of condition. God designed you to flourish "so that" you could be part of his redemptive project in ways that you otherwise could not. He wants you to flourish "so that" people can be encouraged, gardens can be planted,

have life

Jesus said, "I have come that they may have life, and have it to the full." We may have heard that without understanding what Jesus offers. When he says he has come to "give life," what *exactly* does he mean?

We all feel that we know what life is when we see it, but life turns out to be surprisingly tricky to define. So we might start here: *Life is the inner power to make something happen.*

Throw a rock, and it soon stops moving. But put a seed in the ground, and something happens — it sends out a root, takes in nourishment, and grows up to be fruitful. To be spiritually alive means to receive power from God to have a positive impact on your world.

What are some ways God gives life and vitality to you? How can you build these into your life and schedule?

- Nature
- Spiritual friendships
- Worship
- Solitude
- Serving
- Study
- Leading
- Art
- Rest
- Celebration
- Scripture
- Recreation
- Exercise
- Family
- Long talks
- Laughter
- Leading a cause
- Retreat
- Small group
- Other

Saint Irenaeus wrote, "The glory of God is a human being fully alive; and to be alive consists in beholding God."

music can be written, sick people can be helped, or companies can thrive in ways they otherwise would not. When you fail to become the person God designed, all the rest of us miss out on the gift you were made to give.

Jesus once said that with God, all things are possible, and the great thing about life with God is that your next step is always possible. That step toward God is always waiting, no matter what you have done or how you have messed up your life. Jesus was hanging on a cross with a thief hanging next to him, and Jesus turned to him and said, "Today you will be with me in paradise."

There is always a next step.

So I propose a toast: "Here's to Trevor. And to Henri. And to the me you want to be."

PART TWO
flowing with the spirit
»

Chapter 3

Discover the Flow

A flourishing life *is* possible.

After the conversation with my wife about "the list," I kept thinking about how I don't want to wait for circumstances to change in order to live the way I was meant to live. I just have to want it more than I want anything else. I usually allow myself to be preoccupied or pulled in multiple directions because I think I have to devote little chunks of my mind to worrying about how I will solve some problem or finish some project, as if success with them will make me happy and free.

The truth is, a life of freedom and joy is available right now. My main job is to remain connected to God. When my primary focus is being present with him, everything else has a way of falling into place. When my primary focus becomes anything else, my inner vitality suffers, and I become a lesser version of myself.

On vacation one summer, my wife — a veteran water-skier — was teaching our family to water ski. I had only water-skied once or twice before, so it took several trips to feel any confidence at all. I decided I wanted to try using only one ski, but the boat could not generate enough power for me to get up out of the water.

Back in the boat, I noticed a button labeled "power-tilt." I know nothing about boats or engines, but it seemed like a promising button, so we gave it a shot. I heard a whirring sound, which I later learned was the propeller being driven much deeper under the water.

I got back behind the boat, balanced precariously on one ski, and yelled to Nancy, "Hit it!"

The bow of the boat lifted out of the water at a 45-degree angle and moved as if it had been shot out of a cannon. Adequate power to get my body up out of the water was not a problem. Survival was. I gestured wildly for the boat to slow down. However, we had not prearranged signals, and my kids interpreted my waving as a desire to go faster, so they revved the boat full throttle. I was not just up, but was bouncing through the air between landings like a rock skipping across a smooth lake. It did not occur to me to let go of the rope. I eventually came down on my face.

For six months I could not smile with the right side of my mouth.

But I did find out I could ski. I just needed power.

Trying to become the person you were made to be through your own effort is like trying to ski behind a rowboat. We need a "power-tilt" for the soul. Where do we look?

Jesus made staggering promises about his ability to transform human lives:

> "Let anyone who is thirsty come to me and drink. Whoever believes in me, as Scripture has said, streams of living water will flow from within them." By this he meant the Spirit, whom those who believed in him were later to receive.

The King James Bible states it this way: "Out of his belly will flow rivers of living water." The belly is the deepest place inside you — the place where you get anxious or afraid, where you feel hollow or empty when you are disappointed. The Greek word is *koilia*, and we speak of getting *colitis* when rivers of stress run in our belly. Scientists say we have a reptile brain — a "brain in the gut" — that is, neurons in the digestive system that produce feelings of well-being or threat deeper than we can put into words. It is in that very deepest place that Jesus says he will produce vitality.

This life is not something we produce; it exists independently of us. It is the Spirit of God. If we turn to any book in the New Testament, we see a picture of amazing life offered by Jesus through the Spirit.

> "You will receive power when the Holy Spirit comes on you."

Though you have not seen him [Jesus], you love him ... and are filled with an inexpressible and glorious joy.

"Take my yoke upon you and learn from me, for I am gentle and humble in heart, and you will find rest for your souls."

Would you say this describes you? Are you filled with inexpressible joy? Do other people comment from time to time that your belly is flowing with rivers of living water and that you have more or less mastered humility?

I will tell you what I think happens. I think that often people are moved by the vision of Jesus, they are overwhelmed by the hope and beauty of his promise, and they say yes to it. For a time, there is a kind of spiritual honeymoon period. They are filled with love for God, and they are drawn to the Bible. They want to tell other people about their faith. They love to worship. And some things change. Maybe coarse language gets cleaned up. Maybe certain habits get overcome.

But over time this sense of progress stalls out. Instead of life flowing with rivers of living water, I yell at my children whom I love. I worry too much about money or my job. I grow jealous. I use deception to get out of trouble or to get what I want. I pass judgment on people easily, casually, arrogantly. My prayer life is up and down. I am stuck in a gap.

God's plan is for you to become the best version of you, but right now there are two versions of you. There is the you God made you to be — and there is the you that currently exists.

What do you do with the gap?

» Gap Management

Our problem is that we think we have to close the gap through our own ingenuity. Some people think if they just try harder, they can close the gap between the me God made them to be and the me that currently exists. They think they are simply not being heroic enough in their spiritual effort. "I'll read another book. I'll listen to another talk. I'll learn some new disciplines. I'll serve more. I'll work harder. I'll try to be nicer to the people in my life."

You hear about someone who gets up at four o'clock in the morning to pray, and you feel guilty because you think you don't pray enough. So you resolve to do that too, even though you are not a "morning person" — at four o'clock you are dazed and confused and groggy and grumpy, and no one wants to be around you at that time of the morning. Even Jesus doesn't want to be around you at four in the morning. But you think, *Well, this is exhausting and miserable — I certainly don't like doing it — so it must be God's will for my life. It must be spiritual.* You keep it up for several days or weeks or months, but not forever. Eventually you stop. Then you feel guilty. After enough guilt, you start doing something else.

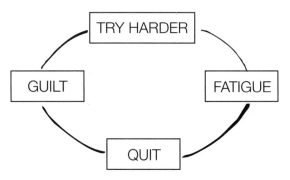

Sometimes we manage the gap by pretending. We learn to fake it. We speak as if we had had deeper spiritual experiences than we really have, as though our sin bothers us more than it really does. We pray as though our voice is throbbing with an emotion that we really have to generate ourselves. Sometimes we play spiritual musical chairs, always searching for a different church or tradition or spirituality that has the magic key. Some people flit from one spiritual experience to another, continually rededicating their lives to God and then falling away, hoping to recapture the emotions they felt when they first met God. Some people quietly, secretly give up. They still hope they will go to heaven when they die, but between now and then they have been disappointed too often to expect change any more. They have gotten used to languishing.

At the beginning of our life with God, we are aware of a gap between God and us, separation from God because of sin.

We come to understand that we cannot bridge this gap by our efforts or good behavior. We cannot earn God's love and forgiveness; it comes only by God's grace. Salvation is given by the grace of God,

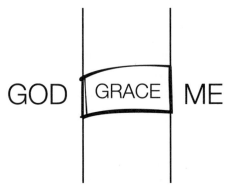

achieved through the power of God, offered through the Spirit of God, and made secure by the promise of God. And so we commit our life to God.

But there is still a gap.

Now the gap is between the me I am right now and the me I'm meant to be — "current me" and "sanctified me." But here's the problem: People think it is our job to bridge that gap by our effort. But we can't. This gap, too, can only be bridged by grace. Self-improvement is no more God's plan than self-salvation. God's plan is not just for us to be *saved* by grace — it is for us to *live* by grace. God's plan is for my daily life to be given, guided, guarded, and energized by the grace of God. To live in grace is to flow in the Spirit.

We have now reached the foundational idea of this book: *The only way to become the person God made you to be is to live with the Spirit of God flowing through you like a river of living water.* The rest of this chapter will gives us a clear picture of what it looks like to live from one moment to the next in flow with the Spirit — not in following rules or trying harder — so that you receive the power to flourish as the me God made you to be.

> God's plan is not just for us to be saved by grace — it is for us to live by grace. ✗

» Flowing with Life

Experiencing the flow of the Spirit, spiritually speaking, is what makes us come alive, and the picture Jesus uses for life in the Spirit in the book of John is a river. Rivers are mentioned 150 times in Scripture, often as a picture of spiritual life, and for good reason. Israel was a desert, so a river is grace. A river is life. We don't know much about the Garden of Eden, but we do know this—a river ran through it.

> A river watering the garden flowed from Eden.
> (Genesis 2:10)

If a river flows, life flourishes. If a river dries up, life dies. So it is with you and the Spirit. The first human being was just a lump of clay until God breathed into him the "breath of life." (In Hebrew the word for *breath* is the same word used for *spirit*.) One of the signs that you are in the flow of the Spirit is a sense of God-given vitality and joyful aliveness overflowing in you.

When our son was three years old, he wanted to pour his own glass of milk out of a very full carton. Nancy was reluctant; we had three small children and spills were a way of life. But our son was so set on it that she couldn't say no, although she did warn him to be careful. His little hands picked up the heavy gallon container, and the milk went gushing into the glass—but wonder of wonders, it stopped just in time. The glass wasn't just full; the milk crowned the top of it. Not a drop was spilled. *Gloria in excelsis.*

But then Johnny was so excited that he grabbed the glass and swung it exuberantly from the counter to the table. The spillover was tremendous.

When someone bumps into me, what spills out of me reveals what is inside of me. That is the idea behind one of Paul's favorite words—*perisseuein*—to "overflow" or "abound" with life. He spoke of people being "full of the Spirit," and the spillover effect was tremendous. Jesus told his followers that when the Spirit arrived, they would receive power. When the Spirit flows in you, you are given power to become the person God designed.

You become you-ier.

» Flowing with Soul Satisfaction

As the deer pants for streams of water, so my soul pants for you, my God.

This psalm got made into a song, and sometimes when people sing it they think it means they are *supposed* to long for God or like church services and church songs. But this psalm is much bigger than that. It means that God is my life-giver and therefore my desire for life cannot be satisfied apart from him.

This is not a picture of Bambi wondering through a leafy-green, stream-laden forest with a slightly parched throat. This is desert country. No rivers, just wadis — gullies that would contain water only in the rainy season. Now the wadis are dried up, and the deer is going to die if it doesn't find water. That is us. We were made for soul satisfaction and simply die without it.

If you want life, you want God. You want him the way a deer dying of thirst wants water. You want God more than you know.

In Jesus' day the Jews celebrated God's gift of water and life at the Feast of the Tabernacles. The chief priest would dip a golden pitcher into the pool of Siloam and lead a parade up to the temple. This was the most joyful moment in the life of Israel. It was said that whoever had not seen the Feast of the Tabernacles did not know joy.

The priest would shout to the crowd, "With joy you shall draw water from the well of salvation!" Then he would pour the water out onto the ground. In the desert land of Israel, where drought was a constant fear, no one poured good water onto the ground. It was a kind of acted-out parable that God would one day satisfy his thirsty people with more water — more life — than they could handle. It was at that feast — maybe at that moment — when a rabbi stood up and cried out in a loud voice, *"Whoever is thirsty, let them come to me and drink...."*

When I am in the flow of the Spirit, sin looks bad and God looks good. When I experience gratitude, contentment, and satisfaction deep in my soul, there is a good chance it is the Spirit flowing within.

» Flowing with the Fruit of the Spirit

There is a river at the beginning of the Bible, and there is a river at the end:

Then the angel showed me the river of the water of life, as clear as crystal, flowing from the throne of God and of the Lamb down the middle of the great street of the city. On each side of the river stood the tree of life, bearing twelve crops of fruit, yielding its fruit every month. And the leaves of the tree are for the healing of the nations.

Even here in California we don't have trees that yield their fruit *every* month. This scene is a picture of supreme flourishing, for the water flows from God, the source of life. In particular, when we are in the flow of the Spirit, we become increasingly full of the fruit of the Spirit: "love, joy, peace, patience, kindness, goodness, faithfulness, gentleness and self-control." The best indicator that I am living in the flow is the growth of the fruit.

A woman sees a father shopping with a fussy two-year-old in his grocery cart. "Be patient, Billy," he whispers. "You can handle this, Billy. It's okay, Billy."

The woman said to him, "I don't mean to interrupt your shopping, but I just had to tell you how wonderfully loving and patient you are with little Billy."

The man replied, "Actually, my son's name is Patrick. *My* name is Billy."

The Spirit is available to whisper to us thoughts of love and joy and peace and patience every moment of our life. *Right now.* All we have to do is stop, ask, and listen.

I can't make myself loving or joyful. A tree's job is not to try to bear fruit; the tree's job is to abide near the river. And the fruit does not ripen overnight.

When I am in the flow of the Spirit, I am moved toward greater love and more joy. And the blessing does not stop with me. The apostle John says the tree bears twelve crops, which calls to mind the twelve tribes of Israel and the twelve disciples of Jesus. In other words, God is giving life to his people.

Then comes the line in the Bible that takes your breath away: "And the leaves of the tree are for the healing of the nations." This is good news, but not just for Israel. Not just for the insiders. It is good news for the world. You and I—the leaves—are to flourish for the healing of the nations. For the healing of the Gaza strip. For the healing of Darfur. For the AIDS ward in the Sisters of Mercy hospital in Addis Ababa. For the apartment building full of loneliness. For the expensive home in the suburbs ripped by a divorce. For the lonely worker at an office party. For the forgotten woman at a homeless shelter.

The Spirit never just flows *in* us; he always flows *through* us so that others might flourish as well.

Anytime you see life flourishing, it is receiving nourishment from beyond itself. This is true of a tree, it is true of you, but it is also true of the world around you. The river can flow in you. The river can flow through you.

When you are in the flow of the Spirit, there is going to be some spill-over that blesses someone else.

» In Flow with the Presence of God

What if God really is at work in every moment, in every place? What if your job is just to jump into the river? What if your job is to figure out, from one moment to the next, how to stay in the flow? How to keep yourself aware and submitted to God's Spirit so that rivers of living water flow through your belly, through the core of your being?

The apostle Paul gives a simple command, which in a sense is all we need to do: "Do not quench the Spirit." The Spirit is already at work in you. Jesus says if you have come to him, if you are a follower of his, the Spirit is there. He is bigger than you; he is stronger than you; he is more patient with your failures and your gaps and your inadequacies and your pretending than you are. He is committed to helping you 24/7. So Paul says, in a sense, your only job is not getting in his way. Just *don't quench the Spirit.*

As we go about life, either we do things that open ourselves to the Spirit's influence in our lives — which Paul talks about in terms of "walking in the Spirit," "keeping in step with the Spirit," or "sowing to the Spirit" — or we do things that close ourselves off to the Spirit. For instance, Paul wrote, "Since we live by the Spirit, let us keep in step with the Spirit. Let us not become conceited, provoking and envying each other."

Here is a simple example of what I mean by closing ourselves off to the Spirit. Nancy and I had dinner with two other couples, some of our best friends, which we always do between Christmas and New Year's Eve. We look back on the past year and talk about high points and valleys, what we have learned and how we have changed. It's an annual highlight.

At one point I was talking about me, and Nancy gave my hand a little squeeze. No one else could see it. Just me. It was a little signal: *You're talking too much. Give someone else a turn.* The old squeeze play. We hadn't worked out the signal before; it was spontaneous. My immediate thought was, *I don't like the squeeze play. I think what I was saying about me was really interesting. I think Nancy is being overly directive.*

Here was the biggest problem: After dinner was over, I didn't say anything to her. I just thought to myself, *It's not a big deal. We don't need to talk about it.* I decided I would rather avoid a potentially unpleasant conversation than honor our relationship, learn more about myself, and wrestle with being honest. (Have you never done such a thing? Am I the only one?) In that decision I cut myself off just a bit from the flow of God's Spirit. In that one small area I quenched the Spirit's leading in my life.

The next day I spent time with another good friend. We talked about our families and marriages, and that incident from the previous night came up. Immediately I knew I had to talk to my wife about the squeeze thing, sooner or later. (Honey, if you're reading this, stop squeezing my hand.)

There was a lag between the time when she first squeezed my hand and the time when I finally talked with her about it. The lag lasted about twenty-four hours during which I resisted the flow of truth in my life. Yet one of the goals of spiritual life is to reduce the lag time of being out of the flow of the Spirit.

Nancy and I had a good talk that night about what the squeeze play meant, about the kind of person I want to be, the kind of person she wants to be, and what kind of marriage we want to have. And in that moment, I was back in the flow.

» Just Plunge In!

The Holy Spirit is always ready to guide you toward God's best version of yourself. Of course, many times I don't want to be guided! I want to blow up at someone, or be greedy, or lie to get out of trouble. I want to quench the Spirit. The more my habits are formed around resentment or anxiety or greed or superiority, the more often I will quench the Spirit. It will take time and wisdom for habits to get re-formed. But the Spirit of God is tenacious. All that is needed in any moment is a sincere desire to be submitted to the Spirit's leading. We need not worry about God's response; a sincere heart never needs to fear that God is upset.

I was traveling on obscure back roads in a part of the country I had never been to before. When I obtained a rental car, the man at the counter said to me, "Along with this car, if you want, you can also get a little box, a guidance system." Have you ever seen one of these? You plug it in and punch in your destination, and a voice will tell you how to get to wherever it is that you are going.

"Do you want to add this to the car?" he asked.

My immediate response was, "No. I'm not going to pay for that. I can find where I'm going without that."

But when I went out to the parking lot, I could not find my car. I could not remember what stall it was in. I had to go back to the counter and tell the man I had gotten lost before I found my car.

I decided to get the box.

There was a voice coming out of the box. You don't even have to look at a screen or follow a map. Someone talks to you. It is a British voice, because people who talk with a British accent always sound smarter. You're just inclined to do what they say. And it was a woman's voice, because ... same thing.

You can get the box. You can have the lady's voice in the car, but that doesn't mean you trust her. If you trust her, what do you do? You do what she says. You go where she tells you to go. If she says, "Turn left," you turn left. If she says, "Turn left," and in your heart you think, *Oh, but I want to turn right,* you remember that verse, "There is a way that seemeth right unto a man, but the end thereof are the ways of death."

To live in the flow of the Spirit means doing what Jesus says. I will mess up a lot. I am going to need his power. I know that, but I form the intention. I say to him, "God, with your help, as best I can, I will do what you say. I will give you my life, my time, my obedience." If that is not my settled intent, then it is best to be honest about it.

There is something else you need to know. At one point when I was driving in the unfamiliar territory, I was quite sure the lady in the guidance system was wrong. She said to go left, and I didn't go left. I went right because I knew she was wrong. Then, in a fascinating response, she said, "Recalculating route. When safe to do so, execute a U-turn." I knew she still was wrong ... so I unplugged her. That is the beauty of that little box—you can unplug her.

And—would you believe it?—I got lost as a goose, which my wife enjoyed immensely. So we plugged that lady back in, and you know what she said?

"I told you so, you little idiot. You think I'm going to help you now? You rejected me. There is no way. You just find your way home by yourself."

No, of course she didn't say those things. She said, "Recalculating route. When safe to do so, execute a U-turn."

That is grace.

God will say to you, "Here is the way home. Execute a U-turn." As soon as you are ready to listen, as soon as you are ready to surrender, that is repentance.

He will say, "I will bring you home." That is grace.

Jesus is the only one with authoritative wisdom about how to live. He is the only one to bring about the possibility of forgiveness for your sin and mine. He is the only one to give any kind of realistic hope of conquering death. To all who approach him, he is the thirst-quencher, the life-giver, the Spirit-bringer. No matter how wrongly you have erred in the past, if you are sincerely ready to listen to and obey God, *you do not have to worry about God being mad at you.*

He is not that kind of God.

Chapter 4

Find Out How *You* Grow

When a young shepherd boy named David was preparing for battle against Goliath, King Saul stepped in to help. But he made the mistake we so often make in other battles: He figured that whatever would be helpful to *him* would also be helpful to *David*. So King Saul—who stood "head and shoulders" above every man in Israel—dressed up David in his own tunic and armor, crowned him with his helmet, and armed him with his sword. David "tried walking around" in them, the Bible says, but it was no use. Saul was a size 52 long and David was a 36 regular. Saul was a warrior; David was a shepherd. Saul was a man; David was a teenager. The very things that would help Saul in a battle would only hinder David. Saul's tunic did not fit. His helmet was too big, his sword was too heavy, and his armor would only slow David down.

Fortunately, David had enough self-awareness and courage to name the problem. "I cannot go in these," David said, "because I am not used to them." David had to set aside Saul's equipment and use what would help *him*—a sling, some stones, and nimble feet—and Saul ended up sending David with the best help he could give: "Go, and the LORD be with you."

The greatest battle of life is spiritual. It is the struggles with resentment and anger and greed and superiority that keep me from living in the flow with God. How often in spiritual life do we get burdened because we try to wield weapons that have helped someone else in the battle? We hear about how someone else prays, or reads Scripture to start or end their day, or worships, or studies, or serves—and we feel guilty if we don't do the same. We get frustrated because what works for someone else is not helpful to us. We are like David, trying to walk around in Saul's armor.

The apostle Paul said to "put on the full armor of God," which includes truth and peace and prayer and faith. Have no doubt, it will fit you. If David had gone into battle using Saul's armor, he would have lost. God knew what Saul needed. God knew what David needed. And God knows what you need.

> For we are God's masterpiece. He has created us anew in Christ Jesus, so that we can do the good things he planned for us long ago. (Ephesians 2:10 NLT)

The Bible does not say you are God's *appliance*; it says you are his masterpiece. Appliances get mass-produced. Masterpieces get handcrafted. God did not make you exactly like anyone else. Therefore his plan for shaping you will not look like his plan for shaping anyone else. If you try to follow a generic plan for spiritual growth, it will only frustrate you. Paul said, "Where the Spirit of the Lord is, there is freedom."

It is time for you to stop walking around in Saul's armor. It is time to get free.

» The Freedom Way

Many approaches to spiritual growth assume that the same methods will produce the same growth in different people—but they don't. Because you have been created by God as a unique person, his plan to grow you will not look the same as his plan to grow anyone else. What would grow an orchid would drown a cactus. What would feed a mouse would starve an elephant. All of those entities need light, food, air, and water—but in different amounts and conditions. The key is not treating every creature alike; it is finding the unique conditions that help each creature grow.

Imagine a doctor's office where every patient is told, "Take two aspirin and call me in the morning." If I have a headache, that is great advice, but if my appendix has just burst, I will be dead before morning. Imagine a store that sells only one kind of shirt — one color, style, fabric, and size — and makes the same deal on pants. There are no "one-size-fits-all" stores, because God made people in different sizes. Imagine a parent who thinks, *No matter how many kids I have, I will treat them each exactly the same way. Each kid will be a blank slate for me to write on, pliable clay for me to mold. They will all be motivated by the same rewards, impacted by punishment the same way, and attracted by the same activities.*

What obliterates these ideas?

Reality, such as actually having children and becoming quickly aware that every human being is different. If we really want to help someone grow, we will have to help them in a way that fits their wiring.

Our great model for this is God himself, for he always knows just what each person needs.

He had Abraham take a walk, Elijah take a nap, Joshua take a lap, and Adam take the rap.

He gave Moses a forty-year time out, he gave David a harp and a dance, and he gave Paul a pen and a scroll.

He wrestled with Jacob, argued with Job, whispered to Elijah, warned Cain, and comforted Hagar.

He gave Aaron an altar, Miriam a song, Gideon a fleece, Peter a name, and Elisha a mantle.

Jesus was stern with the rich young ruler, tender with the woman caught in adultery, patient with the disciples, blistering with the scribes, gentle with the children, and gracious with the thief on the cross.

God never grows two people the same way. God is a hand-crafter, not a mass-producer.

Now it is your turn.

God has existed from eternity — but he has never had a relationship with you before. He wants to do a new thing with you. The problem many people face when it comes to spiritual growth is that they listen to someone they think of as the expert — maybe the pastor of their church — talk about what he does, and think that is what they are supposed to do. When it doesn't work for them — because they are a different person! — they feel guilty and inadequate; they often give up.

God has a plan for the me he wants me to be. It will not look exactly like his plan for anyone else, which means it will take freedom and exploration for me to learn how God wants to grow me. *Spiritual growth is hand-crafted, not mass-produced. God does not do "one-size-fits-all."*

Take the practice of writing in a journal, for example. When I mentioned journaling one time while speaking at a conference on spiritual life, I heard groans. I asked, "How many people do not like to journal?" What amazed me was not just how many hands were raised (the vast majority), but the speed and vehemence with which they were thrust into the air. It was as if people were admitting a secret shame they had been hiding for years. I have repeated this question on numerous occasions, always with the same results—once even at a workshop on journaling!

If you don't like to keep a journal, here is a thought you might like: *Jesus never journaled*. Neither did Abraham or Moses or Ruth. Throughout most of the history of the human race, people loved God without ever picking up a paper and pencil. In fact, in those days most didn't have supplies to journal. Yet people still grew spiritually, examined their souls, fought sin, and learned obedience. "Journal" was not a verb back then; it wasn't even a noun. C. S. Lewis, one of the most influential Christians of the twentieth century, said that he kept a journal until he was converted. Then when he became a Christian, he realized that it was making him preoccupied with himself. So he stopped journaling.

Does this mean that keeping a journal is a bad idea? Not at all! As a matter of full disclosure, I often find it very helpful myself, especially in times of stress or pain. Writing my thoughts in those times helps prevent my self-examination and prayers from slipping into spirals of negativity. You may find that a journal helps you become more aware of God's presence in your life or aids you in praying. If it does, do it.

But you are free. Disciples are handcrafted, not mass-produced. No wonder we get frustrated when we think that everyone is supposed to look like the pastor or the author or whoever is teaching us at the moment about spiritual growth. We learn differently, struggle with different sins, and relate to God in different ways.

> Spiritual growth is hand-crafted, not mass-produced. God does not do "one-size-fits-all."

When Jesus prayed for his disciples, he did not pray, "May they all have identical devotional practices." He prayed, "Father, may they be one with you." The main measure of your devotion to God is not your devotional life. It is simply your life.

> The main measure of your devotion to God is not your devotional life. It is simply your life.

Trying to grow spiritually without taking who you are into account is like trying to raise children on an assembly line. If you train an 80-pound gymnast and a 300-pound linebacker exactly the same, you will end up with two useless 190-pound people.

There is now an online resource designed to help you find a customized way to grow spiritually that will work for someone exactly like you. It is called Monvee, and it involves taking a four-minute assessment tool to help you understand your temperament, learning style, spiritual pathway, signature sin, and season of life.

It will then suggest a personalized plan to help you live more fully in the flow of the Spirit, with recommendations over the next sixty days for what to do with your mind, your time, your relationships, and your experiences to help you grow closer to God.

It has been shaped by people with backgrounds in theology, technology, spiritual formation, and psychometrics. It is like getting customized help for spiritual growth from people with great wisdom about how spiritual growth happens, a plan shaped by people who understand how we are wired.

Look on the jacket of this book, and you will see a code number. Go to the website and enter the code for your own assessment and plan.

A frequent problem in the way we talk about spiritual growth is that there is not much spirit in it — God's Holy Spirit, that is. Only God makes things grow, and that growth is not always predictable. Like a tree beginning to bud, growth always has surprise attached to it.

What, then, do I need to know to learn how God wants to help me grow?

» What Brings Me Life?

If you are looking for a conversation stopper, try asking people this question: *How are your spiritual disciplines going?* Most people think of a very short list of activities that fall in the "I ought to do this, but I don't do it as much as I should, so it makes me feel guilty just thinking about it" category. So here is an alternative question: *What do you do that makes you feel fully alive?*

Everyone knows what it's like to feel fully alive, and everyone longs for that. Maybe you feel alive when taking a long walk at sunset. Maybe it is reading a great book and taking time to savor its thoughts and language. Maybe it is having a talk with lots of laughter in front of a bonfire with a few close friends. Maybe it is watching a movie or a play that causes you to say yes to life. Maybe it is taking a long drive. Maybe you love to play an instrument. Maybe you come alive when you are pursuing a hobby.

A spiritual discipline is simply an activity you engage in to be made more fully alive by the Spirit of Life.

Of course, that is not the same as "doing whatever feels good in the moment." Too much alcohol or too much food or compulsive sexual activity may feel good for the moment, but these activities do not lead us toward life. Eventually they lead to guilt, addiction, or regret.

> ✱ A spiritual discipline is simply an activity you engage in to be made more fully alive by the Spirit of Life.

The things that bring us life are also not simply "what feels comfortable." Giving away money or confessing sin may feel scary in the moment — but so does a good roller coaster ride, which leaves no doubt that I am alive and kicking.

We often assess how "spiritual" we are by how much we are pursuing our distorted list of "what counts" toward spiritual growth instead of by our fullness of life. Working with joy, tipping generously, listening to someone patiently, eating gratefully, reading quietly, playing happily — it all counts! *Every* moment is a chance to live in the flow of the Spirit.

No relationship can last if it is built purely on "should" — not even with my dental hygienist. My wife, my kids — even my dog — don't want me to be with them only because I think I *should*. Because they love me, they give me freedom, and in that freedom desire grows.

Likewise, where the Spirit is, there is freedom. It may seem strange, but when I think of God giving me freedom from the staleness of too many "shoulds," I find that my love and admiration for him grows. I want to be around a God like that!

Sustainable spiritual growth happens when I actually *want* to do what I *ought* to do. This means I have to change how I think about what "counts" as spiritual, for what makes an activity spiritual is not the activity itself. It is whether or not I do it with and through the Spirit. It is the quality of the presence and interaction with the Spirit while I am doing the activity.

» What Is My Temperament?

One of the most common temperament scales — the Myers-Briggs — looks at whether you are introverted or extroverted, whether you prefer data or intuition, whether you are a thinker or a feeler, and whether you like things orderly or open-ended. Each category gets expressed by a letter, so on the Myers-Briggs scale I come out an INFP. I am somewhat introverted, I am intuitive, I am a feeler, and I prefer spontaneity.

Every human being has a temperament, which means certain practices will come more naturally for you than others. Different temperaments are not better or worse, they simply are (although I personally am pretty sure Jesus was an INFP). Everyone needs some time in solitude, but if your personality is marked by being introverted, you have a greater capacity to withdraw from noise and people and tasks to be alone and quiet.

Because I am an introvert, the idea of going off to be alone almost always sounds appealing to me. However, solitude rarely happens by default. Circumstances in my life never conspire to produce a day with no activities or events. I have to choose solitude, and the simplest way is to take my calendar, find a day in the future when I have no commitments, and block it off to go some place I would love to be—out in nature or at a retreat center.

People often wonder how long they should be in solitude. You can experiment, because spiritual practices are about freedom. At first I found that about an hour was all I could handle. Eventually I came to love a day of solitude and found myself feeling free of other people's expectations and demands. When I am alone with God, I remember that all the people in my life are temporary and that their opinions of me don't really matter much.

If you are an extrovert, the notion of a day in solitude may sound like a nightmare. Try it for an hour. Remember, however, that this is not about the time; it's about the Spirit. If you are an introvert and love solitude, it does not mean that you are more spiritual than your extroverted spouse or friend, for whom community and fellowship probably come more naturally. They may have a head start on the very ability to love people that you are hoping God will grow in you when you are alone with him.

One man I know is both an extrovert and a deep feeler. He is in the flow of the Spirit best when he is neck-deep in the soul struggles of another human being. Ironically, even though he is trying to help someone else, it is in those moments when his own soul is healed. He found he needs to schedule several one-on-ones like that every week.

Some people have temperaments that crave regularity, order, and closure. If this is you, then having set times for prayer and lists of whom and what you are praying for may keep you connected to God. I know a woman who could show years of lists of prayers and years of lists of answers, and those lists are priceless to her. But if you have a temperament that craves spontaneity and change, your prayer life is never going to look like that. You may have tried and then given up on the lists, feeling guilty. But that is not because you don't love God; it is because you're just not a list-maker.

God desires to fill you with life, and you cannot get filled up when you are engaged too much in an activity that drains you. It does not mean that you will be less connected to God. Spontaneous people are capable of as much love as well-organized people—they're just messier. A man I know walks regularly and turns his walks into times of prayer. For him, there is something about the act of walking itself that provides enough change in what he is looking at to help his mind stay focused.

» What Is My Pathway?

Author Gary Thomas has written about how we all have what he calls sacred pathways—ways that we find naturally help us experience the presence of God. For instance, because one of my pathways is intellectual, I may find myself drawn deeply to God by a book that might put my wife to sleep. Because one of her pathways is activism, she may find herself intensely aware of God's presence neck-deep in a project that would make me want to take a nap. Often we will recognize our pathways because we find ourselves being changed or making key decisions when we are doing a particular activity. Some people connect to God best through nature. Some are activists, finding God naturally when they are charging into a cause. Intellectuals find their hearts filled with the Spirit when their minds are filled with great thoughts. Some people find the Spirit most alive in them when they are serving. Some connect most naturally with God in solitary contemplation. Others feel closest to God when they are having fellowship with friends. Some sense him nearest in worship.

sacred pathways

Naturalist — finds God in nature

Ascetic — is drawn to disciplines

Traditionalist — loves historical liturgies

Activist — comes alive spiritually in a great cause

Caregiver — meets God in serving

Sensate — senses God through five senses

Enthusiast — loves to grow through people

Contemplative — is drawn to solitary reflection and prayer

Intellectual — loves God by learning

(For more information on these categories, read Gary Thomas's book *Sacred Pathways* [Grand Rapids: Zondervan].)

It is good to be familiar with each pathway, but you will find that one or two are the most gripping for you. When you do identify which ones you resonate with most, you will also find that they are the most sustainable for you, because your desire for them will be highest.

» What Is My Learning Style?

Thankfully, spiritual growth is not restricted to people who like school, for God also wired us to learn in different ways. One man is quite bright and devoted to God, but he hates to read. Consequently, approaches to spiritual growth that require much reading are not going to help him. He has a huge capacity for growth and functions at a high level; he's just not a reader. He learns by listening. He learns from conversations, tapes, and talks.

Others learn mainly by doing. For example, if I try to assemble something, I will read the instructions seven times before trying to put tab A into slot B. But my friend Sam is a hands-on guy. He would try to build a nuclear power plant without looking at directions first. Trial-and-error is the way he learns best, which is great as long as he is not packing my parachute. For Sam, sitting in a church listening to a talk will never be his primary path to growth. An hour of doing is worth ten hours of listening.

Another friend of mine, Lee, learns best when her emotions are deeply engaged. She will be impacted most profoundly by information wrapped up in imagination, art, and other people. Her husband, Wendell, on the

learning styles

Visual — learn best by seeing

Auditory — learn best by hearing

Tactile — learn best by doing

Oral — learn best by saying

Social — learn best in groups

Logical — learn best in linear process

Imaginative — learn best through art, story, and image

other hand, only has an emotion about once a decade. Deep emotion actually interferes with his learning.

You have a natural love of learning. But you have a natural style for learning as well. If someone reads the Bible more than you do, it does not necessarily mean they love God more than you do—they may just love reading more than you do. Try different styles of learning to see which fit you best.

» What Is My Signature Sin?

Precisely because you are uniquely you, you also wrestle with a unique set of temptations. No one sins exactly like you! As we will see in a later chapter, the sins that are most troubling for you are actually connected to your greatest gifts and interests. People who are great at leading are often tempted to use others; people who are gifted at peacemaking can be tempted by avoidance; people with a gift for spontaneity are often tempted by their impulses. Knowing your sin patterns can help remove barriers to living in the flow of the Spirit.

Much of my own signature sin has to do with the need to look better than I really am. This often leads me to want to hide. I was sitting in front of my computer at home not long ago when someone in the family asked if I had a certain phone number. The truth is, I didn't know. I thought perhaps I had it in my cell phone, but I didn't want to take ten seconds to walk to the counter where my cell phone was, see if the number was there, and say it slowly enough for it to get copied down. I was busy. At my computer. Writing a chapter for a book about living in the flow of the Spirit.

But I didn't want to admit any of this. I didn't want the other person to think of me as a time-hog unwilling to serve.

So I just said, "No. Sorry. Can't help you."

Then the tiniest little voice whispered in my mind, *You little pastor scumbag.*

I had to stop, look the other person in the eye, and tell them, "I didn't tell you truth. I lied."

The other person did not respond by saying, "You scumbag." She understood and, unlike that tiniest little voice inside me, was much more gracious. She knew I am capable of much worse than that, and she forgave me. Even in the embarrassment of that moment, I became known more fully and loved more deeply.

Saint Benedict led a community of faith and wrote one of the most famous guidebooks for spiritual growth ever produced, *The Rule of Benedict*. But he built flexibility into it. He speaks of how the abbot must treat each soul differently: "One he must coax, another scold, another persuade, according to each one's character and understanding. Thus he must adjust and adapt himself to all. . . ."

Freedom is the *goal* of growth. A great pianist is free to play notes without worrying about them. A great friend is free to be spontaneous. Spiritual practices are always about freedom.

Also, freedom is needed for the *path* to growth. One pianist might need to practice lots of scales. Another might do better improvising. Another might be helped by sight-reading. The same is true for spiritual growth: You are free to find the path that helps you best.

However, freedom is not the same as self-indulgence. I am not free to become a great pianist by watching TV and eating potato chips all day. I cannot grow in the Spirit if, as Paul says, I use my freedom to "indulge the sinful nature."

When I am aware of my signature sins, I am less vulnerable to them. Knowing where the land mines lie is the first requirement of a safe journey.

» What Is My Season of Life?

How you grow also depends on the season of your spiritual life. When a plant is very young, it often needs external support to help it grow. Tomato plants or young trees, for example, get tied to stakes; vines may need a lattice. But as they grow, the framework that was needed in their early days may actually inhibit growth later on. In spiritual life, structure is often most important when a person's faith is young. You have so much to learn. Worship, prayer, the Bible are all new to you. But as the years pass, what helps in one season may not help in another.

One woman I know loved to study the Scriptures, and she did it regularly for many years. Then her husband died, and she found that in her grief, reading the Bible was not helpful to her. This was not because she was resistant. In her great pain, for many months, it was like dust. So she had to live on what she had already fed her mind. Her hunger for Scripture did return eventually, but for a season of grief she had to receive grace in other ways.

Maybe you have been attending church for years out of a sense of obligation. You show up week after week out of habit, or because someone expects you to, but it is actually increasing the distance between you and God. So here is an idea: Stop going to church. Wait until you want to go again. Find out why you want to go. Trust that if you truly seek, God will bring the desire back to you.

Sometimes people think that because the Bible says "don't give up meeting together," you can never take a Sunday off. But God himself sometimes sent people (including Elijah, Moses, and Jesus) off for more than a month where they weren't around anybody! God's goal is not a perfect attendance record; it is a community of people who actually want to be in community.

Your path to growth will not be quite like anyone else's. It will be unique. It will be you-ier. It won't always be easy. But there is one decision that is always possible—that will always help you grow—and we turn to that now.

Chapter 5

Surrender: The One Decision That Always Helps

There is a God. It is not you.

This is the beginning of wisdom. At first, it looks like bad news because I would like to run the world. I would like to gratify my desires. I would like to have my own way. But once we think about it, this idea turns out to be very good news.

It means that someone far wiser and more competent is running the show. It is his job to be God; it is my job to learn to let him be who he is. The Bible says, "The fool has said in his heart, 'There is no God.'" I suppose the even bigger fool, looking in the mirror, has said, "*There* is a god!" for the oldest temptation is that we "will be like God." Real life, however, begins when I die to the false god that is me.

Jesus said that out of our bellies can flow rivers of living water. The one decision needed for that in any moment is the decision to surrender myself to God. Even when I am not sure what to do, I can place my life in God's hands. John Calvin said that the only haven of safety is "to have no other will, no other wisdom, than to follow the Lord wherever He leads. Let this, then, be the first step, to abandon ourselves, and devote the whole energy of our minds to the service of God." To do this, we will have to face our greatest fear.

» Who Will Drive Your Life?

It is a scary day when parents place their newborn child in a car seat for that child's first day out in the world. As they head down the road, the fragility of life becomes very real. Do you know when the next scary day with your child and the car is?

Sixteen years later. Now you are handing over the keys. They are moving from the passenger's seat to the driver's seat. Up until then, you have been driving. You choose the destination, route, and speed. The person behind the wheel is the one in control.

We live in a neighborhood with circuitous streets, and wherever I am going, even if it's three blocks away, whatever route I take, someone in my family will critique it. "Why are you going this way? This is the long way! You should have gone the other way." I have to tell them, this car is *my car*. These keys are *my keys*. This way is *my way*.

I live in a family where everybody wants to drive.

Many people find Jesus pretty handy to have in the passenger's seat when they require his services.

Jesus, I have a health problem, and I need your help.
Something hard is going on at work, and I'd like it to be different.
I'm feeling anxious, and I want you to give me peace of mind.
I'm feeling sad, and I'd like a little hope.
I'm facing death, and I want to make sure I'm going to heaven.

But these people are not so sure they want Jesus driving, because if Jesus is behind the wheel, they are not in control anymore. If he is driving, they are not in charge of their wallet anymore. They no longer can simply say, "I'll give sometimes when I feel generous, but I reserve the right to keep what I want." Now it is Jesus' money.

When I let Jesus drive, I am no longer in charge of my ego. I no longer have the right to satisfy every self-centered ambition. Now it is his life. I am not in charge of my mouth anymore. I don't get to gossip, flatter, cajole, condemn, lie, curse, rage, cheat, intimidate, manipulate, exaggerate, or prevaricate anymore. Now it is not my mouth — it is his mouth.

I get out of the driver's seat. I hand over the keys to Jesus. I am fully engaged. In fact, I am more alive than ever before. But it is not my life anymore. It is his life.

Have I invited Jesus along for the ride, or is he driving? Who is behind the wheel? Jesus is very clear on this point: *There is no way for a human being to come to God that does not involve surrender.*

"Whoever finds their life will lose it, and whoever loses their life for my sake will find it." (Matthew 10:39)

"I tell you the truth, unless a kernel of wheat falls to the ground and dies, it remains only a single seed. But if it dies, it produces many seeds." (John 12:24)

"Whoever wants to be my disciple must deny themselves and take up their cross and follow me." (Matthew 16:24)

Surrender is not the same thing as passivity. God's will for your life involves exercising creativity, making choices, and taking initiative. Surrender does not mean being a doormat. It does not mean you accept circumstances fatalistically. Often it means you will have to fight to challenge the status quo. It doesn't mean that you stop using your mind, stop asking questions, or stop thinking critically. Surrender is not a crutch for weak people who cannot handle life.

✶ There is no way for a human being to come to God that does not involve surrender.

Instead, surrender is the glad and voluntary acknowledgment that there is a God and it is not me. His purposes are often wiser and better than our desires. Jesus does not come to rearrange the outside of our life the way we want. He comes to rearrange the inside of our life the way God wants.

In surrender, I let go of my life. It is a Copernican revolution of the soul in which I take myself out of the center of the universe and place God there. I yield to Him. I offer obedience. I do what he says. I am not driving anymore.

SURRENDER: THE ONE DECISION THAT ALWAYS HELPS

When spirituality gets discussed in our culture, there are some messages from the Bible that everybody likes hearing:

"No matter how much you mess up, God still loves you." Everyone likes that one.

"You are so busy and exhausted—God wants you to be rested and refreshed." That sounds good too.

But what about these?

> Jesus does not come to rearrange the outside of our life the way we want. He comes to rearrange the inside of our life the way God wants.

"You need to surrender. You are sinful, stubborn, and stiff-necked. You are self-centered and self-promoting, your own desires are very often self-serving, your ability to perceive your own sin is blinded by self-deception, you need to bend the knee, you need to submit your heart, you need to confess your sin, you need to *surrender.*"

Surrender is a hard word.

I will name one person who I know for sure doesn't like to hear that: *Me.*

» Why Surrender?

When someone throws a winning touchdown pass, when somebody hits the game-winning home run, when a doctor says he has good news, or when someone wins the lottery, we all have a reflexive response with our bodies. We raise them high. During such times we are hardwired to stretch our hands toward heaven. We all want the posture of victory and celebration.

There is another posture, however, that expresses surrender. When we are contrite, when we are submitting, we kneel, expressing with our bodies what is in our hearts. When a subject comes before his king, what does he do to humble himself? He kneels to acknowledge that he is in the presence of his master. When a believer in any religion comes to pray to his God, what does he do? He kneels to acknowledge that he is in the presence of his master. When a man asks a woman to become his wife, what does he do? He gets down on one knee to acknowledge ... well, you get the idea.

Exalted high in victory. Bent low in surrender. The two postures seem opposite, but Jesus understood that if you want to experience victory, you must start in surrender. Surrender brings power, and the need to surrender is deeply tied to Jesus' offer of living in the flow of the Spirit. You receive power through the act of surrender that you cannot obtain any other way; you receive freedom through submission that you will otherwise never know.

The Twelve Steps followed by recovery groups lay out a way of life that is the single greatest path to freedom for addicts the world has ever known. But at the core of the steps lies a great paradox: In which of the twelve steps does it say "now *try really hard* to not drink"? In which of the twelve steps does it even say "now *decide* not to drink"? Amazingly enough, the most powerful tool against the most powerful addiction in the world never asks people to decide to stop doing what is destroying their lives. Instead of mobilizing the will, its followers surrender their will. Try to overcome the problem by your will, and it will beat you. Surrender your will, and sobriety becomes possible. Surrender, which we think means defeat, turns out to be the only way to victory. This is not just the case with alcohol. It is also true with other addictions, with habits, with brokenness—and with sin in general.

Why does the will fail? In *The Big Book* of Alcoholics Anonymous, the writer says that when it comes to drinking, we say and feel "*never again.*" But we do it again. *Why?*

> We are unable, at certain times, to bring into our consciousness with
> sufficient force the memory of the suffering and humiliation of even
> a week ago.... the certain consequences that follow taking a drink
> do not crowd into the mind to deter us. If these thoughts occur, they
> are hazy and readily replaced by the old threadbare idea that this
> time we can handle it ourselves.

It is possible to receive power to become the person I want to be. But to do so, I have to hand over the keys.

Another gift of surrender is peace. If I live in the illusion that I am god, I will drive myself and everybody else crazy with my need for control. When I surrender, I don't just let go of my will. I also give up the idea that I am in charge of *outcomes.*

When my children started driving, I would sit in the passenger seat to coach them. I tried to look relaxed, but if I thought they were taking too

"the nature of the will"

In a series of brilliant experiments, psychologist Roy Baumeister has studied the nature and limits of will-power. One key question was, Once you exercise your willpower — say, by resisting temptation for five minutes — does that make your willpower stronger, weaker, or unchanged for the next few minutes?

Baumeister had certain subjects exert willpower by resisting the temptation to eat delicious, fresh, warm, gooey chocolate chip cookies — eating only radishes instead. Another set of subjects did not have to resist eating cookies. Then all the subjects were assigned complex math problems to solve — problems that were actually *impossible* to solve — in order to measure how long people will exercise willpower to persevere in frustration.

The people who had to resist eating chocolate chip cookies gave up on problem-solving much more quickly than the other subjects. In other words, our willpower is easily fatigued. We can use our wills to override our habits for a few moments, but our habits will always beat willpower alone in the long run.

The will is good at big simple choices: getting married, or taking a job, or joining AA. But the will is *very bad* at trying to overcome habits or attitudes that have become embedded in our bodies. Deep change takes more than willpower. It requires God renewing our minds. It requires surrender.

long to hit the brakes, my feet would start pressing into the floor on some imaginary brake on my side. My jaws would clench and my shoulders would hunch, as if my body believed that it could help slow the car by tensing up.

What a relief it is to believe there is someone more competent than me behind the wheel, so that I *do not have to control the outcomes* of my life. I love my children the best I can, but I am not in charge of their destiny. I work the best I can, but I am not in control of the results. I try to make wise choices to save for retirement, but I am not running the stock market. I find that every moment I worry is a chance to practice letting go of the need to control outcomes.

There is a God. It is not me.

» Surrender as a Continual Experience

Surrender is not something we do once and get over. Paul used a striking image in his letter to Rome when he wrote, "Offer your bodies as a living sacrifice...." During a Jewish sacrifice an animal would be killed, then its body would be placed on the altar to be consumed. So what happens if you put a live creature on the altar and say, "Stay there until you're consumed," then light the fire? The creature will jump right off that altar! But Paul encourages us, of our own volition, to crawl back onto the altar. We are called to surrender day by day, moment by moment. In the moment it feels like death, but it is really the only way to life.

For example, suppose someone in the workplace does something to me that really makes me angry. The situation is complicated, so I am not yet even sure of the right way to respond. Without even trying, my mind fills with all kinds of bad thoughts. In the moment, I do not know what I should do. But thoughts come—I know from God—about what not to do:

No murder. *Okay, I won't kill them.*

No violence. *Okay ... I won't have them beaten up.*

No gossip. *But if I agree to no murder or violence, couldn't we leave gossip on the table?*

Surrender means that I will seek to handle the problem facing me in a way that honors God. The options that look attractive to me—avoiding, evading, gossiping, blasting—I relinquish to God. If my hurt runs deep, it will be about five minutes before the revenge fantasies start raging back. I will have to surrender all over again. But I can recognize those fantasies a little quicker and yield a little sooner.

In my life and in your life there is always the question before us, *who is driving?* I can have a rebellious heart, telling God to stay out of my car altogether, that I will go where I want when I want with my life. Or

I can have a divided heart, keeping Jesus in the car, but driving myself, saying to him, "I will keep this area, this pattern, this relationship under my own control. I will hang onto this grudge. I will enjoy the pleasure I get from this habit. I know you want full surrender, but I don't trust you."

The problem is, living with a divided heart makes us miserable. Sometimes we can keep the guilt vague and fuzzy. Sometimes it will be vivid. But if our heart is sensitive toward God and we keep him out of the driver's seat, the guilt will gnaw at us. Only one thing will bring ultimate peace: a surrendered heart.

> I have been crucified with Christ and I no longer live, but Christ lives in me. (Galatians 2:20)

I turn my life and will over to God. I seek to obey the best I can. You lose a life, but you gain a life—a life much better than the one you lost. In the end, it turns out that nothing you lost was really worth keeping anyway.

» The Action of Surrender

Because surrender is so closely connected to our wills, often a price is attached. Sometimes I can *feel* devoted to God, but when it comes time to act, I find that my surrender is only skin deep.

Anticipating this, Jesus often identified the particular area where surrender was needed in a person's life. To a woman caught in adultery he said, "I don't condemn you. Go and sin no more." We need to surrender our sexuality to God. Many times surrender will involve money, because money is all about trust and control. Often surrender will involve an act of self-disclosure about a grudge, attitude, habit, or sin. Sometimes when I am with a friend, I am prompted to talk about a matter in which I have struggled or have failed. My immediate response is generally, *no way.* At other times I may be with someone and feel the need to confront them about something that would make me uncomfortable. My immediate response again is generally, *no way.*

Then I have to decide: *Will I surrender when surrender means doing something uncomfortable?* If it is comfortable, it wouldn't be surrender.

But here again we are never on our own. The Spirit is always available. One of the most amazing teachings of the Scriptures is that in Jesus,

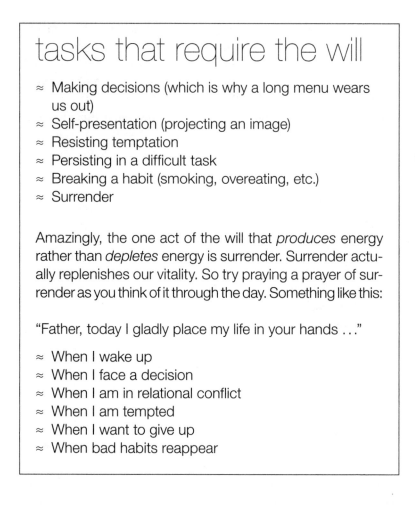

tasks that require the will

- ≈ Making decisions (which is why a long menu wears us out)
- ≈ Self-presentation (projecting an image)
- ≈ Resisting temptation
- ≈ Persisting in a difficult task
- ≈ Breaking a habit (smoking, overeating, etc.)
- ≈ Surrender

Amazingly, the one act of the will that *produces* energy rather than *depletes* energy is surrender. Surrender actually replenishes our vitality. So try praying a prayer of surrender as you think of it through the day. Something like this:

"Father, today I gladly place my life in your hands ..."

- ≈ When I wake up
- ≈ When I face a decision
- ≈ When I am in relational conflict
- ≈ When I am tempted
- ≈ When I want to give up
- ≈ When bad habits reappear

God himself knows the pain of surrender. Jesus knelt in a garden and prayed, "Let this cup pass from me. Nevertheless, not my will, but yours be done." And just as surrender led to resurrection for Jesus, so it does for his followers. The apostle Paul wrote, "For you died, and your life is now hidden with Christ in God. When Christ, who is your life, appears, then you also will appear with him in glory."

What does it mean that you will appear with him "in glory"? It means the day is coming when it will be a glorious thing to be you. One of the noblest thoughts about God ever recorded by a human being came from Moses' encounter on Mount Sinai. Moses asked, "Now show me your glory." We might expect special effects—thunder and lighting and earthquakes and power. But instead God said, "I will cause all my goodness to pass before you."

The most glorious thing about God is how good he is. One day you will share in that goodness. Everything that is small or petty in you will be gone. To glorify God means to be the kind of person people will look at and say, "What a great God God must be to have thought up such a creature!"

That will be you. "In glory." Glorious.

The only way to glory is through humility. The only way to freedom is through submission. The only way to victory is through surrender.

Nancy and I recently decided to take dancing lessons. I grew up Swedish and Baptist, and we were not a dancing people. I also attended a college where it was against the law to dance. But I have been married for twenty-five years, so I guess dancing would be legal now.

We have a terrific dance instructor who, before we began, pulled us aside. "I have a very important question," this instructor said. "You are going to dance now. Who leads?"

There was silence.

I knew the answer, but I wanted to hear my wife say it. A few more seconds of silence, and then through gritted teeth she said, "He leads."

"And who follows?"

Silence. Then, "I follow."

It was hard for Nancy to follow for two reasons. One is that when you aren't leading, you aren't in control. It is hard not to be in control. The other is that when it comes to dancing, I am a thoroughly incompetent leader.

Jesus, however, is a thoroughly competent leader. When you wake up in the morning, you can feel completely confident in saying, "Okay, Jesus, today you lead, and I will follow. Whatever I have to do in my relationships, my body, my health, and my finances are in your hands. I won't try to figure out the rest of my life. I won't try to solve every day. Just today. You lead. I'll follow."

You don't want to miss the dance. It is why you were born. And God leads it, not just for today, but into eternity.

There is a God. It is not you.

Save the last dance. . . .

Chapter 6
Try Softer

Not long ago I went with my wife to a yoga class for the first time in my life. Immediately it became clear to me why yoga will never catch on: They don't keep score. You can't tell who's winning.

Mostly we just stretched, and I am not good at stretching. On a good day I can touch my knees. What made it worse is that most of the other people in the class were clearly double-jointed. There was a middle-aged woman who didn't look particularly fit—I thought I would definitely beat her at whatever you compete at in yoga—but she was a dancer. At one point she did the splits with her legs, bent forward with her torso completely flat on the ground, then tied both her legs around the back of her head. If they had been keeping score, I would have lost at that point on the mercy rule. Afterward, I did ask the instructor if the woman could be tested for performance-enhancing drugs.

As you might imagine, the class was a lot of work and good for my body. But I was struck afterward by a phrase I never heard: *Try harder.* The instructor never said, "Try harder to stretch. Try harder to be flexible. Try harder to contort your body like a fourteen-year-old female Russian gymnast."

When you stretch, you don't make it happen simply by trying harder. You must let go and let gravity do its work. You give permission, opening yourself to another, greater force.

This is not just true when it comes to stretching. As a general rule, the harder you work to control things, the more you lose control. The harder you try to hit a fast serve in tennis, the more your muscles tense up. The harder you try to impress someone on a date or while making a sale, the more you force the conversation and come across as pushy. The harder you cling to people, the more apt they are to push you away.

Sometimes trying harder helps. It can help me clean my room, push through phone calls I need to make, or run another lap. But for deeper change, I need a greater power than simply "trying harder" can provide. Imagine someone advising you, "Try harder to relax. Try harder to go to sleep. Try harder to be graceful. Try harder to not worry. Try harder to be joyful."

There are limits on what trying harder can accomplish.

Often the people in the Gospels who got into the most trouble with Jesus were the ones who thought they were working hardest on their spiritual life. They were trying so hard to be good that they could not stop thinking about how hard they were trying. That got in the way of their loving other people.

The problem when I try harder is that I get fixated on my own heroic efforts. I grow judgmental. I can't let this endure forever. So instead of making vows about how my spiritual life will be perfectly well organized until I die, I seek to surrender my will for just this day. I look for small graces. I try to engage in little acts of service. I pray briefly to accommodate my limited attention span. I look for ways of being with God that I already enjoy. I try to go for half an hour without complaining. I try to say something encouraging to three people in a row. I put twenty dollars in my pocket that I will give away sometime during the day. I take a five-minute break to read a page of great thoughts.

If trying harder is producing growth in your spiritual life, keep it up. But if it is not, here is an alternative:

Try softer.
Try better.
Try different.

A river of living water is now available, but the river is the Spirit. It is not you.

The contemplative Franciscan priest Richard Rohr puts it like this: "Faith does not need to push the river because faith is able to trust that *there is a river.* The river is flowing. We are in it."

Don't push the river.

Trying softer means focusing more on God's goodness than our efforts. It means being more relaxed and less self-conscious. Less pressured. When I try softer, I am less defensive, more open to feedback. I learn better. I stay patient if things don't turn out the way I expected. It means less self-congratulation when I do well and less self-flagellation when I fall down. It means asking God for help.

When I am trying too hard, I cannot stop thinking how nobly I'm behaving. When I take even one step toward growth, my very next thought will often be pride at my goodness — which of course moves me two steps back. True growth always goes in the opposite direction of self-righteousness.

This is the point of one of Jesus' most unusual little stories, sometimes called the "Parable of the Unworthy Servants." Perhaps a better name would be the "Parable of Trying Softer."

> Suppose one of you had a servant plowing or looking after the sheep. Would he say to the servant when he comes in from the field, "Come along now and sit down to eat"? Would he not rather say, "Prepare my supper, get yourself ready and wait on me while I eat and drink; after that you may eat and drink"? Would he thank the servant because he did what he was told to do? So you also, when you have done everything you were told to do, should say, "We are unworthy servants; we have only done our duty."

This seems like a strange parable, especially coming from Jesus, Mr. Servanthood. Why shouldn't the master fix dinner for the servants? But this isn't a story about labor relations. Jesus is addressing our tendency to be over-impressed with how hard we are trying, and he is pointing toward the highest stage of spiritual growth. We might think of our growth — and our perception of our growth — in four quadrants.

Incompetent and unaware. In this stage, not only am I incapable of doing something, but I don't even know how incapable I am. I can't sing, and I don't know how bad I sound. The first cost of incompetence is always the inability to perceive incompetence. In a room where one person is drunk and everyone else is sober, the drunk person is least aware of his intoxication. In the spiritual realm, this is the prodigal son who was wasting his father's money and was not even aware of his own spiritual peril.

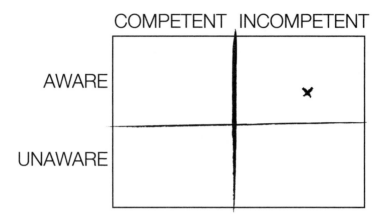

The danger in this stage is living in continued ignorance, and the need is for pain, because pain brings awareness. When the prodigal ran out of money and a famine hit the land, he longed to eat pig slop and "came to his senses." Pain is what we experience when reality crashes into us.

I had a conversation with a lifelong friend awhile back, and he said to me, "You seem so busy that I often feel like I should not contact you. I feel as if I'm usually the one who makes contact if we have contact at all. I'm often afraid that if I call you I'll be one more intrusion on your schedule. It makes me concerned for your life." It was a very painful conversation, but it changed the trajectory of our relationship. Once I was aware of what I was doing, change became possible. This leads to the second stage of growth.

Incompetent and self-conscious. Now I am still incompetent, but I have become aware — or self-conscious — of my incompetence. This is the person who always thought being a parent is easy, that controlling children is just a matter of common sense and setting boundaries — and then one day has a child and actually becomes a parent. This is the person who thought skiing looked easy until she put on a pair of skis. This is the prodigal son "when he comes to his senses." Now he realizes what a miserable failure his approach to life has actually been, and he decides to return home. But he does not think he can come back as a son. The best that he can hope for is to return as a servant.

The danger of this stage is that I will despair over my incompetence and give up. I compare myself to the old-timer who is said to have spent three hours a day on his knees in prayer, and I become so discouraged over my prayerlessness that I give up altogether. I see a family where everyone looks happy, healthy, and overachieving and think my own fathering is hopelessly inadequate. I compare my insides with other people's outsides and decide my insides are too unhealthy to be redeemed. The need in this stage is for hope.

Competent and aware. This is the person who has just received her license to drive, but must monitor where the car is in the lane and plan through every turn. This is the piano player who has to keep thinking which finger goes where. This is the alcoholic on the first day of sobriety, for whom each moment of not drinking seems worthy of applause. These people are constantly thinking about themselves and their efforts at growth. Often they compare themselves to other people, as the elder brother did in the story of the prodigal son.

The danger here is pride. William Lang, who was Archbishop of Canterbury in the first half of the twentieth century, had a painting done of himself that he did not like. He asked the Bishop of Durham what he thought of it, saying that it seemed to portray him as "proud, arrogant, and worldly." The bishop asked him, "To which of those three does Your Grace take exception?"

Stage three lostness can be the worst of all, because it carries its own blindness. People see therapists and pastors every day for anger or anxiety or addiction problems, but rarely does anyone seek help for their pride problem. There are no Betty Ford Treatment Centers for the Insufferably Arrogant, but not because we don't need them.

In another parable about trying harder, Jesus talked about a Pharisee who thanked God that he was not like a sordid little tax collector. Many contemporary Christians read this story and think, *That Pharisee thought he had to earn his way into God's favor, but I'm smarter than he was. My theology is right. Thank God I'm better than that guy who thought he was better than everybody else.*

The need here is for humility. Sometimes it takes a crisis in the area of our greatest pride — reputation, family, spirituality — for our own smugness to be punctured.

Competent and unself-conscious. This is the skier who is flying down the slopes, no longer having to think of herself, free to enjoy the thrill of skiing. This is the father welcoming home his son. In this stage, competence no longer looks heroic — just sane. This is the recovering alcoholic who has been sober twenty years. Sobriety now means not having to think about sobriety all the time, but being free to think of more interesting things.

There was a remarkable village in southeastern France called La Chambon, in which the people risked their lives to protect Jews during World War II. In later years documentaries were made about them; a wonderful book entitled *Lest Innocent Blood Be Shed* was written about them by Philip P. Hallie. But the villagers tended to be irritated by questions that made their risks sound noble or praiseworthy. "What else would you do?" they responded. "You do what needs to be done."

This is the point of Jesus' story. When we truly grow, then obeying God no longer looks like something that requires an appreciation banquet. It just looks like what should come naturally, like something that needs to be done.

Of course, we do not progress through these quadrants strictly in a linear, sequential fashion in our daily lives. We can go back and forth all the time. They can vary from one habit to another. I might be in quadrant four when it comes to alcohol and quadrant one when it comes to anxiety. But they help me remember the goal. The best version of myself lives in quadrant four, where the skier effortlessly glides down the slopes, where the father graciously welcomes his son, where the servant joyfully delights his Master.

There is an old story of an ambitious young person approaching a master and saying, "I want to be your student, your best student. How long must I study?"

"Ten years."

"But ten years is too long. What if I study twice as hard as all your other students?"

"Then it will take twenty years."

There is a river of life all around. But you can't push it.

Try softer.

PART THREE
renewing my mind

Chapter 7

Let Your Desires Lead You to God

Two very athletic nine-year-olds start taking swimming lessons. One begins because he has seen the Olympic Games and wants more than anything in the world to win a gold medal when he grows up. He pictures himself on the podium; he surrounds himself with Olympic pictures; he listens to the national anthem every day. The other kid starts lessons to please his father. Which one is likely to make it to the Olympics?

The one who is swimming for his dream.

Two twenty-year-olds have a goal to save ten thousand dollars. One of them has a dream to buy a used sports car that he loves, that he has wanted since he was sixteen, that will mean a new independence. The other twenty-year-old is saving because he thinks he should. Who do you think will reach ten thousand dollars first, willing to keep track of his expenses, eat cheaply, and forego new clothes?

The one who is saving for his dream.

In Genesis we learn that Jacob fell in love with Rachel so deeply that he agreed to work for seven years to pay her dowry. "So Jacob served seven years to get Rachel, but they seemed like only a few days to him because of his love for her." Who would regard seven years of work as a couple of days?

The one who is working for his dream.

There is no power in life like the power of "got-to-have" desire.

When Jesus described life with God, he told stories about "got-to-have" desire. He said it is like a man who found a treasure buried in the field and joyfully sold everything he owned because he had to have it. It is like a merchant who found a pearl he had been dreaming of his whole life.

Periodically when people listened to Jesus, some of them had this desire awakened in them. They saw how Jesus lived his life. They were drawn to his peace, his courage, or his wisdom. Sooner or later the thought would go off in their brain, *I must have what he has.*

Maybe you already have that burning passion. If so, you can skip this chapter. But too often we are told that we *should* desire God above all things without being told *how.* We cannot conjure up desire on command. So if your spiritual want-to factor wobbles now and then, keep reading.

» You and Your Like-o-Meter

Spiritual growth requires that our life with God move from the "should" category to the "want-to" category, and the most basic assessment we have for any experience or event is what psychologist Jonathan Haidt calls our "like-o-meter." Your like-o-meter was running the day you were born. Taste receptors in babies are pretty well developed, so for them the like-o-meter usually involves what goes into their mouths: "like it — gotta have more" or "hate it — get it out of here." As you continue to grow up, everything registers on your like-o-meter without you having to think about it. Every sound you hear, every conversation you are a part of, every bite you eat either rates positively or negatively on your scale.

Because of this, people also register somewhere on *your* like-o-meter. In the briefest of conversations you will find yourself leaning toward some people. Something in your spirit says, "I like this person. I'm enjoying this conversation." Other people will register negatively on your scale — and at the same time you're doing this, everyone around is rating you on their own like-o-meters. Rarely will we insinuate, "Right now you're about a negative seven on my scale, and if you keep talking you'll sink lower." But it's always going on. So here is a thought to consider:

Do you like God?

That may sound like a strange question, and I don't mean to be glib about God. But if I do not like being with God, I simply will not be with him much. It is good to be honest about this because if you don't like God, there's no use trying to fake him out. The point of this is not to make you feel guilty that you *should* want God more.

"Should" simply does not have the power to get you there.

» The Little Auxiliary Engine That "Should"

"Should" is a kind of auxiliary engine. It is necessary to have this, and sometimes I must do things simply because I should. But if I am running in a marathon, it doesn't matter at mile marker twenty-three whether I think I *should* finish. I will finish because I *want* to finish. "Want" will eventually wear down "should."

Likewise, spiritual growth doesn't mean a life of doing what I *should* do instead of what I *want* to do. It means coming to want to do what I should do. Jesus' point in these stories about desiring the kingdom of God is that when people come to understand how good God is, they *want* him. They don't just love him. They *like* him.

We might look at it this way: When we tell people they ought to do something, we can take that "ought" in two ways—the ought of obligation and the ought of opportunity. The first kind is our duty. You *ought* to pay your taxes. You *ought* to keep your dog on a leash. You *ought* to take your drivers' test. The second kind gives us life. You *ought* to take a break. You *ought* to see the world. You *ought* to taste this cake.

The "ought" of Jesus' message is mainly an ought of opportunity.

When we become aware of this, we feel guilty because our desire for God does not run deep enough—but we cannot make ourselves desire God more by telling ourselves that we should. God is so gracious and patient, wanting us to want him, that he is willing to work with this kind of honesty. That is why we are invited to "taste and see that the LORD is good."

Taste is an experimental word. It is an invitation from a confident chef. You don't have to commit to eating the whole thing; just try a sample— *taste*. If you don't like it, you can skip the rest. But the chef is convinced that if he can get you to take one bite, you are going to want the whole enchilada.

» Use Your Authentic Desires to "Taste and See the LORD is Good"

God made you with desires, and he wants you to desire him most of all — but not only to desire him. Part of trying softer is allowing what we naturally desire around us to lead us back to God. There is a pattern to your desires — certain activities, sensations, people, and thoughts that wake up the "got-to-have" response in you. Those desires are God's gift to you. They are part of the you God wants you to be.

When people enjoy what God has created, his heart is pleased. However, many people think, *If I want to be spiritual, I have to avoid sin, and the best way to avoid sin would be to just do away with desire altogether. If I just didn't want sex or money or food or success, I would be really spiritual because then I wouldn't sin.* But then you wouldn't be human, either. A slab of cement doesn't have to worry about weeds — but it will also never be a garden.

> Lewis Smedes wrote, "God is so great that he does not need to be our only joy. There is an earthly joy, a joy of the outer as well as the inner self, the joy of dancing as well as kneeling, the joy of playing as well as praying."

Uncorrupted by sin, desire is fabulous — fabulous because it is part of God's design. The psalmist says to God,

You open your hand and satisfy the desires of every living thing.
The LORD is righteous in all his ways and loving toward all he has made.... He fulfills the desires of those who fear him.

God is a desire-creating, desire-satisfying God. He made birds with the impulse to fly — they want to do it because God made them to do it. Dolphins swim because God made them with an instinct to swim. God doesn't plant wrong desires in his creatures.

How did Adam know he was supposed to become "one flesh" with Eve? Do you think God put it on his to-do list? "Okay, Adam, name the animals, take out the trash ... and, oh, by the way, don't forget to become one flesh with Eve."

No. Adam looked at Eve, and he discovered he had desire. Where did that desire come from? It came from God.

A beautiful prayer from the *Book of Common Prayer* begins, "Most Holy God, the source of all good desires...." God created desire, and it is God's delight to fulfill desire. I know that my desires are distorted by sin and need to be cleansed, purified, and retrained. This is what Jesus refers to when he says, "Whoever wants to be my disciple must deny themselves and take up their cross and follow me." We must say no to any desires that would keep us from living in the flow of the Spirit. We must always be ready to sacrifice a lesser desire for the sake of living a greater life.

On the other hand, nothing makes a human being more vulnerable to temptation than a joyless life. God's plan is that every time we experience an authentic desire—a God-implanted desire in us—we come to understand more deeply what a good God he is. We learn how God has wired us and what he wants us to do. As a result, we find ourselves loving this great God more and more. This is how we "taste and see" that the Lord is good, and our desire can be part of this river of life that flows in us with power and energy.

> James speaks of the fulfillment of desire when he says, "Every good and perfect gift comes from above, from the Father of all lights who satisfies the desires of those who fear him...."
>
> The writer of Proverbs says, "Hope deferred makes the heart sick, but a longing fulfilled is a tree of life." A desire fulfilled is sweet to the soul.

» Desires in Four Flavors

I would like you to walk through four categories of desires and assess yourself. As you do, be honest, because these categories on the surface might not look spiritual. Maybe you have always thought of them as having nothing to do with God, but if you let them, they can become part of living in the flow of the Spirit. The reality—the *spiritual* reality—is that each one of them has a God-designed foundation in our life.

Material Desires

We all have *material desires*—desires attached to money and clothes and cars and houses. If we could purge away all our sin, we would still desire material things because God created that stuff. All stuff, ultimately, is part of God's creation, and therefore it is all good. And therefore it is desirable.

Do you like money? In Acts 16 we read about Lydia, a businesswoman dealing in textiles, who was the first convert to Christianity in Europe. She had an eye for design and a flair for making money. Imagine the passion and drive it would take for a woman to succeed in business in the ancient world. She was good enough at it that she owned her own home, and it was large enough that it became part of her ministry. Lydia's house became the first meeting place of the first church in the history of Europe. Of all the churches built over all the centuries — Notre Dame, Westminster Abbey, and the Sistine Chapel — the very first one in Europe was the home of this Philippian businesswoman named Lydia.

Maybe you have a flair for money. You enjoy it. You don't admit it to anyone at church, but you do. You love being surrounded by beauty, design, and color. That in itself is not a bad thing. God created beauty. God loves beauty.

If these desires choke your generosity, cause you to live in debt, or create chronic dissatisfaction, then it is time to say no. But it is a good thing to put beauty in your environment that speaks to your soul. When you see that beauty, embrace that God-given joy and thank him that he is such a good God.

In that moment, you can experience the flow of the Spirit in your life.

As the Spirit flows in you, maybe God will give you creative, new ideas about how to share what you have, just as he did with Lydia.

Is it a bad thing to like fast cars? That is a material desire. Maybe God placed a desire for fast cars within you so you could be a policeman, so that you could drive really fast and it would be legal. (My nephew is training with the California Highway Patrol, and it sounds like fun.) Or maybe you drive fast so policemen can have something to do.

If you love engines, if you love to work with your hands, remember that you were made in the image of a creative God who engineered this unbelievable, cosmic machine with forces and energies so transcendently mind-boggling that people devote brilliant scientific careers trying to understand just a tiny bit of it. If you are fascinated with engines, that too is spiritual, a direct reflection of the fact that you are made in the image of this God who is the most creative engineer ever. It counts!

Now, if your desire for cars blocks good stewardship or puts you in debt, it is time to say no. If not, is it possible that enjoying a car might be something you could do with God? And when you are driving, you might say, "God, I invite you to be with me in this moment."

The Spirit could be flowing with you right there—*j-u-s-t* under the speed limit.

Achievement Desires

There have been few people in history more motivated by achievement than the apostle Paul. He was constantly moving, teaching, building, and motivating. He described his life with metaphors such as "I have fought the good fight. I have finished the race." God did not take away Paul's desire to achieve; rather, he harnessed it so that Paul could serve others.

We all have desires to achieve things, because God created us to have dominion. That is why the writer of Ecclesiastes says, "Whatever your hand finds to do, do it with all your might." It is a good thing to want to achieve.

Maybe you have a strong drive in your career. Maybe you are highly motivated by the opportunity to learn. Maybe you just love to accomplish. If your achievement desires are leading you to workaholism, to worshiping status, to neglecting prayer, or to using people, then your work needs redirection. But if that is not the case—if you find yourself growing in God and there's an inner fire in you to achieve—go ahead and achieve. Revel in the joy of exercising godly dominion.

Use your ability to accomplish good for others. And when you are doing it—when you are contributing to a meeting, adding value to a team, or formulating ideas—you will know it is more than just you. As you have relational skills that enable you to bond with clients, you can simultaneously pray for them and bless them. Every now and then stop and thank God that you get to do this, for as you achieve and feel joy in doing so, you are exercising dominion and opening yourself up to the flow of the Spirit.

Relational Desires

In the Old Testament we read about the friendship between Jonathan and David. Even though Jonathan was heir to the throne, he voluntarily gave up power because he knew his friend David was God's choice to be king. Jonathan wanted to be friend more than he wanted to be king. That is unusual in circles of power. Jonathan did not become David's friend because he was pursuing the discipline of spiritual friendship. He simply liked David, and that friendship produced generosity and humility in Jonathan that changed the course of Israel. There have been countless kings whom nobody remembers — but Jonathan's friendship with David has inspired the human race for thousands of years.

We all have relational desires, and maybe you hunger for deep relationships but never really pursue them. You get too busy. If deep relationships don't just fall into your lap, you give up. Deep relationships, however, don't just fall into our lap. Jonathan had to overcome unbelievable barriers to build his friendship with David — and there is a good chance that you will, too, to build a friendship.

My friend Chuck has the spiritual gift of breakfast. He meets people at a southern franchise called the Waffle House. The waitress loves to wait on him because he tips well and makes everybody laugh. He is both really funny and utterly unguarded about his own brokenness, which makes people open up to him like tulips in the sun. And although he often ponders doubts when he is alone, he feels God's presence most powerfully when he sits in the Waffle House and is allowed to see someone's soul. It is not coffee that brings people to him; it is the rivers of living water flowing out of him.

If you have a gift for hospitality, throw parties on a regular basis. The joy you feel when people are gathering and talk is flowing and laughter is resounding and new friendships are being forged comes from God. Your living room can become an outpost of the fellowship of the Spirit.

Physical Desires

Because your body was made by God, you also have appetites for things to eat, drink, touch, and see — *physical* desires. The Old Testament is filled with commands for God's people to feast, eat, drink, celebrate, sing, dance, shout, and make music — all things we do with our bodies. These appetites, desires, and delights can then become a way of remembering how good our God is and can lead us to become more joy-filled people.

You learn to connect the gift — which you already love — with the Giver, whom you want to love more. You start with what you already like and work your way back to its source, to God. You taste and see that the Lord is good.

God loves it when you enjoy stretching or training your body in new skills, or when you enjoy what your eyes see, your ears hear, your mouth tastes, and your skin feels. The physical is not separate from the spiritual; it is the Spirit who makes our bodies come to life.

How do you "connect the dots," learning to connect the gift with the Giver?

≈ Take a moment at the beginning of the day to invite God to be with you.
≈ Consciously say "thank you" to him in the midst of your enjoyment.
≈ Meet with other people who share your joys, so that you add community to your delight.
≈ Reflect on how much sadder the world would be without these gifts, which helps you not to take them for granted.
≈ Put pictures on your screensaver or desk of what enjoyably reminds you of God's goodness throughout your day.
≈ Use a "breath prayer" such as "thank you for my body" or "taste and see" to help you share your experience with him. A breath prayer is a simple, one-sentence prayer (I can say it in one breath) that energizes my soul the way oxygen energizes my body.
≈ Reflect on passages in the Bible that show God delighting in bodies and creatures and fulfilling desires. (Psalms 102 and 103 are excellent in this regard.)

Have you ever had the desire to be physically attractive? (I will ask that once in a while at churches, but no one ever raises their hand.) This needs to be kept in proper perspective, of course, for the writer of Proverbs did warn, "Like a gold ring in a pig's snout is a beautiful woman who shows no discretion." Beauty of character is a greater good than exterior beauty—but God *did* create our bodies. So can we get real? God made us with a love of beauty.

Some stylists I know once started what they called a "hairdressers ministry." At first it sounded odd to me. The only hairstylist I could think of in the Bible was Delilah, and that didn't turn out so well. But serving people by cutting their hair is a good thing, and people will sometimes tell things to the person cutting their hair that they don't tell anyone else.

This group began giving complimentary haircuts to physically challenged and mentally challenged folks, and then they traveled to Costa Rica to serve young women trying to escape a life of prostitution. The stylists cared for bodies without wanting anything in return. They honored and freely served bodies that had not been honored or served for a long time, bodies that had been turned into objects. What they did touches our hearts deeply because our bodies were made by God—they are precious to him.

It is a good thing to eat food you love to eat, wear clothes you love to wear, listen to music that makes you feel glad, and then to thank God that he gave you your body so you can see and hear and touch and laugh and dance. As you open yourself to the flow of the Spirit in your physical desires, you begin to love God more and more, not because you should or because it's commanded, but because when you get to know him, you just can't help it. What else could you do?

Hardly anything gives me more joy than when I get to give to one of my kids. When I do and their face lights up because I have satisfied a deep desire in them, that is the best. Of course, I don't want them to become selfish, and so I often try to monitor their character to know when denial is required. But all of that is remedial stuff. It is not my ultimate goal. I just love it when I can give and they light up.

That is the best.

Chapter 8
Think Great Thoughts

One Saturday night our house was assaulted by an odor so indescribably noxious we had to evacuate. We figured it was a gas leak and called both the gas company and the fire department. As it turned out, a skunk had gotten very close to our house.

I made a few phone calls, but no exterminator would come to look for a skunk, so we figured the problem would go away on its own. Most of the odor faded away, and what lingered we got used to. It didn't bother us—until a visitor would enter and say, "It smells like a *skunk* around here."

A week later I was on the road when my family called to say the skunk had struck again. I had to find someone who specialized in the ways of the skunk—a "skunk whisperer." The man discovered that we had two live skunks and one dead one permanently residing in the crawl space under our house. It cost a lot to get the skunks removed. But it was worth it.

You cannot get rid of the skunk odor without getting rid of the skunk. Our sense of smell has a unique power to evoke emotion, and in our inner lives, our feelings are like aromas. Our positive feelings — joy, pleasure, gratitude — thrill us like the scent of freshly baked bread. Negative feelings — sadness, worry, anger — can make us want to evacuate our lives. When they hit, your mood dips, you lose energy, God seems distant, prayer seems pointless, sin looks tempting, and life looks bleak.

But our feelings never descend on us at random. As a general rule, our emotions flow out of our thoughts. Discouraged people tend to think discouraging thoughts. Worried people tend to think anxious thoughts. These thoughts become so automatic that, like the lingering skunk odor, after a while we don't even notice we are thinking them. We get used to what is sometimes called "stinking thinking."

This can happen to anyone. The prophet Elijah had reached a high point of his life when he defeated the prophets of Baal. Then one event — the opposition of Jezebel — plunged him into fear. Look at his thoughts: he felt worthless ("I am no better than my ancestors"), hopeless ("he ran for his life"), isolated ("I am the only one left"), and unable to cope ("I have had enough"). He actually wanted to die ("Take my life, LORD").

But God is the great healer. He had Elijah take a nap and eat a snack, then he did a little divine cognitive therapy to replace each of these life-killing thoughts. He gave Elijah an epiphany ("the LORD is about to pass by"), filled his future with hope because God would accompany him ("go back the way you came"), revealed that he was not isolated ("yet I reserve seven thousand in Israel"), and infused his life full of meaning because God had a mission for him.

Elijah thought his problem was Jezebel, but there will always be a Jezebel in our lives. The real challenge is between our ears.

The way we live will inevitably be a reflection of the way we think. True change always begins in our mind. The good news is that if God can change Elijah's thinking, he can change ours. What makes people the way they are — what makes you *you* — is mainly the way they think.

> Let God transform you into a new person by changing the way you think. (Romans 12:2 NLT)

Becoming the best version of yourself, then, rests on one simple directive: *Think great thoughts!* People who live great lives are people who habitually think great thoughts. Their thoughts incline them toward confidence, love, and joy. Trying to change your emotions by willpower without allowing the stream of your thoughts to be changed by the flow of the Spirit is like fumigating the house of the skunk smell while the skunks continue to live in your crawl space. But God can change the way we think, and in this chapter we will look at two ways we can open ourselves up to his work: learning to monitor what happens in our minds, and then resetting our minds to a better frequency.

It is time to go after the skunks.

» Learn to Monitor Your Mind

Our thought patterns become as habitual as brushing our teeth. After a while we don't even think about them. We get so used to bitter thoughts or anxious thoughts or selfish thoughts that we don't even notice what we are thinking about.

One of the great barriers to a flourishing mind is sometimes called mindlessness. My body is at the breakfast table with my family, but my mind isn't. It is ruminating over my problems—a repetitive, anxious, dull, low-grade obsession with tasks and problems. I am *absentminded*; my mind has gone AWOL. Other people can tell I am not fully present because my face is less alive and responsive. I talk less, and when I do say something, it is superficial and terse. I don't do this on purpose. It simply becomes a habit of my mind.

The spiritual life begins with paying attention to our thoughts, which is why the psalmist prayed, "Search me, God, and know my heart; test me and know my anxious thoughts." God knows our thoughts better than we do, and he will help us learn what is going on in our mind from one moment to the next.

As I monitor my mind, I will encounter many thoughts that are unwelcome visitors: I get anxious. I catastrophize. I envy. But I will also begin to recognize what kind of thoughts the Spirit flows in. The apostle Paul gives us a great framework for understanding which are the thoughts and attitudes that come from the Spirit. He writes, "The mind controlled by the sinful nature is death, but the mind controlled by the Spirit is life and peace."

Take any thought, especially thoughts that feel weighty or that you find yourself turning over and over in your mind, and ask, *What direction do those thoughts lead me in? Are they leading me toward life—toward God's best version of me? Or in the other direction?*

CHAPTER 8

LIFE & PEACE

(spirit) — THOUGHTS — (sinful)

DEATH

I received a letter a while ago containing a criticism of me. When I read it, I could feel a twinge in my belly, that core Jesus talks about. I thought, *Someone sees junk in me. I'm embarrassed and ashamed. It will never change. Lots of people see it.* I was tempted to feel sorry for myself, because there was truth to my thoughts. But they did not lead to life.

Then I had another set of thoughts, in which my negativity was turned not toward me but toward the writer of the letter: *He has bigger problems than I do. I'm a pastor. Who is he to criticize me?* Then I became defensive and withdrawn, and again I went into a downward spiral.

But there is an alternative. I could say, "Holy Spirit, would you help me? Would you give me the right thoughts?"

When I do that, thoughts like these come: *Yes, what you're feeling is hurt, and part of that hurt is nothing more than wounded vanity. We can deal with that. I still love you with all your junk. Your well-being with me is not at risk. The man who wrote this may see a flaw in you, but nobody really thinks you're perfect anyway, except your mother. It will actually be better for you not to have to pretend. Here's a chance for you to grow.*

This is grace. Even though there are elements of pain in these thoughts, they do not paralyze me. They bring energy. They are true, and they give me ground to stand on. I realize that if I can keep my mind centered on these thoughts, right feelings and actions are likely to flow out of them. The prophet Isaiah said that we will be kept in perfect peace if our mind is *stayed* on God. This is living in the flow of the Spirit.

One of the simplest and most powerful ways to monitor your mind is called the experience sampling method. Program a watch or iPhone to beep at random intervals through the day. When it does, write down (or make a mental note if you're a spontaneous non-journaler) where you were and what you were doing.

92

Then, on a scale of 1–5, monitor your thoughts like this:

	VERY				NOT AT ALL
PEACE	5	4	3	2	1
CONNECTED TO GOD	5	4	3	2	1

Do this for a week, and look for those activities and people that most help you live in the flow of the Spirit. How can you add those? What are the activities and relationships that most block the flow? How can you change or diminish those?

Learn to become aware of the flow of thoughts in your mind without trying too hard to change them. Toddlers who are beginning to walk consistently learn from their falls, but without judgments that paralyze

Here is another exercise for monitoring your mind. Read through the list of words below, which represent the primary patterns that our thinking falls into. As you read through the list, reflect on your own mental habits and think about how other people experience you. Then select which three of the words express patterns that tend to most characterize your thinking. Ask one or two people who know and love you to go through the same list and give you the three words that they think most characterize you.

Grateful	Curious	Stubborn
Defensive	Hopeful	Angry
Self-preoccupied	Passive	Determined
Dissatisfied	Anxious	Engaged
Creative	Courageous	

them. ("Fallen again! What a clumsy oaf I am! I'm crawling the rest of the day. I don't deserve to walk.") Learning to walk in the Spirit takes at least as much grace and strength as learning to walk on two legs, and the Spirit will always help lead us toward God's best version of ourselves. We can picture it this way:

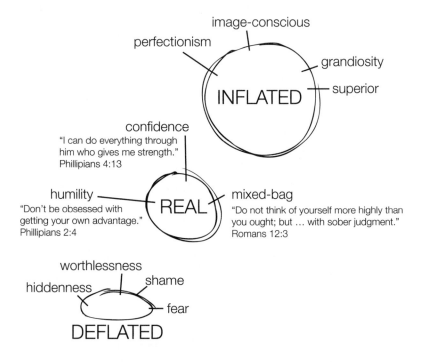

Much like Elijah, we can be tempted to think we are the only one really faithful, the only special or gifted or entitled one. This is related to that old temptation "you will be like God," for when we think of ourselves as god-like, we become obsessed with our own success and happiness and need to prop up an inflated sense of our competence and worth. Then reality hits, and often when this idealized me crumbles, what is left is a deflated, "shattered" me. Like Adam and Eve, we want to run and hide. We think that we have nothing to offer and that everything is awful.

But the Spirit wants to liberate us, both from thinking as if we are God and from thinking as if we are nothing. There is a God; it is not you. He wants to help you be the real you, the best version of you. He wants to help you become you-ier.

So you move to the next step.

» Learn to Set Your Mind

You can't stop thinking wrong thoughts by trying harder to not think them, but you can do something else. You can "set your mind," for the most basic power you have over your mind is that you can choose what you pay attention to. At any moment—including this one—we can turn our thoughts in one direction or another. It is within our capacity to set our minds; that explains why two people can be in the same set of circumstances and yet have completely different experiences.

A friend sent me passages from a dog's diary and a cat's diary as a means to show me the difference a mindset can make:

Excerpts from a Dog's Diary:

8:00 am—Dog food! My favorite thing!

9:30 am—A car ride! My favorite thing!

9:40 am—A walk in the park! My favorite thing!

10:30 am—Got rubbed and petted! My
        favorite thing!

12:00 pm—Lunch! My favorite thing!

1:00 pm—Played in the yard! My
        favorite thing!

3:00 pm—Wagged my tail! My
        favorite thing!

5:00 pm—Milk bones! My favorite thing!

7:00 pm—Got to play ball! My favorite thing!

8:00 pm—Wow! Watched TV with the people! My
        favorite thing!

11:00 pm—Sleeping on the bed! My favorite thing!

Excerpts from a Cat's Diary:

Day 983 of my captivity. My captors continue to taunt me with bizarre, little dangling objects. The only thing that keeps me going is my dream of escape.

Two creatures, identical circumstances, but totally different experiences. What is the difference? It is a way of thinking. Gratitude is one mindset; entitlement is another. John Milton wrote in his epic poem *Paradise Lost*, "The mind is its own place, and in itself can make a heaven of hell, a hell of heaven."

Setting your mind is like setting a thermostat. It is creating a target for the climate. Once you set a thermostat, the heating and air-conditioning will have to adjust in relation to the weather. It is a constant process, but the goal is for the system to create a life-giving climate. So too it is with our minds. Many people try to tell themselves to *stop* thinking negative thoughts — which immediately brings to mind the very thoughts they are supposed to stop thinking.

✳ John Milton wrote, "The mind is its own place, and in itself can make a heaven of hell, a hell of heaven."

Set your mind on things above, not on earthly things. (Colossians 3:2)

Those who live in accordance with the Spirit have their minds set on what the Spirit desires. (Romans 8:5)

There is a better way.

My friend Danny went spelunking in the caves of Iowa. The man guiding took him deep underground, then said he would lead Danny through a passageway into a spectacular chamber. The passageway was small enough that Danny had to stoop at first. Then as it grew still smaller, he had to get on his hands and knees. Eventually the only way to go forward was to lay on his back and push his body forward with his feet. Then the ceiling was so low that when he inhaled he could not move at all! He had to stop, inhale, and exhale, and only then was his chest low enough to allow him to move. By this point it was physically impossible to back out. If the passageway had gotten any smaller they would have lain there and died in that cave.

Danny is a sky-diving, mountain-climbing, hang-gliding thrill-seeker, but there in that cave he felt sheer panic. He was terrified. He tried fighting his fear, but he kept picturing his dead body moldering in the cave. Finally, he told his guide he was about to lose it, and the guide said, "Danny, close your eyes and listen to my voice. I will keep talking, calmly, and guide you through this. We will be okay. I have been here before. I will get you to the other side. But you must listen to my voice. It will not work for you to let your thoughts run wild. Just focus on my voice."

Danny did so. What freed him from panic and fear was *not* trying hard to quit thinking fearful thoughts. It was listening to another voice.

What voice do you listen to when you're in the cave and it's dark, when the ceiling is low and you can't back out? The Spirit longs to flow in our minds all the time. One reason why people have found memorizing Scripture helpful is that it helps us listen to the voice of our guide when we are in the cave. We set our minds on those thoughts that equip us for life. I might miss a second serve, but the Spirit will remind me that I am still God's beloved child. I might be criticized, but the Spirit will remind me that truth and grace are always my friend. The Spirit desires his presence to be a river of life—of love and joy and peace—through each moment of the day.

God's gift of your mind is unbelievably lavish. Before you were born, your body produced about 200 billion neurons, giving you the power to think and react. You had such an embarrassment of riches that by the time you were born, you had killed off around 100 billion of those neurons, and you have never even missed them. Between your second month in the womb and your second birthday, your body was producing 1.8 synapses *per second*. And you weren't even tired!

Your thoughts have enormous power over your life. Researchers have found that tennis players can improve their backhands simply by rehearsing them *mentally*. Neurons that will change you are firing in your mind. Over time, those pathways between neurons were shaped in ways that are absolutely unique to you—and God has no intention of wasting them.

Even twenty years ago, researchers thought the adult brain was genetically determined and structurally unchangeable. But they have since found that even into adulthood the brain is amazingly changeable—it has neuroplasticity. Which synapses remain and which ones wither away depends on your mental habits. Those that carry no traffic go out of business like bus routes with no customers. Those that get heavily trafficked get stronger and thicker. The mind shapes the brain. Neurons that wire together fire together. In other words, when you practice hope, love, or joy, your mind is actually, literally, rewiring your brain!

> Researcher Jeffrey Schwartz, echoing pioneer psychologist William James, writes, "The essential achievement of the will is to attend to one object and hold it clear and strong before the mind, letting all others — its rivals for attention and subsequent action — fade away like starlight swamped by the radiance of the Sun."

Because you were made in the image of God, you have the capacity for what might be called "directed mental force." Ever drop a contact lens on a carpet? Your focus causes your brain to suppress attention to anything that could distract you: lint, color, design, or cookie crumbs. All the kinds of sights simply don't register. Neurons don't fire. You have "set your mind" to look for that contact lens, and it responds as if you were giving a bloodhound a shirt with the scent of a fugitive.

It is amazing how often people think they are the victim of whatever thoughts happen to be running through their heads. It is as if they are passive spectators watching thoughts run across the screen, with no control over what's on it.

But there is a fundamental battle in the spiritual life being waged by the Evil One over the nature of the thoughts that run through your mind. The ultimate freedom that you have, the freedom no one can take away even in a concentration camp, is the freedom to decide what your mind will dwell on. I "set my mind" to look for the presence and goodness of God in my life, the river of living water flowing out of my belly.

A wonderful man I know used to stop by a newsstand each morning to get a paper on his way to work. Each day the worker behind the counter was surly, but this man would respond with unfailing good humor and politeness. A friend who sometimes went with him to work asked him why he remained so kind in the face of so much rudeness. He replied, "Why would I let his unhappiness dictate my attitude?"

Somebody is bussing my table at a restaurant. I don't notice him, as he is just a bit character in the movie of my life. Then the Spirit intervenes. The thought occurs in my mind, *Pay attention. Look in his eyes. This is a man with a family, with hopes and dreams. He is bussing tables because he hopes to provide for his children so that they can have more education and possibilities.* For a moment I come alive. I can tell him thank you and mean it. I can bless him — willing good for him before God. And the world moves a tiny little bit toward flourishing.

Sometimes emotions may be leading us down a destructive path, but the Spirit always offers another way. For instance, someone might say, "I'm in love with him. He's married; I know it's wrong, but I can't help it."

Actually, yes you can. You can pray and ask the Spirit to help reset your heart. You could spend an hour a day every day for a month with women who have lost their husbands to infidelity. Listen to their stories. Look into the eyes of their children. Hear the betrayal. See a broken promise through their eyes. You will think new thoughts.

In the flow of the Holy Spirit, your feelings will change. At any moment you can turn your mind to God. The Holy Spirit is flowing, wanting to renew your mind all the time — as if there is a little network called HSN (Holy Spirit Network). I can tune into the Holy Spirit any moment. I can ask the Spirit to guide my thoughts.

I can pause, and listen.

Joshua Bell is perhaps the world's finest violinist. His parents knew he was something special when he was only four years old and he stretched rubber bands to his dresser drawers and played classical tunes on them, adjusting their pitch by pulling the drawers in and out.

As an experiment, he recently played — unannounced — in a metro station in Washington, DC. The people who conducted this experiment were warned by experts that a crowd would certainly gather; they might need extra security. Surely many people would flock to this once-in-a-lifetime opportunity.

Joshua Bell brought his 1713 Stradivarius violin — which cost millions of dollars — and began to play the six most beautiful songs in his repertoire. The world's greatest violinist playing the world's greatest music on the world's greatest instrument.

But no one stopped. A thousand people walked by. You can see it on video. Children would tug on their parents' sleeves, but the adults were too preoccupied. One woman alone recognized him and stopped to listen. She gave him a bigger tip (twenty dollars) than the other thousand people put together. They were in a hurry, hurrying past Joshua Bell because they had other things to do.

Jesus said, "To what can I compare this generation? ... We played the flute for you, and you did not dance."

The Master is still playing, but listening is optional. Those who have ears to hear, let them hear.

Chapter 9

Feed Your Mind with Excellence

We once lived across the street from a couple who did not get along. The husband worked in security, but his passion was to be a body-builder. He was strong, sarcastic, and self-centered. His wife was small and timid — and angry.

He had to go to work every morning at 6:00, and she got up at 5:00 to fix his lunch. We wondered why she would do this for someone she was so mad at until she explained that she was secretly packing his lunches with enough calories to put weight on Shamu the Killer Whale. She loaded what he thought were dietary turkey sandwiches with butter and mayonnaise. She put extra sugar in his yogurt and made his protein shakes with half-and-half. He worked out a lot, but he could never understand why his body didn't look like the guys in the magazine.

He never knew she was larding him up when he wasn't looking.

Our bodies are constantly being formed by what goes into them. We may not like this truth, we may not heed it, but we can't evade it. Bodies get shaped by what goes into them.

Sometimes our kids are tempted to feed our dog bad things — things the dog should not be fed. When bad things go into the dog, bad things come out of the dog. We know that about dogs, and we recognize the importance of what we put into what we value. We are careful about what fuel we put into high performance cars, commercial airliners, or thoroughbreds. But we may forget this when it comes to our minds.

In this world we are being bombarded by a steady stream of messages from the media, bosses, co-workers, people we date, books, iPods — and from our own thoughts. Our mind will be shaped by whatever we feed it while the Evil One tries to lard up our mind when we're not looking. He will put depression in our thoughts at breakfast, sprinkle temptation in our mind at noon, and slip us a worry sandwich when it's time for bed.

He will try to keep us from noticing what we are putting into our mind.

» A Flourishing Mind Feeds on Life-giving Thoughts

If I want my mind to be full of life, I will have to pay attention to what it is focused on. One of the greatest gifts God has given the human race is Scripture — yet we often turn it into a burden. Sometimes people will ask me, "How many minutes a day am I supposed to read the Bible? Seven? Fifteen? What is the minimum I can read and not have God be mad at me?"

That is the wrong question. God is not mad at us for not reading the Bible. No matter how much we read the Bible, he won't love you any more than he loves you right now. The question is, *What can you feed your mind with so that it can flourish?*

Other people ask, "How much more information about the Bible am I supposed to know? What if I feel guilty because so many people know so much more about the Bible than I do?" But the reason to read the Bible is not to fulfill a spiritual duty or to gain more knowledge. It is to jump in the river. So let us talk about the feeding of our minds — including how we use the Bible. But let's not try harder. Let's try softer.

> Blessed are those ... who delight in the law of the LORD and meditate on his law day and night. They are like a tree planted by streams of water, which yields its fruit in season and whose leaf does not wither — whatever they do prospers.

The phrase "meditate on his law day and night" may sound intimidating, unrealistic, or undesirable. How would I ever get any work done if I spent the whole day contemplating Lamentations? But that's not necessary. That is not the idea.

There is an old saying that if you can worry, you can meditate. Meditating is simply turning a thought over and over in your mind. As you do that, neurons are firing and your brain is rewiring. When you receive information that matters to you, you can't help meditating on it.

When I was in high school, a friend of mine told me about a girl who liked me. I could not believe it, because I knew this girl and she was *way* out of my league.

"This can't be true," I said.

"But it *is* true," my friend said. "I don't understand it either, but it's true."

That night my mind fixated on this thought: *She likes me.* I couldn't stop thinking about it. My mind just went there over and over. *She* likes *me.* So the next day, although I could hardly believe it was true, I called her up and asked her out.

It turned out it wasn't true.

But I had one really good night thinking about it. It was my *delight*, and what I delight in, I can't help thinking about.

What would it look like to delight in the law of the Lord? It certainly is something deeper than being thrilled about a bunch of rules in the Bible. It starts with a vision of being loved by God. God is way out of my league. He is in the *perfection* league; I am in the *fallen* league. This wonderful God, this mysterious, all-powerful, all-holy God—he loves me! Periodically this truth bursts in, and we can't stop thinking about it.

He loves *me*!

When we first learn that, our minds may keep returning to that thought the way they do to a surprise promotion. We can't stop thinking about it. However, the day will come when you *can* stop thinking about it—and not because you're a spiritual failure. Neurons respond to novelty, and what ceases to be novel ceases to cause neurons to fire. If you have been married thirty years, you are able to think about things besides the fact that your spouse loves you. Not because you love that person less, but simply because your neurons have gotten used to that information.

The psalmist is saying that he has actually found ways to carry thoughts of God's love and protection into his mental life—his inner flow—in a way that makes his whole life richer. Being loved by God has become such a deep part of his mental circuitry that now it affects all his other thoughts as well.

There are two ways of looking when it comes to a window. I can look *at* a window. I can notice the glass, see if there are any streaks or dust particles or bubbles in it. Or, I can look *through* a window. I can view the world beyond it by using it as an opening to the world.

Sometimes I look *at* the Scriptures. I study its story. I ask questions. Thoughts of God's goodness, love, and peace lodge in my mind. The idea is that I begin also to look at my world *through* the Scriptures — through the perspective of God's constant care and presence.

» Free to Think about "Whatever …"

In giving instruction about how to feed our minds, the apostle Paul writes, "Whatever is true, whatever is noble, whatever is right, whatever is pure, whatever is lovely, whatever is admirable — if anything is excellent or praiseworthy — think about such things."

The striking word in that command is *whatever*. Our minds are being shaped all the time, but we have great freedom to pursue minds that flourish. As a bee that can find nectar in all kinds of flowers, we are now free — even commanded — to feed our minds on noble thoughts wherever we find them. The Bible itself commands us to look beyond just the Bible to feed our minds.

Let us meditate for a moment on that phrase "whatever is lovely." Think of something that is "lovely" to you. A sunset. A favorite novel. Tiny robins chirping in the nest. The face of someone you love. Music that makes you dance. Let your mind dwell there for a moment. Give it directed mental focus.

You just obeyed the Bible. That "counts." You just opened up your mind a bit to the flow of the Holy Spirit.

What causes your mind to be drawn to what is true, noble, right, pure, lovely, admirable, excellent, and praiseworthy? Maybe it is taking art classes and learning to see beauty you had never noticed before. One man I know spends much of his time in his car, listening to a list of the twenty best works of English fiction. Maybe you are an athlete, and competition stirs you to admire the pursuit of excellence. What causes your mind to be drawn to those things?

God's desire is for you to have a mind that habitually thinks noble, true, pure, admirable thoughts. You have great freedom—*whatever*—to allow the Spirit to rewire your mind. As that happens, the Holy Spirit's goal is not to get you really good at suppressing angry behavior. It is for you to have a mind characterized by an ever-increasing flow of Spirit-guided, truth-based, life-producing thoughts and feelings.

When we read about what is noble, when we see something praiseworthy, we experience what psychologist Jonathan Haidt called "elevation." We actually feel a slight expansion in our chest; we feel lighter in our bodies. Our emotions are inspired, and we want to become more excellent ourselves. That counts as obedience to Scripture. That is spiritual.

The flow of the Holy Spirit is always available. You do not have to wait for anything.

» How to Get Fed from the Bible

We are free to feed our minds from every good source, but there is no source like the Bible. It is a written revelation of who God is and of what God's purposes are for humanity. No book comes close to it in influence or significance. Eugene Peterson writes, "Christians feed on Scripture. Holy Scripture nurtures the holy community as food nurtures the human body. Christians don't simply learn or study or use Scripture; we assimilate it, take it into our lives in such a way that it gets metabolized into acts of love." Yet consumer researchers say that the average Bible owner possesses nine Bibles and is looking for more. Something is lacking.

Scripture has never been easier to obtain, and Scripture has never been more difficult to absorb. The unspoken secret is that many people find the Bible boring. This is both a serious problem and a quite recent one. Ancient Greek had no word for boredom. The word did not have its current meaning in English until the last few centuries. We look at the ancient world, and they had no television, no Internet, no movies, no iTunes, and virtually no books—and we think of how boring it must have been.

But the ancients were not bored. We are the ones who get bored because our capacity to focus our attention, to delight our minds in sustained thought, has been weakened by our dependence on external stimuli.

Do you know what country has produced the most poets per capita of any country in world? Iceland. Why? Well, they have nothing better to do. If you are sitting around in a hut and the sun is gone for the next six months, that is a long time to just listen to wind. So the Icelanders would make up sagas and tell them by the fire, then repeat them, memorize them, embellish them, and delight in them. This gave them something to think about when they were alone, so their society created poets by the bushelful.

Have you ever read through one of the Old Testament genealogies? One begat after another. "These were the chiefs among Esau's descendants: The sons of Eliphaz the firstborn of Esau: Chiefs Teman, Omar, Zepho, Kenaz, Korah, Gatam and Amalek." Did it seem just a tiny bit boring to you? Want to guess who it did not bore? The people who first wrote them. In the ancient culture, they *loved* reading them! Those genealogies meant that they weren't just nomads wandering around. They had a story. They had an identity. They were somebody.

> Knowing your origins, knowing your relations, creates order out of social chaos. This is still practiced in oral cultures. In ancient biblical times, people actually took delight in memorizing these genealogies, in reciting them and handing them down. The act of memorizing genealogies was a skill that was greatly admired. It gave them a challenge and huge satisfaction when they were able to memorize that list. They were reciting the Bible, but it was also much like a game.

Part of why delighting in the Scriptures is harder for us than for the ancients is that we have many more tempting alternatives. When David was watching sheep, he had nothing better to do, so he wrote psalms, memorized them, and sang them. They shaped his mind. "The LORD is my shepherd; I shall not want...." The pasture became an outpost of God's kingdom.

In a world with so many *easy* options to amuse or distract our minds, we all have to learn to be fed by the Bible.

Read the Bible with Curiosity

We can learn much from the Bible if we just ask questions: *Who is the author of this book? Who was the audience? Is the writing a par-*

able, instruction, a letter, or history? How would the people to whom the words were first written have understood it? Often the biggest barrier to our becoming learners is what we think we already know.

> Philosopher-educator John Dewey wrote, "Genuine igno-rance is profitable, because it is likely to be accompanied by humility, curiosity, and open mindedness; whereas ability to repeat catch-phrases, cant terms, familiar prop-ositions, gives the conceit of learning and coats the mind with varnish, waterproof to new ideas."

A friend of mine, a pastor of a church in the Midwest, was delivering the children's sermon one Sunday and quizzed the kids to see how much they knew about the Bible. "See that man with two stone tablets in his hand standing on a mountain?" he asked, pointing to the stained-glass windows. "Can anyone tell me his name?"

"Moses," said one girl.

"Very good. How did you know?"

"Because the name underneath the man says, 'Moses.'"

My friend had looked at the window a hundred times, but had never seen the names.

Our brains are wired to fire in the face of novelty and to shut down under familiarity. This means that when we read Scripture we will be most engaged if we ask questions and look for something we had not noticed before.

One of the most important resources in reading the Scripture is one we always carry around with us — our imagination. When you read a Bible story, take time to recreate the details. In John 21, for example, Jesus has prepared a breakfast of fish over a charcoal fire when the disciples come in from fishing. What does the water sound like, lapping against the boat? What is the smell of the charcoal fire and the fish sizzling in the pan? I imagine the light of an early sunrise streaking the sky. How does it feel to be Peter as Jesus calls his name? How would it feel if it were me, if I had denied Jesus, as Peter had? When I enter into the story, it comes alive and God can speak to me in a new way through a passage I may have read many times before.

Read the Bible with Integrity

A woman I know leads a small group of friends who are reading the Bible together, and one of them recently said, "I have come to realize that I don't believe the Bible is true." Her group cheered for her—not because the unbelief is good news, but because she had finally gotten honest enough to name her doubts.

One of the barriers to feeding my mind through Scripture comes when I am confused or unsure whether I can believe a story, but try to force myself to believe it or avoid reading it so that my faith doesn't get disturbed. Only when I read the Bible with an utter commitment to pursuing what I believe to be true, however, is it able to feed my mind.

So when you read the Bible and you have doubts, don't "try harder" to believe. "Try softer." Let God know about your doubts; he already knows about them anyway.

Read Scripture with Expectancy

Sometimes people bring energy to a gathering; sometimes they just show up. My wife used to head up a ministry to twenty-something folks who were mostly single. I knew, even with my eyes closed, if I was in their presence, just by the smell. They smelled great. In regular church services, with mostly old married people, no one cares how they smell. But when people are hopeful of meeting someone, there is electricity in the air. And a scent in the air. They are alive.

It is the same with God. If I really believe that I may meet with God, I don't just show up. My mind is awake. I am hoping and looking for something beyond myself. If my wife hands me the sports page to read, she doesn't care if I scan it casually. But if she hands me a long letter she has spent hours writing for our twenty-fifth anniversary, it is not time for a casual scan. I approach that reading with a different attitude.

I can't *make* myself be excited about reading the Bible, and it isn't wise to try. How it must disappoint the Spirit if he is waiting to flow through our thoughts, but we are too distracted to hear him.

But if I come to Scripture with an attitude of expectancy, that changes things.

Read Scriptures with an Active Mind

I am thinking of a song that I bet you can sing even if you have never heard a recording of it. We don't know who wrote the lyrics. In fact, it doesn't even have lyrics. It was written by some anonymous genius, and it doesn't contain a single word. But it is the most important song you ever learned.

It is the ABC song.

Until the past few centuries, almost all human knowledge was condensed into forms such as the "alphabet song." To this day, we still use such devices to learn how long the months are ("thirty days hath September ...") or rules of grammar ("I before e, except after c ..."). Television networks spend billions of dollars getting jingles to burrow their way into brains. (I have a hard time remembering my cousins' names, but I can tell you all seven people on Gilligan's Island because I could sing the theme song in my sleep.)

When I study something, I take its order into my mind. I internalize it. It belongs to me; it becomes part of me. Whole new worlds suddenly become available to me.

National Public Radio did a series in which people talked about what they believe in. One person featured was a woman from India who had been sold into marriage at age twelve and abandoned by her husband at fifteen. A few years later she was able to attend a literacy class, where she was mesmerized by the alphabet. When she learned to read the letters in her name, she found it had been mispronounced all her life. The discovery that the alphabet had the power to change her name—and more so, her identity—captivated her. She could not stop saying it, learning it, and reading it.

When this Indian woman's mind became alive to the alphabet, to written words, she became a different person. She received dignity. She was able to work. She could raise her children toward a better future. She had been "dead" to the ABCs. Now she is alive to them.

When I read Scripture, I ask God to put it into my bones the way the ABCs are, so that I am able to read his presence in my world—so that I can learn my new name. We were made for so much more than what the average mind gets filled with.

Read the Scriptures the Way You Watch a Movie

Sometimes when a group of people are together, one of them will mention a movie that everyone has seen, and suddenly a discussion surrounding the movie comes alive. People talk about their interpretations of what happened with great vigor. Nobody "tries harder" to watch a movie, but everybody is engaged. However, when it comes to the Bible, the conversations become stilted. People are so concerned with making sure they get the "right" answer that everyone backs out of the conversation.

> Researcher Ellen Langer has studied how our minds work and found we learn best when we view a situation from several perspectives — when we see novel information being presented, when we notice the context in which we are learning, and when we are forming new categories because of what we have learned. Playful curiosity creates much more learning than anxiously filling in the blanks with right answers.

One reason the ancient rabbis read the Scriptures so much is that they created so many wonderful arguments. In the middle of Genesis, for no apparent reason, there is a long list of genealogy of the Edomites. The Edomites were Israel's bitter enemy — yet the rabbis debated over how they made it in Scripture. Could it be that God loves the Edomites too? I grew to love the Bible in college when a group of students and teachers would meet every Friday afternoon, not as a class, but to muse and argue and wonder about why the Bible mentions holy wars or why in the New Testament God is never the subject of the verb for anger. Sometimes we would laugh over our disagreements — as when, after seeking several times to convince me of something, a friend who is much smarter than me shrugged his shoulders and said, "Well, you can't hand a football to a man with no arms."

Because there was space around that table for musing and questions and disagreements, our imaginations and critical thinking were engaged in ways that would never happen if the Bible were simply a series of grocery lists and instruction principles. The characters in the Bible are not sterile moral object lessons; they are real people with flaws and ambiguity through whom God somehow works.

People just like you and me.

Sometimes Try Memorizing Scripture

I know: Memorization scares us. But I also know people who have memorized every episode of the television show "The Simpsons" without trying.

Before written languages were developed, memory was the only way to learn. In our day, memorizing has gotten a bad name as "rote learning." But memorizing never makes our mind a duller place — just the opposite! When we have stored wonderful words in our memory, we will have a much richer inner life than someone who does not. While other people will need external stimulation — such as watching TV or listening to music or going online to keep their minds from drifting into chaos — we will have the joy of being able to savor great words and wonderful ideas without aid.

Eva Hermann spent two years in a Nazi prison camp. She wrote how a young cell mate from a Catholic orphanage one day happened to recite the prayer of Saint Teresa:

> *Let naught trouble thee;*
> *Let naught frighten thee;*
> *All Things pass.*
> *God alone changeth not.*
> *Patience can do all things.*
> *Whoever has God, has everything.*
> *God alone sufficeth.*

When the girl saw how much this helped Eva, she began to repeat the prayer at the end of every day. Eva later wrote of how her time in prison was transformed by the words she had memorized:

We should not imagine that a litany is thoughtless mumbling: real strength can come from it.

"The words were like a stream which carried his soul along with it," says Sigrid Undset somewhere of a person praying. During many a walk in the courtyard I have permitted myself to be carried along by such a stream, by repeating again and again the words of a Psalm: for example, Psalm No. 90, "O God, Thou art our refuge and our strength."

Eva wrote that she met God in a Nazi prison camp in a way she had never met him anywhere else. The words we carry in our minds are available to transform any moment.

When there is a verse that speaks to you, write it on a card. Put it on a mirror in your bathroom, on your Blackberry or calendar, or in your car. If you are an auditory learner, listen to the Scripture being read on CDs or on an iPod. If you are a visual learner, light a candle and read these words: "God is light, and in him there is no darkness at all."

Don't Just Read it … Do Something

A businessman known for his ruthlessness, arrogance, and religiosity once told Mark Twain he intended to visit the Holy Land before he died, in order to climb Mount Sinai and read the Ten Commandments aloud. "I have a better idea," Twain said. "You could stay here in Boston and keep them."

We would rather cogitate on what we do not know than actually do the things we know we ought to do.

Organizations often suffer from inertia. A company may know they need to improve quality control, so they discuss it, listen to presentations about it, read books, look at state-of-the-art systems — but never actually get around to doing it. Their problem is not one of ignorance. Their problem is one of knowing too much, but doing too little.

People would rather debate protein versus carbs, French cooking versus vegetarian, lifting weights versus cardio. Just spend more carbs than you take in. It's not rocket science.

People love to debate individual stocks versus mutual funds versus real estate. Just save more than you spend. It's not rocket science.

People would rather debate doctrine or beliefs or tradition or interpretation than actually do what Jesus said.

It's not rocket science. Just go do it. Practice loving a difficult person or try forgiving someone. Give away some money. Tell someone thank you. Encourage a friend. Bless an enemy. Say, "I'm sorry." Worship God.

You already know more than you need to know.

When I taught tennis, unskilled novices would agonize over which racquet to buy — whether to use nylon or gut strings, whether to string them up at sixty-five or seventy pounds. When they would go practice, they couldn't even hit the ball with their strings. They needed a nylon frame.

✱ We would rather cogitate on what we do not know than actually do the things we know we ought to do.

Don't debate minutiae. Just go practice.

The most influential talk in the history of the world, Jesus' Sermon on the Mount, ends with a striking story that addresses exactly this knowing/doing gap: "Therefore everyone who hears these words of mine and puts them into practice is like a wise man who built his house on the rock…."

This is our challenge.

> Be doers of the word, and not merely hearers.
> (James 1:22 NRSV)

It is easier to be smart than to be good. You don't need to know more from the Bible; you just need to do what you already know.

We don't become doers on our own, of course. As we read the Scripture, we ask the Spirit to help us understand what to do in response, and the intersection of what the Scriptures teach and how our lives unfold will give us a never-ceasing stream to actually do what Jesus says. And when we forget, another chance will come along.

I was picking up a prescription one Saturday afternoon before a church service, and because I was in a hurry, I had called the night before to make sure it would be there. But when I got there, the man behind the counter told me it wouldn't be ready until the next week. Apparently there was a mix-up between the medical people, the insurance people, and the pharmaceutical people.

"But I've got to have it," I replied. I was scheduled to leave the United States the next day.

"Well, it's not ready," the clerk said.

"But the automated system told me last night it would be ready today."

"There is a flaw in the automated system then," he told me.

All of a sudden I felt unbelievable anger well inside me. *A flaw in the system?* I wanted to say, *There's a flaw in you!* I didn't say that, because people from my church might have been around. (That is an occupational hazard of being a pastor.) But with every gesture and tone that I could, I expressed contempt and irritation with the man behind the counter. I didn't simply *feel* anger, I *wanted* to feel it. I indulged it. I wanted to make him feel small. I was amazed at my own ugliness.

When I returned to the church, I opened a Bible in my office and read a single phrase—"love one another"—and had to call a friend to tell him there was an inner jerk inside me that's scary.

Then, after I got back from my trip, I went to the pharmacy to tell the man behind the counter I was sorry for being so irritated and how much I appreciated his help.

And I was back in the flow.

Chapter 10

Never Worry Alone

When our daughters were three and five years old, we took them to a hotel with a swimming pool. We had a long, stern talk about the importance of water safety and the risk of drowning.

My talk may have been a little too effective.

As Laura was jumping into my arms while I was in the water, three-year-old Mallory slipped from a sitting position on the edge of the pool. She was underwater for less than a second, but when I pulled her up, she was sobbing.

"I drowned!" she cried. "I drowned! I drowned!"

From her perspective, it was terrifying. From my perspective, however, it was actually kind of funny.

"No, honey," I replied sympathetically. "You didn't drown. You were only underwater for a second. You're fine.... So let's not tell Mommy about this."

Mallory was never in danger. I knew that even though she didn't. Her father was always watching her, able to scoop her out of trouble at a moment's notice. I was what you might call "a non-anxious presence."

Jesus knew that no earthly situation has the power to put you outside God's care. You are always in the hand of your Father. So when death itself comes for us, it will be like Mallory dipping in the pool, and we will come up saying, "I drowned! I drowned! I drowned!" and the Father will say, "I had you the whole time."

Try a thought experiment: Imagine not being afraid any more. Imagine facing financial difficulties or an irate boss with inner poise and resolve. Imagine receiving bad news and generating constructive ways to solve the problem rather than spiraling through the worst-case scenarios. Imagine facing rejection and obstacles without giving in to discouragement. Imagine acknowledging the mistakes you have made, moving confidently into the future. Imagine doing all of this with God as your partner and friend. Now imagine people around you coming to you when they are upset or discouraged because they find that your peace of mind is contagious.

The mind controlled by the Spirit is life and peace, and what you are imagining is your mind immersed in the Spirit's flow. There is a phrase that wonderfully describes the role the Spirit wants to play in our minds: *The Spirit is a non-anxious presence.*

» God's Transforming Non-Anxious Presence

A non-anxious presence works like this: A group of people at home or work face a problem, and as one person after another hits the panic button, pretty soon everyone is anxious. They repeat each others' worries and ratchet them up another few degrees. It is contagious.

Then they notice someone among them who isn't afraid, someone fully aware of the problem but calm and able to plan with quiet confidence. That spirit begins to spread. Everyone begins to calm down. That one character brings the gift of a non-anxious presence. It brings the assurance that people's well-being is not at risk.

Jesus was once napping in a boat with his friends when a storm came. They woke him up, terrified, and Jesus looked out at the storm and said, "Peace, be still." And it was.

Jesus was a non-anxious presence. He carried peace with him. He did not say, "If you follow me, you will never have problems," for Jesus himself faced big problems. He was always getting into trouble and eventually got killed.

Peace doesn't come from finding a lake with no storms. It comes from having Jesus in the boat.

God does not want us to live in worry or fear. He wants us to live with bold confidence in his power. "For the Spirit God gave us does not make us timid, but gives us power, love and self-discipline." In the Bible, we see a pattern in which God rarely sends people into situations where their comfort level is high. Rather He promises to be with them in their fear. It is God's presence — not comfortable circumstances — that brings people to the best version of themselves.

> Peace doesn't come from finding a lake with no storms. It comes from having Jesus in the boat.

God told Abraham to leave everything familiar and go to a land he did not know, and he told him that God himself would give birth to a new nation that would change the world. Abraham went, and a nation was born.

God told Moses to confront Pharaoh — the most powerful man on earth — and that God himself would use Moses' faithfulness to deliver his people. Moses confronted, and God delivered.

God told Joshua that if he would be a strong and courageous leader when everyone wanted to return to slavery, God would go with them and give them the land. Joshua was strong and courageous, and God himself gave them the land.

Over and over we see this pattern repeated. David faced the giant Goliath, Elijah faced seven hundred prophets of Baal, and Daniel faced a den of lions — and always there was God in the midst of their fear.

The pinnacle of this pattern is reached in Jesus himself, who said to his followers, "In this world you have tribulation." Nobody had more tribulation than him. But after his death and resurrection, he sent his Spirit to be a non-anxious presence for a whole new community. When Stephen was martyred, Paul rose up to take his place. When Paul was executed, Timothy carried on the torch. Lest we think those stories of courage are all in the past, historian Everett Ferguson calculates that more Christians have been killed for their faith in the past fifty years than in the first three hundred years of the church.

So here is Jesus' word for us when someone doesn't like us, when we get a bad review at work, or when the economy dips south and our 401(k) — which remains the envy of 95 percent of the human race — is down 30 percent: "My peace I give you," Jesus promised. "I do not give to you as the world gives. Do not let your hearts be troubled and do not be afraid."

"For the Spirit God gave us does not make us timid, but gives us power, love, and self-discipline." ✗

The peace of Jesus is something much deeper than self-help techniques to manage stress. It is deeper than anxiety reduction to make life more pleasant. It is the settled conviction that goes down to the core of your being — to your belly where rivers of living water can flow — that all things are in God's hands. Therefore all things will be well, and you can live free of worry, burden, and fear.

Before we go any further, we need to pause for one very important caveat: *Everybody* worries.

»A Word to the Worry-Prone

Some people don't just worry occasionally. They worry recreationally.

Maybe you are a *champion* worrier. Maybe you can't remember the last time you were not worried. If you ever find yourself not worried, you get worried that there is something you *should* be worried about. And so you worry until you figure out what it is. Sometimes when you hear messages or read books about worry, they can do more harm than good, because what you take away is, *I shouldn't worry so much. I guess I just don't trust God enough.* Then you worry about how much you worry.

Much of our tendency to worry comes from the raw material we were born with. In his book *Emotional Intelligence*, Daniel Goleman writes that from birth, 15–20 percent of children are prone to timidity. They are finicky about new foods, reluctant about new places, and shy around strangers. From birth, their hearts beat faster in new situations. They are genetically predisposed to more guilt and self-reproach. This is so predictable among mammals that exactly the same proportion of cats as humans is prone to timidity. Cats are less curious and are less likely to

a test to worry about

This is a little quiz adapted from Harvard researcher Edward M. Hallowell. Score yourself on each question from 0 (not at all) to 3 (definitely yes).

1. Do you wish you worried less?
2. Do worries sometimes pop into your mind and take over your thinking like annoying, little gnats?
3. Do you find compliments and/or reassurance hard to take?
4. Are you more concerned than you wish you were with what others think of you?
5. How much do you procrastinate?
   (Have you still not finished the last question?)
6. Do you avoid confrontations?
7. Do you ever feel compelled to worry that a certain bad thing might happen out of an almost superstitious feeling that if you don't worry about it, the bad thing will happen, while if you do worry about it, your worrying might actually prevent the negative outcome?
8. Do you "worry about your worry"? Do you sometimes feel God is disappointed at your lack of faith?
9. Are you worried about what your score will be on this quiz?

If you scored a 0, you are either a remarkably confident person or else you are in complete denial.

If your score is 9 or less, worry does not trouble you much.

If you are between 10 and 18, you may often find yourself troubled by anxiety.

If you scored over 18, it may well be that worry is a major source of pain in your life. You may want to talk about this part of your life with some trusted friends, and it may be that telling a doctor or finding a good counselor could be helpful.

go to new territory, and they kill smaller rodents. About 15 percent of cats are just born timid.

Is that a spiritual problem? Are timid cats simply not close enough to God?

No. God is not distant from any of his creatures.

People who wrestle with deep anxiety or panic attacks are some of the most courageous people I know. If you wrestle with chronic worry, don't compare yourself with someone who doesn't. Don't waste time feeling guilty about worry. Guilt may be just what is needed by someone lying, stealing, or lusting. But guilt simply does not help when it comes to worrying. If you only wrestle slightly with worry, don't pass judgment on a chronic worrier. Only God fully understands a person's inner wiring, and the Spirit wants to be a non-anxious presence in *every* life.

We will talk about two ways to grow out of timidity. One of them you will like a lot. The other one you will like only a little, but it will grow on you.

» Let Love Cast Out Fear

Paul said that when we live in the flow of the Spirit, he does not make us timid, but instead gives us power and love. This is not the only place in the Bible where we see a close connection between receiving love and living in power. The apostle John makes the same association in one of the most famous statements in the Bible: "There is no fear in love.... perfect love casts out fear."

> "There is no fear in love. . . . perfect love casts out fear."

When we live in the flow of the Spirit, we let the perfect love of God wash over us until our fear begins to leave. Modern science has confirmed what John wrote so many centuries ago. Love and fear are literally incompatible in our bodies.

Every child has two needs:

• The need to explore. This is how we learn, grow, develop.
• The need to be safe. If a child doesn't feel safe, she won't explore.

Researchers find that one parent more than the other will push the child to explore, to take a chance, to run a risk, to trust that a little danger's a good thing. Generally, though not in every case, it tends to be the father. Likewise, one parent tends to be the comforter, the soother, the safety net. Again, researchers find that this tends to be the father. (So does this mean that researchers find that moms don't do a whole lot? Just kidding!) Actually, any parent can give both gifts — roots and wings — and every human being needs that secure base from which to explore and grow.

When we experience fear, our body activates the sympathetic nervous system. Our heart races, our breathing grows faster and shallower, our muscles become more tense, and blood leaves the brain and for the heart.

Then we run to our non-anxious presence: our comforter, protector, and parent. As we are held, reassured, and loved, the parasympathetic system takes over. Our heart slows down, our breathing grows deep and even, our muscles relax, and blood flows back to our brain. A little voice inside us says, "I can go out and face the world again...."

Even within our physical body, this is literally true: Perfect love casts out fear.

There is a wonderful picture of this you can see on YouTube if you enter the name "Harry Harlow." Dr. Harlow was a research psychologist in the mid-twentieth century who became famous for his studies of monkeys and their need for love. He found that if little monkeys had perfect conditions for hygiene and food but did not have another monkey present, they languished. Monkeys that had cloth diapers on the floor of their cage did better; they seemed to get what Harlow called "contact comfort" — because they had an innate need for touch that communicated love and strength.

Then Harlow designed two kinds of moms for each cage: a mom made of wire with a bottle of milk so the monkey could be fed, and a terrycloth mom who offered no food — nothing but touch. Much to Harlow's surprise, the monkeys spent less than an hour a day with wire mom and seventeen hours a day with terrycloth mom.

Harlow decided to see what the monkeys would do when they were scared. He devised a mechanical monster with flashing eyes, chomping teeth, waving arms, and a clanking noise — something straight out of a 1950s "Mr. Wizard" television science program — designed to scare the monkey. First the monkey is playing quietly and happily alone. Then one wall of his cage slides up, and he beholds the monster. He is terrified. There is no hesitation. He leaps to his terrycloth mom in a single bound.

Harlow notes that the monkey is not just running *from*. He is running *to* — running to the love that reassures him and drives out fear. Harlow says that contact with his protector "changes his entire personality." He is transformed by love.

At first when the monkey leaps on his terrycloth mom, he is shivering with fear. He wraps his whole body around hers, as if to get her reassurance in as many cells as possible. He is mainlining love and strength. Then he stops shaking. His breathing slows down. The little fellow rotates his head to look at the monster. Then he turns his whole body toward it. His expression changes from fear to menace. He gives a little baby rhesus monkey snarl. Now he is threatening the monster. Perfect love casts out fear.

This is a picture of the mind directed by the Spirit, for God does not give us a spirit of timidity. He gives a mind of life and peace. He calls himself our Comforter, and he will be our refuge, our rock, our fortress, and our safety. He longs to hold us, love us, and watch over us. Perfect love casts out fear.

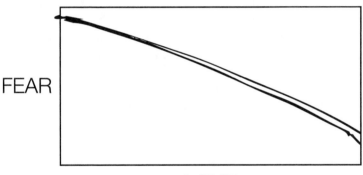

FEAR

LOVE

The kind of anxiety the Spirit wants to free us from is not just the thoughts that are alarming, because such thoughts may alert us to real danger. Toxic anxiety, however, causes our negative, self-defeating, and persistent thoughts to keep cycling over the same ground. Instead of prompting us to take action, they paralyze us. If I worry about finances it will go like this: *Things are not going well financially. The market is probably never going to turn around. I won't have enough for retirement. I am not even saving properly right now. I have never been good with money. I don't understand money really well. I haven't been giving as I should. I can't expect God to bless me. I have to do something to make me feel better. I guess I'll go buy something expensive.*

What are ways in which you most readily experience the love of God, in which his love casts out fear in your body? You have freedom to experiment with all this. God's will is not for intimacy with him to be one more thing you have to worry about!

God wants to love you—and in loving you, to cast out your fear.

Maybe it comes when you are alone with God. Maybe it happens when you pray with a few people. Maybe you find it when reading about the life of Jesus. Or it might come when you are singing a hymn or listening to music.

Often the Spirit will use other people to help love cast out fear. Psychiatrist Edward Hallowell says it like this: *Never worry alone.* When anxiety grabs my mind, it is self-perpetuating. Worrisome thoughts reproduce faster than rabbits, so one of the most powerful ways to stop the spiral of worry is simply to disclose my worry to a friend.

Not long ago I had to speak in front of a large gathering. For some unknown reason, every time I thought about it, I recalled how I fainted twice when giving talks years ago. I could feel the same tightness in my body, and I was afraid it might happen again. For some time I was so embarrassed about this fear that I kept silent. Finally I told a friend, who said he would pray for me; I felt such a relief that I wondered why I hadn't told him sooner.

In fact, when I gave the talk, I started by telling the whole audience about this fear. Now there were thousands of people with concerned expressions, worrying about me fainting during the talk. But I wasn't worried at all. I felt relieved that I didn't have to pretend I was okay. The simple act of reassurance from another human being became a tool of the Spirit to cast out fear—because peace and fear are both contagious.

> ✱ Never worry alone. One of the most powerful ways to stop the spiral of worry is simply to disclose my worry to a friend.

When Israel was to go occupy the Promised Land, God gave them very interesting instructions: "Is anyone afraid or faint-hearted? Let him go home so that the others will not become disheartened too." In an army, in a workplace, on a team, or in a ministry, negativity, fear, and discouragement are contagious. But courage is contagious as well.

God's part in the process is that his peace, "which transcends all understanding, will guard your hearts and your minds in Christ Jesus." By this, Paul means not just peace from God; he is talking about the peace that God *himself* has, the serenity that characterizes God's own eternal being. *That* peace will guard our hearts and minds — and here Paul uses a military term for "guard." It is the word the ancient Greeks used for soldiers who stood guard to protect the city.

"The peace of God, which transcends all understanding, will guard your hearts and minds in Christ Jesus."

Airport security personnel diligently screen every passenger in order to preserve peace and security. Two months after 9/11, I saw that I was just behind a casual acquaintance who happened to be traveling on the same flight. Going through security, I was pulled out of line for some reason and had to go through the security process a second time. The other man went on ahead. He got on the plane and was sitting in the front row as I boarded. In front of passengers and crew as I boarded, this man said, "I wonder why they made you go through security again and not me. Maybe it's your beady, little terrorist eyes." Then he said, "I guess we shouldn't have been talking about bringing those explosives on board, huh?" I made no eye contact. I kept my head down, took my seat, and said nothing. About five minutes later, he got up, took his luggage out of the bin, and was escorted off the plane.

I waited until we took off, then asked one of the flight attendants, "What happened to that guy?"

"Do you know him?" she asked.

"Not very well."

He spent the rest of the day in the San Francisco Airport with four law enforcement officers — and my name ended up on the suspect list.

Airports have resolved that they are not going to board anyone who could threaten the well-being of that plane. They screen anything that can be destructive. In the same way, every thought is a passenger traveling in our mind. Each one has a little spiritual charge that is either positive or negative. Some equip us to deal with life: *God loves me. God is with me. God will guide me. I am never alone.* Some rob us of peace: *I can't handle this. I am alone. I may not be adequate.*

The promise of God is that the Spirit will stand guard over our mind. It's not just our trying harder. When I tell him my concerns, I am "putting off worry." When I ask for his help, I am "putting on peace." And although it takes effort at first, over time it becomes a habit of the mind. This is why prayer is the single most fundamental spiritual discipline when it comes to putting off anxiety and putting on peace.

> ✱ "Instead of worrying, pray. . . . It's wonderful what happens when Christ displaces worry at the center of your life."

Prayer—turning any concern over to God when we feel it—is the part we play in allowing the peace of God to stand guard over our mind.

» Take Direct Action to Face Your Fear

Living in peace is not something that involves only our inner thoughts. It also flows from what we actually do. The Spirit will help us grow in peace by leading us in circumstances we would be tempted to avoid in fear. Here our role is to move forward, embracing challenges despite our anxious thoughts.

Hearing messages about how God will take care of us is not by itself sufficient to remove anxiety from our life. In order to open ourself up to the flow of the Spirit, we need to continually expose our mind to certain thoughts and information—but we also need to engage in certain actions. We will need to step out in trust.

I used to take my kids to a summer camp that has a ropes course thirty feet off the ground. It has several sections with colorful names such as "Jacob's Ladder" and "the Leap of Faith." The very last section is called "The Screamer." Want to guess why?

Before going up on the ropes course, we all get a little lecture from the staff, who tell us how strong the harnesses are, how the ropes we are attached to could literally support tons of weight, and how the metal carabiners clipping everything together are virtually indestructible. They explain to us that up on the ropes is a perfectly safe place to be. We have no reason to worry—and in fact face more danger in the car on our drive home.

Everybody hears the same lecture. No one disputes the facts. We all nod our heads. We all believe what they say. But when we get up on the ropes, our stomachs don't believe they are safe. Jesus said that "out of your bellies will flow rivers of living water," but that doesn't feel like what is flowing out of them the first time we are thirty feet up. That is certainly not what is flowing out of our armpits and sweat glands.

The first time you go across ropes, you're afraid. Thoughts flow automatically: *This is too high. This is not safe. I'm gonna fall.* That flow of thoughts has not been changed by the lecture. Your mind has not been renewed. The second time up, you are afraid, but maybe a little less.

But consider the staff. They have been on the ropes hundreds of times — all summer — and because they have put themselves through this experience time and again, their automatic thoughts have changed. Their stomachs and armpits have become convinced that up on the ropes is a perfectly safe place to be. Their minds have been renewed.

> Therefore, I urge you, brothers and sisters, in view of God's mercy, to offer your bodies as a living sacrifice, holy and pleasing to God — this is true worship. Do not conform to the pattern of this world, but be transformed by the renewing of your mind. (Romans 12:1–2)

The pivotal moment during a ropes course comes when you are strapped in, ready to climb, and you say to your instructor, "On belay" — which I would be tempted to think is a French phrase meaning "I've lost my mind." Actually, to belay a rope means to make it absolutely secure, to fasten it to something immovable. It means that now you are connected to something that will keep you from falling, and you will entrust your body to what you say you believe. You will walk by faith. On belay.

The instructor says, "Belay on."

You say, "Climbing."

Your instructor says, "Climb on," and you are on your way.

You could listen to the lecture about the safety of carabiners a thousand times; you could repeat the whole thing by memory — but that alone would not remove the fear from your body the first time you are on the ropes. Yet, once you say "on belay" often enough, it is just a matter of time before your thoughts begin to change.

Information alone will not bring about the transformation of the whole person. We may read book after book, hear talk after talk, listen to sermons—maybe even read the Bible—but still remain just as anxious as we ever were before. There is no way to get the peace of God from our head to the rest of our body besides trusting God enough to directly confront our greatest fear.

Larry needed to confront his boss, but his boss was a powerful steamroller. Larry was intimidated simply by the sound of his voice. When Larry thought about confronting him, Larry's palms got sweaty. His mouth got dry. His wife told him to lick his palms. He read the psalms, he prayed, he thought of how God loves him unconditionally. But he decided not to have the confrontation, and for the moment he felt much less anxious. But he was misusing both the Bible and prayer.

The Bible and prayer were not given to us as forms of anxiety avoidance. In the long run, anytime we avoid doing the right thing out of fear, we die a little inside. When we really place ourselves in the flow of the Spirit's peace is when we say "on belay" to God.

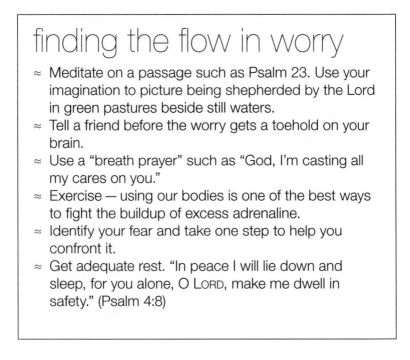

finding the flow in worry

≈ Meditate on a passage such as Psalm 23. Use your imagination to picture being shepherded by the Lord in green pastures beside still waters.
≈ Tell a friend before the worry gets a toehold on your brain.
≈ Use a "breath prayer" such as "God, I'm casting all my cares on you."
≈ Exercise — using our bodies is one of the best ways to fight the buildup of excess adrenaline.
≈ Identify your fear and take one step to help you confront it.
≈ Get adequate rest. "In peace I will lie down and sleep, for you alone, O LORD, make me dwell in safety." (Psalm 4:8)

You are worried about money. Everything in you tells you to hoard it, to hang on to it, to obsess over it. Instead you say "on belay": You manage it wisely. You give it generously. You put it in the trust department.

You are worried about a project at work. Instead of procrastinating, you say "on belay." You give it your best effort with God's help. Each time your worry returns to your mind, you give it to God in prayer.

Your fear of failure tempts you to avoid risk, but instead you say "on belay": *Okay, God, I will take the risk even though I don't know the outcome yet.*

We go through this life one time. Some wonderful things will happen to us; some dreams will come true. Some terrible things will happen to us, bringing with them pain, problems, and disappointment. Of that we can be certain. But we can go through this life worried—or we can go through it at peace.

> *Life is too short,*
>> *joy is too precious,*
>>> *God is too good,*
>>>> *our soul is too valuable,*
>>>>> *we matter too much*
>> *to throw away a single moment of our one and only life on*
>>> *anxious striving.*
> *For the Spirit God gave us does not make us timid.*

On belay.

PART FOUR
redeeming my time

»

Chapter 11

Let Your Talking Flow into Praying

By the time our third child was born, I figured we had been through this drill before and knew what to expect. The doctor was at my wife's bedside for the birth, and everything was going according to plan—until he got a look of deep concern on his face.

"There is a problem," he said.

The umbilical cord had wrapped around the baby's neck, cutting off oxygen to the brain. The doctor had been pretty talkative up to that point, but all of a sudden he wasn't talking at all. Everyone was quiet and focused, and all I could do was say, "Oh God, oh God, oh God, oh God. Make it be okay. Don't let anything happen to that little life."

A few seconds later the doctor was able, inside, to cut the cord. Blood spurted out all over the place, and I started to feel dizzy and queasy.

"I have to sit in a chair somewhere," I announced, "because I'm going to go down." (That did not win me a lot of points with anyone.) So I sat with my head between my knees for the next several minutes while the doctor finished delivering the baby—a beautiful, healthy little boy.

"Is everything okay?" Nancy asked.

"Yes, Mrs. Ortberg," the doctor replied. "Your son and your husband are both pinking up at the same time."

When we are desperate, we call out for God. When we reach the end of our rope, it is only human to reach out to God. When we are thrilled, we thank God. When we are crushed by guilt, we cry out to God.

You pray more than you know. Even in school, we pray. People get concerned about legal issues with that, but experience tells us that as long as there are tests in school, there will be prayer in school, silent though it may be.

> Richard Foster says, "Countless people ... have such a 'stained-glass' image of prayer that they fail to recognize what they are experiencing as prayer and so condemn themselves for not praying."

If someone were to ask you, "How is your prayer life?" what would be your answer? Is the state of your prayer life determined by how long you pray or how often? Is it measured by how many people you are praying for, or how much faith you are praying with, or how many prayers get answered?

If you believe in God, you have already begun to pray — to enter into a dialogue with him — because believing in God means believing he is always present, always listening to what you say. To come to believe is to begin to pray, because of the constancy of God's presence. So let us look at the connection of prayer with "the rest of our lives."

» Is God In on Your Conversation?

We can better understand prayer by thinking about being present with another person, and how being with somebody shapes what we say about them. Sometimes we speak *to* another person. Let's call that Person A. Sometimes, though, we are talking to somebody else about Person A, but we are also speaking in *front of* Person A, so the presence of Person A still influences your words. Then there is a third scenario. Sometimes we talk about Person A in their *absence*, and now what we say may be quite different.

1. Speaking *to* someone.
2. Speaking *in front of* someone.
3. Speaking *in the absence of* someone.

True confession: Have you ever spoken about someone, in their absence, with words you would not have used if they were present? Mark Twain was once riding a train home from Maine after three weeks of highly successful fishing — even though the state's fishing season was closed. He bragged about his huge but illegal catch to the only other passenger in the club car. The passenger grew increasingly glum during Twain's story. When Twain finally asked him who he was, the stranger explained he was the state game warden.

"Who are you?" the warden asked.

"To tell the truth," Twain said, "I'm the biggest liar in the whole United States."

Often when I am speaking *to* someone or *in front of* someone, I hide my real heart. If I am in a job interview, on a first date, or talking to someone in authority, I filter what I say. I may not intend to do this, but I can't help myself. When I am speaking to or in front of somebody — perhaps a boss, a teacher, or a policeman — there is a dynamic at work in my body to manage what I say in light of that person's presence. There is always a sense of effort or strain attached to this, so I long for some place where I can go to be "my real self," where I do not guard my words or body language to manage the impressions of another person.

Now let us bring God into the picture. The reality with God is that we are never speaking or acting in his absence. The psalmist said, "Where can I go from your Spirit? Where can I flee from your presence? If I go up to the heavens, you are there; if I make my bed in the depths, you are there." However, God allows us to sometimes feel as if we are away from him, which I think he does for a reason. Do you ever drive differently when you see a squad car behind you? Why? It is not because your heart is changed. It is not because you see that squad car and think, *Oh, I want to be a good driver.* You don't want to get a ticket! You don't want that little light flashing in the rearview mirror.

You see, God doesn't want forced compliance. God is so immense that if he were "too visible," people would give forced compliance without expressing their heart. So God makes it possible, in enormous love, for us to live as if he were not there.

This reality leads to some dissonance in our spiritual lives. I went to a Christian college, and there was a long-running tradition to determine who was going to pray before meals — the thumbs game, we called it. Everyone would raise their thumbs, and whoever raised their thumbs last was the one to pray. Then we would bow our heads, and that person would say, "Oh God, we love you so much, it's so good to pray to you!"

It didn't occur to me at the time, but years later I thought, *You know, God must be up in heaven saying, "Hey, if it's so good to pray to me, how come the loser of the thumbs game is always the one who has to do it?"* It was as if, when we played the thumbs game, we believed God was not watching. Then when we went to pray, suddenly we were aware that God was tuning in. This is why sometimes people speak in one voice but pray in an entirely different voice. We live with a kind of spiritual split personality.

Anytime I sin, I must remove any thought of the presence of God from my conscious awareness. Then when I pray, I have to put him back in my mind's focus. The goal of prayer is not to get good at praying, as many people think. The goal of prayer is not to try to set new records for how much time we spend praying. *The goal of prayer is to live all of my life and speak all of my words in the joyful awareness of the presence of God.*

Prayer becomes real when we grasp the reality and goodness of God's constant presence with "the real me." Jesus lived his everyday life in conscious awareness of his Father. For example, when he went to raise Lazarus from the dead, he began by "looking up to pray." In our day, most people close their eyes when they pray. But praying with one's eyes open was common for Jewish people in that day. Among other things, it reminded them, *God is right here, right now, in my real world.*

> The goal of prayer is to live all of my life and speak all of my words in the joyful awareness of the presence of God.

> "Father, I thank you that you have heard me. I knew that you always hear me, but I said this for the benefit of the people standing here, that they may believe that you sent me."

Jesus knew the Father was listening not just when he prayed, but all the time, whenever he spoke. God was always responding to Jesus' words, whether they were addressed to the Father or addressed to someone else. For Jesus, the line between praying and just speaking became very thin. Sometimes when Jesus healed a person, he would speak directly to the person he was healing. Sometimes he would speak directly to his Father. It didn't really matter which one he did because he was always speaking in front of the Father and the Father was always responding.

God is the constant gracious listener to our every thought, and prayer begins when we bring what we most naturally think about before God.

» Talk to God about Your Problems

Think about the major categories of your life: your relationships, your financial life, your job, your emotions, your habits, your moral decisions, your health and physical appearance, your mortality. Can you identify at least one problem?

If you can, you have a wonderful prompt for prayer.

One of our illusions is that the reason we worry is because we have problems. If I just didn't have problems, we think, I wouldn't worry anymore. The good news is, *your problems are going to go away.* The bad news is, that won't happen until the day you die. You will be amazed at how your problems stop bothering you then. Until then, however, life will be full of problems.

There is an old equation that helps us understand the dynamics of attention: We tend to be preoccupied by our problems when we have a heightened sense of vulnerability and a diminished sense of power. Today, see each problem as an invitation to prayer. Maybe you are mad at someone. Tell God! An amazing example of this is found in the life of Elisha. One day he was set upon by a gang of young toughs: "Go on up, you baldhead!" they said to him. The Bible says that Elisha turned toward them and called down judgment from heaven, and forty-two of them were chased away by two bears. It doesn't seem like the prayer of a spiritual giant, but Elisha prayed what was in him. Maybe God will send a bear or two down after someone you are mad at. Probably not, but you will never know if you don't pray.

Either way, God will use your problems to grow a better you.

» Talk to God about What You Want

Paul said that we are to pray "in everything," and the implications of that little two-word phrase are enormous. Often we don't pray because our real thoughts seem unspiritual:

- I wonder if I will get a year-end bonus.
- I wonder if I am putting on too much weight.
- I wonder if my boss thinks I am doing well.

When I pray, I end up praying about things I think I *should* be concerned about: missionaries, world peace, and global warming. But my mind keeps wandering toward stuff I am genuinely concerned about. The way to let my talking flow into praying is this: *I must pray what is in me, not what I wish were in me.*

Shel Silverstein once wrote the "Prayer of the Selfish Child": "Now I lay me down to sleep, I pray the Lord my soul to keep, And if I die before I wake, I pray the Lord my toys to break, So none of the other kids can use 'em. Amen." Children come to their parents with all kinds of requests: wonderful, foolish, generous, *and* selfish.

✱ *I must pray what is in me, not what I wish were in me.*

What matters to parents, however, is that their child comes to them. They know that they can guide the child's growth — as long as their child speaks openly with them. It is the hidden heart, not the selfish heart, that is hardest to change.

This is *"in everything"* kind of prayer. I don't wait to clean up my motives first. I don't try to sound more spiritual than I am. I don't pray what ought to be in me. I pray what's really in me. The "in everything" prayer is the most common kind in the Bible. I just try to attach one sincere rider: "Nevertheless, not my will but yours be done."

As long as we have unsolved problems, unfilled desires, and a mustard seed of faith, we have all we need for a vibrant prayer life.

Chapter 12

Temptation: How Not to Get Hooked

Recently my wife and I went fly-fishing for the first time. Our guides told us that "to catch a fish you have to think like a fish." They said that to a fish life is about the maximum gratification of appetite at the minimum expenditure of energy. To a fish, life is "see a fly, want a fly, eat a fly." A rainbow trout never really reflects on where his life is headed. A girl carp rarely says to a boy carp, *I don't feel you're as committed to our relationship as I am. I wonder, do you love me for me or just for my body?* The fish are just a collection of appetites. A fish is a stomach, a mouth, and a pair of eyes.

While we were on the water, I was struck by how dumb fish are. *Hey, fish, swallow this. It's not the real thing; it's just a lure. You'll think it will feed you, but it won't. It'll trap you. If you were to look closely, fish, you would see the hook. You'd know once you're hooked that it's just a matter of time before your enemy reels you in.*

You'd think fish would wise up and notice the hook or see the line. You'd think fish would look around at all their fish friends who go for a lure and fly off into space and never return. But they don't. It is ironic. We say fish swim together in a school, but they never learn.

Aren't you glad we are smarter?

The governor of a large state has brains, charisma, power, and unlimited potential. He also has an emptiness that he feeds with paid sexual liaisons, and when they are made public, they cost him everything.

A brilliant teacher wins every argument she ever enters. She dominates every conversation. Everyone knows how smart she is — and everyone avoids her. Her misery is the one problem she is not smart enough to figure out.

The leader of a large company is thought of as successful, but everyone in his inner circle feels used. He does not even know how alone he is, for no one will tell him.

Temptation is painful to us because when we give in, it doesn't hurt us from the outside; it hurts from the inside. Temptation tries to get our appetites and will to override our deepest values. Temptation will strike where we are most vulnerable, but life in the flow of the Spirit is about more than avoiding temptation. In fact, temptation will also come to us where we most need to grow. If I need patience, there will be some difficult people in my life to help me develop it. If I am tempted by envy, there will be a shining star in the office next door to help me learn grace. Each temptation I face offers a step in the direction of the me I want to be.

But how can I stay in the flow when I am tempted?

»Ask for Help

Nothing makes temptation more powerful than isolation, but we do not face temptation alone. Paul said that "no temptation has seized you except what is common to human beings. And God is faithful; he will not let you be tempted beyond what you can bear. But when you are tempted, he will also provide a way out so that you can stand up under it." For Joseph, when he was being propositioned by Potiphar's wife, this literally meant running out of the room.

I think the single most common "way out," however, involves talking about our temptations with another person. A friend of mine wrestles with gossip, but early on in our relationship he made one of the most candid confessions I have ever heard: "If you want to keep something confidential, don't tell me — I leak like a sieve!"

There was something so disarming about his honesty that instead of being pushed away, I was drawn to him. This temptation was simply the dark side of his giftedness—he was one of the most delightfully verbal people I have known. We began to talk and pray over why he was drawn to gossip, where it got him in trouble, and how he could get free. He eventually became one of the friends to whom I trusted my deepest secrets.

»Ask, Where Will This Lead?

In the flow of the Spirit, it actually requires more mental gymnastics to walk down the wrong path than to walk down the right one. We disguise most of these gymnastics from ourselves, but they are there all the same. The first thing we must do if we are going to give in to temptation is wrapped up in the single word *quench.*

"Do not quench the Spirit," Paul says. Any time I have a desire, the Spirit will prompt me to set it before God and ask the question, "Lord, what do you want me to do with this?" Or I can simply ask regarding any course of behavior, *"If I walk down this road, where will it lead in the long run—toward or away from the me I want to be?"*

God will never lead us to manage a desire in a sinful way. If I want to walk down the wrong road, I must begin by silencing God's divine voice within me. I must be careful not to pray about this desire with a submitted spirit. I must make sure I don't talk about this desire with wise friends who will hold me accountable. I must make sure I don't look carefully at passages of Scripture on the subject and reflect on them. I must do all these things without recognizing I am doing them. I must keep myself in a state of spiritual and mental vagueness where God is concerned.

This response may become so habitual that we don't even notice. In a restaurant an attractive waitress walks past a husband and wife at a table. The husband starts staring at her. He can't take his eyes off her. He's not thinking of this woman as a person, as someone's sister or daughter. She is just body parts, and he is using her to get a little surge of sexual gratification. He thinks nobody notices—but of course someone notices. His wife feels humiliated.

This is "the look" Jesus warned about when he spoke of "committing adultery in your heart." This does not mean that noticing someone attractive is sinful. The sense of attraction is a good thing. Rather, Jesus warns about looking for the purpose of lusting. An element of will has come into the look, and the husband is allowing his mind to wallow in it. It may have become so habitual that he is hardly even aware he is doing it.

The Spirit will pull us another way, however. Maybe we get "caught" and embarrassed. Maybe we feel a twinge of conscience. Either way, the Spirit wants to remind us of who we were created to be.

»Remind Myself of My Deepest Values

The battle against temptation is a noble fight, but if we simply try to repress a desire, it will wear us out. We need to have a very clear picture of what kind of person we want to become, and why. For instance, one day I wrote down all the reasons why I would like to handle sexuality in an honorable way: what it might do to my wife if I didn't, how my children would be affected, what would happen to my work and ministry, how it would feel to be haunted by guilt and failure, and the inability of sexual gratification to last.

Job put it this way: "I made a covenant with my eyes not to look lustfully at a girl." I deliberately seek to not look at a woman who is not my wife for the purpose of deriving sexual gratification. Suppose I am at a health club and out of the corner of my eye I see a woman and think that if I look over at her, then maybe I'll be able to experience a little sexual pleasure. The next thought that comes because of what Job said is, *I don't have to look. I can not look.* The thought that follows is, *Instead of missing out on a little thrill, by not looking I will have a power I didn't know I had. I can be free, and that freedom produced by the Spirit feels good.*

> *Real freedom is not the external freedom to gratify every appetite; it is the internal freedom not to be enslaved by our appetites.*

Temptation promises that we can be free to gratify our appetites as much as we want. See a fly, want a fly, eat a fly. Temptation promises freedom, but it makes us a slave. There is always a hook. Real freedom is not the external freedom to gratify every appetite; it is the internal freedom not to be enslaved by our appetites, to have a place to stand so that we are not mastered by them. For we are something more than a stomach, a mouth, and a pair of eyes.

» *Monitor Your Soul Satisfaction*

When we are hungry, anything on the menu looks good. When our soul is dissatisfied, sin begins to look tempting. That is why it is important to notice the level of soul satisfaction in our life.

On the dashboard of any car are certain lights that tell us how hot the engine is running or when we are about to run out of oil. They are commonly called "idiot lights"—I suppose because only an idiot would ignore them. Likewise, the main light on the dashboard of our heart is our "soul satisfaction" light. This is why in the Bible there are so many commandments that call us to joy: "The joy of the LORD is your strength" and "Rejoice in the Lord always; again I will say, rejoice!"

Why do intelligent people keep getting hooked? What makes those with high IQs so vulnerable to temptation, when it is obviously such a dumb step? We become vulnerable to temptation when we are dissatisfied with our lives. The deeper our dissatisfaction, the deeper our vulnerability, because we were made for soul satisfaction. We cannot live without it. If we do not find soul satisfaction in God, we will look for it somewhere else, because we will look for it. Then it becomes an idol. What was called idolatry in biblical times we often talk about today as addictions. Our lives get all wrapped up around them. That is why Jesus begins the Sermon on the Mount, not with rules about morality, but with good news to speak right to the yearnings of the soul: *blessed.*

Blessed.

Blessed are not just the winners that society says are blessed. Blessed are not just the super models. Blessed are not just the rich and powerful who can attract trophy partners. Blessed are the wrinkled. Blessed are the misshapen. Blessed are those who never got asked to the prom, who never got asked to dance. Blessed are the single; blessed are the married. Blessed are the prostitutes, the addicted, the shamed, and the regretful.

Blessed, blessed, blessed. Blessed are you, not because you can have every desire fulfilled, but because you are not your desires. Blessed are you because you are more than a stomach, a mouth, and a pair of eyes. Blessed are you because what you really ache for is to be loved by and connected to God, and now Jesus says that love, that life, that connection is yours if you want it through him.

Do you want it?

» Don't Stay Down!

It is instructive that while the devil is called the Tempter, he is also called the Accuser. As soon as he gets someone to give in to temptation, he will switch hats and try to convince us that because we have yielded to temptation, we are beyond redemption.

The Spirit is just the opposite, always seeking to "deliver us from evil." When we do give in, the flow of the Spirit moves us toward forgiveness, redemption, and healing.

I was running on a beach early one morning, discouraged by the lack of progress in my own life and feeling that I was still wrestling with the same selfishness and fear that I had many years ago. Because it was so early, the beach was deserted. Then I saw a man walking toward me—a big old guy, bald as could be, wearing only a long pair of floral swimming trunks, great big paunch leading the way. He looked like Santa Claus on summer vacation.

I intended to just give him the jogger's nod of acknowledgment and keep moving down the beach, but he was having none of that. Looking me right in the eye, he stuck his right arm all the way out to the side and silently held a huge hand in the air. He walked right up to me. He was insisting on a high five. The man had *attitude*. I smacked his hand with mine, and he gave me a nod of satisfaction, as if to say, "We're connected now. It is good that we share this beach together. I am glad you are here."

Immediately I had this thought—whether or not it is from God, only God knows: *I am glad you are here. I am not neutral about your existence. This is a little picture of grace. Do not be discouraged, not even about your own failings.*

To this day, every time I remember the man on the beach, I think about God.

Blessed.

Chapter 13

Recognize Your Primary Flow-Blocker

USA Today once ran an article about the ten most difficult things to do in sports. Number five was returning a professional tennis serve. Number four was hitting a golf ball long and straight (even though it's just sitting there on the tee). Number three was pole-vaulting over fifteen feet. Number two was driving a race car at megaspeed without dying. But the hardest feat in athletics is hitting a professionally thrown baseball.

A few years ago, a friend of mine named Ned Colletti, who was vice president of the San Francisco Giants baseball team, asked if I would speak at a chapel service. He offered to let me take batting practice with John Yandle, the batting practice pitcher for Barry Bonds. I thought it would be a good chance to benchmark my athletic skills.

I never played organized baseball, but as a kid growing up we played on a vacant lot where the best pitcher around was Steve Snail. In fifth grade I could hit his pitches better than anyone else in the neighborhood. (There was only one other kid in the neighborhood, and she was in first grade—but I was still best.)

I did pretty well against Snail, I thought. *Let's see how this goes.*

At the batting cage in AT&T Park, John wound up and let go, and I heard the sound of the ball hitting the net behind me.

He's not just lobbing them in there, I thought. *He wants to see if I can hit his best stuff.*

John wound up again, and the second time I swung, the ball had already been in the net several seconds by the time my bat got over the plate. So I kept starting my swing earlier until eventually I would begin my swing about the same time I saw him start his windup. I hit several foul balls and a few dribblers that might have gone fair. I was feeling pretty good.

Then he said, "Do you want me to put a little zip on one?"

Those *had* been his lobs.

"Sure!" I said. "It's been hard to time these slow balls."

He wound up. I never saw it.

I asked him if that was his best pitch.

"No," he said, "you wouldn't want to see that."

"What level player would hit that well?" I asked.

"A good high school player would crunch it," he said, "and a good college player would strike out a high schooler with his eyes closed. Minor league guys would throw shutouts to college guys. Put a major league arm against minor leaguers and it's no contest."

John sent a scouting report to Ned Coletti: "John Ortberg — bats right, throws right. Took ten minutes of batting practice. As a hitter, John makes a good pastor."

That day I learned there is a vast chasm between sandlot baseball in Rockford, Illinois, and Major League talent in San Francisco. It's not just that I wasn't good — I didn't know enough to know how "not good" I was.

A study done a few years ago showed that the first sign of incompetence is our inability to *perceive* incompetence. We deceive ourselves about our intelligence, for example. I may think I'm pretty smart until I read about a student who did not miss a single question on the SAT, ACT, and PSAT combined. We deceive ourselves about our talent, for people at a karaoke bar sing with far more confidence than reality would allow. We deceive ourselves about our appearance. A grandpa friend of mine boarded an airport tram and noticed an attractive young woman sitting nearby who smiled at him. He thought to himself, *I've still got it.* "Excuse me, sir," she said. "I can stand. Would you like to take my seat?"

Nowhere does this inability to have an objective, accurate, reality-based view of our performance show itself more than in the spiritual realm. When it comes to moral character, the purity of heart, the duplicity in our actions, how many of us have given serious thought to how our lives would grade out—not by the standard of the neighborhood sandlot where we can always find a first-grader to outperform—but in the eyes of a holy, just, righteous, and truth-telling God? That is why the most dangerous force in the world is not sickness or injury or bankruptcy.

It is sin.

Sin is a word not often thought about seriously in our time. Neal Plantinga writes, "Nowadays, the accusation *you have sinned* is often said with a grin, and with a tone that signals an inside joke...." Sin has become a word for hot vacation spots (Las Vegas is Sin City) and dessert menus: "Peanut Butter Binge and Chocolate Challenge are sinful; lying is not. The new measure for sin is caloric."

But sin is the deadliest force because it takes us out of the flow of the Spirit. Imagine the consequences if we did not have a word for cancer or depression. We must identify and understand that which threatens our ability to flourish, and only sin can keep us from becoming the person God wants us to become. All other challenges face us from the outside. Sin works its way inside, strangling our soul.

» Your Own "Original Sin"

We used to have a car with a bumper sticker that read "I poke badgers with spoons." It is a line from a British stand-up comedian named Eddie Izzard.

Eddie grew up in the church and heard early on about the doctrine of original sin, but he was a little fuzzy on the concept. He assumed it meant that priests get tired of hearing the same old boring confessions, so they want somebody who won't just confess sin—they want someone who will confess *original* sin.

He figured that instead of old stand-bys such as greed and lust, he would come up with something that no one has ever confessed before: "I poke badgers with spoons." My wife thought it was so funny, she had it printed on a bumper sticker and put it on her car. We finally peddled the car to another family—on the condition that they had to keep the bumper sticker.

Debates have raged for centuries over the notion of original sin. The theologian Augustine said there is a fundamental moral stain that gets passed on to every human being even before they are born. The classic counterargument was raised by a monk named Pelagius, who claimed that every human being is a blank slate, a morally neutral free agent who has a clean shot at perfect innocence.

Pelagius clearly never had children.

The Bible never actually uses the phrase "original sin," but the writers of Scripture (and any moderately perceptive observers) know that we are remarkably prone to do things that we know are wrong. We have a staggering capacity for self-deception and self-justification.

There is a kind of "original sin" in another sense. Your sin is intimately connected to the passions and wiring God gave you. Sin doesn't look quite the same in anyone else as it does in you. Like your fingerprints, your signature, or your bowling style, your sin pattern is unique to you.

» Needed: A Deeper Understanding of Sin

Author Richard Lovelace noted that for many centuries people who wrote about the soul understood sin's complexity and ambiguity. They knew how much of our character lies beneath conscious control. They understood how superiority and judgmentalism creep into champions of morality and how someone who appears to be dissipated by greed or lust may be capable of nobility and love.

But by the nineteenth century, much of what was written about sin grew superficial and simplistic: Divorced people are bad; married people are good. Sexual sinners are bad; chaste people are good. The "world" — which in Scripture is identified with that broken reality that runs through each of us — became shorthand for talking about people who don't go to church, as in "we're not like 'the world.'" We turned sin into a grocery list of "thou shalt nots."

People latched onto Sigmund Freud and modern psychology partly because they needed language about the human condition that recognizes the complexity and ambiguity in every one of us. We learned how to speak about our psyches, but we still need a way to speak about our souls. No one recognized more clearly than Jesus that some people who look like "huge sinners" actually have hearts that are tender for God.

Others who are thought to be (and think of themselves as!) spiritual giants are actually walking heaps of pride and envy.

Living in the flow of the Spirit requires talking about sin in a way that is balanced, honest, and redemptive.

» Signature Sins

We do not get tempted by that which repulses us. Temptation rarely begins by trying to get us to do something that is 180 degrees in the opposite direction of our values. It starts close to home with the passions and desires that God wired into us and tries to pull them a few degrees off course. That subtle deviation is enough to disrupt the flow of the Spirit in our life, so coming to recognize the pattern of sins most tempting to us is one of the most important steps in our spiritual life.

Author Michael Mangis writes about what he calls "signature sin." It is based on the idea that my life has certain patterns, relationships, temperaments, and gifts that are unique to me — yours does too. My fingerprint is unique and could be recognized by an expert; my sin is similarly patterned. Certain temptations are especially troubling for me, and some sins are more appealing than others. Even if we both struggle with the sin of lashing out in anger, I am likely to have it triggered and express it in different ways than you do. In other words, we don't sin at random. Our sin takes a consistent and predictable course. When a car or a body begins to wear out, it is not equally vulnerable at every point; there are inevitably a few areas that are most distressed that will be the first to go under pressure. So it is with our souls.

My sin pattern is so characteristic that it can be used to identify me. It is my sin profile, and anyone who knows me well will recognize my sin profile in a moment. In fact, other people often know my sin profile better than I do myself.

Because we live in a physical environment, we sometimes speak of leaving a

> The pattern of your sin is related to the pattern of your gifts.

carbon footprint. But we also live in a spiritual environment and leave a sin footprint, which damages our spiritual environment. This is part of the power of temptation, because *the pattern of your sin is related to the pattern of your gifts.*

Just as home-run hitters also strike out a lot, the areas of our gifts and passions will also indicate our areas of vulnerability. Extroverts who can inspire and encourage can also be prone to gossip. People who love to learn will be tempted to feel superior and talk down to others. Those who are spontaneous and have a great appetite for life will struggle with impulse control. Good listeners may become passive enablers. Optimists wander toward denial. Tell me your gifts, and I'll tell you your sins.

Greek mythology spoke of the nemesis, your mortal enemy. Your nemesis is like you in almost every way, except that he is the ruined version of you. Sherlock Holmes's nemesis was Professor Moriarity, also a brilliant man—but like Holmes would have been if Holmes had gone wrong. You are your own nemesis, your own biggest problem, because there is a relationship between the best version of you and the worst version of you. What they have in common is that both of them are *you*.

Mangis identifies nine of these patterns, using an ancient system called the enneagram. It is somewhat controversial, because it is used by many different spiritual traditions, but it is thought to have originated out of considerations of the seven deadly sins and the fruit of the Spirit, and it can be applied in a Christian framework. (For a few other references, see Richard Rohr's book *The Enneagram*.)

These nine patterns are as follows:

Reformers have a deep love of perfection. They naturally have a high standard of excellence, and their greatest fear is to be flawed. (They also make good surgeons and excellent golfers.) At their best, they are crusaders, watchdogs, and prophets. But they wrestle with perfectionism and self-righteousness. They will be tempted to judge others whose standards are not so high.

A friend of mine in Chicago, a surgical pathologist, fits the reformer profile. He was charming and eligible, but he cycled in and out of relationships because no one could ever quite measure up. I once asked him if he thought there was any connection between his inability to find a woman good enough to marry and his profession—cutting up dead tissue and putting it under a microscope to see what is wrong with it. Reformers are prophets and idealists who call us to be our best selves—but they can also be hard to live up to.

Servers love to be needed. They are natural caregivers who will fluff up your pillow even if it doesn't need fluffing. They remember birthdays and are the first ones up to do the dishes. Often servers work in positions where they support someone else, and they will feel most comfortable in a social gathering when they have something to do.

While they are drawn to help, their helping can sometimes come out of their *own* neediness. As a result, they can drain others if their giving becomes a form of taking. Underneath their servanthood sometimes lurks low self-esteem that demands to be fed but can never get filled up. Sometimes servers marry an addict because that forms a kind of symbiotic relationship.

Achievers love to conquer challenges and perform before others. At their best, they are motivated to grow, stretch, and learn. They can inspire and move people to action, and they often like to be in front of crowds. Giving a talk, which is the most common fear in America, often energizes them. If they don't have a chance to develop and shine, they will lose motivation. Achievers want to make an impact on the world around them.

Their temptation is that they can live for their image, idolizing their own performance. Unredeemed, they will be prone to measure their success in terms of applause and recognition. When John the Baptist said about Jesus, "He must increase, but I must decrease," he was stating the surrender that comes most difficult to an achiever. In the book of Acts we read about a character named Simon Magnus who offered to give Peter money in exchange for a dose of the Spirit that would let Simon have a spectacular ministry. An unredeemed achiever can turn what looks like serving God into serving himself.

Artists love beauty and carry inside a strong desire to be unique. They love to express their individuality in bold ways and enjoy living on the margins. In different eras they were beatniks, hippies, or punk rockers. They often have a very strong sense of what kind of look they want to effect or what life they want to create that they cannot express in words but that emerges in art or action.

While they bring color and flair to a world that might otherwise be drab, their sensitivity can enslave them to emotional swings, and their desire to be special can become preoccupying. Their temptation is connected to the need to be different. In their need to be special and stand out, they may look down on "ordinary people." They want to be bohemian—unless they live in Bohemia.

Thinkers like to know—*everything*. At their best, they are the investigators, scientists, and inventors among us. They love to discover truths that no one else has ever seen and to master a body of knowledge, a skill, or a hobby on their own. They often have amazing memories for the information that they are interested in, and they are often quite introverted. If you are a thinker, you probably like your own space.

While thinkers love knowledge, knowledge can "puff up." Sometimes thinkers love being right more than they love the people around them. They often don't express emotion or affection directly; more often they will express it through gestures or indirection. So it can feel as if they are takers and not givers.

Thinkers do not like to lose an argument, and in their minds that has never happened. They don't like to be interrupted, and they can go into solitude for hours, if not days. That doesn't mean that they are more spiritual; they just have a low need to be around people. Thinkers are not fun to argue with—unless you are one.

Loyalists were born to be part of a team. They crave a cause to which they can give themselves and a community that they can believe in. At their best they help everyone else become better. They are usually quite bright and often articulate, although they may not volunteer their thoughts. But they can grow cynical when they feel let down—which is inevitable at times. They are tempted to want to shift responsibility to somebody else.

Of all animals, dogs are most famous for their loyalty, and oddly enough the ancient Greek word for dog is *kunos*, from which we get the word *cynic*. Loyalists' suspicion of God is that he is fickle, hard, or unfair, and their signature sin is fear. When Jesus told the parable about the three servants and the talent, the third servant—the one who buried his gift because he was afraid the master was hard and cruel—was behaving like a bruised loyalist.

Enthusiasts are wired to be the life of the party. They can add zest and color to the lives of everyone around them, and in their perfect world they would be the bride at every wedding and the corpse at every funeral. The enthusiast will often have a gift for storytelling—and they may talk about themselves a lot. If you talk with them about their problems, they may listen to you at first, but they are like Teflon—it just doesn't seem to stick with them.

I was in a restaurant with a friend, and every time we ordered something, the server said "superb" or "excellent choice" or "brilliant." We finally asked her, "Do you ever say, 'That was really stupid,' or, 'That's going to taste terrible'?" The mask came off, and she said, "No. In the kitchen we actually have a list of affirmations, and every time somebody orders something, we have to give them one of those affirmations."

Enthusiasts do not need a list of affirmations because they are *always* saying "cool," "awesome," "wow," "fabulous," or "great." They can live for years without seeing the pain or darkness in other people or themselves. They are also tempted to make life revolve around the pursuit of positive feelings — the desire for gratification — and they become miserable if they feel they are not getting enough attention.

Commanders are created to understand power and leadership, to know how it works and to feel a natural pull toward it. If this is you, being strong is very important to you. You have a need to lead. Opposition actually energizes you, but power can become an end in itself, and you can get frustrated when you are not getting your own way. Other people may be frightened by you if they don't agree with you.

> Winston Churchill was a commander who was easily bored by agreement and whose greatest moments were inspired by opposition. He once said that British Prime Minister Clement Attlee was a modest little man with much to be modest about. He had a running battle with Lady Astor, who once said to him, "Mr. Churchill, if I were your wife I would put poison in your coffee!" To which Churchill famously replied, "Lady Astor, if I were your husband I would drink it." When Adolf Hitler came to power in Germany, Churchill found the enemy that he had been waiting for his whole life.

When we took our dog for obedience training, the instructor said, "When you're giving your dog an order, you must always be above your dog. Never get down and look your dog in the eye when you're giving him an order, because you must establish your dominance. If the dog wants to go outside and scratches at the door, you never respond to the dog and let him go out. You make the dog do a trick first, and then you let him go out the door."

I immediately thought of someone I know who treats people this way, someone with an instinctive understanding of how power works and who always seeks the dominant position. If you are a commander, you do not like to be coached, taught, corrected, or led.

Peacemakers have a natural love for serenity and tranquility; they thrive when life is calm. Peacemakers love the verse, "How good and pleasant it is when God's people live together in unity!" Peacemakers can make excellent therapists and mediators, and in their redeemed state they bring reconciliation to families, neighborhoods, and workplaces.

But peacemakers can be tempted to seek peace at any price, using their relational skills to blend in and avoid taking initiative or assuming risks because of their undue attachment to comfort. They often suffer from "terminal niceness" when courage is required instead. A peacemaker friend of mine used to leave the table to empty the wastebasket anytime a conflict broke out at dinner time.

REFORMER

Strengths: Lives with an internal standard of what is good, noble, and beautiful. Calls others to live better lives

Weaknesses: Can be arrogant when unredeemed. Has high standards that can lead to a secret, inner sense of inadequacy

Example: The prophet Amos, who carried a plumbline to show Israel the standard God expected of society

SERVER

Strengths: Lives out love in action. Has a natural other-centeredness that makes people feel cared for

Weaknesses: Can use "giving" to manipulate others. Sometimes mistakes servanthood with fear or low esteem

Example: Martha, who was busy serving while her sister Mary sat at Jesus' feet

ACHIEVER

Strengths: Has a strong desire to grow. Has the ability to accomplish things and add value in the lives and world around them

Weaknesses: Has the temptation to be preoccupied with one's own success. Sometimes uses other people to receive applause or approval

Example: *Solomon, who sought achievement in education*, finance, culture, statecraft, and the arts

ARTIST

Strengths: Loves beauty and goodness. Brings imagination to life, love, and faith

Weaknesses: Finds that the need to be different can become an end in itself. Can be tempted to give in to impulses and live an undisciplined life

Example: King David, who had strong gifts as a poet, dancer, and composer of many psalms

THINKER

Strengths: Is a discoverer, inventor, and lover of logic. Holds a passion for truth — even when it is costly

Weaknesses: Having conviction of being right can lead to arrogance. Can be tempted to withdraw from relationships and love

Example: The apostle Paul, who loved to study, reason, explore, and teach

LOYALIST

Strengths: Is faithful and dependable when the chips are down. Loves to be part of a great team

Weaknesses: Is prone to skepticism or cynicism. When threatened, can be pushed into isolation by fear

Example: Elisha, who became Elijah's steadfast companion and protégé

ENTHUSIAST

Strengths: Has high capacity for joy and emotional expression. Has enthusiasm that is contagious for others

Weaknesses: Can have a need to be the center of attention. Has a need to avoid pain that can lead to escape or addiction

Example: The apostle Peter, who was the first one to leap out of the boat — even if it meant sinking

COMMANDER

Strengths: Has a passion for justice and desire to champion a great cause. Has charisma to lead that inspires others

Weaknesses: Has a need for power that can cause others to feel used. Sometimes relies on fear and intimidation to get one's own way

Example: Nehemiah, who was moved to action — rallying followers and defying opponents — when he heard Jerusalem was in ruins

PEACEMAKER

Strengths: Has a natural ability to listen well and give wise counsel. Has an easygoing, low-maintenance relational style

Weaknesses: Has a tendency to smooth things over and avoid conflict. Is passive

Example: Abraham, who was a peacemaker with his wife, his nephew Lot, and foreign leaders — even attempting to mediate between God and Sodom and Gomorrah

- Which category best describes you?
- Tell a friend or two, and see if it matches their observations of you.
- What does this tell you about your sin pattern and temptation?

It is critical to learn the patterns at the core of the me you want to be and the corresponding sin patterns, for no one is more vulnerable than the person who lacks self-awareness. Jesus warned about people who go around taking specks out of others' eyes while failing to notice the two-by-four in their own. My signature sin is my own two-by-four—so appealing to me that it is my biggest danger, so close to me I am apt not to see it.

As I become more aware of my signature sin, I sometimes wish I could be like someone else. I fall into the "achiever" category, so I sometimes think I would be less sinful if I were a "server." But every category wrestles with sin, only in different ways. Knowing every category has its own hidden temptations helps me be less likely to envy someone else when I am doing badly and less likely to judge someone else when I think I am doing well.

Knowing our signature pattern also tells us what we need to be most fully spiritually alive. If you are a reformer, you will need to be aware of the risk of self-righteousness, but you will also know that you have been wired by God with a passion for justice and that this passion is a good thing. You will feel God's presence most fully when you can express it with freedom and love.

Finally, knowing other people's patterns helps us live in community better. As we learn about others' patterns, we become more patient with those whose signature sins are different than ours. We can make sure helpers don't always get stuck in "serving" mode; we can encourage peacemakers to speak honestly when they are angry. We grow into a way of talking about our sin so that we challenge each other in ways that include laughter and lightness about our common brokenness.

I had lunch last week with a friend and co-worker who tends to be a peacemaker. At the end of our lunch, he had one more thing to tell me, which was to remind me of a group conversation we had both been part of a week earlier where I had communicated frustration and anger in inappropriate ways. He was gently telling me that I had sinned, and it was not fun for me to hear that. One difficulty of being in relationship with this guy is that he only sins about once a decade. But I am watching him very carefully, so that when it happens I can be there for him too.

For when we know ourselves and each other, when we walk in love, we are free to be called to the best version of ourselves—God's hand-signed version of ourselves.

That is the signature we really want.

Chapter 14

When You Find Yourself Out of the Flow, Jump Back In

The one pair of eyes into which you can never gaze is your own. There are parts of yourself you will never see without a mirror, camera, or outside help.

So it is with your soul.

In one sense, you know yourself better than anyone in the world. You alone have access to your inner thoughts, feelings, and judgments. In another way, you know yourself worse than anyone else can know you, for we all rationalize, justify, minimize, forget, and embellish—and we do not even know when we are doing it.

There is a me I cannot see.

Carol Tavris and Elliot Aronson have written a wonderfully disturbing book called *Mistakes Were Made (But Not by Me)*, which charts the mental tricks we play to deceive ourselves. We all fall for the self-serving bias. We claim too much credit and too little blame. Most faculty members rate themselves as above average teachers, and virtually all high school students rate themselves as above average in social skills. Most people in hospitals due to car crashes *they* caused rate themselves as above-average drivers. Even when people have the notion of self-serving bias explained to them, most people rate themselves as above average in their ability to handle the self-serving bias.

We suffer from the fundamental attribution error. When I see bad behavior in you, I attribute it to your flawed character. When it happens in me, I attribute it to extraordinarily trying circumstances. When you yell at your kid, you have an anger problem. When I yell, it's my kids' fault for misbehaving.

We are also guilty of confirmation bias. We pay attention to experts who agree with opinions we are already committed to, ignoring or discounting contrary evidence.

Our memories are not simply faulty; they are faulty in favor of our ego. People remember voting in elections they didn't vote in, voting for winners they did not vote for, and giving money to charities that they never gave to. They remember their children walking and talking at ages earlier than they did. (I know these are findings of credible research, but I can't remember who the researcher was—I think it might have been me.) The book *Egonomics* tells of a survey in which 83 percent were confident in their ability to make good decisions, but only 27 percent were confident in the ability of the people they worked closely with to make good decisions.

We are all viewing ourselves in the fun house mirror. People who know me well can always see these trends in me more easily than I see them in myself. This is why we are often stunned when someone else sees past our defenses into our souls. It is not that they are geniuses. It is just that I am sitting right in my blind spot.

» Acknowledge Your Own Blind Spot

Apart from the flow of the Holy Spirit, we can't even see our sin. Here is a vivid picture of how this works: When we lived in Chicago, there was a season when we would often get heavy snow. (It started in August and ended in June.) To melt snow and ice, the street crews would cover the roads with rock salt, which ended up coating car windshields. At night, driving by headlights in the dark, you don't know the film is there. Then the sun comes up, and sunlight is 500,000 times more intense than moonlight. The intensity of the sunlight illumines all the salt on the windshield, and suddenly you can't see out of it. You can't go anywhere. You have only two choices: Get the windshield cleaned up, or drive only at night. Avoid the light.

> This is the verdict: Light has come into the world, but people loved darkness instead of light.... (John 3:19)

We connive with each other not to see sin.

In South Africa I talked about apartheid with many church leaders who are about my age. Several of them said that they didn't favor it and knew it was a bad idea—but they look back now and ask, *Why didn't we say more? Why didn't we protest it?*

There was a system that sustained the sin of apartheid. If you were white, you talked mostly with other whites. The evil and injustice of it all did not enter your mind with sufficient force to move you to act. Millions of victims lived in injustice and cruelty, and the evil still ripples out.

> The same dynamic that sustained apartheid is always at work in us when it comes to greed, gossip, judgment, hypocrisy, flattery, bitterness, and hatred. Our insensitivity to sin is as dangerous as the inability to feel pain. However, the awareness of sin cannot be recovered simply by trying to crank up the volume. Merely *saying loudly and often* that sin is bad will not create the tectonic shift needed in our souls. You don't have to work hard to get people to hate cancer. They just have to love life. If they love life, people will always be opposed to whatever can destroy it.
>
> "The thief comes only to steal and kill and destroy; I have come that they may have life, and have it to the full." (John 10:10)

» Invite the Spirit to Examine Your Soul

Trying to see the truth about myself is like trying to see the inside of my own eyeballs. "Who can discern their own errors? Forgive my hidden faults," the psalmist asked. Fortunately, we are not left on our own. The Spirit is already at work in us. Our job is simply to listen and respond.

Once, in the middle of the night, Nancy and I were lying in bed and there was a tremendously loud beeping sound. Nancy gave me an elbow to the ribs and said, "What is that sound?"

I knew that if I acknowledged hearing the sound, it would be my job to go check it out. So I said, "What sound?" But I had to say it very loudly so that she could hear me over the tremendously loud beeping sound.

And she said, "That tremendously loud beeping sound."

"Oh, *that* sound! Let me go find out."

I went into the hallway, found the problem, and took care of it. When I got back to bed, Nancy asked, "What was it?" I told her it was the smoke detector.

"What made it stop?"

I told her I took the battery out.

"You can't do that," she said. "There could be a fire in the house somewhere."

"Nancy," I explained patiently, "we're upstairs. There's no smoke, we can't smell anything, there's no heat coming from anyplace. I checked. Do you smell any smoke? I don't smell any smoke. It was clearly a battery problem. Trust me. I took care of it."

We went back to sleep.

The next morning I had an early breakfast meeting, so while everyone else in the family was still sleeping, I went downstairs to leave the house. There were some odd malfunctions. The hall lights downstairs didn't work. The garage door wouldn't open automatically. That was strange, but I didn't think much more about it. Forty minutes into breakfast the server asked me if I was John Ortberg.

"Your wife called," she said. "She asked you to come home. She said the house is on fire."

I went home. Fire trucks were parked all over the cul-de-sac. I watched the outside of our white house turning brown, great clouds of smoke escaping into the neighborhood.

It turns out that a few delinquent birds built their nest inside the chimney casing. It eventually started smoldering and set off that loud beeping sound. Because we didn't do anything (and when I say "we," it is my way of saying that mistakes were made, but not by me), a fire started behind the wall and did unbelievable damage. All from a little bird's nest. A stupid little bird's nest. What kind of an idiot would take the batteries out of a smoke detector so he could sleep better during a fire?

That would be me.

The smoke detector wasn't my enemy; the fire was my enemy. The smoke detector was simply trying to help me.

I have a life. That's my house. I have a soul. You do too. Do you hear any beeping sounds there?

Beeping can sound like this: A parent neglects his children. They complain, misbehave, or increase the level of conflict around the house, and the parent has a nagging sense of failure. But instead of looking closely at his parenting — instead of talking directly about it with his children — he buries himself more fully in work, hobbies, or television.

A woman feels a twinge of pain when she sees a documentary about famine in Africa. She vaguely wonders about how little money she gives. But she doesn't like the discomfort, so she distracts herself by going shopping.

An angry man blows up at those closest to him. His "beeping sound" is his loneliness. He takes the batteries out of the smoke detector by drinking a little more, convincing himself his relatives are all difficult people.

Guilt is not my enemy. Sin, which blocks off life, is my enemy. The Spirit will often bring a sense of conviction, and when he does, the best response is not to suppress the guilt, but to get out of bed, take a look around the house, and put out the fire before it does more damage.

» Don't Get Used to the Beeping

One of the most poignant statements in the Bible is about Samson, who had been created by God to be a man of great strength and power. After a lifetime of disobedience, Samson had pushed God out of his life. At a great moment of crisis, he rose to exert his strength, but we are told that Samson "did not know that the LORD had left him." He had lost all sensitivity to God's divine presence in his life.

I too am insensitive. I don't know the truth about myself. But God will help reveal to me what truth I am able to handle. Our bodies have an amazing capacity to warn us about what ails them, if we learn to read the signs. Some warning signs are obvious: Chest pains may indicate heart trouble. But some are remarkably subtle: Shortened eyebrows could signal hyperthyroid problems; yellow bumps on our eyelids can mean high cholesterol; a diagonal crease in our ear lobe is linked to risk of heart attack. It makes you want to go look in a mirror, doesn't it?

In the same way, God will enable us to find the truth about our souls if we are patient and open and willing. The psalmist asks God to do the fearless searching inventory, for only God can give enough grace, strength, and truth to overcome our distorted vision. Left to myself, I will rationalize or excuse or defend myself. I will "call evil good and good evil," as Isaiah says. Or I will be neurotic about it. Madame Guyon, a wise writer on spiritual life, warned against "depending on the diligence of our own scrutiny rather than on God for the knowledge and discovery of our sin." So let's try. Allow your thoughts and responses to be guided by the Spirit.

One of the most important metaphors the Bible uses for sin is that of clothing. It speaks of "putting off" anger, slander, rage, greed, sexual impurity, and so on. And then it speaks of "putting on" those characteristics that flow from life in the Spirit. One of the ways you can think about sin is to use the acronym R.A.G.S. Those characteristics we are to "put off" by and large fit into one of these four categories:

R.A.G.S.

Resentment: mismanaged anger and bitterness

Anxiety: an inability or refusal to trust God; sins of passivity and timidity

Greed: mismanaged desire of all kinds

Superiority: self-righteousness and contempt for others

To make it concrete, you can respond with an A, B, or C response

"A" means things are going well

"B" means there is not much change either way

"C" means this is a matter of concern

Let the Spirit prompt you as you walk through this.

Resentment

≈ What is your irritability these days?
≈ Are you becoming less and less easily irritated?
≈ How about bitterness and unforgiveness?
≈ Do you attack or withdraw from others?
≈ Is your handling of resentment getting better, getting worse, or in neutral?

Pause for a moment. Does the Spirit bring to mind anyone with whom you need to reconcile? Seek to set things right.

Anxiety

≈ What is the discouragement factor in your life these days?
≈ Do you find that you are more frequently allowing concerns to motivate you to prayer?
≈ Do you have more or fewer fears these days about money, your job, or what other people think of you?
≈ Do you allow your fears to keep you from doing what God wants?

Greed (and Mismanaged Desire)

≈ Are you becoming more or less a victim of your appetites now than you used to be?
≈ Is self-control going up, down, or in neutral?
≈ Are you living with more openness and less hiddenness than you used to, living more of your life in the light?
≈ Do you find that what you desire and enjoy is increasingly in line with what God wants for you?

Superiority

≈ Respond to this statement: "I have become so humble, I amaze myself." (It's hard to give yourself an "A" on this one.)
≈ Are you becoming less self-preoccupied these days?
≈ Do you find yourself thinking more about other people and God as well as the work God has for you to do?
≈ How often in conversations do you remark on the positive characteristics of others?
≈ How often do you tell negative stories or communicate cynicism?
≈ Are you spending more or less time serving?
≈ How much clarity did you have? Often we have to grow before God can show us deeper and more subtle layers of sin.
≈ Where did you find yourself "B" or "C"? Are there any particular behaviors you need to go back to apologize for or clean up?
≈ Find a close friend and talk with him or her about what you are learning.

» Recognize the "Ministry of Conviction"

Jesus said that when the Holy Spirit came, he would convict people of sin. But conviction is not simply the same thing as "getting caught." After we moved from California to Illinois, I was driving home from preaching—a short mile-and-a-half drive—and got pulled over.

"Do you know why I pulled you over?" the officer asked.

I hate that question.

"You came to a stop sign, but you didn't come to a complete stop. You just came to a roll. I noticed your license plates. In California they may be fine with it if you slow down to a roll at a stop sign, but you're in Illinois now, and in Illinois stop means *stop*."

I told him that I was sorry, that I was distracted because I was coming home from church—did I mention I work at a church? Did I mention I work for God?

He told me he would let me go if I would say a Mass for him.

Sometimes people get caught doing something wrong and feel pain. But pain is not necessarily conviction over sin. It may just be embarrassment over being caught. Sometimes pain is pain over how other people are thinking about them. If no one knew, they would not be in pain.

Conviction is not the same thing as fear of punishment. Conviction is when I get a glimpse of what I am capable of, as in, *How did I become the kind of man who can do* that? *How did I become the kind of person who cheats on tests? How did I become the kind of person who tells lies to get what I want? How did I become the kind of person who is so cowardly about what I say?*

When God is at work in me, however, the pain is not about other people knowing or about consequences. That is all external. The pain of conviction is internal—over who *I am*. I respond by asking, *God, please send as much light as I can stand. Clean off the windshield of what I cannot clean.*

Cleanse me.

» The Indispensible Hope

Repenting of our sin is never despairing of our sin; it is always done in hope. Guilt may be an important stop on the journey, but it is never meant as the end of the line. We get our car checked by a mechanic, not so we can blame the car, but so it can get fixed.

Repenting is a gift God gives us for our own sake, not his. Repenting does not increase God's desire to be with us. It increases our capacity to be with him.

Ever see an animal repent?

We have a dog and a cat. Our dog sleeps in a little house every night, and he always gets a treat before he retires. He expects it. He feels entitled to it. When I stand up after 9:00, he goes crazy with anticipation. He stands at the door of the closet where the treats are and won't go into his house without a treat.

But sometimes the dog does a bad thing. When that happens, and when we find the bad thing, he does not expect a treat. He will run from us. He will actually kennel himself without a treat. He knows he's been bad.

Sometimes our cat does something wrong. Do you think the cat repents? No. Do you know why? Cats are evil. Somebody once said the difference between a cat and a dog is that a dog has a master, while a cat has staff.

We often think we need to repent because God is mad at us and needs some time to cool off. We think of repenting as a way of punishing ourselves so that perhaps God will be less severe with us.

> Low self-esteem causes me to believe I have so little worth that my response does not matter. With repentance, however, I understand that being worth so much to God is why my response is so important.

Repentance is not low self-esteem. Low self-esteem causes me to believe that I have so little worth that my response does not matter. With repentance, however, I understand that being worth so much to God is why my response is so important. Repentance is remedial work to mend our minds and hearts, which get bent by sin. When David murdered Uriah and slept with Bathsheba, he went a year without repenting. He had to train his mind to separate his deed from his worship of God. Then his friend Nathan told him a story about a wealthy man who stole the one sheep a poor man possessed. Notice what happens: David looks at Nathan's story through the eyes of the wronged person, and he feels compassion for the victim and indignation for the oppressor. Then Nathan says to David, "You are the man!" For the first time, David sees his deed from the perspective of those he has hurt. He now *thinks* and *feels* differently.

Repentance is always done in the gracious promise of forgiveness.

» Can We Really Expect to Change?

Imagine an alcoholic going into an AA meeting and hearing, "We re so glad you're here! We want you to know that you are loved and forgiven through nothing you have done. Of course, don't expect to change. Don't expect to stop drinking. We don't like it when people suggest sobriety is possible. We believe it breeds arrogance and self-sufficiency when people think in terms of actually not drinking. We have a little bumper sticker: 'Twelve-steppers are not sober, just forgiven.'"

The whole point of Alcoholics Anonymous (which grew out of an attempt to recapture classic Christian spiritual practices) was to bring freedom from a spiritual power (what the *Big Book* calls the "cunning, baffling, powerful, patient" enemy of addiction) that was destroying lives.

Sometimes people are afraid that if they don't change fast enough, God will get impatient with them. They don't generally use these words, but they wonder, *How much sin can there be in my life before I need to start worrying? Is there a level of sin that is acceptable for a Christian, then if you go higher you're in danger—like with the level of mercury in Lake Michigan? Is there a limit to impurity such as the Food and Drug Administration has? Is the standard high like that for homogenized milk, or is it like the standard of purity required for hot dogs, with lots of room for junk? Is it possible to be a Christian and just never grow?*

The issue is not whether God will get tired of forgiving sins. Forgiving is always the right response to sincere repentance. God is not worried that he might be taken advantage of. He is not afraid that some bad boy will use his charm to put one over on heaven.

The danger is not that God won't respond to our sincere repentance; the danger is that we might become so ensnared in the distorted thoughts that sin inevitably produces that we become simply unable to repent.

It is because of this that sin is to be taken so seriously. Paul told the church at Galatia, "Brothers and sisters, if someone is caught in a sin, you who live by the Spirit should restore that person gently. But watch yourselves, or you also may be tempted."

When the Spirit is helping us, we don't turn to that person in a judgmental way, because we are in no position to judge the amount of spiritual growth that has taken place in someone else. Missionary Frank Laubach preached the gospel to a tribe that had a long history of violence. The chief was so moved by Laubach's presentation that he accepted Christ on the spot. He then turned to Laubach in gratitude and said, "This is wonderful! Who do you want me to kill for you?" That was his starting point.

Only God knows what everyone's starting point is.

» Cling to a Bigger Hope

The bigger hope I cling to in the face of sin is not my goodness, but God's.

This year we had a daughter graduate from Azusa Pacific University. My wife spoke at the commencement, so we gathered with a group of fifty or so faculty, alumni, and administration before the ceremony. A few dozen people had graduated fifty years earlier, and they were there also to celebrate with their freshly minted co-alums.

At one point, Jon Wallace, the university president, pulled three seniors into the center of the room and told us all they were going to be serving under-resourced people in impoverished areas for several years after graduation. The graduating seniors said a few words about where they were going and why, and we applauded. They thought that was why they were there. Then Jon turned his back to the rest of us, faced the three students, and told them the real reason they were in the room.

"Somebody you do not know has heard what you're doing," Jon said. "He wants you to be able to serve the people where you are going without any impediment. So he has given a gift. He has asked to remain anonymous, but here is what he has done for you."

Jon turned to the first student and looked her in the eye. "You have been forgiven your school debt of $105,000."

It took a few moments for the words to sink in. The student shook her head at first. The thought registered. She began to cry at the sheer unexpected generosity of a mountain of debt wiped out in a moment by someone she had never met.

Jon turned to the next student. "You have been forgiven your debt of $70,000."

Jon turned to the third student. By this time she knew what was coming. But it was as if she could not believe it was happening until she heard the words. "You have been forgiven your debt of $130,000."

All three students were trembling. Their lives had been changed in a twinkling by the extravagance of someone they had never met. All of us who watched were so moved, it was as if we had experienced the forgiveness ourselves. There was not a dry eye in the room. (I wanted so badly to say, "I have a daughter who's graduating this weekend....")

An unpayable debt. An unseen giver. An unforgettable gift. And the freedom of the debtors becomes a blessing to the world.

Grace.

The joy of forgiveness.

There is a bigger debt we labor under. We give it labels such as regret, guilt, shame, or brokenness — sin. But God was in Christ reconciling the world to himself. We know what is coming, yet we need to hear the words just the same: Forgiven. Forgiven.

Forgiven.

PART FIVE
deepening my relationships

≫

Chapter 15

Try Going Off the Deep End with God

Researchers once surveyed people about their favorite room in the house. The top answer was the kitchen. People love that one. Most husbands' top answer was the bedroom. Want to guess what the top answer was for mothers of young children?

The bathroom.

Why? You lock the door. You keep those little rug rats out of there for at least a couple of minutes. You keep your husband out of there for at least a couple of minutes. The idea is that you find some place where you know you are alone. You are free of stress. You find sanctuary—a holy place.

God wants to give us sanctuary. There is another kind of presence when we are gathered together, but there is a unique way in which we experience the presence of God when we are alone.

I have one friend who finds this special solitude with God at a little Italian restaurant. Another friend experiences it most often while driving country roads. One finds it on airplanes. Another likes to go to a retreat center in the hills of Malibu Canyon. Still another finds it in the early hours of the morning in his office. You will recognize the place where you can be yourself before God.

Sometimes we are to pray privately. It is good to pray with people, but when I am praying and other people are listening, the fact that I am aware they are listening changes how I pray. Being alone with God, however, I can fully be myself.

In Jesus' day, almost no homes had private bedrooms. The "room" he refers to when he said, "When you pray, go into your room, close the door and pray to your Father," might be a supply room where they kept feed and tools or a few small animals. That would be the only place where there might be a door. It would be the most humble room in a humble home.

✳ **Being alone with God, you can fully be yourself.**

> "When you pray, go into your room, close the door and pray to your Father, who is unseen. Then your Father, who sees what is done in secret, will reward you." (Matthew 6:6)

What is your room?

» Speak to God about Your Deepest Concern

Dutch theologian Abraham Kuyper wrote that there is a similarity between the structure of each individual life and the structure of the tabernacle in the Old Testament, which was divided into three compartments.

There was the outer court, where everyone had access. Likewise, there is a public you. You too have an outer court, which is you when you go to work, shop, or play. This is your appearance or your image, and everyone sees this part of you.

In the tabernacle there was also an inner chamber called the Holy Place. Not everyone had access to this area, and most were not allowed in. You too have a holy place, the place where you only allow certain people to enter, such as your friends or family. You decide who comes in and who doesn't, and no one can force their way in. Someone may hold power over you vocationally or financially, but that does not allow them entrance. Maybe someone wormed their way in, and you have to see a therapist to get them out. But ultimately everyone gets to decide who they allow in that inner chamber.

Then there was one more chamber — a very small, carefully guarded place, deep inside. It was the most sacred, and they had a beautiful name for this: the Holy of Holies. It was entered only by the chief priest, and there was room there for only one person and God.

This is the mystery and depth and amazing truth about *you*, because whether you are young or old, high or low on the totem pole, you have one of these places inside you too. Only God is allowed in there. No other human being can come into your Holy of Holies.

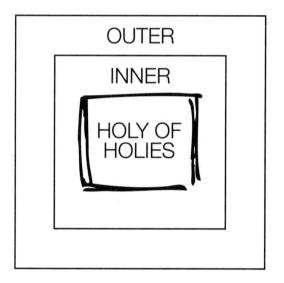

Early in our marriage I used to say to Nancy, "I know you so well, I know you better than you know yourself." Do you think she took that as a compliment? No. That is one of those "how could you be so dumb as to say that?" comments of mine, because there are depths in each one of us no one else will *ever* know — even if we wanted them to know. That is not because we are closed mouthed or secretive. There are parts of us we simply cannot put into words. There are depths in us that we don't even know ourselves.

In the Bible we often see characters addressing their own soul. The psalmist says, "Bless the LORD, O my soul," and, "Why are you downcast, O my soul?" Recognition of the unconscious, of thoughts and desires living far beneath my awareness, was around long before Sigmund Freud. The soul is so deep that I do not even know it fully myself.

You carry your soul around with you all the time. It may be filled with joy and peace; it may be empty and neglected. People who just look at the outer you—sometimes even people who are in the inner court—do not see your soul.

No one knows about this but you and God.

» Private Prayer Is Your Soul Alone with God

Jesus prayed. We are told that when he was baptized, "as he was praying, the heavens opened," and the Spirit came upon him. The flow of the Spirit is closely connected to prayer, and Jesus immediately went into forty days of fasting and prayer.

Jesus prayed *when his life was crowded and draining.* After he began his public ministry, privacy became difficult. "The news about him spread all the more, so that crowds of people came to hear him and to be healed.... But Jesus often withdrew to lonely places and prayed."

Jesus prayed *when he faced important choices.* When it was time to select his closest friends, he sought guidance. "One of those days Jesus went out into the mountainside to pray, and spent the night praying to God. When morning came, he called his disciples to him and chose twelve ... [as] apostles...."

Jesus prayed *when he was sad or frightened.* During Jesus' ministry his cousin, John the Baptist, was arrested and eventually executed. "When Jesus heard what had happened, he withdrew ... privately to a solitary place" to be alone with his Father.

Jesus prayed *when he needed strength for his work.* One morning, "while it was still dark, Jesus got up, left the house and went off to a solitary place where he prayed." When Simon Peter came looking for him,

Jesus said, "Let us go somewhere else — to the nearby villages — so I can preach there also. That is why I have come."

Jesus prayed *when he was worried about people he loved*. When he was about to die, Jesus knew that his disciples would fail. He told Simon Peter, "Satan has asked to sift all of you as wheat. But I have prayed for you, Simon, that your faith may not fail. And when you have turned back, strengthen your brothers."

Jesus prayed *when he faced an insurmountable problem*. "Jesus went out as usual to the Mount of Olives, and his disciples followed him." He said, "Pray that you will not fall into temptation." Then "he withdrew about a stone's throw beyond them, knelt down, and prayed, 'Father, if you are willing, take this cup from me; yet not my will, but yours be done.'"

When Jesus prayed, things happened. One time he took Peter, James, and John with him up on a mountain to pray, and "as he was praying, the appearance of his face changed, and his clothes became as bright as a flash of lightning."

I often find myself feeling guilty when I read those descriptions of Jesus at prayer, but I am not sure guilt helps us pray much more over the long haul. So consider this question: Do you think Jesus prayed a lot because he *wanted* to pray, or because he thought he *should* pray?

If you ever feel guilty about your praying, know that someone who is better at it than you is already at work. Scripture says, "God's Spirit is right alongside us helping us along. If we don't know how or what to pray, it doesn't matter. He does our praying in and for us, making prayer out of our wordless sighs, our aching groans. He knows us far better than we know ourselves ... and keeps us present before God."

I think Jesus *wanted* to pray. I think that for us to pray much, or deeply, we need to move from what we think we *should* do to what we *want* to do. But that won't happen if we simply tell ourselves that we have to pray more. So let us put "shoulds" aside for a moment. How can we begin to pray in a way that will help us *want* to pray?

Almost twenty years ago, I felt frustrated at my own lack of prayer. So

I found a kind of prayer coach, who advised me to spend a few moments after praying just jotting down what had gone on while I was praying. The single most frequent observation for me was that while I was praying I was aware of being very tired.

"Did you tell the Lord about this?" my coach asked.

"No."

"Do you think it would be a good idea to talk to him about this?"

"Yes."

I began to learn that although I was trying to set aside time to pray, I had a hard time being *fully present*. We all know what it is to be with another person when their mind is a million miles away. I began to think that is how God felt when I was praying. After a period of frustration, my prayer coach had the suggestion I mentioned earlier; to go outside alone and simply invite Jesus to come with me.

The next day I went to the ocean, took my shoes off, started to run, and invited Jesus to come along. I found the strangest thing. When I thought I was *supposed* to be talking to him, I found it effortful and difficult. Now that all I had to do was invite him, I couldn't stop thinking about him. My mind kept reflecting on his being with me. I found myself wanting to point out the pelicans and the waves to him. People and concerns would pop into my mind, and I would find myself telling Jesus about them.

Everything changed.

» The Spirit Will Invite You to Pray

We can look for cues that embed prayer into our daily lives. In the Bible we are commanded to practice hospitality. In ancient times this usually involved hosting overnight visitors; now it might start with welcoming a telephone call that feels like an interruption. Out of habit I may find myself answering with a grudging spirit. *What do you want? Make it fast. You're bothering me.*

But there is another way. Wil Derske, a Benedictine monk, writes about the monastic value of hospitality and says that to accept a phone call is an opportunity to receive a guest. We can pause a moment before answering, in order to change our inner attitude from irritation to welcome. Derske says he will say a prayer of blessing just before taking the call: *Benedicamus Domino* — it might be the Lord!

Another way to accept the Spirit's invitation to pray is what might be called "paper prayers." Hezekiah was king of Israel when he received a letter from the much more powerful king of Assyria. The Assyrian king demanded the capitulation of Israel and warned Hezekiah not to trust in God. He warned that resistance meant that they would have to "eat their own filth and drink their own urine" before they died.

Hezekiah took the letter, went up to the temple, "and spread it out before the Lord." Then he prayed, beginning by remembering God's greatness: "O LORD Almighty, God of Israel, enthroned between the cherubim, you alone are God over all the kingdoms of the earth. You have made heaven and earth. Give ear, O LORD, and hear; open your eyes, O LORD, and see."

What piece of paper would you spread out before the Lord? Maybe it is a financial statement that is overwhelming. Maybe it is a divorce certificate or a medical diagnosis or a pink slip or a flaming e-mail. Any piece of paper that causes distress can be an invitation to prayer, a candidate to be spread out before the Lord.

» Use Your Body in Prayer

Body language is an important part of communication, and we can use our bodies in many ways to help us pray. We saw earlier that in Bible times people generally prayed with their eyes open. A friend of mine who knows church history said people closing their eyes and bowing their heads to pray did not become common practice until the 1800s — and then it was mostly to get children to settle down in Sunday school. There are records in Scripture of people praying as they stand, kneel, lie prostrate on the ground, sit, stretch out their hands, lift faces toward the sky, or bow them toward earth.

I find that my mind often works better in prayer when my body is moving. My wife and I take walks in our neighborhood, and there is one very steep hill that I usually run up. It takes two minutes and twenty seconds on a good day, and my heart is beating like a hummingbird's wings by the time I reach the top. Not long ago, I was running and was seized by the thought that this time I could not make it. So I began to repeat, "I can do all things through Him who strengthens me." Repeating that, one step at a time, I made it to the top. I was facing a difficult conflict at the time — my own king of Assyria. At the top of the hill the thought came, *Just as I received the power to go up the hill, I will receive the power to face the conflict.* And the flow of the Spirit came in a running prayer.

You are free to use your body and posture to help you turn your mind and heart to God:

- ≈ In confession, I often have my head bowed and will kneel; it helps me remember and experience the humility of the moment.
- ≈ In worship, you may want to turn your face toward the sky.
- ≈ Asking for guidance, I will sometimes place my palms upward as a way of expressing with my body "whatever you want...."
- ≈ When praying with someone, say at a restaurant, I may look that person right in the eye while talking to God: *Father, I am so grateful for this person. You know what they need. Give them what is required by their hearts.*
- ≈ To praise God, I will often use music to sing prayers.

» When Your Mind Wanders — The Spirit Is There Too

Does your mind ever wander when you pray? Sometimes it is good for us to take a few moments at the beginning of a prayer to slow down our mental metabolism and help us focus. It can be helpful for us to look at a candle or meditate on a verse or a word. But I have discovered that sometimes my wandering thoughts themselves can guide me into prayer.

I begin praying, and then I imagine myself being wildly successful at something. Or I replay a conversation with a person I am upset with. Or I try to figure out how to solve a problem I am worried about.

I used to think of those kinds of thoughts as obstacles to prayer, but I have come to think of them as prayers waiting to be offered. Maybe the reason they pop into my mind is not simply my short attention span, but rather what my mind is really concerned about. Instead of trying to suppress these thoughts, it is better to begin to talk to God about them. And just like that, I am back in the flow of prayer. Indeed, we are free to pray in the ways that will best help us live in the joyful awareness of God's presence.

» Let God's Face Shine on You

God gives us a remarkable picture of what can happen in prayer when we watch a parent and a little child. Imagine a one-year-old who looks at you and holds his gaze. You are charmed. He looks shyly at first, tilting his head away and looking out of the corner of his eye. You do the same. It's fun. He turns his face to look directly at you. You mirror the turn. There is a sudden noise behind him, and he looks startled — and you mirror his surprised look. He is so startled that he is getting ready to cry, so you shift into a smile. He does the same, and he is soon gurgling with joy.

We are hard-wired for this interaction. In fact, it is more than a game. When a child makes eye contact like this, when someone lets him know through their own body that they understand what he is feeling, his brain and nervous system make crucial connections inside his body. He is experiencing what is called "neural integration." When his amygdala gets terrified, it gains rapid access to his cerebral cortex, which can tell him to calm down while it works on solving the problem. By playing the face game, you are literally giving the child peace. Therefore, he wants to play. No one has to tell a child they should play. Children are hard-wired for it. It heals them. They find delight there.

In the Old Testament, God instructed Moses to give the Israelites the following blessing: "The LORD bless you and keep you; the LORD make his face to shine upon you; ... the LORD lift up his countenance upon you, and give you peace."

Is this what happened when Jesus prayed?

Prayer was not an energy-drainer for Jesus; it was an energy-giver. So it can be for us, if we come to see God's face shining on us. When I meet with a critic who wants to argue with me, I lose energy. When I meet with my best friend, I gain energy. God wants to meet with us as our friend.

The ability of love to speak to the deepest places of our hearts never goes away. Have you ever noticed how people in love sometimes speak to each other in baby talk? It is immensely intimate and private — and it's off-putting to a third party. If you do it, I wouldn't want to hear it. But we do it because it is the tenderest language we know.

Jesus' prayer life demonstrated this intimacy, because he called God "Abba," an Aramaic word much like "Dada" or "Momma." (Jesus spoke in Aramaic, and some portions of the New Testament are written in Aramaic rather than Greek.) "Abba" was a Jewish child's first word, because it was so easy to say. Somehow when Jesus was with God, the tender love that an adult offers to a child to give strength is what he received from his Father. It rewired his nervous system.

It does not stop there, for Jesus told his followers that they could have this same experience. This is why Paul wrote that by the Spirit we too can say, "Abba, Father." This is what happens when we are praying in the flow.

> God's Spirit touches our spirits and confirms who we really are. We know who he is, and we know who we are: Father and children. (Romans 8:16 *The Message*)

Prayer, more than any other single activity, is what places us in the flow of the Spirit. When we pray, hearts get convicted, sin gets confessed, believers get united, intentions get encouraged, people receive guidance, the church is strengthened, stubbornness gets melted, wills get surrendered, evil gets defeated, grace gets released, illness gets healed, sorrows are comforted, faith is born, hope is grown, and love triumphs.

In prayer—in the presence of God—we come closest to being fully ourselves.

Chapter 16

Make Life-Giving Relationships
a Top Priority

When I turned fifty, my sister Barbara brought two stacks of boxes that were four feet high. When I opened them, I found they were filled with the foods of our youth. She had brought for me all kinds of food that I had loved, that were part of life growing up in Rockford, Illinois, and that I hadn't eaten in thirty-plus years.

There was a bag of "Mrs. Fisher's Potato Chips," which you can only get in Rockford. These chips are just grease and fat and salt and vinegar. Fabulous! Barbara brought almond tarts with white frosting that we used to get at a Swedish bakery that, sadly, went out of business years ago. Barbara had to track down a baker and get him to teach her how to make those tarts. She also brought a box of homemade popcorn, because our grandmother used to pop popcorn in bacon grease. She would fry up bacon, pop popcorn in the bacon grease, and then throw the bacon into the popcorn. Nobody in my grandmother's family lived to be very old — but we ate well.

When I grew up, we had "Sara Lee Banana Cake," so another box from Barbara had banana cake in it. I was a frosting guy, and Barbara was a cake girl. I would give her my cake, and she would give me her frosting. They don't make it anymore, but there is a group of "Sara Lee junkies" online who track down these recipes and swap them. My sister went online, found the recipe, and practiced it for months.

Only my sister could have gotten me those gifts. Love in a box. Our life together in food.

I was struck by how much a part of my life Barbara is. For fifty years I have been loved, believed in, and called to my best self by this remarkable, slightly older woman. My sister Barbara was my first and best friend. We played "spies" together, shared secrets, and went through school, church, piano lessons, plays, college, adult life, and therapy. When she gave me that birthday food, it struck me that as the body is nourished by food, so the soul is nourished by people.

More than anything else, we are shaped by people. Some naturally help me live in the flow and make me want to be the best version of myself. They see that best of me when I cannot see it. They cheer me on when I grow toward it. They get in my face when I move away from it. They encourage me when I am tempted to give up.

Plus I like them.

» The Power of Connectedness

God uses people to form people. That is why what happens between you and another person is never *merely* human-to-human interaction — the Spirit longs to be powerfully at work in every encounter. Referring to this dynamic, some writers of Scripture speak of "the fellowship of the Spirit." *Fellowship* has become a churchy word that suggests basements and red punch and awkward conversation. But it is really a word for the flow of rivers of living water between one person and another, and we cannot live without it.

An academic journal called *The Journal of Happiness Studies* publishes studies using the tools of research to identify what makes human life flourish. When researchers look at what distinguishes quite happy people from less happy people, one factor consistently separates those two groups. It is not how much money you have; it is not your health, security, attractiveness, IQ, or career success. What distinguishes consistently happier people from less happy people is the presence of rich, deep, joy-producing, life-changing, meaningful relationships.

Spending meaningful time with people who care about us is indispensable to human flourishing. Social researcher Robert Putnam writes, "The single most common finding from a half-century's research on life satisfaction, not only from the U.S. but around the world, is that happiness is best predicted by the breadth and depth of one's social connections."

Connectedness is not the same thing as knowing many people. People may have many contacts in many networks, but they may not have any friends.

Part of what it means to be made in God's image is our capacity for connectedness, because God created human beings and then said, "It isn't good for man to be alone." Paul paints a picture of that connectedness in writing to the church in Ephesus that they are "being rooted and established in love."

When a tree puts roots into the ground, those roots are able to take in nutrients and water, and the tree grows and has life and strength—but *only* if it is rooted. In the same way, we are rooted and our souls are nourished in the love of God and other people. We experience this both physically and emotionally when we connect with somebody.

You are walking down the street, and someone you know smiles at you. They care about you through words, through touch, through listening, through prayer together. Whenever there is an exchange of genuine caring, it is as if the roots of your soul are getting fed. Every life has to have that connectedness.

How necessary is it? British scientist Donald Winnicott found that children who play in close proximity with their mother are more creative than children playing at a distance from her. Winnicott found that children are naturally inventive, curious, and more likely to take risks in what might be called the "circle of connectedness." When they are within this circle, they take more risks. They show more energy. If they fall down, they are more likely to get back up. They laugh more than children who are outside the circle.

Why? It is not that Mom is doing for the child what the child could do for himself. She is not solving problems for this little kid or generating ideas about how he ought to play. Instead, when love is present, when that child feels safe and cared for in her presence, something gets released in his life. He gets a little stronger. He gets bolder and more creative. Love releases life in that child that would otherwise remain dormant and unsummoned.

When you are loved, it is not just that you receive more from someone else, but also that you become more yourself. *You-ier.* Love brings the power to become the me I want to be. Loving people are literally life-givers. That is connectedness.

As children grow older and capable of more abstract thought, the circle gets bigger. When they are a one-year-old, maybe they want to be within a few inches of their mom. When they are two, they can be several feet away, but still in the circle. When they are three, the circle may be as big as a house.

How about when they are fifteen—how far away do they want to be then? The circle is now the size of the solar system. They want to be tracing the orbit of Haley's Comet.

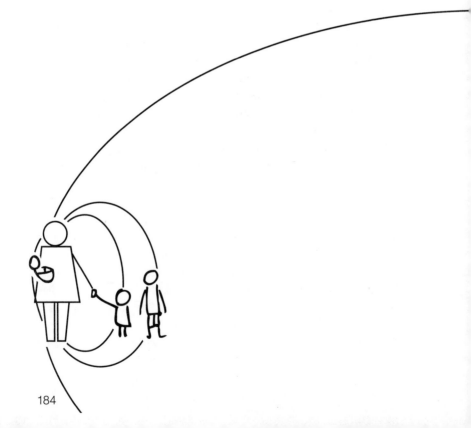

When love is working correctly, this sense of connectedness becomes internal. Initially, it is a very physical connection. When life begins, there is actually physical attachment. As we get older, we carry it around inside of us, and eventually we can take it with us wherever we go.

Likewise, we flourish when we are connected with God and people, and we languish when we are disconnected. Emotionally, isolated people are more prone to depression, anxiety, loneliness, low self-esteem, substance abuse, sexual addiction, and difficulties with eating and sleeping.

Physically, the destructive aspects of isolation are powerful. Even animals that are isolated experience more extensive arterial sclerosis than animals that are not isolated. A friend of mine used to have a dog and a cat, and the dog and the cat fought for ten years. Then one year the cat died, and the dog didn't want to eat. Day after day the dog wouldn't eat, until six weeks later the dog died. That is the power of connection.

People who are socially disconnected are between two and five times more likely to die from any cause than those who have close ties to family, friends, and other relationships. People who have bad health habits like cigarette smoking, overeating, elevated blood pressure, and physical inactivity — but who still remain connected — live longer than people who have great health habits but are disconnected.

> We see the physical, life-giving power of connection in Winston Churchill. He had a wonderful marriage with his wife, was deeply connected to his family, his friends, his nation, and his work. His health habits were terrible. His diet was awful. He smoked cigars all the time. He drank too much, had weird sleep habits, was completely sedentary — yet he lived to be nearly ninety. Somebody asked him, "Mr. Churchill, do you ever exercise?" He replied, "The only exercise I get is serving as a pallbearer for my friends who died while they were exercising."

Spiritually, as John says, "Anyone who does not love remains in death." When we live in isolation, we are more likely to give into temptation or discouragement. We are more likely to become self-absorbed. We are more likely to spend money in selfish ways. Not only do *we* suffer when we live in disconnectedness, but then other people whom God placed around us get cheated out of the love God intended us to give them.

> *"Loners who care only for themselves spit on the common good." (Proverbs 18:1* The Message*)*

We were designed to flourish in connectedness. This does not mean that we have to become more extrovert. Some of the shyest people I know have some of the deepest friendships. Flourishing in connectedness does mean that we will have to learn to identify who the life-giving people around us are, as well as discover how to give the power of connectedness to others, so that we can cultivate those relationships.

So let's open the boxes and look at the gifts connectedness brings.

» The Gift of Delighting

Love is mostly something you do, not something you feel. The circle of connection is marked by servanthood. "You, my brothers and sisters," Paul says, "were called to be free. But do not use your freedom to indulge the sinful nature; rather, serve one another humbly in love," because what marks God's kingdom is when people serve one another.

A therapist I know asked a client how he knew when his marriage of several decades had gone bad. "It was when she stopped putting toothpaste on my toothbrush in the morning," the man said. When they were first married, whoever got up first would put a roll of toothpaste on the other spouse's toothbrush. Then somewhere along the line, they stopped squeezing for each other and squeezed only for themselves.

A son drives for five hours to be with his mother on her birthday. A friend mentions a book he is interested in; his friend remembers and finds a copy to give him for no visible reason. A middle-aged couple in a restaurant see a young husband and wife with little money and secretly pay their check. A father knows how much his daughter likes having a clean car, so he sneaks over to wash it for her by surprise. People in a small group email each other throughout the week as a way of expressing their care.

A wise man once said that just as the three laws of real estate are "location, location, location," the three laws of relationship are "observation, observation, observation." People who give life to us are people who notice us. They know what we love and fear. When we work to truly notice someone else, love for them grows. When we work to truly observe another person, in that self-forgetfulness our own soul flourishes.

If you can't do great things, Mother Teresa used to say, do little things with great love. If you can't do them with great love, do them with a little love. If you can't do them with a little love, do them anyway.

Love grows when people serve.

» The Gift of Commitment

One of the marks of the early church was their commitment to connectedness because they knew connectedness doesn't just happen. They met together every day. They ate together with glad and sincere hearts. Over time, however, that value began to fade. So the writer of Hebrews said, "Let us consider how we may spur one another on toward love and good deeds, not giving up meeting together as some are in the habit of doing." In other words, keep committed to community.

I have never known anyone who failed at love yet succeeded at life. I have never known anyone who succeeded at love yet failed at life. We need love to live.

> Robert Putnam made a staggering comment: "As a rough rule of thumb, if you belong to no groups but you decide to join one, you cut your risk of dying over the next year in half." It is difficult to imagine anyone not interested in cutting their risk of dying in half. That is why the new motto for small groups at the church where I serve is, *"Join a group or die."*

In sports, the more an athlete needs encouragement from the fans, the less likely he or she is to get it. Rarely do fans of a losing team think when a slumping player comes up to bat: "Let us consider how we can spur him on to good deeds." Too often, people who need the cheers the most get them the least.

Every day, everyone you know faces life with eternity on the line, and life has a way of beating people down. Every life needs a cheering section. Every life needs a shoulder to lean on once in a while. Every life needs a prayer to lift them up to God. Every life needs a hugger to wrap some arms around them sometimes.

Every life needs to hear a voice saying, "Don't give up."

» The Gift of Love

The deepest words of the soul are the simplest: "I love you."

My father grew up in a Swedish home where he knew he was loved, but love didn't get expressed much verbally. So when he and my mom formed a family, they wanted to make sure they said those words. And so I grew up hearing those words: *I love you, Johnny.*

> Let no debt remain outstanding, except the continuing debt to love one another, for whoever loves others has fulfilled the law. (Romans 13:8)

My dad is actually John Ortberg Sr., and I am John Ortberg Jr., so I was always "Johnny." Those were the last words I would hear at night: "Love you, Johnny." I would hear them when I got discouraged or sad. I would hear them when I felt lonely. I would hear them when I messed up.

My mom always said two things when she was really worried. One of them was, "I thought you were dead in a ditch somewhere." And it wasn't just "dead." You would think "dead" would be bad enough, but it's not just dead. It's "dead in a ditch." You might have been dead in a lovely meadow or something. That wouldn't be so bad, but dead in a ditch—that was awful.

The other was, "I was afraid someone had hit you over the head." Not just "hit you"—that would be bad enough. But "hit you over the head" because the head is such a vulnerable place. If she was *really* worried about us, she would combine them: "I was afraid someone had hit you over the head, and you were lying dead in a ditch."

Which is another way of her saying, "I love you."

Maybe there is someone in your life who just needs to have you look them in the eye and say it: *I love you.* The Spirit of God is at work in us all the time, prompting these expressions of love.

I was driving someone else's car yesterday morning, and I noticed that the gas tank was about empty, so I stopped and filled it up with gas. I can give a small gift of love like this in other ways, such as noticing what kind of coffee delights someone in a coffee bar and surprising them with it. I can let someone who is obviously in a hurry cut in front of me in line at a grocery store when I am not rushed. I can notice something admirable about one of my kids' friends and write a note to their parents to congratulate them.

Every moment is an opportunity to practice a gesture of love.

» The Gift of Joy

In the circle of connectedness we learn what a good thing joy is. One time my sister, brother, and I came home from school, and my mom had put on some kind of a rejuvenating facial mud mask that hardens and makes your face look like you are 187 years old. With all the wrinkles and cracks, she looked like something from a science fiction movie.

"Mom," we said, "take that off your face. That looks terrible!"

She looked at us sadly. "Children, I can't take it off. I haven't put anything on my face. This is a skin condition. It just happened today. I went to the doctor, and he said there's nothing that can be done. This is it."

"Mom, stop teasing us. It's awful! Take it off now."

"Children, stop saying this. You will make me feel bad. My face will look like this for the rest of your lives, so get over it."

We lost it. My little brother started to weep. My sister ran to call my dad. I kept pleading. Finally my mom couldn't take it anymore, so she told us the truth and she laughed and laughed.

We all ended up in therapy.

> A cheerful heart is good medicine, but a crushed spirit dries up the bones. (Proverbs 17:22)

We hunger for joy. "Satisfy us in the morning," writes the psalmist—but not with more money or power or applause. "Satisfy us in the morning with your unfailing love so that we may sing for joy and be glad all our days."

Joyful people make us come alive.

When the book of the law was read to the people in Nehemiah's day, they were overwhelmed by inadequacy and guilt. Nehemiah gave to them and us a remarkable statement: "The joy of the LORD is your strength." We know we love joy, but we often forget the power of joy. Joy gives us the strength to resist temptation. It brings the ability to persevere. Joy is the Velcro that makes relationships stick. Joy gives us energy to love. A person who brings joy to us is an oasis in a desert land. We don't just need air and food and water. We need joy.

> A twenty-year study of more than 4,700 people found that joy is contagious. People who become happy make it more likely that their friends will become happy, for happiness travels through relational networks like ripples on a pond. It is so robust that it continues through three degrees of separation, so you are more likely to increase in happiness if even a friend of a friend of a friend becomes happy. Having a happy friend is more likely to increase your happiness than getting a $5,000 raise. So if you get a $5,000 raise, try giving it to your friend. He will be happy, and you will both win.

»The Gift of Belonging

When I am loved, I belong to someone and they belong to me. This is why the most common designation for people in Jesus' community is "brother" or "sister."

When our family moved from Illinois back to California, our oldest daughter was entering college and wrestled not with just leaving the family, but with having all of us leave the home where she had grown up. She told us an unforgettable metaphor that a very wise friend used to explain her situation. It is as if she were getting her boat, sailing away from the dock, and then turning to find her dock was going away too. It is hard to be a little boat heading out to sea when you have no more dock to return to.

As our daughter spoke, I looked over at Nancy. She was immediately thinking of her own life growing up. In her family there was lots of independence early on, but not so much all-togetherness. "It's like I got a boat right away," she said, "but I never had a dock!"

I was struck by just the opposite. We prized closeness, but independence was the bigger struggle. "I had a great dock," I said. "I just never got my boat!"

When you were born, God gave you a boat—your life—designed to be an adventure for all your days on the earth. God also created a dock—your family—that could be the place of safety and security to give you the courage to sail.

Belonging. This is God's gift to us.

One day God says to the angels, "I have an idea. I am going to create the family."

An angel asks, "What is it?"

"I am very excited about this idea," God says. "Of course, I am excited about all my ideas. One of the great things about being God is you just never have a bad idea—but this one is special. *Family* is going to be the way I connect people in love. It will work like this. Adult people will sign up to take care of a tiny little stranger."

"Are they going to get paid?" the angel asks.

"No, that little stranger is actually going to cost them a lot of money. Not only that, but the little stranger won't even be able to talk at first. It will just cry and scream, and you will have to guess why. It will make you lose sleep. It will make messes all the time that you have to clean up. It will be utterly vulnerable. You have to watch that kid twenty-four hours a day, seven days a week. Then when it's two, that little stranger will be able to say words like "no" and "mine," and it will throw tantrums. And then I am thinking about inventing puberty. I am not too sure about that one yet, but if I do, they will get these strange things called hormones that will go crazy. Odd things will happen to their bodies. They will get pimples, their voices will crack, and their limbic systems will melt down. Then they will grow up, and just when they are mature and beautiful and interesting and able to contribute, they will move away. That's the idea. What do you all think?"

The angels shuffle around and look at their feet. *Who's going to tell him?* they think. *Lord, who would sign up for that? Why would they do it?*

Here is where God really gets excited. "They won't even know why. They will just look at that little body, those little hands and feet, and they will think that this tiny little stranger is beautiful, even though he looks like every other baby and all babies look like Winston Churchill. Then one day that little stranger will smile at them, and they will think they have won the lottery. That little stranger will say 'Dada' and 'Mama,' but it will say 'Dada' first because daddies are just so self-sacrificial and noble and ... how I love them. But moms are good too. So it will say 'Dada' and 'Mama,' and then those little arms and hands will open up and reach out and wrap around that neck, and it is going to feel to that grown up that for the first time now they understand why arms and hands were created.

"What it's really all about is just grace.

"Children, the new generation, will learn that they are prized and belong before they have ever done a single thing to earn it. The old generation will learn that when they give, they will receive. When they give the most, they receive the most.

"And then one day I will tell them, *Human race, I am your Father. You are my daughter; you are my son.*

"They will get it and they will be undone."

Teilhard de Chardin wrote, "Someday, after we have mastered the winds and the waves, the tides and gravity, we will harness for God the energies of love, and then for the second time in the history of the world man will have discovered fire."

connectedness inventory

When something goes wrong, do I have at least one friend I can easily talk with about it?

Yes   No

Do I have a friend I can drop in on at any time without calling ahead?

Yes   No

Is there someone who could accurately name my greatest fears and temptations?

Yes   No

Do I have one or more friends whom I meet with regularly?

Yes   No

Do I have a friend I know well enough to trust their confidentiality?

Yes   No

If I received good news like a promotion, do I have a friend I would call immediately just to let them know?

Yes   No

If I can't say 'yes' to most of these questions, I may want to look for a small group to join, or invite someone out for coffee as a first step toward connecting.

Chapter 17
Be Human

In the church, we have a sin problem.

The problem is not just that we sin—everyone has *that* problem. Our problem is that we can't talk about it. Our problem is that we pretend we don't have a problem. We are comfortable with stories about people who *used* to sin, and people often get invited to give testimonies as long as they have happy endings, the way television sitcoms used to in the 1950s: *I used to have a problem, but then I met God, and now I'm doing much better.*

Imagine going to see a counselor and saying, "I only want to talk about problems I *used* to have. Please do not ask me to acknowledge having any current problems. It would be embarrassing. I'm afraid you might reject me."

Why would anyone go to a counselor to try to convince the counselor that they don't need a counselor?

Why would anyone go to church to try to convince the people there that they don't need a church?

Years ago in southern California, I was part of a small group in which we were all relatively new husbands. We talked about our adjustments to married life, our sexuality, our jobs, our faith, and our money. We went to movies, baseball games, and weekends in Palm Springs. But one day one of the guys didn't show up, and we found out that week that he had struggled with compulsive gambling for years. This put him in huge financial problems, which then led to financial dishonesty at work. Eventually he got fired and got divorced. He had lived in fear, compulsion, and self-loathing for years — but none of us knew. Maybe he didn't have the courage to tell us. Maybe we sent subtle signals that talking about such deep problems would be unwelcome. I found myself wondering afterward, *How deep did the roots of these issues go in his life? When did they start? If we could have talked about them, would his life have gone differently? How much did my own need to look better than I am contribute to a culture of superficiality?* All I know for sure is that what should have been the place of greatest safety and healing was not.

People are okay telling a doctor that their body has a problem or telling a mechanic that their car has a problem. Couldn't sinners be okay telling other sinners they have a sin problem? If I want God (or anyone else, for that matter) to love the *real* me, I will have to work at getting real.

David was Israel's greatest king — but he was also a polygamist. He was a terrible father. He coveted another man's wife, committed adultery with her, attempted to deceive the husband, eventually had the husband murdered, and covered up his crime for a year. He was a liar, an adulterer, a coveter, and a murderer. As a friend of mine noted, no one at the time was wearing a "What Would David Do?" bracelet.

Yet he was called "a man after his [God's] own heart."

Is it possible for someone to be struggling so deeply with sin and yet still long for God at the same time?

I heard a Christian leader speak about the two great sins that plagued his spiritual life. One was that there were times when he was on an airplane and was not as bold in witnessing to the passenger next to him as Jesus would have been. His other confession was that there were times when his mind wandered while he was praying. He expressed great angst over these sins.

What hope does that leave for those of us who, as the author Anne Lamott says, do things that make Jesus want to drink gin out of the cat dish? Even in writing this, I confront a strange problem. If a pastor confesses to serious sin, people think he should leave the pastorate. If he only confesses to safe, non-scandalous sins, people think he is inauthentic and hypocritical. So at this moment I find myself wanting to make some confession that will look vulnerable and honest, yet not be so scandalous as to cost me my job. I cannot confess sin without sinning in the act.

You don't have to be victorious to join Alcoholics Anonymous—just needy. There are no "recovered addicts," only people in the process of recovering, because as soon as sobriety leads to self-righteousness, for disaster to come is just a matter of time.

However, relationships grow deep when people become real, which is to say, honest about the sin common to us all.

» The Spirit Flows in Transparency, So Come As You Are

I have a recurring problem that periodically requires treatment. It is a little embarrassing to mention, but recently it became very troublesome, and I had to go to the urgent care center. Andrew, the medical student on call, asked me what the problem was, and I didn't want to tell him. Want to know?

I'll tell you anyhow.

I had wax in my ears that had been building up over time, and then, when I went swimming, water got behind the wax until I could barely hear. People would come up to me after church, and I couldn't tell if they were saying "hi" or confessing deep sin.

So I finally went to the urgent care center, but I didn't want to name my problem. When I at last told Andrew, my vulnerability melted when he smiled.

"That's *tremendous!*" he said. "We're going to get that wax right out. I love getting wax out. It's one of the things I do best. All kinds of people have that problem. I'm a wax specialist."

Andrew took out a high pressure hose and an ice pick and removed a piece of wax the size of a small grapefruit. He said, "Man, your body really produces a lot of wax." I felt much better, and he was so happy to get it out.

My wife used to be a nurse, so when I arrived home, she asked, "Did you bring the piece of wax home? Can I see it?"

"I just left it there," I said. "But I could go back and see if they saved it or something."

Why was I embarrassed about my wax? Andrew is my friend. My wife was so proud of me, she wanted to see it. Their acceptance helps me accept that I am a wax machine. Now I don't care who knows.

When you can step into openness and stop pretending, you find yourself coming alive. Hiddenness and pretense are always the enemy of flourishing.

There is an old but uncertain story about the derivation of the word *sincere*. The ancient Romans used to prize Greek sculptures for their aesthetic excellence. The statues were already a few centuries old, however, and some of them had cracks or gaps where marble was missing. Vendors discovered that if they put wax in the sculptures, these figures looked great—for a season. The wax looked like real marble, but over time, the wax would yellow and harden until it became apparent that the statue was not totally authentic. So if vendors wanted to sell a statue and it was all marble—the real deal through and through—they would mark it *sine*, the Latin word for "without," and then *cera*, the Latin word for "wax."

Sine cera. Without wax.

When the Christian church started, people met together in their homes "with glad and sincere hearts"—without wax—because now there was a circle of connectedness where everyone could come on in just as they were.

Where hearts are sincere, they will be glad.

In writing to this early community of believers, the apostle Paul said, "Accept one another, then, just as Christ accepted you, in order to bring praise to God." Acceptance is more than just being liked by someone. Jesus didn't say to me, "John, if you just clean up a bit, if you just dress better, and read the Bible more, *then* I'll let you into my family." Of course he is going to help me become my best self, but I don't have to pretend to be any better than I am to be in Jesus' circle. *How* did Jesus accept you? Just the way you are. When someone knows the embarrassing, humiliating truth about me and still accepts me, I come alive.

A few friends and I from college days get together once a year for an extended weekend to experience the fellowship that comes from knowing each other deeply over a long period of time. Most of the time I was with them, I tried to listen to myself speak as I might hear someone else, and I was struck by how much of what I say is designed to show how smart, how clever, or how funny I am, often at someone else's expense. I found myself making my achievements sound more impressive than they are. I wasn't sure that—if I were not me—I would actually *like* me.

I read recently that one sign of narcissism is that the desire to be admired is stronger than the desire to be liked. It was painful to read that, because I thought of how much it describes my own wound. While I was telling these things to my friends, I was suddenly seized by the thought of how *lucky* I was to have friends who love me, for I am broken. When I am in superficial relationships, I can forget my brokenness. But when I am with people who know me deeply and accept me fully, their acceptance touches my brokenness as a doctor touches the injured place on a patient's body. Their very touch begins to heal, and through the mystery of the fellowship of acceptance, God's Spirit flows.

> Henri Nouwen wrote, "When we honestly ask ourselves which person in our lives mean the most to us, we often find that it is those who, instead of giving advice, solutions, or cures, have chosen rather to share our pain and touch our wounds with a warm and tender hand. The friend who can be silent with us in a moment of despair or confusion, who can stay with us in an hour of grief and bereavement, who can tolerate not knowing, not curing, not healing and face with us the reality of our powerlessness, that is a friend who cares."

»Give the Gift of Confession

One of the most important moments of my spiritual life was when I sat down with a longtime friend and said, "I don't want to have any secrets anymore." I told him everything I was most ashamed of. No wax. I told him about my jealousies, my cowardice, how I hurt my wife with my anger. I told him about my history with money and my history with sex. I told him about deceit and regrets that keep me up at night. I felt vulnerable because I was afraid that I was going to be outside the circle, to lose connection with him. Much to my surprise, he did not even look away.

I will never forget his next words.

"John," he said. "I have never loved you more than I love you right now." The very truth about me that I thought would drive him away became a bond that drew us closer together. He then went on to speak with me about secrets he had been carrying.

I can only be loved to the extent that I am known.

If I keep part of my life secret from you, you may tell me you love me. But inside I think that you would not love me if you knew the whole truth about me. I can only receive love from you to the extent that I am known by you.

I cannot be fully loved unless I am fully known.

To be fully known and fully loved is the most healing gift one human being can give another. James writes, "Confess your sins to one another, and pray for one another, so that you may be healed." We are all forgiven, recovering sinners, and no one can be secure in a relationship if they are loved only because they are smart, pretty, strong,

> You can only be loved to the extent that you are known.

or successful. Sin isolates us, and sin and isolation will make us sick in our soul and even our body. Confession and then prayer, connectedness to each other and to God, ushers in the Spirit and helps bring healing.

» No Pedestals

It is a remarkable thing how the writers of Scripture never do what churches are so tempted to do, which is put people on a pedestal. To illustrate how grittily honest the biblical writers are about human nature, answer this question: *Who in the Bible would you say had the best marriage?*

Adam and Eve had their honeymoon in paradise, and it all went downhill from there. Abraham lied that Sarah was his sister — twice — and impregnated her servant, Hagar. Isaac and Rebekah spent their marriage battling because he favored Esau and she favored Jacob. Jacob had children by two wives and the wives' servants. About all we know of Moses' wife, Zipporah, is that they had an argument over circumcising their son and she called Moses a "bridegroom of blood." David was a disaster as a husband; Solomon was worse. When Job's life got hard, Mrs. Job told him to "curse God and die!" I am not making this up: Someone online said they thought the best marriage in the Bible was between Noah and Joan of Ark.

In fairy tales, life is a difficult adventure until you get married — and then you live happily ever after. But nowhere in the Bible do a couple get married and then live "happily ever after." Marriage doesn't save anyone. Only Jesus does that.

The Bible is remarkably transparent about the flaws and brokenness of the marriages of every character — yet how often in churches do couples sit in silent agony? They have an image of spiritual success to project, but under the surface the reality is that they have not slept together for months. Or there is verbal or physical abuse going on. Or they have a young daughter who is pregnant and they don't know what to do. Or one of them is a secret alcoholic. Or they are facing bankruptcy.

Often the people who need help the most receive it the least, because that would mean leaving the pedestal. But what if real people could be as honest as the Bible about marriage? In a community gathered around a cross, there is no room for pedestals. In the Bible, marriage is not the fulfillment of our dreams; it is a place where we learn.

» Recognize the J-Curve

Experts in the learning field sometimes talk about the J-curve, a graph measuring performance, in which someone initially does worse before they start improving. Their progress looks like a letter "J" when graphed, with an initial dip before things head upward.

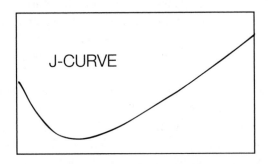

If you have been hitting tennis backhands the wrong way, when someone teaches you the correct grip, proper form, and right footwork, when you begin to try to hit them the right way — you will actually hit them worse than when you were trying the wrong way! If you stick with it, however, eventually your backhand will be far better than before. But you have to accept that at first it will be worse.

When the disciple Peter first exercised enough faith to get out of the boat, he sank and looked worse than any of the other disciples. When he tried to defend Jesus, he cut off a man's ear. When he promised to be loyal, he fell flat on his faith. When he tried to advise Jesus, he was a devil's advocate.

Eventually, though, Peter's faith and boldness and loyalty and wisdom enabled him to become a leader of the church. But he got worse before he got better. Notice that this did not surprise or discourage Jesus. In fact, Jesus was so patient with his disciples that we might think of the J-curve as the Jesus-curve. He will never stop helping a follower of his who is sincerely seeking to grow.

Jesus will always lead us toward growth, and growth always requires risk, and risk always means failure. So Jesus is always leading us into failure. But he never gives up on a student just because he or she fails.

If you haven't been confronting when you should and you begin, you will do it badly at first. If you have rarely encouraged people, your initial attempts may be clumsy. If you have never shared your faith with someone, the first time you do it you may stumble all over yourself.

Go ahead and stumble. Failure isn't falling down; failure is refusing to try. We ought to celebrate failure.

We are living on the J-curve.

» The Gift of Honest Language

Being human means being honest about what we want, but all too often we can wallpaper over human difficulties with a veneer of pious language. There is the story about a boy who comes home and doesn't see his mom is visiting with their pastor. He holds a rat in his hand. "Mom, you'll never guess what. There was a rat running around behind the garage. I saw it and threw a stone and hit it. It just laid there, so I went over and stomped on it. Then I picked it up and threw it against the wall as hard as I could. And I picked it up and threw it again." Then he sees that the pastor is there and that if looks could kill, he would be a dead kid. He holds the rat high in the air and adds in a pious voice, "And then the dear Lord called him home."

When we try to look more spiritual, we actually make ourselves less human. Pretending always cuts us off from the flow of the Spirit. Author Scott Peck once wrote of a couple who constantly used "God talk" to cover up their cruelty and attempts to control. In the Ten Commandments we are told not to take the Lord's name in vain. Usually we think about this in terms of using profanity, but maybe it happens more often when we hide behind spiritual language.

We were in a small group many years ago with a very diverse group of people. One of them was a teacher with a traveling ministry doing "Holy Ghost Explosion Revival" meetings. One of them was uninitiated enough that she did not know whether "Jesus" and "Jesus Christ" were the same person. The uninitiated one was once talking about her most dysfunctional relationship with a former boyfriend who had belittled her and betrayed her and abused her in humiliating ways. "Now he has cancer," she said, "and I hope he dies."

"You can't say that!" said the teacher. "You have to pray for him. You have to pray that he will be healed. The Holy Ghost can heal him right this moment. I'm going to pray right now. You've just got to love him!"

"But I don't love him. I hate him. I hope he dies."

Why is it that the psalms are so full of human anger, that they express so much raw, unfiltered hostility and lust for vengeance and fury and demands for divine justice to come pretty quickly—and that the prayers prayed in churches feel so ... well, decaffeinated? Is it possible that God could actually handle our anger?

There is an old hymn that includes the lines, "Just as I am, without one plea." This song speaks of coming to God without hiding, knowing that I am loved simply as a gift. A few people in my life allow me to relate to them "just as I am," and I cling to them the way a drowning man clings to a raft.

If ever there were a true "just as I am" church, if ever there were a community where everybody could bring all their baggage and brokenness with them without neat and tidy happy endings quite yet, if ever there was a group where everyone was loved and no one pretended—we could not make enough room inside the building.

in the flow ≈

- ≈ Who is the friend I am most transparent with?
- ≈ What are my secret regrets and temptations? Is there someone I could talk with about them?
- ≈ Spend some time reflecting on your regrets and temptations. Schedule some unhurried time to meet with the person you trust most deeply. Share with them — at a level appropriate to how well you know and trust them — the condition of your heart and soul.
- ≈ Laugh at yourself at least once today.

Chapter 18

Find a Few Difficult People to Help You Grow

Some people tempt me out of the flow of the Spirit. They judge me, and I feel discouraged. They dislike me, and I feel rejected. They are a black hole of need and drain me. They throw roadblocks in my path and discourage me. They anger me. They scare me. They depress me. Plus I don't like them.

The playwright George Bernard Shaw sat next to a pompous bore at a dinner party one evening. After listening to an interminable monologue of useless information, Shaw observed, "Between the two of us we know all there is to know."

"How's that?" asked his fascinated companion.

"Well," replied Shaw, "you seem to know everything except that you're a bore. And I know that!"

Shaw and Winston Churchill famously found each other to be difficult. Shaw once sent two tickets to Churchill to the opening night of one of his plays, with instructions to "bring a friend—if you have one." Churchill sent them back because he was busy opening night. He said he would come on "the second night—if there is one."

We all have difficult people in our life, but hear this: God can use them to help you become the best version of you—maybe even more than the people you like. Jesus said,

> You're familiar with the old written law, "Love your friend," and its unwritten companion, "Hate your enemy." I'm challenging that. I'm telling you to love your enemies. Let them bring out the best in you.... If all you do is love the lovable, do you expect a bonus? Anybody can do that. If you simply say hello to those who greet you, do you expect a medal? Any run-of-the-mill sinner does that. In a word, what I'm saying is, *Grow up*. You're kingdom subjects. Now live like it. Live out your God-created identity.

Other people don't create your spirit; they reveal your spirit.

In fact, if God wants to grow some quality in you, he may send you a person who tempts you to behave in just the opposite way. If you need to develop love, then some unlovable people will be your greatest challenge. If you need to develop hope, maintaining it in the face of discouragers will make it strong. If you want to grow in your ability to confront, a hard-to-confront intimidator will give you serious practice. As lifting weights strengthens a muscle and cardio exercises strengthen a heart, difficult people can strengthen our ability to love.

Why does God allow difficult people in my life?

What other kind are there?

If God were to get rid of all the difficult people in the world—if he were to remove everybody with quirks, flaws, ugliness, and sin—you would get awfully lonely.

We always wish that God would give us a life without difficult people in it. But how many great characters in the Bible had difficult people in their lives? Moses had Pharaoh, Elijah had Jezebel, Esther had Haman, Jacob had Laban, David had Saul, John the Baptist had Herod. Even Jesus had Judas. If God loves you and wants to shape you, he will send some difficult people your way. But take heart. You are the difficult person he is sending to shape somebody else!

If we can learn to have rivers of living water still flowing through us in these relationships, we will be unstoppable.

» Recognize the Impact

We are far more affected by the impact of people on our lives than most of us realize. We are always—*always!*—being energized or drained by every interaction.

Dr. Jill Taylor was a thirty-seven-year-old, Harvard-trained brain scientist who suffered a massive stroke. The left side of her brain, which regulates speech and linear thinking, was devastated. For many months she lay in a hospital bed, unable to carry on a conversation. She writes of how even though she could not understand the words people were saying to her, she became intensely aware of whether the people approaching her were enhancing her sense of life or depleting it.

> I experienced people as concentrated packages of energy ... although I could not understand the words they spoke, I could read volumes from their facial expression and body language. I paid very close attention to how their energy dynamics affected me. Some people brought me energy while others took it away.

At a level deeper than words, deeper than exchanging information, every interaction with another person is a spiritual exchange. Some people are life-bringers to us. They increase our energy, deepen our hope, add to our joy, and call out the best in us. Other people are life-drainers. They add to our anxiety and invite us to cynicism. We find ourselves becoming defensive, depressed, or exasperated.

How do we grow through difficult relationships?

» Keeping God between You and Me

Before some friends of mine went on a trip, they dropped their hunting dog off at a summer camp. I didn't even know there were such places. It was a refresher course on obedience school to retrain their dog, to make sure that every time he gets a command, his response is prompt, eager, wholehearted, unquestioning obedience. When he came home, it was as if he were a new creature. It was summer camp and reform school all wrapped up into one.

Wouldn't it be nice if there were such places for people? If there were, they would be full. Of course, that's what kills us, because we can't fix *people*. There is a good reason for this, however: Everyone has a soul. Everyone has a "Holy of Holies," where only that person and God can meet. Only God can touch the deepest place of another's soul. We may think, *I can intimidate, lecture, flatter, manipulate, reason, cajole, reward, or withdraw to get the behavior I want out of that person.* And maybe I can, out on the outer edges of their personality; but I can't touch the deepest part of another person. Only God can.

Prayer is the closest we come to being able to influence people at their deepest level, to be able to go with God into another person's soul, because always between me and the most inner part of another person stands Jesus. The most direct way to another person is not talking to them. The most direct way is talking to Jesus.

I can remember as if it were yesterday the hardest conversation I have ever had. It was with a person I had known more than a decade, over long-standing and complicated problems in our relationship. I had avoided speaking truthfully about our problems for years, so picking up the phone to schedule the talk felt like the hardest thing ever. I was afraid the conversation would be grueling and painful, that we would not see eye-to-eye. It ended up being worse than that!

But here was the thought that enabled me to have the talk: *I do not have to control the outcome. I do not have to make the other person agree. I don't even have to do the talk well. I just have to show up. The rest is up to God.*

At the end of the conversation, even though it had not produced the results I wanted, I felt alive because I was trusting Jesus with a challenging relationship. When I keep God between you and me, I begin to be less afraid of you.

Another time I was desperately concerned about someone I love, whom I wanted to fix, but they would not let me fix them. A wise friend said the best thing I could do was to pray, offering "gentle, non-frantic prayer." When God is present, prayer does not have to be frantic. When I keep God between me and you, I begin to be less controlling.

In driver education we learn to reduce accidents by keeping the right distance between ourselves and other cars — one car-space of distance for every ten miles per hour of speed. In spiritual education we learn to keep a kind of spiritual space between ourselves and the souls around us. That space is where God flows between you and me. Jesus advised, "When someone gives you a hard time, respond with the energies of prayer, for then you are working out of your true selves, your God-created selves. This is what God does."

» What Makes Someone Difficult for You?

The space between me and my enemy is the space where love can grow. Many studies have been done on what causes us to like someone. Out of all the causes — physical attractiveness, IQ, ability, personality type — the number one factor that determines whether or not you will like another person is whether or not they like us. If they like you, you will like them. If they don't like you, you will not like them.

This is humbling.

If there is someone I have never liked and then I find out that they have said something good about me, I think, *Man! This person is more on the ball than I thought. This is a person with some hidden depth in them.*

That person could be wonderful in every other respect, but their dislike of us shapes our perceptions more than anything else. *Gandhi doesn't like me? I always thought he was a little shallow.*

God's not that way. God loves people who love him. He loves people who don't love him. He doesn't do it because he has to. He doesn't say to himself, *Well, I am God, so I guess I'm stuck with having to love people. Boy, I sure wish I didn't have to!*

God does it because love is the only way to life.

» Staying in the Flow with the Spirit Takes a Quarter-Second

Anger is prone to take me out of the flow. This is why Paul wrote,

> Do not grieve the Holy Spirit [in other words, don't cut yourself off from the flow of the Spirit] with whom you were sealed for the day of redemption. Get rid of all bitterness, rage and anger, brawling and slander, along with every form of malice.

Difficult relationships can give the Evil One a foothold, but God has wired us so that in times of intense difficulty we have a kind of built-in moment to turn to the Spirit for help. As we noted in chapter 15, the primary place in the brain that processes strong negative emotions such as rage and fear is called the amygdala. When this is removed from certain animals, they become incapable of rage and fear. Normally, when input comes into the brain, it goes to the neocortex for processing. In about 5 percent of cases, however, when something extremely emotional happens, it goes to the amygdala, and the thinking part of the brain gets short-circuited.

Mom is in a grocery store, in a hurry, so she is tense. She has her three-year-old next to her and her eighteen-month-old in a shopping cart. Suddenly the three-year-old grabs a box of cocoa puffs.

"Put it down," says Mom.

But the three-year-old is determined to have them.

"Put it down!" Mom repeats.

At this point the eighteen-month-old, who has been holding a glass of jelly, throws it to the ground from the cart, and it shatters. What happens to Mom next is what researchers call "an amygdala hijack." The amygdala takes over the thinking process, and Mom goes ballistic. She picks up the three-year-old, drapes him over one arm, carries him doubled over like a pretzel, and she is shaking the shopping cart. The kid is yelling, "Put me down! Put me down!" Mom is out of control, suffering from what researchers call "cognitive incapacitation." Rational thought is no longer an option.

But there is an aspect of our circuitry that gives us hope.

Impulses formed in the brain can be measured during neurosurgery. I decide that I am going to move my hand, and then that impulse travels to the hand. But in between the brain activity and the movement of the hand, there is what one researcher calls the "life-giving quarter-second."

There is a quarter-second between when that impulse takes place in your brain and when that action takes place in your body. And that quarter-second — although it doesn't sound like very long in the life of the mind — is huge. The apostle Paul wrote, "In your anger do not sin ... and do not give the devil a foothold." That quarter-second is the time when the Holy Spirit can take control. That is when you can give the foothold to the Holy Spirit or you can give it to sin. That one quarter-second in your mind can be an opportunity to say, "Spirit, I've got this impulse right now; should I act on it?"

It was a long hot day, the car had broken down once, the air conditioning wasn't working, the kids weren't behaving, and Nancy wasn't being too good either. I tried enticing the kids into "the quiet game," but they weren't going for it. I got lost. I was frustrated. The kids spilled food. Finally, the noise level went beyond what I could bear. There was a life-giving quarter second, but I blew right past it. I wasn't interested. And I used language on my kids that I had never used before, that I never thought I would.

It is amazing how the desire to hurt someone you love can be so strong in your body one moment and then lead to such pain when you indulge it. But another piece of good news is that when you blow it — and you will blow it — God sends another quarter-second right behind.

And you can get right back into the flow.

» Learning from the Master

No one mastered the art of dealing with difficult people better than Jesus did. He had lots of practice. The Romans wanted to silence him; Herod wanted to kill him; Pilate washed his hands of him; religious leaders envied him; his family thought he had lost his mind; his towns-people wanted to stone him; Judas betrayed him; soldiers beat him; the crowds shouted for his crucifixion; and his own disciples ran out on him. Yet Jesus never prayed for God to remove difficult people from his life.

If he had, there would have been no people left at all.

Sometimes even prayer can be misused as a way of avoidance. Some-times people will ask God to remove a difficult person from their cir-cumstances because they are too anxious to confront the person honestly. If God answered that prayer the way they wanted, they would actually lose the opportunity for growth that is his great desire for them.

Jesus' teachings about dealing with difficult people flowed out of deep, intimate, painful experiences and wisdom. They have influenced world civil rights leaders and movements like no other words ever spo-ken, from Mahatma Gandhi to Martin Luther King to Desmond Tutu. We will look at two of Jesus' teachings here: How you deal with those who insult you, and how you deal with those who would use you.

Insulters

Jesus begins, "You have heard that it was said, 'Eye for eye, and tooth for tooth.' But I tell you,... If anyone slaps you on the right cheek, turn to them the other cheek also." The "eye for an eye" statement comes from the Hebrew Scriptures, and although it sounds harsh to us, it was actually an enormous step forward in the ancient legal world. When there were no policemen, no Constitution, and no Bill of Rights, powerful people might kill someone for a slight injury. So this law limited retribution by teaching proportional justice.

But it still leaves us with a problem. My instinct is that if someone hurts me, I will hurt them back—and the pain I experience always seems worse to me than the pain I cause the other person. A group of subjects was paired up, and people received pressure against their finger. Then they were told to exert the same amount of pressure on the other person's finger. When it was their turn, they always inflicted more pain than they received. Always. The result is an "eye-plus-a-little-something-extra" for an eye.

But Jesus gives another option. A key for understanding him comes from his mention of the "right cheek." Society in Jesus' day was built around shame and honor. The left hand was considered unclean; it was not to be used for eating—or for hitting. So a blow to the right cheek would be done with the backhand. It was a way to publicly insult someone. The main intent was not physical harm, but public disgrace. A backhanded slap was something done only to a social inferior, such as a slave or a child.

When someone insults us, what should we do? Everyone expects one of two responses: retaliation or cowering. Jesus is saying, "Your safety and your honor are in the hands of your heavenly Father."

So now we can get creative.

One possibility is that we could turn the other cheek. Our enemy can't backhand our left cheek. Either he has to fight you as an equal, which he doesn't want to do, or he has to find a nonviolent, nondestructive way to resolve conflict.

Who do you get insulted by? "Slaps" in our day often take the form of barbs, digs, and "backhanded" comments. Someone demeans your idea at work. Someone accuses you falsely at home. A relative says something judgmental about you. What is your first instinct: retaliation, fear—or both?

Now, with the Spirit there is a new possibility. Don't run and hide. Don't strike back. Confront the other person with honesty and strength. Be creative, patient, and active. Work toward reconciliation.

Users

Jesus gives another case study: "If anyone forces you to go with them one mile, go with them two miles." His listeners would have understood this situation, for Roman soldiers were allowed to force Jews to carry a burden a mile for them.

This is the kind of person who would use us, thinking of us not as a person, but as a tool. What do you do in that situation? Jesus invites people to see their enemy as a human being. This Roman soldier is a young boy, a stranger here, probably poor himself. All he receives is local hostility. So here is an idea. You finish the mile, look him in the eye, and say, "You look tired. Can I give you a little more help? Can I go with you another mile?"

That would blow the soldier's mind. Nobody does that! Who sends in a tip to the Internal Revenue Service?

Often when someone is difficult to me, I want to think of them as deliberately unlikable rather than as a real person with their own story. A friend offered to introduce English essayist Charles Lamb to a man whom Lamb had disliked for a long time by hearsay. "Don't make me meet him," Lamb said. "I want to go on hating him, and I can't do that to a man I know."

We can give the gift of empathy. We remember that the person we don't like is also a human being. We put ourselves in their place. We take the time to imagine how they feel, how they're treated. We ask what would help them become the best version of themselves, and in turn the interaction becomes an opportunity for me to practice becoming the best version of myself. We actually *need* difficult people to reach our full potential. (If you don't have enough, take the Monvee online assessment mentioned earlier and hone in on the "difficult people" section.)

» Being the "Difficult Person"

I once gave a talk about difficult people that I thought was terrific. That is, until I found out that someone I knew quite well and worked with closely told another friend about who his difficult person was.

It was me.

I wanted to run and hide when I heard that. He was not a casual acquaintance either, and I realized that I had been speaking and behaving in ways that were painful and life-draining to someone quite close to me. Our conversations often left him feeling that he was just an audience. He got clear signals that I regarded my opinions as more accurate and important than his. All this left him wanting to hide. On top of that, I had been clueless.

It is hard enough to try to reconcile something wrong that we have done. But to heal what we have *been*—to overcome being the difficult person for somebody else—requires grace from a higher source. My own defensiveness and embarrassment made me want to hide. We were able to overcome this somewhat, though I am afraid it remained in a high-maintenance category. But I have never forgotten the emotion of discovering that I was someone else's difficult person. I hope it has made me more aware in other relationships. I know it has made me more grateful for grace.

Maybe you have difficult people who haven't just troubled your world but have rocked it. Shattered it.

What happens then?

CHAPTER 18

» The Reconciling Power of Tenacious Love

Often we find our difficult people right in our own family. One of the great stories about shattered relationships is the biblical story of Joseph and his brothers. You may remember that Joseph was hated by his brothers because he was his father's favorite. Joseph is then betrayed and sold into slavery by his brothers—but the end of Joseph's story looks odd to us.

His brothers head to Egypt to get food and don't recognize Joseph, who is now serving as the prime minister. Because they don't recognize him, he puts them through some odd circumstances. He gives them a feast, but gives the youngest brother Benjamin "five times more" than anyone else. Why does he supersize Benjamin's meal? He then sends them on their way, but frames Benjamin for stealing a silver cup. He tells the brothers they can have their food and go home, but that Benjamin must be left behind to die. Isn't he being a little passive-aggressive?

Children between the ages of two and four average 6.2 fights per hour. That's about ninety fights per day, or about three thousand fights per year. If you are parenting little kids, no wonder you're tired!

The reality is that there is something beautiful in this story that serves as the climax to the book of Genesis. Up to this point in Genesis there has not been the healing of a broken relationship through confession and repentance at the expression of forgiveness. In the accounts of the brokenness of Adam and Eve, Cain and Abel, Isaac and Ishmael, and Jacob and Esau there is no record of true reconciliation.

But now it will happen.

Here are Joseph's brothers, one more time with their youngest brother, Benjamin, whom their father loves, and they can be rid of him. This time, however, they don't even have to do anything. They don't have to sell him into slavery. As far as they know, it is Benjamin's own fault. All they have to do is not lift a finger, and the favorite is gone once more.

But Judah stands up:

> But Benjamin is so young. It would kill my father. Let me take the place of the boy. I know the law must be upheld. I know the debt

must be paid. I understand. Let me pay it. Let me pay it. Let his punishment fall on me. I love him too much. I love my dad too much. I'll pay it. I'll pay. Take me.

For the first time in the Bible, in this story of God's, we see the possibility of a substitutionary act of suffering on behalf of someone to save someone else. We see that maybe a community could be healed by the voluntary atonement of one person who is willing to suffer the punishment that belongs to somebody else.

> In the ancient world the rabbis had a saying, "Full repentance is shown when a person is subjected to the same situation in which he had sinned ... in which he had fallen once before ... only this time, he does not sin." The rabbis said that Judah was the ultimate example of true repentance. The second time around, Judah gets it right.

Now Joseph knows that the hearts of his brothers have changed, and this strange charade ends. He weeps so hard that the Egyptians could hear him sobbing through the thick walls. That is the power of reconciliation.

Where in your life is there a relationship that needs reconciliation? Maybe you have been so badly hurt by somebody who lied or cheated or betrayed you, and that hurt goes so deep, that you are thinking right now, *He doesn't deserve it!*

Probably not. Neither did Joseph's brothers. Neither do I. Neither do you.

Do it anyway.

> God was in Christ, reconciling the world [the whole world] to himself." (2 Corinthians 5:19 KJV)

Do it because another young dreamer came into the world, and he too was stripped of his robe. He too was betrayed and deserted by his brothers.

He too loved sacrificially so that love could prevail in the end.

PART SIX
transforming my experience

»

Chapter 19

Let God Flow in Your Work

Once there was a man who loved to work.

He loved creating value. He loved the way his work made him grow. He didn't always like the problems he ran into, but he felt joy when he came up with a solution that … well, *worked*.

He loved being a part of a team. He managed people and felt it was what he was born to do. He liked getting to know his co-workers; he asked about their lives and families and interests. He loved when a team got inspired about an idea. He loved watching people gain new skills and confidence. He valued the chance to spot each person's abilities and help them move toward becoming the best version of themselves. He even enjoyed getting ready for work. Sometimes in the shower he would yell, "Focus!" to himself just to get psyched up. He liked looking ahead at what each day would hold. He enjoyed the feeling at the end of the day when he could look back on how he had been productive.

He didn't tell people at his church this, but secretly he felt the presence of God more at work than he did at church services. He often found himself praying for ideas and wisdom. He would get excited when a solution to some problem seemed to pop into his head. When it was time for evaluations, he looked forward to the chance to learn and grow. His joy at work made him a better husband, father, friend, and volunteer. The skills he learned at work made him better at other relationships. His children grew up believing that the chance to work was a gift.

When he was sixty-five, someone asked him if he was going to retire. He looked up the word *retire* in the Bible, but he couldn't find it. So he just kept working. After a while he cut back to part-time, and eventually his work was all volunteer.

When he was very old and ill, all the people he had loved and worked with over the years gathered around his sickbed. They thanked him for how he had enhanced their lives. He thought of all the joy and purpose that his work had given him over the years, and these were his final words:

I wish I could have spent more time at the office.

I'm not sure where the cliché first arose that at the end of life no one wishes they had spent more time at work, but it wasn't in the Bible. In the Bible, everyone works. Dennis Bakke, in a wonderful book called *Joy at Work*, notes that most of the heroes in the Bible had what we would think of as secular vocations. Isaac developed real estate, Jacob was a rancher, and Joseph was a government official (in charge of agriculture, the economy, and immigration policy) who served a pharaoh in a foreign land that did not honor Israel's God. Joseph did not decide he could serve God best by leaving his well-paying government job and starting a non-profit, faith-based organization to do charity work. Moses spent forty years as a sheepherder, Esther won a beauty pageant and went into government service, and David worked in animal husbandry, the military, and statecraft. Daniel was an immigrant who attended Babylon's version of Oxford and became prime minister. Lydia was a successful business-woman in textiles. Paul was a tent-maker.

Perhaps the ultimate expression of how much God values work is Jesus the carpenter. Jesus spent more than three-quarters of his working life in the building profession, fashioning benches and tables and probably involved in construction. The word we translate *carpenter* comes from the Greek *tekton*—from which we get our word *technology*—and would include the ability to do stone or masonry work.

The Bible is a book written by workers about workers for workers, but too often in discussion about spiritual life our work gets ignored. Or all we get are warnings: "not too much," "not too hard," or "not too long." One writer on spiritual life lamented how some pastors call their work space an office rather than a study, "thereby further secularizing perceptions of pastoral work." By this line of thinking, "study" is somehow by its nature "spiritual," but "office work" is "secular."

Yet far more human beings will spend their lives in offices than in studies. Most adults spend about half their waking lives at work. Your work is a huge part of God's plan for your life, and God intends the Spirit to fill and energize workplaces. Work that gets done in offices and elsewhere — building up people, creating teams, managing the resources of creation — desperately requires the guidance and energy of the Spirit.

The fourth commandment covers all seven days of the week, not just the Sabbath: "Six days you shall labor and do all your work ... for in six days the LORD made the heavens and the earth." I have often heard sermons designed to make people feel guilty about not keeping the Sabbath, but I have never heard a sermon designed to make people feel guilty about not honoring the six-day work week. The point is not how many days or hours we are punching the clock. The point is that just as God made and loves the Sabbath, so he also made and loves work.

So how do we find God in our work? How do we allow our work to move us toward the person God wants us to become?

» First, Discover Your Strengths

Do you know the first person in the Bible who was said to be "filled with the Spirit of God"? Here's a hint: It was not Adam, Noah, Abraham, Joseph, Moses, Elijah, Daniel, Mary, Jesus, Paul, Jonah, or the whale.

It was Bezalel.

That name doesn't ring a bell?

Bezalel was not a prophet, priest, king, or apostle. He was a craftsman, skilled in design. He had an eye for color and a flair for management, so when it was time to build a tabernacle for the people of Israel, he oversaw the job.

> See, I have chosen Bezalel son of Uri, ... and I have filled him with the Spirit of God, with wisdom, with understanding, with knowledge, and with all kinds of skills — to make artistic designs for work in gold, silver and bronze, to cut and set stones, to work in wood, and to engage in all kinds of crafts.

Imagine being Bezalel. From your youth you love to work with your hands. You don't know that God is involved in this — but he is! He has actually placed these desires in you, which will one day bless people around you. When you are working, the joy and power you feel is actually the presence of the Spirit.

"Discover your strengths" is a phrase made famous by Marcus Buckingham and what has been called the "strengths movement." It calls us to stop focusing on improving weaknesses rather than naming and developing strengths—which also reflects God's design. God did not say, "Moses, your craftsman skills are weak. Let's have you stop leading this people for a while, and work on improving your craftsmanship skills." God's plan was that the community would be enriched when people were doing what he had created them to do.

> Each of us has certain strengths. We were born with them, they will always be our strengths, and we delight in them. Work happens best when we discover these strengths, put them to use, and focus on developing them. Trying to improve our weaknesses is like trying to teach a rabbit to swim or a snail to race. God's design for work is best when it goes "from strength to strength." (If you haven't discovered your strengths yet, the book *Now Discover Your Strengths* by Buckingham and Donald O. Clifton is a great place to start.)

According to Marcus, the simplest definition of a strength is an activity which, when you do it, makes you feel strong. There are certain activities that thrill and challenge you, and others that bore and drain you. When you discover this, you are not simply engaged in "career planning"—you are studying the handiwork of God. It matters that you do this, because the single little patch of creation that you are most responsible for stewarding is your own body.

> Dorothy Sayers said, "Work is not, primarily, a thing one does to live, but the thing one lives to do. It is, or it should be, the full expression of the worker's faculties, the thing in which he finds spiritual, mental, and bodily satisfaction, and the medium in which he offers himself to God."

God himself works with strength, freedom, and joy. When you discover your strengths, you are learning an indispensible part of what it means to be made in the image of God. When you help other people discover their strengths, you are helping the image of God to be restored in another human being. You are part of the work of redemption—the liberating of work from the curse. You are doing the work of the Spirit.

George comes alive when he picks up a guitar. Emily comes alive when she leads a team. Rick comes alive when he counsels someone who is hurting. Verna comes alive when she finds someone she can help.

Speaking is my craft. When I get to read, study, and think, then figure out how to communicate it all in front of a group of people—trying to sense the room and gauge where people's hearts and minds are, thinking about what to say next, listening to the Holy Spirit—I feel as if every single cell of my body has been switched on.

That's work—just what you and I were made for.

» Understand What You Receive When You Work

Amazingly enough, research shows that the best moments of our lives don't come from leisure or pleasure. They don't involve sex or chocolate. They come when we are totally immersed in a significant task that is challenging, yet matches up well to our highest abilities. In these moments, a person is so caught up in an activity that time somehow seems to be altered; their attention is fully focused, but without having to work at it. They are deeply aware without being self-conscious; they are being stretched and challenged, but without a sense of stress or worry. They have a sense of engagement or oneness with what they are doing.

This condition is called "flow," because people experiencing it often use the metaphor of feeling swept up by something outside themselves. Studies have been done over the past thirty years with hundreds of thousands of subjects to explore this phenomenon of flow. Ironically, people experience it far more in their work than they do in their leisure. In fact, the time of week when "flow" is at its lowest ebb in America is Sunday morning, because so many people do not know what they want to do. Sitting around does not produce flow.

I believe this picture of "flow" is actually a description of what the exercise of dominion was intended to look like. God says in Genesis that human beings are to "rule" over the earth, or to exercise "dominion." We often think of these words in terms of "dominating" or "bossing around." But the true idea behind them is that we are to invest our abilities to create value on the earth, to plant and build and write and organize and heal and invent in ways that bless people and make the earth flourish.

Draw a graph in which the vertical axis represents the strengths God has given you and the horizontal axis represents the challenge of the task before you. If your skill level is very high, but the challenge of the task is too low, you experience boredom. If your skill level is too low, and the challenge of the task is too high, you experience frustration and anxiety. But when the level of the challenge you face matches the level of the skills you possess — then you are set up for flow.

All skill is God-given, and we are invited to live in conscious interaction with the Spirit as we work, so that he can develop the skills he gives us. Work is a form of love. We cannot be fully human without creating value.

We do not work mainly for money, recognition, promotion, applause, or fame. We work for flow. We live for flow. We hunger for the experience of flow, and when it is present, something happens in our spirit as we connect with a reality beyond ourselves and partner with God. This is why the psalmist says, "Unless the LORD builds the house, those who build it labor in vain." Flow is part of what we experience in that partnership, and in that, God in turn uses flow to shape us.

Bezalel experienced flow when he crafted wood, David when he played the lyre, Samson when he used his strength, Paul when he wrote a brilliant letter, Daniel when he ran a government, Adam when he gardened, and Jesus when he carpentered. If other people report to you, whether in paid or volunteer activities, one of the great spiritual acts of service you can perform is to ask whether they are experiencing flow in their work and seek to help them experience more flow.

When we are working in the flow of the service of God and his kingdom, when we are experiencing flow in activities that enhance and bless the lives of others around us — then we are working in the Spirit.

Then we are growing rich.

When we work, we grow. Marcus Aurelius wrote, "When you arise reluctantly in the morning, think like this: 'I arise to accomplish a human task. Should I then complain, when I am about to do that for which I was born, and for which I was placed on earth? Or was I created to pamper myself under the blankets, even if that is more pleasant. Were you born, then, to enjoy and, generally to feel, but not to act? Don't you see the plants, the birds, the ants, the spiders, the bees who all perform their own tasks and in their own way helping to let the cosmos function? Don't you then want to do your work as a human? Don't you hasten to do what is befitting your nature?"

Chapter 20

Let Your Work Honor God

Journalist William Zinsser's first job was writing for the *Buffalo News*. Traditionally cub reporters often start by writing obituaries, but Zinsser was frustrated with his assignment. *I could be doing Pulitzer Prize-winning investigative reporting*, he thought to himself, *and I'm stuck writing obituaries*. Writers don't win Pulitzers for obituaries. Finally he worked up enough courage and asked his editor, "When am I going to get some decent story assignments?"

"Listen, kid!" his crusty old editor growled at him. "Nothing you write will ever get read as carefully as what you are writing right now. You misspell a word, you mess up a date, and a family will be hurt. But you do justice to somebody's grandmother, to somebody's mom, you make a life sing, and they will be grateful forever. They will put your words in laminate."

Things changed.

"I pledged I would make the extra calls," Zinsser said. "I would ask the extra questions. I would go the extra mile."

That is essentially from the Sermon on the Mount — write obituaries for others as you would want others to write an obituary for you — obituaries that deserved to be laminated—because someday, somebody will. Zinsser eventually moved on to other kinds of writing, including a book on writing itself that has sold more than a million copies. But none of it would have happened if he had not devoted himself to obituaries.

God himself can only bless me in my circumstances today. If I cannot experience the Spirit in the work I am doing today, then I can't experience the Spirit today at all.

My friend Andy Chan headed up the placement office for the Stanford School of Business, helping graduates find work. He says that someday he wants to write a book called *The Myth of Passion*. This is the myth that somewhere out there is the perfect job, the idealized calling that fits my soul the way a key fits into a lock, and if I could just find that job, torrents of passion would cascade out of my heart like water going over Niagara Falls. We have this romanticized idea that we will find "job-love at first sight."

Passion for our work is not usually a subterranean volcano waiting to erupt. It is a plant that needs to be cultivated. It is a muscle that gets strengthened a little each day as we show up—as we do what is expected of us, and then some.

Paul wrote, "Don't just do the minimum that will get you by. Do your best. Work from the heart for your real Master, for God, confident that you'll get paid in full when you come into your inheritance. Keep in mind always that the ultimate Master you're serving is Christ. The sullen servant who does shoddy work will be held responsible. Being Christian doesn't cover up bad work."

Maybe it would help to put a little sign on your desk: "For God's sake—do your best!"

» My Best Self Works Wholeheartedly

We almost never get to know ahead of time the full significance of what we do or don't do in our work. We are simply told, "Whatever your hand finds to do, do it with all your might."

Judaism, Christianity, and Islam all trace their roots to Abraham—not a priest, but what we would think of today as a rancher. When he was "now old and well advanced in years," he realized the time had come to find a wife for his son Isaac. Since there was no eHarmony, he assigned the task to the "chief servant in his household, the one in charge of all that he had."

The servant set out with a caravan of ten camels to the region Abraham had directed him. Finding a wife for your boss's son was a high-stakes assignment that required considerable thought. So the servant began his work with a prayer: "O LORD, God of my master Abraham, give me success today...."

Do you ever pray to ask God to make your work successful? People sometimes wonder if it's okay to pray for work to be successful. Of course! If success is becoming my god, I will have to find a way to dethrone it. But generally speaking, if you can't pray for the success of what you're doing, start doing something else!

When the servant arrived in the town of Nahor, a young woman named Rebekah greeted him and offered to get the servant a drink. When he had finished drinking, Rebekah said, "I'll draw water for your camels too, until they have finished drinking." We are told she "quickly" emptied her jar into the trough and "ran" back to the well to draw more water. It all sounds fairly unremarkable, until you read between the lines:

> One gallon of water weighs eight pounds;
>> a thirsty camel can drink up to thirty gallons of water;
>>> and there were ten camels.
>>>> Do the math.

Rebekah is running to the well. This girl is drawing three hundred gallons of water for a stranger. She does all that could be reasonably expected of her and then some.

This was the pivotal moment of her life. Because of her act of service, Rebekah became the wife of Isaac and went on the adventure of a lifetime, becoming part of sacred history. To this day, her name is remembered and revered by people of faith.

But Rebekah did not know all this was at stake. She did not offer to draw three hundred gallons of water because she knew what the reward could be. It was simply an expression of her heart.

We often hear people say that we should put family above work. Oddly enough, we will not find this thought expressed in the Bible. I will say that again: Nowhere in the Bible does it say that family is more important than work. What the Bible does say is that love matters above all. Families are to be one vehicle through which we express love. Our work is to be another. We will be accountable for our families; we will also be accountable for our work. Often, from a biblical perspective, families were (and are) a place where work gets done.

When we discover the gifts God has given us and the passions that engage us, and we put them to work in the service of values we deeply believe in—in conscious dependence on God—then we are working in the Spirit. Then our work is helping each of us to create the me I want to be.

We are the ones who make our work significant—not the other way around.

» Make Work Part of Your Calling

In our first year of marriage Nancy and I went to Ireland to visit the town of Kilrush at the mouth of the Shannon River in the County Clare, where Nancy's grandmother had been born. While Nancy was visiting some of her relatives, I met a man named Father Ryan.

Father Ryan had actually assisted the priest who helped christen Nancy's grandmother in that remote village in an obscure corner of Ireland, where they seldom saw Protestants. So when Father Ryan found out that I was a pastor at a Baptist church, he wanted to talk shop.

"So you're a Baptist, are you?" he said to me. "Tell me, do you believe in God?"

"Yes," I replied.

"Do you believe in Mary?" he asked slyly.

"Yes," I said again—though we didn't go into detail.

Then we talked about our job descriptions, and he told me what a priest does. "We christen them when they're born. We marry them when they get wed. We hear confession and pronounce forgiveness over their souls. We preach over them when they die. We do it all. We hatch 'em, match 'em, patch 'em and dispatch 'em."

When Nancy came into the room, I introduced her to Father Ryan.

"Ah," he said, "your calling comes with benefits."

A priest is sometimes described as one who represents God to the earth and the earth to God. But the reality is that that was the original job description of the human race. We were made in God's image to continue his work of making the earth to flourish and then, by our flourishing, to give voice for the whole earth to praise God. All work was designed by God to be priestly work. It is not just professional clergy or missionaries who are called by God.

The scholar N. T. Wright has a wonderful image of this. Picture human beings as mirrors set at a forty-five degree angle between heaven and earth. We were created to reflect God's care and dominion to the earth, and we were made to express the worship and gratitude of creation up to God. This is what we do when we work.

You have a calling. You have been gifted. You are a priest.

This is not just something that relates to volunteering at a church. Your work is a primary place—maybe *the* primary place—where your calling gets lived out. Maybe we should issue robes to electrical engineers, clerical collars to accountants, and vestments to auto mechanics every once in a while just to remind us of this.

In his book *Habits of the Heart*, sociologist Robert Bellah describes three orientations people take toward their work. The first is to treat your work as a job. When you do this, you focus on it as a way to get money and pay bills. When asked, most people list money as the primary reason why they work. In the words of that old bumper sticker, "I owe, I owe, so off to work I go." But if your focus is mainly on what you receive from your work, you will most likely come to resent it.

A second orientation is to approach your work as a career. Here your motivation will be higher, but your focus is on advancement and prestige. In a career orientation, your feelings about your work are based on how much success it is creating for you. If your career is not going well, it may feel to you as if your worth is on the line.

The third orientation is to look at your work as a calling. The language of vocation or calling is widespread, but it is rooted in the life of faith. If there is a "calling," then there is someone making the call. That someone is God. That is why you cannot do just anything you want. You are not the call-er; you are the call-ee.

Any work that has meaning, that can be a blessing to people and to the earth, can be a calling. A doctor or pastor might get sucked into viewing work as a means to get a good income, and therefore they only have a job. A garbage collector, however, may see what he does as part of making the world a cleaner and safer place and therefore have a calling.

On our street lives an older woman with many health problems, and a younger woman helps care for her. Often in the afternoon the two of them walk very slowly down the street. The younger woman holds her tightly, makes sure her walk is safe, tries to make her laugh, and listens to her heart. She has a calling.

Lottery winners often make the same comment: "Winning the lottery is not going to change my life." But six months later they have quit their job and bought a new house. A survey of one state's lottery winners had two main findings. One, a majority were more unhappy now than before winning. Two, none of them would give up the money they had won. People whose primary motivation for work is money will always feel resentful and dissatisfied. It is perhaps not so ironic that the song "Take this job and shove it" was famously recorded by a man named Johnny Paycheck.

Isaiah wrote, "When a farmer plows for planting, does he plow continually?... Does he not plant wheat in its place?... His God instructs him and teaches him the right way.... All this also comes from the LORD Almighty, wonderful in counsel and magnificent in wisdom." God wants to meet you in your work.

> Miroslav Volf says, "All human work, however complicated or simple, is made possible by the operation of the Spirit of God in the working person; and all work whose nature and results reflect the values of the new creation is accomplished under the instruction and inspiration of the Spirit of God."

» View Work as Service to God

I have a friend who used to work at Disneyland, and he said that when he was trained, there was one value emphasized above all others: What puts the magic in the Magic Kingdom is servanthood. They are told that when you are in the kingdom, when you walk through those gates, you serve. Whatever your job is, you are a servant.

You treat every encounter with people as if they were your personal guest. If they need directions, escort them. If they ask a question and you have heard it a hundred times, answer it as if you have never heard it before.

There is a ride called the Jungle Cruise, and the most common question asked of the Disneyland staff about it is, "How long is this ride?" So the staff is given a prepared, standard answer: "The Jungle Cruise is an exciting adventure ride that lasts ten minutes." They are supposed to repeat that every time.

Well, one employee had been asked it once too often, so when a couple asked, "How long is the Jungle Cruise?" he looked at them and

in the flow at work ≈

- ≈ Ask God to make your work go well *today*.
- ≈ Continually seek to identify and develop your God-given strengths rather than focusing on improving your weaknesses.
- ≈ Take five-minute breaks throughout the day to relax, get refreshed, and ask God for strength to work well.
- ≈ Identify the larger meaning of your work that makes it a calling.
- ≈ Periodically review your attitude — get water for the camels.
- ≈ Solicit feedback on how you can grow.
- ≈ Make friends with the people you work with.
- ≈ Seek to enjoy your work.

said, "Three days." That couple got out of that line, left the park, went back to the Disney Hotel where they were on their honeymoon, packed up their suitcases, checked out of their hotel, and came back to the line at the Jungle Cruise. The next day that Disneyland employee was gone, and someone else was standing at the line and saying, "The Jungle Cruise is an exciting adventure ride that lasts ten minutes."

Jesus said that what puts the magic into his kingdom is serving, because "the Son of Man did not come to be served, but to serve." His is not a kingdom about status and climbing ladders and getting attention. The best you is built by serving, and God's kingdom is one of those kingdoms where if you don't want to serve, you won't really want to be there. Sometimes God will interrupt us in our work, not to give us a chance to show off our giftedness, but simply to give us a chance to serve.

Jesus tells a story about three men who are given bags of money and then are accountable to their master. The first man received five talents' worth — a talent being a unit of weight — and he "went and traded with them, and gained five more talents." He had skill, initiative, drive, and broad scope to make decisions. He made a 100 percent profit and was commended by his master.

The second man had a smaller talent share, but was equal in his work. His commendation was just as big. In the life of the Spirit, visible outcomes do not determine the gift given or the gift received.

But the third man buried the single talent he was given. He punched the clock. He called in sick. He did not dream, try, dare, or do. His job review did not go well.

In the end, he too said, "I wish I had spent more time at the office."

Think about your work today. If Jesus were your direct supervisor, would you have done your work any differently than you did? How would you have done repairs, answered phones, typed documents, or taught classes if Jesus were checking your work?

In this world, the hardest work sometimes is the most overlooked. A husband came home from the office one day, and the house was a mess. Dirty clothes were all over the floor, dirty dishes filled the sink, the kids were crying, the beds were unmade, the bathrooms smelled bad, and the TV set was blaring. He asked his wife what was going on.

"You know how you ask me every night what did I do all day?" she said. "Well, today I didn't do it."

> Martin Luther once said, "What you do in your house is worth as much as if you did it up in heaven for our Lord God."

The day is coming when God will look at his faithful servants and say, "Well done." He will say it to faithful employees who give themselves diligently to work that never earns much human recognition. He will say it to workers who know they could have climbed higher if they had cut corners or manipulated others. He will say it to single parents who cared for kids — bathing them, feeding them, cleaning up after them — when they were tired and thought nobody was looking.

Somebody is looking. Someone is keeping track.

It *is* worth it.

Chapter 21

You Have to Go through Exile before You Come Back Home

Imagine you have a child and you are handed a script of her entire life laid out before you. Better yet, you are given an eraser and five minutes to edit out whatever you want. You read that she will have a learning disability in grade school. Reading, which comes easily for some kids, will be laborious for yours. In high school your child will make a great circle of friends, then one of them will die of cancer. After high school she will get into the college she wanted to attend, but while there she will lose a leg in a car crash. Following that, she will go through a difficult depression. A few years later she will get a great job, then lose that job in an economic downturn. She will get married, but then go through the grief of separation.

With this script of your child's life before you and five minutes to edit it, *what would you erase?* That is the question psychologist Jonathan Haidt asked in this hypothetical exercise. *Wouldn't you want to take out all the stuff that would cause them pain?*

We live in a generation of "helicopter parents" who constantly swoop in to their children's lives to make sure no one is mistreating them and that they experience one unobstructed success after another in school, sports, and relationships. Whoa! If you could wave a wand and erase every failure, disappointment, and suffering, are you sure it would be a good idea? Would that enable your children to grow into the best version of themselves? Is it possible that in some way people actually need adversity and setbacks — maybe even something like trauma — to reach the fullest level of development and growth?

Paul believed that as we live in the flow of the Spirit, suffering can lead to growth. Suffering can actually produce more flourishing people.

> We rejoice in the hope of the glory of God. Not only so, but we also rejoice in our sufferings, because we know that suffering produces perseverance; perseverance, character; and character, hope. And hope does not disappoint us, because God has poured out his love into our hearts by the Holy Spirit, whom he has given us. (Romans 5:2–5 NIV)

» Three Attitudes toward Adversity

There are many ways to look at the ups and downs of our futures, and philosopher Robert Roberts describes three attitudes we can hold: hope, despair, and resignation.

Hope is the belief that my future holds good prospects. I genuinely *desire* what I think this future holds, and I *believe* this future prospect to be on the way. Hope is not hype. Of course, hope involves waiting, and hope can include uncertainty, so it can be scary. But when I hope, I delight in the thought of the future. I welcome tomorrow. You can always tell if you are around a hope-er.

Despair, on the other hand, creeps in if I desperately want something but believe it will not happen. In despair, my longing is still strong, but I believe that it will go unfulfilled. The thought of the future becomes painful: *This depression will never go away. I will never be loved.* Despair paralyzes. The soul cannot survive for long with deep despair. Despair is so toxic, people will manage it by *resignation.*

Resignation is a kind of halfway house between *hope* and *despair.*

In resignation, I ratchet down my desire, trying to convince myself that what I wanted so badly isn't a big deal. *The job is not that great. She's not that pretty, and there are plenty of other fish in the sea. When it comes to aging or taxes or being a Chicago Cubs baseball fan, learning to accept the inevitable with serenity is the course of wisdom.* But can resignation alone sustain a life?

The best version of you is a hoper, because the Spirit of life is a Spirit of hope. The Spirit never leads us to despair, and there is always hope—which is not based on circumstances, but rather is an inner disposition. In fact, researchers have identified a personality variable they call *dispositional optimism*, a capacity to anticipate the future.

Give yourself a five-second hope test by answering yes or no to these two statements:

- In uncertain times, I usually expect the best.
- If something can go wrong for me, it usually will.

If you answered yes to the first question and no to the second, you will naturally love this chapter. If you answered any other way, you will *need* this chapter, because the good news about hope is that it can be learned!

» Normal Life and Crisis

In what we call "normal life," we drift along under a set of assumptions that may work for a long time: I may feel secure because I have a certain amount of money. I have an identity because I have a certain job, title, degree, or list of achievements. I have a purpose because I am going to achieve more than I already have. Life seems to "work."

Then a crisis comes. Maybe it's a financial crash. Maybe you lose your job. Maybe you lose someone you love. You go to the doctor's office and find you have a malignancy. There is a scandal, and you lose your reputation. Your son or daughter rejects you, running down a road that violates everything you believe in.

Any crisis carries in its wake the question, *What can I build my life on that circumstances cannot rob me of? What really matters?*

NORMAL   NORMAL

CRISIS

Sometime ago someone came into my office and told me to check my rear passenger tire. It appeared to be getting low, so I took it to the service station to get it patched. After a few months, somebody else told me the same thing. For several months, I would have to reinflate it, then it would slowly leak out. Eventually, the car doctor said, "This tire is tired and worn out. It's time to face reality. You have to get a new tire."

Then last weekend my car wouldn't start. It was a battery problem. I thought I could get the battery recharged, but the car doctor said, "This battery is tired and worn out. It's time to face reality. You have to get a new battery."

At breakfast, after too much coffee and too little sleep the night before, I noticed my wife looking at me with a tender look, and I asked her, "What are you thinking?"

"You're looking tired and worn out," she said.

I did not like where this was headed.

What do you do with a broken person? I can resign myself to a tire that can't be reinflated or a battery that can't be recharged. But what if the problem is closer to home? Ernest Hemingway wrote, "Sooner or later, the world breaks everyone, and those who are broken are strongest in the broken places."

Sometimes that is true. But sometimes people write beautiful things and believe them to be true — or hope that they are true — and yet they don't help. Hemingway himself had a brokenness that couldn't get stronger, and he ended his life because the pain was too great.

Something happens to us amid adversity.

For a long time, researchers have looked at what enables some people to endure suffering. But over the last decade or so, the focus has shifted from looking only at how some people make it through to how people are able to go through adversity and actually come out the other side stronger than before. Just as there is a condition called "post-traumatic stress disorder," researchers are now talking about "post-traumatic growth."

One line of thinking is that adversity *can* lead to growth. Another line of thinking is that the highest levels of growth cannot be achieved *without* adversity. It may be that somehow adversity leads to growth in a way that nothing else does.

But adversity does not automatically bring growth. It can cripple people, and much of the outcome depends on how people respond to adversity. Jonathan Haidt writes about three ways in which post-traumatic growth can happen. I modify them here a bit, add a fourth, and look at how God can grow us in adversity.

1. *Rising to a challenge reveals abilities hidden within you (and beyond you!) that would otherwise have remained dormant.*

It is in adversity that we find out what we are really made of, just as we find out what is inside a tube of toothpaste when it gets squeezed. People often say, "I could never go through what that person went through. I would die." Then they go through it. Their heart keeps beating. Their world goes on.

We don't know what we are capable of until we have to cope.

I cannot ensure my circumstances will work out the way I want them to, but I can always ask, "How would the person I most want to be face this situation?" We don't even have to believe in the Bible to see this. Wise people have always understood the connection between suffering and growth. Meng Tzu, a Chinese sage from the third century BC, said,

> When heaven is about to confer a great responsibility on any man, it will exercise his mind with suffering ... place obstacles in the path of his deeds, so as to stimulate his mind, harden his nature, and improve wherever he is incompetent.

But nowhere do we see this idea displayed more prominently than in the Bible. God could have let Abraham stay in the comfort of Ur, Moses stay in the splendor of Pharaoh's courts, and Aaron stay in the safety of the crowd. He could have kept David away from Goliath; Shadrach, Meshach, and Abednego out of the fiery furnace; Daniel out of the lion's den; Elijah away from Jezebel; Nehemiah out of captivity; Jonah out of the whale; John the Baptist away from Herod; Esther from being threatened; Jeremiah from being rejected; and Paul from being shipwrecked. But he didn't. In fact, God used each of these trials to bring people closer to himself — to produce perseverance, character, and hope.

One of the classic stories of adversity in the Bible is about Joseph. At the beginning of his life, Joseph is the favorite son of his father, envied by his brothers, with dreams of being the one everybody bows down to. Then he is kidnapped by his brothers and ends up serving as a slave in the home of Potiphar. He loses his home, his culture, his security, and his status as favorite son. What does Joseph have left? He is in a strange bed, in a strange house, in a strange land, with no friends, no prospects, and no explanation. But he has one gift — and that one thing makes all the difference.

Scripture says, "The LORD was with Joseph. . . ." Joseph is not alone.

What happens to someone who loses everything but God, then finds out that God is enough? As a powerless stranger, he experiences the presence of God in his life in a way he never did in the comfort of his own home. Rivers of living water begin to flow from his belly that he had never known before, because hope comes from the promise that "we know that in all things God works for the good of those who love him." God wasn't at work producing the circumstances Joseph wanted. God was at work in bad circumstances producing the *Joseph* that God wanted.

> God isn't at work producing the circumstances you want. God is at work in bad circumstances producing the *you* he wants.

One of the most misquoted "verses" you will never find in the Bible is this one: "God will never give me more than I can handle." Huh? Are you kidding me? Where is that one? Poverty, holocausts, genocide, war—people are given more than they can handle all the time!

The Bible does say that no temptation is given to people without a way out, but that is about temptation, not adversity. The Bible does not promise that you will only be given what you can handle. In fact, the one certainty of your life is that you will die—and you definitely can't handle that! You will never be placed in a situation God can't handle. Nothing—including death—will place you beyond his flow of living waters.

Maybe you are in a situation—a relationship or a financial condition—that is not what you wanted. You want to lie down and die. But when you don't—when you show up, when you offer the best you have—something good is happening *inside* you that far outweighs whatever is happening *outside* you.

Jesus was facing adversity when he told his followers that if they had faith, they could command a mountain and it would be cast into the sea. When my focus is on the mountain, I am driven by my fear. When my focus is on God, however, I am made alive by my faith. But if I did not have the mountain, I would not know that faith could be in me.

Your circumstances—even the best of them—are temporary. But you—the person you become—go on forever.

2. *Adversity can deepen relationships.*

Somehow suffering can soften a heart and deepen friendships in a unique way.

> The Trappist monk Thomas Merton wrote, "As long as we are on earth, the love that unites us will bring us suffering by our very contact with one another, because this love is the resetting of a Body of broken bones."

Nancy went to nursing school with a classmate we will call Shelly, who was intelligent, engaging, and beautiful — everyone loved her.

Shelly fell in love and married Steve, an architect and basketball player who looked like a male model. They had more good genes than any couple has a right to expect. But when Shelly walked into her bridal shower, she was grieving that everything was not as it should be: she had broken a nail putting gas in her car.

"But it's okay," she said in her deep southern drawl. "Steve said that once we're married, I will never have to put gas in my car again."

To resurrect a phrase from those days, *gag me with a spoon.*

On that day, a trial was a broken nail. But storms have a way of coming to every life.

Shelly and Steve were married and wanted to have children, but were disappointed for years, through two miscarriages and the pain of watching other people walk baby strollers and complain about their lack of sleep. They wished that little cries would keep them up at night, but finally Shelly was diagnosed with a condition that was treatable, and she eventually gave birth to a little girl.

By this point they had reached an age when they thought it better not to have any more children, so Steve went through a surgical procedure. The next month, Steve was hurt playing basketball and knocked unconscious. In the emergency room, the doctor took one look at his x-rays and turned pale:

"Don't move; don't breathe deep; don't have a deep thought," the specialist said.

The staff put him in traction and flew in a surgeon, who told Steve that if he had so much as sneezed or turned the wrong way, he could have ended up quadriplegic or dead. Steve could die during the operation.

But he didn't, and the surgery was a success.

Because of all this, the doctors never did check to make sure Steve's minor surgical procedure to avoid having more children had been effective. Next month, Shelly called to tell us she was pregnant. They hadn't planned on this. A few weeks later she called back, and for the first thirty seconds all she could do was groan.

The baby still inside her had been diagnosed with severe heart defects and massive cognitive deficits. Friends did not know what to say. Some said, "Your baby will be healed. God has told us. You just have to have faith. We'll pray — you watch."

Steve and Shelly watched. They prayed. The baby was not healed. All that the doctors said came true.

Others said, "People will be watching you. Don't grieve. Don't look sad. Show how much faith you have." Another person said, "God must love you very much to give you a retarded child." I won't even tell you what that response did to them.

If they were writing this, Steve and Shelly would tell you that their little baby is precious to them beyond words. They would tell you they have grown through this pain. They would also tell you they would give all that growth back in a heartbeat if it meant health and wholeness for their child.

Loss is not simply something to be recovered from. Hope does not mean returning to happiness as soon as possible. God comes to us in our grief and shares it. In that shared grief, we find love. "Mourn with those who mourn," Paul says. Love meets in shared suffering and broken souls like no other kind of love.

One of the most common results of people who go through deep grief is that they come to have a deeper appreciation for other people. People diagnosed with a serious illness often describe this paradox. They hate having their body invaded by the illness, but they wake up to how much people matter. They quit wasting time and emotion on what doesn't count.

Recently I visited a twelve-step group, and one of the most powerful moments came when the members and newcomers introduced themselves. It is always the same liturgy. They say who they are and name their brokenness — something we almost never do in normal public gatherings.

"I'm Dale. I'm an alcoholic."

Know what everybody says back? "Hi, Dale!" In other words, *We are glad you're here. You're one of us. Hi, Dale!*

Alcohol is not one of my limps — I have enough other ones — but it was very healing to hear everyone, and I felt that I wanted to say, "My name's John, and I'm an alcoholic," simply because the warmth of belonging in that room was so healing. To say, "My name is John, and I'm a Presbyterian pastor" would sound as if I were in denial.

Somehow prisoners, addicts, or those grieving can meet and identify with each other in ways that people in "normal life" forget.

God comes to us in our grief, and because he shares our grief, it begins to mingle ever so slightly with hope.

We cling to each other, and love meets in shared suffering and broken souls like no other kind of love.

As a young woman, Joni Eareckson Tada became paralyzed and has been in a wheelchair for decades. She would tell you every day she wishes she could walk. She would also tell you she has met God and loved people, in ways she couldn't have imagined on her own, because of that chair. She has been used to inspire thousands because of that chair in ways she otherwise never would. That chair is part of the curse. And yet still she thanks God for the chair.

3. *Adversity can change your priorities about what really matters.*

A friend named Bill Dallas has written a book, *Lessons from San Quentin*, in which he talks about how the moment of his greatest suffering became the turning point of his life. He had been living for money, possessions, success, beauty, pleasure, and parties — and doing quite well. But he took a few wrong turns, got involved in financial dealings that were less than transparent, and ended up in the San Quentin prison. There the strangest thing happened.

He met God. Bill found a group of men serving life sentences who had found God, and there he discovered people with a greater sense of peace and a deeper experience of community than people he had known in penthouses and office suites. More and more, they were becoming the best version of themselves.

As with Joseph, the Lord was with Bill in prison. Bill says that if he were to visit one more place before he dies, it wouldn't be the Eiffel Tower or the Great Wall of China or the Taj Mahal. It would be that prison cell where he met God.

It is as if in normal life we step onto a treadmill and begin running after something — money, security, or success — when adversity knocks us off. Suffering enables us to see the folly of chasing after temporal gods, and when people suffer, they often resolve to not return to their old way of life when things normalize. But the key to accomplishing that is taking action before normal life takes over again. We have a finite window of time to make changes; otherwise we will drift back to our old patterns. Bill changed his work, his lifestyle, his friends, his habits, and his God so that when he was released from prison, his life normalized, but his values and trajectory had been transformed.

> Danish philosopher Søren Kierkegaard said, "Affliction is able to drown out every earthly voice... but the voice of eternity deep in the soul it cannot drown."

As always with the Spirit, a response to his work is needed on our part. If you merely say, "I'm going to remember this new perspective that I've learned," when your life returns to normal, you will get back on the treadmill. But if you have courage to make changes in your life, something can happen in your soul. The Spirit will bring the courage if you keep asking while the experience of adversity is fresh. Ultimately, adversity can produce hope because of a reality much larger than you and I.

That reality is that God is a redemptive God.

4. *Adversity points us to the Hope beyond ourselves.*

What do you think was the largest single publication in the 1960s? What book, magazine, or print product do you think outstripped everything else? It was actually a catalog — and it was not produced by Sears Roebuck or Montgomery Ward.

It was produced by a company called Sperry and Hutchinson, better known as S&H. Ever hear of S&H Green Stamps? No?

At their height, S&H printed three times more stamps than the United States government. They published enough catalogs to more than circle the earth. If you saved enough of their stamps, you could get ... a toaster. Or another appliance. One school in Erie, Pennsylvania, saved 5.4 million green stamps and bought two gorillas for a local zoo.

You would take these stamps to a place called a redemption center to be exchanged. Redeemed. The company is still around, online, and offers what are called greenpoints. Amazingly enough, they are still accepting stamps. If you find any in the attic, you can still turn them in. It's not too late.

With endless patience, at infinite cost to himself, God had been waiting since the beginning of history — watching, suffering, loving — until in the fullness of time he sent his only begotten Son to a redemption center on a hill called Calvary. What does he want to redeem? *Everything.* All creation is groaning for redemption, Paul says. God wants to redeem you.

When circumstances look bleak, when the stock market is down, or when your morale is sinking or your assets are shrinking or your health is collapsing, you may wonder, *Is* anything *going up?*

Yes.

The chance to trust God when trusting isn't easy is wide open. The prospect for modeling hope for a hope-needy world is trending upward. And the possibility of cultivating a storm-proof faith is always going up. This is so because certain truths remain unchanged: God remains sovereign, grace beats sin, prayers get heard, the Bible endures, heaven's mercies spring up new every morning, the cross still testifies to the power of sacrificial love, the tomb is still empty, and the kingdom that Jesus announced is still expanding without needing to be bailed out by human efforts.

God is still in the business of redemption, specializing in bringing something very, very good out of something very, very bad. Julian of Norwich was a woman who could attest to that, living as she did during the Black Plague-infested fourteenth century. She was a great hoper, who sang a song of hope from the depths of the trials of her day:

> *But all shall be well,*
> *And all shall be well,*
> *And all manner of things shall be well...*
> *He did not say, "You shall know no storms, no travails, no disease,"*
> *He said, "You shall not be overcome."*

PART SEVEN
flowing from here on out
»

Chapter 22

Ask for a Mountain

Everyone is looking for just the right logo. Companies spend millions of dollars to find a little icon that will communicate what they offer in a memorable and compelling way. Nike's logo is a little checkmark-looking symbol we call a swoosh. It is actually a stylized version of the wing from the Greek statute "Winged Victory," and the word *Nike* itself comes from the Greek word for victory. Their logo is a swoosh; their brand is *success*.

Apple's logo is, well, an apple. There is a story on the Internet that it was derived from the biblical tree of knowledge, but that may be urban myth. The logo, however, has come to represent the meeting of technology and intelligence at our fingertips. Their icon is an apple; their brand is *smart*.

McDonald's logo is so well known that as bad as I am at art, this is the one that always gets recognized even when *I* draw it. The Golden Arches. On every continent they mean joy and gratification—the Happy Meal. Their logo is a pair of arches; their brand is *pleasure*.

Mercedes-Benz's logo is a three-pointed star inside a circle. Inevitably, when I draw this one, people think it is the peace sign, but nobody is selling peace. The company chose a three-pointed star to express their engines' dominion in land, sky, and sea. Their logo is a star-in-a-circle; their brand is *power*.

If you were to choose a logo for your life, what would it be?

All four logos are known around the planet, but none of them is the *most* famous logo in the world, the one symbol that has been around for centuries. You see it on tombstones and T-shirts, chapels and necklaces; it is the single most famous logo the world has ever seen.

A cross.

Because it has been around so long, people often look at the cross without thinking what it means. There is a story about a woman who walks into a jewelry store and asks for a cross. The clerk replies, "Do you want an empty one, or one with a little man on it?"

The cross was not empty.

Crosses were a way of killing people. Devised by the Persians and popularized by Alexander the Great, the cross was perfected by the Romans as a means of deterring rebellion. It was intended to be both painful and humiliating; the English word "excruciating" comes from the Latin word for crucifixion.

Jesus himself said, "Whoever would come after me must deny themselves, take up their cross, and follow me." It was this image that came to represent the movement associated with Jesus.

Think about how strange this is: In its beginnings, this little movement called Christianity struggled under persecution, trying to attract people to become part of their cause, and the symbol they used to represent their message was not an icon of success, knowledge, pleasure, or power. They chose a symbol universally understood to represent scandal, failure, and death.

Who would choose a means of execution as their company logo? Imagine the electric company hiring a marketing consultant who advises them to make their primary image a little electric chair, with the catchy little slogan underneath, "The power is on."

When Jesus invited his followers to "take up their cross," it was not a call to annihilation. It was a call to spiritual greatness in the divine conspiracy of sacrificial love. Human beings were offered a cause worth living for, dying for, and being resurrected for. God was reconciling all things to himself, and evil, sin, death, and guilt were about to receive their eviction notice.

The cross was not empty. There was a man on it.

Now you and I have something worth living for, dying for, and being resurrected for—something more than success, smarts, pleasure, or power. The God of the cross is renewing and creating all things to flourish through the power of sacrificial love.

And we get to be a part.

» Ask God for a Glorious Burden

We sometimes yearn for a problem-free life, but that would be death by boredom. It is in working to solve problems and overcome challenges that we become the person God wants us to be. Every problem is an invitation from the Spirit, and when we say yes, we are in the flow.

So don't ask for comfort. Don't ask for ease. Don't ask for manageability. Ask to be given a burden for a challenge bigger than yourself—one that can make a difference in the world, one that will require the best you have to give it and then leave some space for God besides. Ask for a task that will keep you learning and growing and uncomfortable and hungry.

There can be no learning without novelty. There can be no novelty without risk. We cannot grow unless there has been a challenge to what is familiar and comfortable. The Spirit leads us into adventure. The Spirit leads us into a dangerous world. To ask for the Spirit is to ask for risk.

A friend of our family decided to change his name. Actually, he was leaving his first and last name alone, but he wanted to add a middle name: *Danger*. Seriously! (This is a true story—I have seen the paperwork.) He felt he had always been a compliant, middle-of-the-road, play-it-safe kind of person, and he wanted to do something to stake out a new identity.

It requires a lot of legal work to get your name changed, and this friend had to go to court multiple times. On the day of his final court appearance he was last on the docket. One of the cases before him involved two parties suing each other, who got so aggressive they had to be escorted out of the courtroom.

Everything finally went according to plan, and the judge granted my friend's request. As he was walking out the door, however, the bailiff stopped him. "Be careful. Those two men who got kicked out have started fighting in the parking lot. It's dangerous out there."

My friend knew this was a once-in-a-lifetime opportunity, and he showed the bailiff his paperwork. "It's okay," he said. "*Danger* is my middle name."

The Spirit wants to make you a dangerous person. The Spirit wants to make you threatening to all the forces of injustice and apathy and complacency that keep our world from flourishing. The Spirit wants to make you dangerously noncompliant in a broken world.

Ask God for a mountain.

» Finding Your Challenge

Caleb was one of twelve scouts sent to explore the Promised Land when Israel had left Egypt. When the scouts returned, ten of them said that the assignment was impossible and they should return to slavery in Egypt. Only Caleb and Joshua trusted God and said, "We can certainly do it."

Because of Israel's unbelief, Caleb had to spend forty years of his life wandering through the wilderness. By the time the Israelites crossed the Jordan River, he was eighty years old. Then another five years passed beyond that before the various tribes of Israel were assigned land to occupy. As Caleb described it years later,

> "I was forty years old when Moses ... sent me from Kadesh Barnea to explore the land. And I brought him back a report according to my convictions, but the others who went up with me made the hearts of the people melt with fear. I, however, followed the LORD my God wholeheartedly."

If you have a negative attitude and a small faith when you are forty, there is a good chance you will not have a negative attitude and a small faith when you are eighty-five, because there's a good chance you won't ever make it to eighty-five. Psychologist Martin Seligman studied several hundred people in a religious community and divided them into quartiles from most to least optimistic and faith-filled. He found that 90 percent of the most optimistic, faith-filled people were still alive at the age of eighty-five. But only 34 percent of the most negative, pessimistic people made it to that age.

Another study, the largest of its kind, tracked over 2,000 adults over the age of sixty-five in the southwestern United States. Optimistic people — faith-filled people — had better health habits, lower blood pressure, and feistier immune systems and were half as likely to die in the next year as negative people. If you have a positive attitude, you are likely to live a decade longer than people with a negative attitude. Are you happy to hear that? If not, you could be in serious trouble.

Twelve spies went out, but only Joshua and Caleb had faith. *We can do it!* they said. *Let's go do it.* The other ten, however, said, *It cannot be done. Let's go back and be slaves in Egypt.* Forty-five years later, Caleb was as feisty as ever. Want to guess what happened to the other ten by then? They were all dead. None of them made it to Caleb's age.

Faith is an amazing life-giver.

A friend of mine named Mark married a woman named Pauline Brand. Her father was Paul Brand, a great doctor who wrote a book with author Philip Yancey. Brand was also a brilliant doctor who devoted his life to serving many of the poorest of the poor. Yancey says he admires Paul Brand more than any other man he's known.

But maybe even more amazing than Paul's life was the life of his mother, Evelyn Brand. When she was a young woman she felt called by God to go to India. As a single woman in 1909, a calling like that required a truckload of faith and an equal amount of determination. She married a young man named Jessie and together they began a ministry to people in rural India, bringing education and medical supplies, and building roads to reduce the isolation of the poor.

Early in their ministry they went seven years without a single convert, but then a priest of a local tribal religion developed a fever and grew deathly ill. Nobody else would go near him, but Evelyn and Jessie nursed him as he was dying. He said, *This God, Jesus, must be the true God because only Jessie and Evelyn will care for me in my dying.*

The priest gave his children to them to care for after he died—and that became a spiritual turning point in that part of the world. People began to examine the life and teachings of Jesus, and in increasing numbers began to follow him. Evelyn and Jessie had thirteen years of productive service, then Jessie died. By this time, Evelyn was fifty years old, and everyone expected her to return to her home in England. But she would not do it. She was as feisty as Caleb.

She was known and loved for miles around as "Granny Brand," and she stayed another twenty years under the mission board she had served so faithfully. Her son, Paul, came over when she was seventy years old, and this is what he said about his mom: "This is how to grow old. Allow everything else to fall away until those around you see only love."

» Do Something Difficult

Caleb's desire for challenge was both God's gift to him and his gift to God. As he prepared to enter the Promised Land, this is what he said:

So here I am today, eighty-five years old! I am still as strong today as the day Moses sent me out; I'm just as vigorous to go out to battle now as I was then. Now, give me this hill country that the LORD promised me that day. You yourself heard then that the Anakites were there and their cities were large and fortified, but, the Lord helping me, I will drive them out just as he said.

Hill country is much more difficult to occupy than flat ground, but that is exactly what Caleb asked for—the hardest challenge. He had to face the Anakites, Israel's most formidable opponents, the ones talked about in Numbers 13 of whom the people said, "We saw the descendants of Anakites there. We seem like grasshoppers next to them."

Caleb asked for the hardest enemies—in the most dangerous territory.

Caleb was eighty-five years old, so you would think he was going to ask for a nice condo at Shalom Acres. But what he wanted was the privilege of a really hard assignment. He chose another battle before he checked out. *God, just give me the hill country.*

» "Give Me the Hill Country, God"

God has wired us so that our bodies, minds, and spirits require challenge, and we flourish especially when we face challenges for a cause greater than ourselves. We experience the flow of the Spirit most deeply when we focus on challenges that enrich the community and when we cease to be preoccupied with our own advancement.

When Joshua—like Caleb, one of the two faithful scouts—became the new leader when Moses departed, Caleb could have withdrawn or sulked. Instead, Caleb's engagement in life just kept growing. He immersed himself among the people around him. As his generation all died out he had to develop a whole new circle of friends as an older man. He became mentor, guide, and cheerleader for an entirely new generation, and he did it to such an extent that they all said they wanted eighty-five-year-old Caleb to lead them when they went to the hill country.

Challenges undertaken for the greater good bind us to people. The pursuit of comfort, however, leads to isolation—and isolation is terminal.

Dr. Marian Diamond, a researcher on aging at the University of California at Berkeley and one of the world's leading neuroanatomists, found that deliberately induced challenges are required to keep our brains healthy and developing. In one experiment, a group of rats was given food directly, while another group had obstacles placed in front of their food dish. Rats that had to overcome obstacles developed a thicker cortex and more dendrites, were able to navigate other mazes more quickly, and were able to solve problems more proficiently than the comfortable rats. The fewer problems that a rat had, the faster its brain went downhill. If you love a rat, give it problems.

Dr. Diamond also wanted to explore the effects of isolation on aging. She found that if twelve rats were in a cage together—a little community of rats—and given challenges, their brains developed more and had a thicker cortex than if they were given a challenge in complete isolation. Then she wanted to see how this worked with older rats, so she took rats that were six hundred days or older, the equivalent of a sixty-year-old human being. Same results.

She was invited to present her findings in Germany, and she found that the rats they were working with there lived to be eight hundred days old. This troubled her, because her rats started dying up to two hundred days earlier. So she told her researchers that there was one item they had not given their rats, and that they were going to start: They decided to give those rats love. The rats would face the same challenges as before, but after each challenge the researchers would pick up the rat and hold it in their hands, press it against their lab coats, pet it, and speak kindly to it. They would say, "You are one sweet rat," or whatever it is you say to affirm a rodent.

When they started loving those rats, those critters did more than break the eight-hundred-day barrier. At 904 days they were not only still alive, but still developing thicker cortexes. They had more developed brains under challenging conditions because facing challenges in community gives life and isolation destroys it.

> "Listen to me, house of Jacob. . . . Even to your old age and gray hairs I am he, I am he who will sustain you. I have made you and I will carry you; I will sustain you and I will rescue you." (Isaiah 46:3–4)

Life is not about comfort. It is about saying, "God, give me another mountain." It might look like Granny Brand. It might look like Caleb. It might be a story that gets told—or it might not. No one may know about your story but you and God. It doesn't matter.

Living the adventure God planned, becoming the person God created you to be, is not one pursuit among many. It is why you were born.

It is worth wanting above all else.

» Knowing Your Mountain

How will you recognize your mountain? There is no formula. Just as in every other area of your growth, your mountain will not look exactly like anyone else's. But often you will recognize it because it lies at the intersection of the tasks that tap into your greatest strengths and the needs that tap into your deepest passions. Yet know this for sure: *God has a mountain with your name on it.*

When Rich Stearns became engaged as a young man and new Christian, his fiancée wanted to register for china. But he said to her, "As long as there are children starving in the world, we will not own china, crystal, or silver." Then, as he entered the corporate world and started climbing the ladder, he discovered his remarkable gifts of leadership. He loved strategic thinking, team-building, and mission achievement. Twenty years later he became the CEO of Lennox, the top producer of luxury tableware — fine china — in the country.

One day he received a phone call from an organization called World Vision, asking if he would consider getting involved with them. So Rich went to Rakai, Uganda, an area considered ground zero for the AIDS pandemic. In that village he sat in a thatched hut with a thirteen-year-old boy with the same first name — Richard. One pile of stones outside the door marked where they had buried the boy's father, who had died of AIDS, and another pile of stones marked where they buried his mother, who also died of AIDS. That kind of thing happens every day in Africa.

Rich talked for a while with the boy — now the head of the household trying to raise his two younger brothers — and asked him at one point, "Do you have a Bible?"

Yes, the boy said, and he went into the other room and brought back the one book in their house.

"Are you able to read it?" Rich asked, and at that the boy's face lit up.

"I love to read the gospel of John because it says Jesus loves children," the boy said.

Indeed, as the song goes, Jesus loves "all the children of the world." There has never been anybody like Jesus to bring good news to a thirteen-year-old boy in a thatched hut, with a pile of stones where a mom and a dad ought to be.

Richard left his job and his house and his title and asked God for one more hill.

The logo of World Vision consists of its name with a little field of color and a shining star next to it. The star brings to mind the apostle Paul's call to people to "shine like stars" in an often-dark world. It is also reminiscent of the star that announced the presence of God to the world at Bethlehem. Even *World Vision* is only a little part of a larger and more wonderful vision we find at the beginning of John's Gospel: "In the beginning was the Word, and the Word was with God, and the Word was God ... and the Word became flesh, and dwelt among us."

What we translate in English as "word" comes from the Greek word *logos*. It is where we get our word "logo."

Jesus is God's logo.

It is as if God has said, "I want my icon, my character, my representation, my will, my symbol to be wrapped up in one single expression. It is Jesus. He is it."

Jesus is God's logo. If you want to know what a life can look like when it is lived with the Spirit flowing from the belly, look at Jesus. On a mountain called Calvary, on a splintered cross, the sin that needed to be cleansed, the price that needed to be paid, was finally and fully paid by Jesus.

At the end of the day, we do not have a program, plan, platform, or product to help the world. We have a Savior. We do not point to success, knowledge, pleasure, or power. We point to a cross.

What is *your* logo?

We saw earlier part of the story about Evelyn Brand. Here is the rest of her story.

Toward the end of her life, everyone called her "Granny Brand." She had spent her life in India, including twenty years of widowhood, and at age seventy she received word from her home mission office in England that they were not going to give her another five-year term. They felt that she was simply getting too old.

But she was also stubborn.

A party was held to celebrate her time in India, and everyone there cheered her on. "Have a good trip back home," they all said.

"I'll tell you a little secret," she announced. "I'm not going back home. I'm staying in India."

Evelyn had had a little shack built with some resources that she had smuggled in. Then she bought a pony to get around the mountains, and this septuagenarian would ride from village to village on horseback to tell people about Jesus. She did that for five years on her own. One day, at seventy-five years old, she fell off and broke her hip. Her son, Paul Brand, the eminent doctor, said to her, "Mom, you had a great run. God's used you. It's time to turn it over now. You go on back home."

"I am not going back home," she said. *God, give me the mountain!* She spent another eighteen years traveling from one village to another on horseback. Falls, concussions, sicknesses, and aging could not stop her. Finally, when she hit ninety-three years old, she could not ride horseback any more. So the men in these villages — because they loved Granny Brand so much — put her on a stretcher and carried her from one village to another. She lived two more years and gave those years as a gift, carried on a stretcher, to help the poorest of the poor. She died, but she never retired. She just graduated.

If Granny Brand had a logo, it would not point toward success, smarts, pleasure, or power. It would be the stretcher on which she was carried up and down the mountains to pour out the end of her life in sacrificial love.

What a remarkable logo!

Your deepest longing should be to be alive with God, to become the person God made you to be, and to be used to help God's world flourish.

That is the life available to you every moment. It is the life found in Jesus, the man on the cross, who mastered sin in his death and mastered death in a tomb and who now dispenses life with unrivaled authority. It is available to you in this very moment, no matter what your situation. God is at work in this hour, and his purpose is to shape you to be not only his servant, but his friend. Out of your belly shall flow rivers of living water. Blessed are you.

Ask for a mountain.

sources

Chapter 1: Learn Why God Made You

14: "For we are God's handiwork": Ephesians 2:10.

16: "Know that the Lord Himself": Psalm 100:3 NASB.

16: "If anyone is in Christ": 2 Corinthians 5:17.

18: "Don't let anyone look down": 1 Timothy 4:12.

19: "I saw the Holy City": Revelation 21:2.

20: "The Spirit and the bride": Revelation 22:17.

Chapter 2: The Me I Don't Want to Be

22: Henri Nouwen, *Can You Drink This Cup?* Notre Dame, IN: Ave Maria Press, 1996, 89.

27: "We know that in all things": Romans 8:28.

28: "Rule-keeping does not": Galatians 3:12 *The Message.*

28: "I have come that you": John 10:10 paraphrased.

30: "When I came to die": From *Walden.* Quoted in William Irvine, *On Desire.* New York: Oxford University Press, 2006, 267.

30: Gordan MacKenzie, *Orbiting the Giant Hairball: A Corporate Fool's Guide to Surviving with Grace.* New York: Viking Press, 1998, 19.

30: A vision of languishing: Ezekiel 37.

30: "Grows and builds itself up": Ephesians 4:16.

31: "I have come that they": John 10:10.

31: Irenaeus, *Adversus Haereses.*

32: "With God, all things are possible": Mark 10:27 paraphrased.

32: "Today you will be with me": Luke 23:43.

Chapter 3: Discover the Flow

36: "Let anyone who is thirsty": John 7:37–39.

36: "You will receive power": Acts 1:8.

37: "Though you have not seen him": 1 Peter 1:8.

37: "Take my yoke upon you": Matthew 11:29.

40: "Breath of life": Genesis 2:7.

40: "As the deer pants for streams": Psalm 42:1.

41: "Whoever is thirsty": John 7:37 paraphrased.

41: "Then the angel showed me": Revelation 22:1–2.

42: "Love, joy, peace": Galatians 5:22–23.

43: "Do not quench the Spirit": 1 Thessalonians 5:19 NASB.

43: "Since we live by the Spirit": Galatians 5:25–26.

45: "There is a way that seemeth right": Prov. 14:12; 16:25 KJV.

Chapter 4: Find Out How *You* Grow

47: "Head and shoulders": 1 Samuel 9:2 NRSV.

47: "Tried walking around": 1 Samuel 17:39.

47: "I cannot go in these": 1 Samuel 17:39.

47: "Go, and the LORD be with you": 1 Samuel 17:37.

48: "Put on the full armor of God": Ephesians 6:11.

48: "Where the Spirit of the Lord is": 2 Corinthians 3:17.

50: C. S. Lewis, *Surprised by Joy*. New York: Harcourt Brace, 1955.

51: "Father, may they be one with you": John 17:21 paraphrased.

58: Saint Benedict: Quoted in Will Derske, *The Rule of St. Benedict for Beginners*. Collegeville, MN: Liturgical Press, 2003, 47.

58: "Indulge the sinful nature": Galatians 5:13.

59: "Don't give up meeting together": Hebrews 10:25 paraphrased.

Chapter 5: Surrender: The One Decision That Always Helps

60: "The fool has said in his heart": Psalm 14:1; 53:1 NASB.

60: "Will be like God": Genesis 3:5.

60: "Out of our bellies can flow": John 7:38 paraphrased.

60: John Calvin, *Institutes of the Christian Religion*, Book III, Chapter 7, Section 1: Quoted in Dallas Willard, *Renovation of the Heart*. Colorado Springs: NavPress, 2002, 143.

64: Alcoholics Anonymous, *The Big Book*, 4th Edition. New York: Alcoholics Anonymous World Services, 2002, 24.

65. Roy Baumeister: M. T. Gailliot, N. L. Mead, and R. F. Baumeister, "Self-Regulation." In *Handbook of Personality: Theory and Research,* 3rd edition. Edited by O. P. John et al. New York: Guilford Press, 2008, 472-91.

66: "Offer your bodies as a living sacrifice": Romans 12:2.

67: "I don't condemn you": John 8:11 paraphrased.

68: "Let this cup pass from me": Matthew 26:39 KJV.

68: "For you died, and your life": Colossians 3:3–4.

68: "Now show me your glory": Exodus 33:18.

69: "I will cause all my goodness": Exodus 33:19 MLB.

Chapter 6: Try Softer

72: Richard Rohr, *Everything Belongs: The Life of Contemplative Prayer*. New York: Crossroad, 2003, 143.

72: "Suppose one of you had a servant": Luke 17:7–10 NIV.

72: Prodigal son: Luke 15:11–32.

74: William Lang: Source unknown.

74: Jesus talked about a Pharisee: Luke 18:9–14.

75: Philip P. Hallie, *Lest Innocent Blood Be Shed: The Story of the Village of Le Chambon and How Goodness Happened There*. New York: Harper Perennial, 1994.

Chapter 7: Let Your Desires Lead You to God

79: "So Jacob served seven years": Genesis 29:20.

80: Who found a treasure: Matthew 13:44.

80: Who found a pearl: Matthew 13:45–46.

80: Jonathan Haidt, *The Happiness Hypothesis: Finding Modern Truth in Ancient Wisdom.* New York: Basic Books, 2005.

82: "Taste and see that the LORD": Psalm 34:8.

82: Lewis Smedes, *How Can It Be All Right When Everything Is All Wrong?* San Francisco: HarperSanFrancisco, 1992, 20.

82: "You open your hand": Psalm 145:16 NIV.

82: "One flesh" with Eve: Genesis 2:24.

83: *Book of Common Prayer*, Evening Prayers, Collect for Peace.

83: "Whoever wants to be my disciple": Mark 8:34.

83: "Every good and perfect gift": James 1:17.

83: "Hope deferred makes the heart sick": Proverbs 13:12.

84: Lydia: Acts 16:11–15.

85: "I have fought the good fight": 2 Timothy 4:7.

85: "Whatever your hand finds to do": Ecclesiastes 9:10.

85: Jonathan and David: 1 Samuel 20.

87: "Like a gold ring in a pig's snout": Proverbs 11:22.

87: Delilah: Judges 16.

Chapter 8: Think Great Thoughts

90: Elijah and Jezebel: 1 Kings 19: 1–18.

91: "Search me, God": Psalm 139:23.

91: "The mind controlled": Romans 8:6.

92: Kept in perfect peace: See Isaiah 26:3 KJV.

94: Like Adam and Eve: Genesis 3:8.

96: John Milton, *Paradise Lost*, Book One, lines 254–55.

98: Jeffrey Schwartz, *The Mind and the Brain: Neoplasticity and the Power of Mental Force.* New York: Harper Perennial, 2003, 325.

99: Joshua Bell: See www.boncherry.com/blog/2009/03/04/a-violinist-in-the-metro-subway/

100: "To what can I compare": Matthew 11:16–17 NIV.

Chapter 9: Feed Your Mind with Excellence

102: "Blessed are those": Psalm 1:1–3.

104: "Whatever is true": Philippians 4:8.

105: Jonathan Haidt, *The Happiness Hypothesis: Finding Modern Truth in Ancient Wisdom.* New York: Basic Books, 2005. See also http://www.virginia.edu/insideuva/2001/26/haidt.html and http://psycnet.apa.org/?fa=main.doiLanding&doi=10.1037/1522–3736.3.1.33c (accessed 3 September 2009).

105: Eugene Peterson, *Eat This Book: A Conversation in the Art of Spiritual Reading*. Grand Rapids: Eerdmans, 2006: quoted in Richard Foster, *Life With God: Reading the Bible for Spiritual Transformation*. New York: HarperOne, 2007, 1.

106: "These were the chiefs": Gen 36:15.

106: "The LORD is my shepherd": Psalm 23:1 KJV.

107: John Dewey: Quoted in David Marcum and Steven Smith, *Egonomics: What Makes Ego Our Greatest Asset (or Most Expensive Liability)*. New York: Simon & Schuster/Fireside, 2008, 168.

110: Ellen Langer, *Mindfulness*. New York: Da Capo Press, 1990, ch. 1.

111: Eva Hermann, "In Prison — Yet Free." Philadelphia: Tract Association of Friends, 1984. www.tractassociation.org/InPrisonYetFree.html (accessed 3 September 2009).

111: "God is light": 1 John 1:5.

112: Mark Twain: See www.inspirationalstories.com/1/181.html

112: "Therefore everyone who hears": Matthew 7:24–25.

113: "Love one another": John 13:34.

Chapter 10: Never Worry Alone

115: "Peace, be still": Mark 4:39 KJV.

116: "For the Spirit God gave us": 2 Timothy 1:7.

116: "In this world you have tribulation": John 16:33 NASB.

116: Everett Ferguson, *Backgrounds of Early Christianity*, 3rd Edition. Grand Rapids: Eerdmans, 2003.

117: "My peace I give you": John 14:27.

117: Daniel Goleman, *Emotional Intelligence: Why It Can Matter More Than IQ*. New York: Bantam Books, 1994.

118: Edward M. Hallowell, *Worry: Hope and Help for a Common Condition*. New York: Ballantine Books, 1998.

119: "There is no fear in love": 1 John 4:18.

122: "Is anyone afraid or faint-hearted?": Deuteronomy 20:8.

123: "Which transcends all understanding": Philippians 4:7.

124: "Instead of worrying, pray": Philippians 4:6–7 *The Message*.

125: "Out of your bellies will flow": John 7:38 paraphrased.

Chapter 11: Let Your Talking Flow into Praying

132: Richard Foster, *Prayer*. New York: HarperOne, 1992, xi.

133: Mark Twain: Quoted in *Homiletics* 19, no. 1, January–February 2007, 50.

133: "Where can I go from your Spirit?": Psalm 139:7–8.

134: "Looking up to pray": John 11:41 paraphrased.

134: "Father, I thank you that you have heard me": John 11:41.

135: "Go on up, you baldhead!": 2 Kings 2:23 NIV.

136: "In everything": Philippians 4:6 NIV.

136: Shel Silverstein, *A Light in the Attic*. New York: HarperCollins, 1981.

136: "Nevertheless, not my will but yours be done": Mark 14:36 paraphrased.

Chapter 12: Temptation: How Not to Get Hooked

138: "No temptation has seized": 1 Corinthians 10:13 NIV.

138: Potiphar's wife: Genesis 39.

139: "Do not quench the Spirit": 1 Thessalonians 5:19 NASB.

139: "Committing adultery": See Matthew 5:28.

140: "I made a covenant with my eyes": Job 31:1 NIV.

141: "The joy of the Lord is your strength": Nehemiah 8:10.

141: "Rejoice in the Lord always": Philippians 4:4 NASB.

142: "Deliver us from evil": Matthew 6:13 KJV, NASB.

Chapter 13: Recognize Your Primary Flow-Blocker

143: *USA Today*: From a series of articles published in February 2003.

144: Study on incompetence: Source unknown.

145: Cornelius Plantinga, *Not the Way It's Supposed to Be: A Breviary of Sin*. Grand Rapids: Eerdmans, 1995, 2–3.

145: Eddie Izzard: Standup routine, date unknown.

146: Augustine and Pelagius: See further, for example, in Earle E. Cairns, *Christianity through the Centuries: A History of the Christian Church*, 3rd Edition. Grand Rapids: Zondervan, 1996, 130–31.

146: Richard Lovelace, *Dynamics of Spiritual Life: An Evangelical Theology of Renewal*. Downers Grove, IL: InterVarsity Press, 1979, 99ff.

147: Michael Mangis, *Signature Sins: Taming Our Wayward Hearts*. Downers Grove, IL: InterVarsity Press, 2008.

148: Sherlock Holmes: See the novels by Sir Arthur Conan Doyle.

148: Richard Rohr, *The Enneagram: A Christian Perspective*. New York: Crossroad, 2001.

149: "He must increase": John 3:30 KJV.

149: Simon Magnus: Acts 8:9–25.

150: Parable about the three servants: Matthew 25:14–30.

151: Winston Churchill, on Clement Atlee: Quoted in Alec Douglas-Home, *The Way the Wind Blows*. New York: Fontana, 1976.

151: Winston Churchill, on Lady Astor: Quoted in Consuelo Vanderbilt Balsan, *The Glitter and the Gold*. Maidstone, Kent, UK: George Mann Books, 1953.

151: "How good and pleasant it is": Psalm 133:1.

155: Jesus warned about people: Luke 6:41–42.

Chapter 14: When You Find Yourself Out of the Flow, Jump Back In

156: Carol Tavris and Elliot Aronson, *Mistakes Were Made (But Not by Me): Why We Justify Foolish Beliefs*. Wilmington, MA: Houghton Mifflin/ Mariner, 2008.

157: David Marcum and Steven Smith, *Egonomics: What Makes Ego Our Greatest Asset (or Most Expensive Liability)*. New York: Simon & Schuster/Fireside, 2008, 41.

159: "Who can discern their own errors?": Psalm 19:12.

160: "Did not know that the LORD": Judges 16:20.

161: "Call evil good and good evil": Isaiah 5:20.

161: Madame Guyon: Quoted in Richard Foster, *Prayer: Finding the Heart's True Home*. New York: HarperOne, 1992, 30.

165: "You are the man!": 2 Samuel 12:7.

166: "If someone is caught in a sin": Galatians 6:1.

166: Frank Laubach: Cited by Dallas Willard in personal communication.

Chapter 15: Try Going Off the Deep End with God

172: "When you pray, go into your room": Matthew 6:6.

172: Abraham Kuyper: Cited by Richard Mouw in a public address.

174: "Bless the LORD, O my soul": Psalm 103:1 KJV.

174: "Why are you downcast": Psalms 42:5, 11; 43:5.

174: "As he was praying, the heavens opened": Luke 3:21 TLB.

174: "The news about him spread": Luke 5:15–16.

174: "One of those days Jesus went out": Luke 6:12.

174: "When Jesus heard what had happened": Matthew 14:13.

174: "While it was still dark, Jesus got up": Mark 1:35, 38.

175: "Satan has asked to sift all of you": Luke 22:31.

175: "Jesus went out as usual": Luke 22:39–42.

175: "As he was praying": Luke 9:29.

175: "God's Spirit is right alongside us": Romans 8:26–27 *The Message*.

176: Will Derske, *The Rule of St. Benedict for Beginners*. Collegeville, MN: Liturgical Press, 2003.

177: "Eat their own filth": 2 Kings 18:27 NIV.

177: "O LORD Almighty, God of Israel": Isaiah 37:14–17.

177: "I can do all things through Him": Philippians 4:13 NASB.

179: "The LORD bless you": Numbers 6:24–26 NRSV.

180: "Abba, Father": Romans 8:15; Galatians 4:6.

Chapter 16: Make Life-Giving Relationships a Top Priority

182: "The fellowship of the Spirit": See, for example, 2 Corinthians 6:14; 13:14; Philippians 2:1; 1 John 1:6.

183: Robert Putnam, *Bowling Alone: The Collapse and Revival of American Community*. New York: Simon & Schuster, 2000, 332.

183: "It isn't good for man": Genesis 2:18 TLB.

183: "Being rooted and established": Ephesians 3:17.

183: Donald Winnicott, *The Maturational Processes and the Facilitating Environment*. London: Hogarth Press, 1960.

186: "The only exercise I get": Source unknown. Also attributed to nineteenth-century U.S. Senator Chauncey Depew.

186: "Anyone who does not love": 1 John 3:14.

187: "You, my brothers and sisters": Galatians 5:13.

187: "Let us consider how we may": Hebrew 10:24–25.

188: Putnam, *Bowling Alone*.

190: "Satisfy us in the morning": Psalm 90:14.

190: "The joy of the LORD is your strength": Nehemiah 8:10.

190: "A twenty-year study of more than 4,700 people": "Infected with Happiness," *San Francisco Chronicle*, 5 December 2008, A1, 14.

192: Teilhard de Chardin: Quoted in Alan Loy McGinnis, *The Friendship Factor: How to Get Closer to the People You Care For*. Minneapolis: Augsburg Press, 1979, 192.

Chapter 17: Be Human

195: "A man after his own heart": 1 Samuel 13:14.

195: Anne Lamott, *Traveling Mercies: Some Thoughts on Faith*. New York: Doubleday/Pantheon, 1999.

197: "With glad and sincere hearts": Acts 2:46.

197: "Accept one another, then": Romans 15:7.

198: Henri J. M. Nouwen, *The Road to Daybreak: A Spiritual Journey*. New York: Doubleday/Image Books, 1990.

199: "Confess your sins to one another": James 5:16 NASB.

199: "Bridegroom of blood": Exodus 4:26.

199: "Curse God and die!": Job 2:9.

200: "When the disciple Peter": See Matthew 14:28–31; John 18:10; John 13:36–38 and 18:15–18; Matthew 16:22–23.

201: M. Scott Peck, *Further Along the Road Less Traveled: The Unending Journey Toward Spiritual Growth*. New York: Simon & Schuster/Touchstone, 1993, 211.

202: "Just as I am, without one plea": Words by Charlotte Elliott; tune by William B. Bradbury.

Chapter 18: Find a Few Difficult People to Help You Grow

203: George Bernard Shaw: Source unknown.

204: "You're familiar with the old written law": Matthew 5:43–48 *The Message*.

205: Jill Taylor, *My Stroke of Insight: A Brain Scientist's Personal Journey.* New York: Viking Press, 2008, 74.

206: "When someone gives you a hard time": Matthew 5:44–45 *The Message.*

207: "Do not grieve the Holy Spirit": Ephesians 4:30–31.

208: "Life-giving quarter-second": Daniel Goleman, *Emotional Intelligence: Why It Can Matter More Than IQ.* New York: Bantam Books, 1994.

208: "In your anger do not sin": Ephesians 4:26–27.

209: "You have heard that it is said": Matthew 5:38–39.

210: "If anyone forces you to go with them": Matthew 5:41.

211: Charles Lamb: Source unknown.

212: "But Benjamin is so young": Genesis 44:30–34 paraphrased.

Chapter 19: Let God Flow in Your Work

218: Dennis Bakke, Joy at Work: *A Revolutionary Approach to Fun on the Job.* Seattle: PVG, 2006.

218: Eugene H. Peterson, *Working the Angles: The Shape of Pastoral Integrity.* Grand Rapids: Eerdmans, 1987, 67.

219: "Six days you shall labor": Exodus 20:9, 11.

219: "See, I have chosen Bezalel": Exodus 31:2–5.

220: Marcus Buckingham: See Marcus Buckingham and Donald O. Clifton, *Now Discover Your Strengths.* New York: Simon & Schuster/Free Press, 2001.

220: "From strength to strength": Psalm 84:7.

220: Dorothy Sayers, *Creed or Chaos: Why Christians Must Choose Either Dogma or Disaster (Or, Why It Really Does Matter What You Believe).* New York: Harcourt, Brace & Jovanovich, 1949, 53.

222: "Rule" and "dominion" over the earth: Genesis 1:26, 28 TNIV, KJV.

222: "Unless the LORD builds the house": Psalm 127:1 NRSV.

223: Marcus Aurelius: Quoted in Will Derske, *The Rule of Benedict for Beginners.* Collegeville, MN: Liturgical Press, 2003, 17.

Chapter 20: Let Your Work Honor God

224: William Zinsser, *On Writing Well: An Informal Guide to Writing Nonfiction*, 2nd Edition. New York: HarperCollins, 1980, 176.

225: Andy Chan: Personal communication.

225: "Don't just do the minimum": Colossians 3:22–25 *The Message.*

225: "Whatever your hand finds to do": Ecclesiastes 9:10.

225: "Now old and well advanced": Genesis 24:1 NIV.

227: N. T. Wright: Lecture at InterVarsity Conference on Human Flourishing, December 2008. See http://thesuburbanchristian.blogspot.com/2008/12/tom-wright-on-human-flourishing.html (accessed 21 September 2009).

228: Robert Bellah, *Habits of the Heart.* Berkeley: University of California Press, 1985.

229: "When a farmer plows for planting": Isaiah 28:24–26, 29 NIV.

229: Miroslav Volf, *Work in the Spirit: Toward a Theology of Work*. Eugene, OR: Wipf & Stock, 2001, 114.

230: "The Son of Man did not come": Matthew 20:28; Mark 10:45.

230: "Went and traded with them": Matthew 25:16 NASB.

231: Martin Luther: Quoted in Leland Ryken, *Work and Leisure in Christian Perpsective*. Portland, OR: Multnomah, 1987, 130.

Chapter 21: You Have to Go through Exile before You Come Back Home

232: Jonathan Haidt, *The Happiness Hypothesis: Finding Modern Truth in Ancient Wisdom*. New York: Basic Books, 2005.

233: Robert C. Roberts, *Spiritual Emotions: A Psychology of Christian Virtues*. Grand Rapids: Eerdmans, 2007, 148ff.

235: Ernest Hemingway: Source unknown.

236: Meng Tzu: Quoted in Haidt, *The Happiness Hypothesis*, 135.

237: "The LORD was with Joseph": Genesis 39:2.

237: "We know that in all things": Romans 8:28.

237: No temptation is given to people: See 1 Corinthians 10:13.

237: They could command a mountain: See Mark 11:23.

238: Thomas Merton, *Seeds of Contemplation*. Boston: Shambala, 2003, 74.

239: "Mourn with those who mourn": Romans 12:15.

240: Joni Eareckson Tada: See, for example, *Joni: An Unforgettable Story* (Grand Rapids: Zondervan, 1976) and *A Lifetime of Wisdom: Filled with God's Precious Rubies* (Grand Rapids: Zondervan, 2009).

240: Bill Dallas, *Lessons from San Quentin: Everything I Needed to Know about Life I Learned in Prison*. Wheaton, IL: Tyndale, 2009.

241: Søren Kierkegaard, *Christian Discourses*, translated by Walter Lowrie. 1941; reprint, Princeton: Princeton University Press, 1971.

242: All creation is groaning for redemption: See Romans 8:22.

242: Julian of Norwich, *Revelations of Divine Love*, ch. 27, Revelation 13.

Chapter 22: Ask for a Mountain

246: "Whoever would come after me": Matthew 16:24; Mark 8:34; Luke 9:23.

248: When the scouts returned: See Numbers 14:3–4.

248: "We can certainly do it": Numbers 13:30.

248: "I was forty years old when Moses": Joshua 14:7–8.

248: Martin Seligman, *Learned Optimism: How to Change Your Mind and Your Life*. New York: Simon & Schuster/Free Press, 1998, 7ff.

248: "Faith-filled people": Seligman, *Learned Optimism*, ch. 1.

249: Paul W. Brand and Philip Yancey, *Fearfully and Wonderfully Made*. Grand Rapids: Zondervan, 1980.

250: "So here I am today, eighty-five years old!": Joshua 14:10–12.

250: "We saw the descendants of Anakites there": Numbers 13:33 paraphrased.

250: Joshua became the new leader: See Deuteronomy 34:9; Joshua 1:1–3.

250: Marian Diamond, "Optimism about the Aging Brain," *Aging Today*, May-June 1998. See http://www.asaging.org/at/at–193/diamond.html (accessed 21 September 2009).

252: Rich Stearns, *The Hole in Our Gospel: What Does God Expect of Us? The Answer That Changed My Life and Might Just Change the World.* Nashville: Thomas Nelson, 2009.

252: "All the children of the world": From "Jesus Loves the Little Children." Words by C. Herbert Woolston; tune by George F. Root.

252: "Shine like stars": Philippians 2:15 NIV.

253: "In the beginning was the Word": John 1:1, 14 KJV.

The Me I Want to Be DVD Group Study

Becoming God's Best Version of You

John Ortberg

If God has a perfect vision for your life, why does spiritual growth seem so difficult? Pastor and bestselling author John Ortberg has some intriguing answers to that question, and he has organized his thoughts and God's words into a straightforward and timely guide for living your best life in *The Me I Want to Be*.

This DVD group study will show how God's perfect vision for you starts with a powerful promise. All those who trust in God "will be like a tree planted by the water that sends out its roots by the stream. The tree does not fear when heat comes; its leaves are always green. It has no worries in a year of drought and never fails to bear fruit" (Jeremiah 17:7-8).

John Ortberg urges you to recognize your brokenness, understand that God is the project manager, and follow God's directions. He also helps you gauge your spiritual health and measure the gap between where you are now and where God intends you to be.

Learn to be a thriving and flourishing Christ-follower as you study these five sessions.

The Me I Want to Be sessions include:

1. Discovering the Spirit
2. Renewing My Mind
3. Redeeming My Time
4. Deepening My Relationships
5. Transforming My Experience

DVD: 978-0-310-32078-4
Participant's Guide: 978-0-310-32079-1
Curriculum Kit: 978-0-310-32081-4

ZONDERVAN®
.com

Share Your Thoughts

With the Author: Your comments will be forwarded to the author when you send them to *zauthor@zondervan.com*.

With Zondervan: Submit your review of this book by writing to *zreview@zondervan.com*.

Free Online Resources at
www.zondervan.com

Zondervan AuthorTracker: Be notified whenever your favorite authors publish new books, go on tour, or post an update about what's happening in their lives at www.zondervan.com/authortracker.

Daily Bible Verses and Devotions: Enrich your life with daily Bible verses or devotions that help you start every morning focused on God. Visit www.zondervan.com/newsletters.

Free Email Publications: Sign up for newsletters on Christian living, academic resources, church ministry, fiction, children's resources, and more. Visit www.zondervan.com/newsletters.

Zondervan Bible Search: Find and compare Bible passages in a variety of translations at www.zondervanbiblesearch.com.

Other Benefits: Register yourself to receive online benefits like coupons and special offers, or to participate in research.

ZONDERVAN®

ZONDERVAN.com/
AUTHORTRACKER
follow your favorite authors

WORLDVIEWS

WORLDVIEWS
Crosscultural Explorations of Human Beliefs

NINIAN SMART

CHARLES SCRIBNER'S SONS
NEW YORK

Copyright © 1983 Charles Scribner's Sons

Library of Congress Cataloging in Publication Data

Smart, Ninian, 1927–
    Worldviews, crosscultural explorations of human
beliefs.
    Bibliography: p.
    Includes index.
    1. Religions.   2. Ideology.   I. Title.
BL80.2.S62   1983   291   82-16877
ISBN 0-684-17811-7
ISBN 0-684-17812-5 (pbk.)

1 3 5 7 9 11 13 15 17 19   F/C   20 18 16 14 12 10 8 6 4 2
1 3 5 7 9 11 13 15 17 19   F/P   20 18 16 14 12 10 8 6 4 2

Printed in the United States of America.

TO MARILIS

Preface

I HOPE this book will be a good introduction to the modern study of religion. To study human beliefs and the feelings and practices which accompany them we need to go beyond traditional religions, even though much of this book is about how we might get to know them better. So I have given the book a rather broader scope than might be thought usual for one who writes out of the tradition of the history and philosophy of religion. In brief I pay attention to all the major forces of belief and feeling which animate our world.

This book is for students of all ages and explorers of all walks of life. I hope it may be a stepping stone to richer knowledge and clearer understanding. Mostly it is about knowing other people; such knowledge is at the heart of humanistic education and the social sciences.

I owe a lot to students and colleagues in Lancaster, England, and in Santa Barbara, California. I have benefited especially from teaching large classes of often eager students in California, for whom the study of religions and the analysis of worldviews is for the most part new. I learned much from this experience; but I have also learned from the many good discussions I have had with M.A. students, especially in Lancaster, often fresh from their own experiences in various countries and occupations.

I am grateful to Steven Vertovec for helping with the preparation of the manuscript. I am also grateful for the encouragement and advice of Edith Poor and Helen McInnis of Charles Scribner's Sons, and for the happiness of working again with a publishing house which commissioned my longest book, *The Religious Experience of Mankind*, to which this is a sort of young companion.

NINIAN SMART

Tremezzo, Lago di Como, Italy

Contents

WORLDVIEWS

Introduction

WE know more about each other today than we have ever known before. Among the branches of learning and science which have formed this knowledge, the study of religion has a central place. As an educational experience it provides fine training for our world. The reason is simple: human beings do things for the most part because it pays them to do so, or because they fear to do otherwise, or because they believe in doing them. The modern study of religion is about the last of these motives: the systems of belief which, through symbols and actions, mobilize the feelings and wills of human beings. In addition to examining traditional faiths, the modern study of religion also looks at secular symbols and ideologies— at nationalism, Marxism, democracy—which often rival religion and yet in an important sense are themselves religious. Thus, the modern study of religion helps to illuminate worldviews, both traditional and secular, which are such an engine of social and moral continuity and change; and therefore it explores beliefs and feelings, and tries to understand what exists inside the heads of people. What people believe is an important aspect of reality whether or not what they believe is true.

The English language does not have a term to refer to both traditional religions and ideologies; the best expression is perhaps *worldviews*. In this book I shall use *worldviews* in a general sense to refer to both religion and ideologies, and also to refer specifically to secular ideologies.

With electrons or moons or eggs or chestnut trees there is no need to understand what they think. Science does not have to worry about any conscious insides that such things might have. They can be treated just as physical objects (although as it turns out they are composed mainly of space). But with human beings things are otherwise. Why did Caesar cross the Rubicon? What were the roots of the Iranian Revolution? Why did the Holocaust occur? Why is Roderick happy? The answers to such questions must make some reference to what folks feel, the ideas they have, the structures of belief of their society—in a word, to human consciousness. The study of religions and secular worldviews—what I have termed "worldview analysis"—tries to depict the history and nature of the beliefs and symbols which form a deep part of the structure of human consciousness and society.

This modern study of religion is not much more than a century old, although its roots lie in the last decades of the eighteenth century and the period known as the European Enlightenment. For most of human history, people have had rather rudimentary ideas about their own and other people's beliefs. Often imprisoned within a culture or a credo, they have not had the desire or the chance to venture on a more detached and sensitive exploration of religion. Too much tied up with their own concerns, they have often found it easier to dismiss the faiths and feelings of others as heretical, devilish, ignorant, or antisocial, and this has been so especially in the West. Yet paradoxically, the modern study of religion started in the West, and through comparative research, historical inquiry, and a broadening of sympathies this study has opened up the entire sweep of religious experience. The study has gone far beyond its Western origins. Important work on religions is being done in India, China, Japan, Africa, and elsewhere. The modern study of religion is becoming global. This is natural. Our contemporary world is now bound together tightly. We live in the age of the global city.

The most compelling pictures in our times are those magical photographs of the Earth, taken from halfway to the moon: the shining blue ball bandaged lightly in its atmospheric wool, the dim shapes of great continents showing darkly through the gaps. Ours is no longer the wide, wide world of older days, nor is Earth any more just a fecund, soil-clad floor out of which life emerges, as our ancestors might have pictured it. The images of the Earth we now have tell us that we live together on a little ball, bound together, and to it, in a web of air and food. And the very cleverness which took men so far aloft to take those photographs also allows us to send a missile to our enemies in half an hour, or to fly for fun to the farthest continent in hardly more than a day. If, that is, we have the money for missiles and fun: most people do not.

The fact that human civilization is now so tightly knit that its every crisis sends ripples around the globe, is one reason why the modern study of religion, with its emphasis on understanding rather than preaching, is so important. Even if we do not agree with one another it is vital that we should at least understand one another. We have a long way to go in achieving this understanding, however; the importance of the modern study of religion has not, on the whole, penetrated fully to people's consciousnesses—whether in academic life, in government, in the media, or in business.

There are two reasons why this is so: one has to do with older conceptions of what it means to study religion; and the other has to do with the compartments into which knowledge is carved. The heart of the modern study of religion is the analysis and comparison of worldviews; from this broader point of view, the problems caused by the older images of religion and by the compartmentalization of religious studies can readily be seen. But before coming to that let me say a word about what I mean by "the modern study of religion."

The modern study of religion takes religion as an aspect of life and tries to understand it historically and crossculturally. It applies the insights of various disciplines—such as psychology, anthropology, sociology, and linguistics—to illuminate its dynamics. It is parallel to, and sometimes overlaps with, political science and economics. We are all to some degree or other political animals, because power is a fact of life; and we are all economic beings, for financial exchange is a fact of life. But we are all also religious beings, for orientation to life is itself a fact of life; and we are all in one way or another so oriented. We are not, of course, necessarily religious in any formal or traditional sense. Many people are agnostics, atheists, nonobservers of customary tradition. But whether we have spelled it out to ourselves or not, each one of us has a worldview, which forms a background to the lives we lead. The modern study of religion has as one main focus the exploration of such worldviews: particularly the more widely held belief-systems and especially those of a traditional kind, such as varieties of Christianity or Buddhism.

A Native American proverb says, "Never judge a man 'till you have walked a mile in his moccasins." Much of what the modern study of religion involves is such moccasin-walking. It is a kind of voyage into other people's and our own living hearts, a travel into the sentiments and ideas that animate people, often at the deepest level. It means travel too into the past, swimming upstream along the river of time, trying to reach the mind of Paul or Buddhaghosa or Confucius. It is in itself a noble and imaginative task, to find out what the world looks like from another person's or society's point of view. It is difficult, though, and that is one reason why I shall spell out some of the ways it can be made easier.

The modern study of religion is not perceived by most people very clearly as yet, for they usually and not surprisingly identify the study of religion with traditional patterns—learning catechisms, going to seminary, studying the texts of the faith, or training to be a minister, priest, or rabbi. Such traditional confessional (as we may call it) study continues, and is necessary if traditions are to maintain themselves. But it is not the same as the modern study I have described. It does not pretend to be crosscultural. Its main concerns are with the truth of one's own faith, not with the understanding of other worldviews. It starts from the assumptions of faith. It does not need to be dispassionate.

People thus often think of the religious expert—Billy Graham, Pope John Paul II, the Dalai Lama, a seminary professor, a learned rabbi—as a spokesperson for a particular faith. And that is fine if what is wanted is an expression of faith or opinion starting from the particular tradition to which the spokesperson belongs. But such persons are part of the traditions for which they speak: they are part of what the modern student of religion seeks to understand. They are themselves part of the data. Thus, though the Pope is the authority for Catholics, others may know more about religions, including Christianity, than he does. For example, it is my job, as a religious scholar, to understand religion; it is his, as a religious leader, to *be* religion.

If older conceptions of religious study as preparation for preaching get in the way of people's understanding the significance of the modern study of religion, so does the compartmentalization of knowledge. Thus, a student goes to one department to study Christianity, typically, but to study Marxism she goes to another; to study the social meaning of Judaism she goes to one department, but to study the social meaning of Australian aboriginal religion she goes to another; to study modern existentialism she goes to one department, but to study Zen she goes to another. The study of worldviews is not only crosscultural, but crossdisciplinary; it occurs in the contexts of religion, political science, sociology, anthropology, philosophy, Oriental studies, and others.

If a visitor from another world were to come down and hover invisibly over our planet he would see religions and ideologies in conflict, and he would see people moved by symbols both modern and traditional. Would such a visitor so easily distinguish the Olympic stadium from the temple, or the hammer and sickle from the Islamic crescent, or the psychiatrist from the priest? Would he carve up the world the way we do in the modern West? Such a visitor, reporting back home to some far galaxy, might say: "These humans have all kinds of orientations to the world, and all kinds of symbols, and all kinds of ways of training their minds and feelings. Some they call religions, when there is some kind of looking upward to a heavenly sky or inward into the depths of their being. Mostly these ways of thinking and acting have had a very long history (by their standards), up to three or four thousand years."

And if that is what a dispassionate observer would say, does it not call in question our compartments? The modern study of religion is beginning—rightly—to look toward breaking these down, and analyzing all worldviews and human symbols together, whether they are traditional or not.

Thus, a main part of the modern study of religion may be called "worldview analysis"—the attempt to describe and understand human worldviews, especially those that have had widespread influence—ranging from varieties of Christianity and Buddhism to the more politically oriented systems of Islam and Marxism, and from ancient religions and philosophies such as Platonism and Confucianism to modern new religions in Africa and America. To see how they work we must relate ideas to symbols and to practices, so that worldview analysis is not merely a matter of listing beliefs. A Christian's belief in Christ is a matter of experiencing him and partaking of him in the communion service; a Buddhist's belief in the impermanence of things is a matter of seeing this impermanence revealed through meditation; the Marxist's belief in the labor theory of value is a matter of readiness to act against what she perceives as exploitation. In a word, belief, consciousness, and practice are bound together.

An educated person should know about and have a feel for many things, but perhaps the most important is to have an understanding of some of the chief worldviews which have shaped, and are now shaping human culture and action. It is for this purpose that I here try to present some of the main elements and themes of the modern study of religion.

But beyond knowing the geography of human consciousness, a person may wish to explore his own orientations, to try to articulate his own beliefs, to reflect about life and the world: to form or clarify the basis of his own worldview. Such a goal goes beyond the comparative study of worldviews: it is itself a quest. This too can form a living part of the modern study of religion, for once we have traveled into other minds and times we may want to return to our own lives. What do these symbols mean to me? Toward which orientation should I set my own soul's face?

Here the student of worldview analysis becomes the self-explorer, the quester. As we shall see, there can be a fruitful interaction between quest and analysis. But initially the modern study of religion is less involved in judgment than description. And that itself is an exciting but difficult task. And if, as we have suggested, we should not judge a person until we have walked a mile in his moccasins, then we must embark first upon the description of religions and religion. However, that in turn requires us to reflect about ways and means, about methods and lines of approach.

In chapter 1 I shall give a more detailed map of the study of religion and worldviews. In chapter 2, so that we may bear in mind the general character of worldviews, I shall present an inventory of the major faiths and belief-systems found in today's world and in the past. In chapters 3 through 8 I shall discuss some of the theories and themes arising out of various disciplines used in the study of religion. These six chapters correspond to the six dimensions of religion, to which I shall come in a moment. In chapter 9 I shall consider what is happening at the developing edge of human belief and practice, and on into the future. In the last chapter I consider what the individual can do to continue his exploration of worldview analysis or to carry further his own quest.

The model of six dimensions of religion (which I have described in *The Religious Experience of Mankind*, chapter 1, and elsewhere) is a useful device for trying to get a rounded picture of a religion. The six dimensions are the doctrinal, the mythic, the ethical, the ritual, the experiential, and the social.

1. Doctrinal. A religion typically has a system of doctrines. Christianity holds that the world depends on God, that God is Three in One—namely, Father, Son, and Holy Spirit—that Christ is both God and man, and so on. These are part of the doctrinal dimension of Christianity. They tell Christians about the nature of God and his relationship to the created world and the human race.

2. Mythic. Typically a religion has a story or stories to tell. But they are not just any old stories—they are ones which quiver with special or sacred meaning. In the field of religion such stories are called myths. The word does not imply, as it does in everyday speech, that such stories are not true, just "myths"; but often "myth" is used technically to refer to stories of the gods or other significant beings who have access to an invisible world beyond ours. Thus, the mythic dimension of Christianity focuses on the story of the Fall, when the first man and woman alienated themselves from God and were driven from their earthly paradise; the subsequent contracts between God and the people of Israel as part of his plan to save the human race from its state of alienation; the coming of Christ and his death and resurrection; the beginning of the Church which carries forward the work of salvation; and the promise that Christ will come again to earth to wind up human history in a great climax of judgment and bliss.

3. Ethical. A religion has an ethical dimension. Believers are enjoined to observe certain rules and percepts. Thus, in Christianity Jesus commanded his followers to love one another and to love their enemies. There are also the commandments derived from the Old Testament, which forbid killing, adultery, stealing, and so forth.

These three dimensions—the doctrinal, mythical, and ethical—form a web of belief, but the beliefs are only truly understood in the context of experience and practice. So in Christianity, doctrines about God are not just about some neutral and remote being who created the universe; God is a being who is actively worshipped. Christians pray to him, and he brings his influence to bear upon a person's inner life (such influence being referred to usually as "grace"). The story of his dealings with humanity implies that somehow the Christian can identify with the story by taking part in certain acts and practices: for instance, in the Lord's Supper or Mass, the Christian is involved in a replay of the last events of Jesus's life, and absorbs his life-giving power through partaking of the bread and the wine, which present afresh the body and blood of the Savior. Thus myth is often conjoined to ritual acts which replay them and so convey their meaning to believers in a concrete way.

4. Ritual.   So, typically a religion has a ritual dimension. Christianity, for example, usually involves its followers in acts of worship, praying, singing hymns, hearing the appointed passages from the Bible, and such sacraments (rituals through which God's grace is conveyed) as baptism and communion (the Lord's Supper, Eucharist, Mass, Liturgy—different branches of Christianity use different words).

5. Experiential.   Ritual helps to express feelings—awe and wonder, for instance—and can itself provide a context of dramatic experience, when the believer feels immediately and strikingly the presence of God. In Christianity, there is often emphasis on the experience of conversion, or being "born again"; while the monastic tradition (especially important in Catholic and Eastern Orthodox Christianity) is often the means of nurturing the experience of inner illumination in which the mystic feels a kind of union with Christ. Such experiences are part of the *experiential* dimension of religion.

6. Social.   Any tradition needs some kind of organization in order to perpetuate itself. It thus embeds itself in society. In Christianity the churches provide a strong *social* dimension.

For reasons of continuity in the overall argument, I shall, in the various chapters mentioned above, deal with the dimensions in a different order than listed here. I'll first discuss the experiential dimension, since experience has played and still plays such a central part in the history of religion. Consider Paul's conversion on the Damascus road, and the experiences of the risen Christ among the other apostles; consider the light which lit up the Buddha's mind under the Bo Tree; consider the tremendous, even painful experiences of Muhammad while receiving revelations from Allah; look to the lives of mystics and prophets and others in a variety of faiths. All these testify to the way experiences can dynamize religion and so dynamize the world. Thus a whole Islamic civilization had its roots in Muhammad's experiences, a whole Buddhist civilization in the Buddha's enlightenment, a whole Christian civilization in the experiences of the Hebrew Prophets and of the early Church. There were many other factors indeed, but the experiential dimension had an explosive and creative part to play. So in chapter 3 we will explore the varieties of religious experience and problems about their power and meaning.

In chapter 4 we will see how myth works and how it remains in secular form a powerful ingredient in today's world, as human beings search for new identities and find them partly in the story of their past. In chapter 5 we shall see how religious doctrines are formed, in interaction with myth and experience, and how they relate to other areas of human knowledge such as modern science. In chapter 6 we will learn how moral values themselves reflect the understanding of the world found in vision, story, and doctrine, and how far we can see a universal ethic among the great traditions. In chapter 7 we turn to the ritual dimension, and the way symbols are used, while in chapter 8 we shall see how religion operates socially.

In these explorations there will be a chance to see how the modern study of religion can throw light on theories of the individual and of society. For we are able to look upon such theories from a crosscultural perspective: Does Freud's account of religion work for Buddhism? Can the Marxist analysis of religion successfully explain the varieties of religious forms and the persistence of religion in the modern world? What is the relation between religion and the rise of capitalism? To what extent do theories of religion depend upon an estimate of the truth of religion? Many questions flow from the writings of some of the great thinkers of modern times—Sigmund Freud, Karl Marx, Rudolf Bultmann, Mircea Eliade, Max Weber,

Carl Gustav Jung, Ludwig Wittgenstein. We may only touch upon these figures and themes, but at least we shall have opened up perspectives on a strange and enchanting landscape, beckoning us forward to further thoughts about the enigmas of our existence and the forces which drive human processes onward.

It may seem strange that it is possible to illuminate so much of modern life and theory by beginning from the study of traditional religions. Many people think that religion, for all its spurts of resurgence here and there, is on the way out—destined in the end to wind up as fairy tales. But it happens that symbols often work most powerfully when they are unseen and unrecognized. The historian of religion is sensitive to the way symbols help to shape our existence, and is therefore able to perceive them more easily in our daily world. This is a perception he or she shares with the depth psychologist. Thus, if we hear it said that "modern men" no longer need religion, we need to see what kind of loaded notion *modernity* is. Doesn't it carry with it some kind of myth? Isn't there the suggestion that we have entered a new era in which science and technology will help to solve our problems, leaving behind the superstitions of the past? Doesn't it dress itself in lasers and rockets and glittering machines? Doesn't its fantasy life flow in science fiction? Doesn't it, in its myth of history, suggest the superiority of those nations and cultures that can devise the best machines and systems of management? Such a notion as *modernity* has much of the force and power of older religious symbols, but the apostles of secular modernity would not thank me for saying so. They have made a judgment about religion, a negative one. In fact, by drawing a line between the secular and the sacred they have already made a value judgment (secular is modern and good, religion is old and bad). So they feel that calling the cult of modernity a kind of religious attitude, as I have just done above, undermines and challenges the very distinction which helps to give them a sense of superiority. Nevertheless, it may be illuminating for us to see how the symbol of modernity works, and in this the historian of religion will have some insights to share. Thus it is that the modern study of religion (and note, by the way, how I too am implicitly calling on the values of modernity) starts from the old in order to throw light upon the new.

But in speaking of the modern study of religion we should not attempt to create a closed compartment. It is convenient to think of worldview analysis as a field of study, but it must by necessity over-lap with many other disciplines and approaches. Already in my list of famous names I have hinted that it overlaps with depth psychol-ogy (Freud and Jung), economic history (Marx and Weber), New Testament studies (Bultmann), the history of religions (Eliade), and philosophy (Wittgenstein). But equally we could look to literature—you can learn much about worldviews through Shakespeare and Dostoyevsky and Steinbeck; or to art history—you can learn much through Giotto and Indian sculpture; or to music. The symbolic life of human beings ranges across the humanities and the social sci-ences. The modern study of religion presents a perspective on the whole of human life.

So let us then accept the invitation to enter our world, and see it with new and yet old eyes.

Exploring Religion and Analyzing Worldviews

WHAT I have called the modern study of religion has evolved from a number of dramatic shifts in thinking and knowledge occurring mainly in the last century.

Developments in the Nineteenth Century

The nineteenth century saw the vast spread of Western colonial conquest. It brought Europe into ever closer ties with the peoples of the East and the southern hemisphere. This was a great spur to scholarship in Asian and other languages. These languages helped unlock the religious treasures of Islam, of India, of Buddhism, of the Chinese tradition, and of Africa. People in the West could begin to think about the place of Christianity, and for that matter Judaism, among the great religions of the world. Already the material for the comparative study of religion was being accumulated.

The nineteenth century also saw the publication of Darwin's controversial theory of evolution. This new way of thinking about the origin of the human race challenged earlier Western beliefs about the way mankind was created by God. It called into question the literal truth of Genesis. But more, it suggested that not only had the human race evolved, gradually and over a long period of time, but that socially and in other ways it was still evolving. There were a number of new theories suggesting ways in which religion itself had evolved. Such theories were backed up by data collected by the new science of anthropology, the study of small-scale societies. By supposing that the cultural development of (say) Australian aborigines corresponded to a similar stage of development in an earlier phase of human evolution, anthropologists thought they could chart the history of human development in general—and, in this case, the history of religion.

Anthropologists hypothesized that humans graduated from animism (belief in living powers dwelling in material and natural objects), to polytheism (belief in many personalized gods), to monotheism (belief in one God), and maybe beyond, to atheism. Most of these theories are now no longer thought to be valid, partly because they often reflect the assumption of Western culture that it has achieved the highest stage of development and achievement—a possibly arrogant value judgment rather than a scientific diagnosis. Still, ideas of cultural evolution greatly influenced speculations about patterns of similarity among the myths, symbols, and rituals of widely distant societies.

The theory of evolution also, as it happened, combined with a whole series of developments in history, archaeology, and language study, throwing new light upon the ancient Middle East and on the early stages of Jewish and Christian history. The new approaches suggested it was possible to treat the Bible not so much as a sacred, infallible scripture, but rather as a collection of historical documents for the scholar to probe. To some degree this brought a challenge to Christian orthodoxy, and even now there are debates about the literal truth of the Bible. But this shift in attitude was a stimulus to look at the scriptures of all nations and traditions more dispassionately. And this gave further impetus to the formation of what one scholar, Max Müller, called "the science of religion," and what others have referred to as the history of religions.

Another school of nineteenth-century religious thought helped to breed new psychological and social theories. It was the notion that God is a projection: that is, he is like a picture thrown on a screen, who seems real to us and existing "out there," but nevertheless really has his source in human feelings or human culture. This idea was taken up by Karl Marx, who saw traditional religion as a side effect of the economic relations within feudal and capitalist societies. Human beings, unable to master earthly economic and social problems, project their desires upon the universe. There is a heaven awaiting the oppressed, while at the same time the ruling classes use the divine authority figure to serve their interests and keep workers and peasants in subjection. Later a different theory of projection was formulated by Sigmund Freud, only the emphasis was more on the dynamics of the nuclear family and the child's developing feelings about his father and mother, rather than on society as a whole. God is Father writ large. Such projection theories were a stimulus to social and psychological explorations of religion.

But these theories were themselves open to criticism; for didn't they presuppose a view about the world, a view in which God is an illusion, and material forces can explain human development? And isn't Marxism itself possibly a sort of projection, offering the illusion of a material paradise in the human future, rather than a heaven in the sky? Doesn't Freudianism itself become a sort of religion, with psychoanalyst as priest? Why shouldn't the view that religion is our illusion itself be an illusion?

Whatever theory we may end up with about religion, and whatever comparisons we may wish to make about religions, we first face the problem of describing religions and secular worldviews as they actually are. And this is where modern scholars of religion have looked for a way of "moccasin-walking" which begins not with claims of religious truth or cultural superiority, but which tries to treat religions and secular worldviews on their own terms. It is a way which respects the standpoint of the believer.

Such an approach is sometimes called the *phenomenological* method, following the German philosopher Edmund Husserl (1859–1938). Husserl tried to describe experience as it actually is, without the distortions created by prior beliefs and assumptions. Phenomenology asks that we step back and look afresh at our own feelings, perceptions, and the whole flow of consciousness. Can we see a rose afresh without thinking of all the associations the word "rose" suggests? Phenomenology is a little like the method of some contemplatives engaged in religious meditation (in the Buddhist tradition, for instance). But for our purposes Husserl's philosophy need not detain us, for the word "phenomenology" (the study of what appears) has been used in a less technical way by historians of religion. What they borrow from Husserl is the idea that the believer's world can be described without introducing the assumptions and slant of the investigator. For various reasons I think it is best not to use the word "phenomenology," but rather the phrase "structured empathy."

Empathy literally means "feeling in": it is getting at the feel of what is inside another person or group of persons. It is not quite the same as sympathy, "feeling with" (*pathy sym* rather than *pathy em*), for sympathy means I *agree* with the other. Even I do not agree with the other person, however, I can still have empathy. For instance, we might feel what it is like to have been a Nazi revering Hitler without in any way sympathizing with her, or with Hitler's aims. Feeling what her worldview is like would help us to understand why Hitler was as successful as he was. But even more important, empathy helps us to better grasp the facts—for the facts include the way she feels and thinks about the world.

This is why, too, the empathy needs to be *structured*. We have to comprehend the structure of another's world: and in general, we have to try to understand the structures of belief inside the head of the believer. So what is it like to be a Buddhist in Sri Lanka or a Catholic in Ireland? We need to know quite a lot about Buddhist ideas and practices as found in Sri Lanka, and quite a lot about Roman Catholic beliefs and practices as found in Ireland.

I shall return to all this, for there is much more to be said. But for now let us agree that the neutral, dispassionate study of different religions and secular systems—a process I have called worldview analysis—has been an important ideal in the comparative study of religion. It emerged in the nineteenth century as a way of treating the world's religions on their own terms.

For we must remember that, in the past, most of the Western study of religion has been thought of as Christian theology—the study of the texts, history, and doctrines of the faith on the assumption that Christian faith, being true, was superior to all others. When other religions were studied, they were usually compared—unfavorably—to Christianity. They were studied, for instance, as background for Christian missionary work in Africa, Asia, and elsewhere. At worst they were regarded as examples of religious idolatry, and at best as incomplete pointers to the higher truth to be found in Christ. Hinduism, for example, was a religion in which, as the nineteenth-century Anglican bishop Heber wrote in a famous hymn: "The heathen in his blindness/ Bows down to wood and stone." Either that, or else it was regarded as a religion whose noblest aspects needed completion by Christ, who is, to quote the title of a book by a famous Scottish missionary to India, J. N. Farquhar, "The Crown of Hinduism." But historians of religion engaged in worldview analysis see things more dispassionately. The inferiority or superiority of Hinduism is, in their view, a matter of judgment, bias, evaluation, or belief; but it is neither relevant nor helpful in describing what Hinduism is, what it feels like, what its many faces are.

The worldview analyst has struggles on two fronts. To the right are those "traditional" believers (Christian and otherwise—but since we are speaking chiefly of Western scholarship, it is mainly traditional Christians and Jews we have to consider) who regard a more dispassionate and nonjudgmental description of the world's beliefs as an implicit threat to the faith. To the left are those humanists and Marxists who think that religion is irrational and so has to be explained away as some kind of projection. Both groups forget that religions are what they are and have the power they have regardless of what we may think about their value, truth, or rationality. They also forget that in a plural world, questions of the truth of any one religion over any other are debatable—and so we have to listen to one another.

The "Comparative" Study of Religion

For a long time, and especially in Europe, a strange division arose between religious scholars who belonged largely to Christian faculties of theology or divinity schools, and scholars engaged in the comparative study of religion. It was as though all religions other than Christianity (and, by implication, Judaism because it belonged to the same tradition of "revealed" religion) were to be treated as a separate group. It was sometimes argued that Christianity is unique and cannot seriously be compared to other religions. Only in the

1960s did the English-speaking world, and to some degree northern Europe, arrive at a broader and more integrated conception of the study of religion in which various religions and worldviews, Christianity included, are dealt with together. Thus, the modern study of religion emerged partly out of the comparative study of religion and looks at Christianity, too, as a "world religion"—not as the exclusive concern of Christian scholars.

But I should add that many of the best historians of religion have been Christians. Although there have been problems among those Christian theologians who think that comparative religion makes people comparatively religious (to echo a famous and disdainful quip by the Roman Catholic writer Ronald Knox), many Christians have had a more encouraging view of the modern study of religion. (Actually, as far as my experience goes, Knox is quite wrong.)

So far, in sketching some of the threads woven into the fabric of religious studies, I have used, interchangeably, the phrases "history of religions" and "comparative study of religion." Both phrases have somewhat confusingly been in vogue.

People have used "the comparative study of religion" because, as a famous slogan has it, "If you know one, you know none." This means that knowledge of one religion can throw light upon another, and knowledge of another upon one's own, or that of one's own culture. For instance, in a number of traditions water is a symbol of chaos, and so even of death: knowing this helps to illuminate the ritual of total immersion practiced by many Christians at baptism. The devotee dies to the world and then rises again out of the waters of chaos and death with the risen Christ. Another example is this: some Christian mystics say that it is impossible to refer to God with words, for in the higher stages of the path of meditation all words and images disappear. It turns out that similar things are said in Buddhism and in the Hindu tradition. So this similarity of expression suggests that there may be here some kind of universal human experience, and that the comparative study of religion helps bring this universality to light.

Moreover, if I cross the frontiers of my own culture and travel into the minds and hearts of another tradition, I am bound to make some kinds of comparisons, even if only in realizing that I must not read the assumptions of my own background into the lives of other people. If I as a Christian explore the meaning of the Sabbath for a

Jew, I must become aware of deep differences in attitude, despite the use of a common word, namely "Sabbath." In order to understand the Buddhism of Sri Lanka or Thailand I must put behind me the thought that the supreme focus of faith is God, for the Buddhism of Sri Lanka does not focus on a Creator and has quite a different picture of the universe from that found in Genesis. I must not start from the assumptions of baseball in trying to understand cricket. Exploring another tradition should bring contrasts, not just similarities, to the surface; and this is what making comparisons means. So, in an important sense, every time I cross the mental frontiers of my tradition and society I am engaged in a comparative study. And indeed, comparative study is possible within traditions and societies, as well as outside them. I am an Episcopalian, and the adjustments I need to make in order to understand what it is like to be a Southern Baptist or a Mormon or a New England Catholic are already considerable. I must not assume that I know my neighbor. And even if for some purposes it is useful to talk about Christianity or Buddhism, it is in fact more realistic to speak of Christianities and Buddhisms. Each has more than fifty-seven varieties. In brief, then, the whole enterprise of crosscultural understanding is comparative.

It also happens that modern scholars of religion have done much work on themes and types, looking at similar phenomena across the board. I have mentioned mysticism—here trying to see if there is a single shining core of inner experience to be found among those in different religions who engage in meditation. Another example is this: there are recurring patterns in different stories of creation and in myths of catastrophe, such as the story of the Flood. Or, we can see how there are types of religious leadership in both East and West—there are monks and nuns, priests, prophets, and other ecstatic visionaries. Or again, the notion of religious sacrifice seems to be a widespread religious phenomenon. All these observations are to do with *types* of religious phenomena.

Somewhat confusingly, a number of well-known writers (such as Gerardus van der Leeuw, the Dutch scholar, Geo Widengren, the Swede, and Mariasusai Dhavamony, the Indian) have used the term "phenomenology of religion" when referring to their comparative studies of religious themes and types. We thus have another meaning for that over-long word, "phenomenology." I think it is clearer if we refer to this particular kind of study as "typology" or "thematic comparison," or perhaps even "morphology," the cataloging of forms.

But although it is true that there is a comparative element in the study of religion, the phrase "comparative study of religion" is rather awkward and has in any case begun to fall rather out of fashion. It sometimes had negative connotations: as we have seen, in the old days it could be a conscious or unconscious means of expressing Western superiority when other faiths were compared to their detriment. Partly because of the influence of the modern Chicago school of religion, led by Mircea Eliade, and partly because the International Association for the History of Religions uses the term, it is more common now to talk of "the history of religions." This covers both the writing of the history of individual faiths as well as thematic reflections about contrasts and comparisons.

Some like also to use the word "crosscultural" to express the fact that we have to see world religions together. The term has the following great merit: it suggests that the traffic is not all from one culture to others, but can cross in differing cultural directions, East and West and North and South. The message here is that we should not be busy merely imposing Western themes and categories on non-Western faiths, but that we should also be using Eastern and other categories to throw light on Western religion. Thus, for example, a major element in the Hindu tradition is the fervent worship of a personal God, thought of as Vishnu, or Krishna, or Shiva, or the divine female Kali. (About the last, an anecdote is told: A Hindu swami, or religious teacher, was once pressed to tell on television what God is really like; he surprised his American white male interviewer by saying "She is black.") Anyway, such devotion—or faith— is called *bhakti,* an important strand both in Hinduism and in later Buddhism. It is reasonable, vis-à-vis Christianity, to say that many Protestant hymns and Paul's theology also express a variety of *bhakti.* There are many other non-Western categories which could with profit be used across the board. We could begin to ask questions like "What is distinctive about Christian *bhakti?*" So the modern study of religion can well be looked on as crosscultural.

This makes sense; we do, after all, live on the same globe. We are now moving into a period of global civilization in which we begin to share one another's ancestors and achievements. Beethoven is played in Tokyo and Indian music in New York, and the citizen of the world can draw on the ancestral wisdom of both Socrates and Confucius and the art of Paris and Nigeria. So too can the modern study of religion become genuinely crosscultural, and therefore global.

These comparative themes become especially important when we begin to test wide-ranging theories about religion. For instance, the great sociologist Max Weber (1864–1920) hypothesized that Protestantism was a main factor in the rise of capitalism in the West. To test his theory, he looked at how things fared outside Europe, in the Islamic, Indian, and Chinese worlds. For if we say that certain religious factors A and B give rise to result C in one culture, then we need to discover whether A and B are present in other cultures which do *not* manifest C. Either they are not so present, or at least, not jointly; or, if they are so present, then we should look for some further factor D which tell us why A and B gave rise to C in one culture but not in the others. We cannot put human societies and human histories into a laboratory, but we can use global history as a kind of laboratory. This is where the social sciences can make use of crosscultural comparison. Weber was a major crosscultural pioneer in the fields of religion and economics. He described religious attitudes which, in his view, greatly influenced the rise of capitalism. The Protestant faith, according to Weber, placed great emphasis on inner-worldly asceticism, in which the faithful lived actively, but austerely, *in* the world (rather than living the more contemplative life of the monastery, which other faiths emphasize). In particular, Weber identified the influence of Protestant reformer John Calvin, whose teachings, coupled with his establishment of a religiously controlled state in Geneva, were important. These factors motivated the middle classes to work hard and spend moderately, and were thus central to the rise of capitalism. What, by the way, do we say about the Buddhist and Confucian values lying deep in the social structures of Japan? How far have they been the source of Japan's great technological and economic miracle?

The fact that the modern study of religion is crosscultural helps to strengthen the belief that we should include secular worldviews within its scope. For although it may seem to us in the West that the division between secular and sacred is "natural," and that political ideologies such as Marxism belong to a different category from religions, other, non-Western perspectives may not necessarily divide human realities the same way. Thus, if we look to China, we find that Maoism comes as a direct alternative to the old tradition of Confucius, which likewise contained a philosophy on how to run society. They both play in the same league.

We can sum up what has been said or implied about the modern study of religion as follows:

First, it is plural, dealing with the many religions and secular worldviews of the globe.

Second, it is open-ended in the sense that it includes consideration of belief-systems and symbols lying beyond the frontiers of traditional religions.

Third, it treats worldviews both historically and systematically, and attempts to enter, through structured empathy, into the viewpoint of the believers.

Fourth, it makes thematic comparisons which help to illuminate the separate traditions.

Fifth, it is polymethodic: it uses many methods drawn from various disciplines—history, art history, philology, archaeology, sociology, anthropology, philosophy, and so on.

Sixth, it aims to show the power of religious ideas and practices and their interactions with other aspects of human existence.

Seventh, it can set the scene not only for an educated understanding of the world and its various belief-systems, but also for a personal quest for spiritual truth.

A central part is played in all this by the process of structured empathy. It is the way we cross our own horizons into the worlds of other people.

Exploring Italian Catholicism

Let us see what structures are involved in trying to understand a particular form of Christianity. Suppose we are trying to understand the nature and shape of Roman Catholicism in Italy.

First, we have to reckon that it is part of the family of faiths known as Christianity, and some general picture needs to be gained of the main teachings and practices of the religion. It is useful here to use the six dimensions as an inventory, and we have already seen something of the general structure of Christianity from our discussion of these.

But second, particular features of Roman Catholicism need to be understood. There is, for instance, the fact that it is *Roman*. Think of the many tendrils of meaning and association the word "Rome" trails with it. Rome is the eternal city, the hub of the old Empire, still lively in the consciousness of the Italian: it remains a center of pilgrimage. Incidentally, pilgrimage is an important religious theme in the great traditions—consider Banaras in India beside the holy Ganges River; Mecca, the annual meeting point of millions of Muslims; Jerusalem, whither many a medieval traveler went with great peril and hardship, and where Jews and Christians still flock eagerly today. Think of Compostela in Spain, and Guadalupe in Mexico. The idea that one should travel to the "center" of one's cosmos, the spiritual hub of the universe, is an old one.

The centrality of Rome goes with the centrality of the Pope, successor of Peter—who was martyred in Rome perhaps on the very spot where St. Peter's now stands—and of Paul, the great apostle who ended his days in the imperial capital. Thus Rome is an ingredient in the continuance of the Christian myth, stretching back through the Resurrection and the life of Christ to the Jewish hinterland of the faith. It stretches forward through the life of the Church, which has a divine essence, was founded by Christ, is animated by the Holy Spirit, is led by Peter's successors, and is the earthly vehicle for the transmission of the divine teachings and the life-giving rituals of Christianity.

This mythic dimension of Roman Catholicism, then, is the story or set of stories which give the faithful a sense of identity and belonging to a divinely instituted organization. The central element in their experience of the Church is the heart of its ritual dimension, namely the Mass. We cannot truly understand the power and meaning of Roman Catholicism without having a sense of the Mass.

This raises some questions of method. How can I have that sense without in some way participating in the Mass? I can of course rely somewhat on films and literary works which may present the Mass, and this may be a vital help in the search for empathy. It would be better to attend at least one or two Masses as a sort of participant. In the field of anthropology, living with the people one is trying to understand is commonly called "participant observation." It is a way of doing fieldwork. In religion too fieldwork is important. Even if it is not always feasible for the explorer of religion to do it, it is something that he or she should bear in mind, for there will be many opportunities in life for travel and for explorations, and if a person remains truly interested in understanding her fellow human beings then these opportunities can provide ways of deepening knowledge.

If one is trying to enter into the minds of those who attend Mass (I am here assuming that the person seeking to do so is not Roman Catholic), one has to suspend one's own beliefs. It is not the point to say, "These practices are based upon a set of doctrines which I do not share." It is vital, by contrast, to think what it would be like to believe those things. One's own biases and commitments fall away. This suspension of one's own assumptions is sometimes referred to (following Husserl) as *epochē* (pronounced ep-och-ay, with *och* rhyming with loch, *ay* rhyming with day). Another word which is used is "bracketing," for one "brackets out" one's own beliefs for the time being.

This may seem difficult, but the difficulty depends partly on the person. A religious fanatic, for instance, may find it impossible to practice such bracketing. Certain kinds of religious commitment may stand in the way of understanding. Sometimes firm atheists, too, find it hard to enter into the spirit of religion. But generally, I think it is not too hard for people to have enough awareness of themselves to be able to draw a line between their own beliefs and feelings, and those of others.

The Mass as a ritual needs quite a lot of explanation. The participant observer can often do with a running commentary. The observer has to see it as the central way in which the faithful perceive themselves as having access to the power of Christ: he or she has to understand how the bread and wine not only symbolize, but actually (from the point of view of the faithful) *contain* the substance of Christ himself. She has to see how, for the Catholic, the central religious "specialist" is the priest. It is not the preacher, for instance, although preaching is one of the priest's functions; nor is it the monk, although in fact monks are part of the fabric of Catholicism and often have priestly functions. He or she must understand that the rite of the Mass is central to Catholic Christianity, and it is the priest who is authorized to conduct the rite: he is the one who can bring into being again and again this great encounter between

Christ and the faithful. So the participant observer must not only try to see the Mass through the feelings of the faithful, but also through their complex beliefs—beliefs which relate to, among other things, the institutions and nature of the Church.

Traditionally, a bell is rung at the moment during the Mass when the bread and wine are consecrated—when, that is, they cease being ordinary articles of food and drink and become the sacred substance of God himself. Sometimes the bells of the campanile or church tower are also rung, tolling solemnly. This solemn moment has its own feeling. It is *numinous,* to use a word coined by Rudolf Otto (whose work will be discussed in the next chapter): it contains mystery and inspires awe. The faithful bow in silence before the solemn event. The observer, too, has to have a sense of this solemnity, this numinous feeling.

This is one place where religion tends to differ from secular worldviews. The latter do not have such a vital concern with this sense of the Other, this feeling of divine presence, this perception of unseen Power. But even so there are parallels to traditional religion. In Moscow, tourists—who are, in effect, pilgrims—line up daily to look at the embalmed body of the great Lenin, chief founder of the Revolution, and so of the new world in which they live. Such magical figures as the Beatles have had similar effects of strange power upon their fans; the death of John Lennon had many of the overtones of a solemn religious event, for he summed up in his person, for the "believers," a set of values—peace, love, the music of gentle protest. In the heyday of the Cultural Revolution in China the reverence for the power of Mao's thought and person reached religious proportions.

With the sense of the power of Christ in the sacrament, the pious Catholic also believes that Christ's goodness and holiness are such that the person who takes communion, that is, receives into herself the substance of Christ, must be in the right state. She must not be in a state of sin, which is a kind of impurity and at the same time an alienation from, a being cut off from, God. So it is that the Church has the institution of confession: here the faithful unburden themselves of their sins and receive forgiveness from God through the priest. Their sins are no longer dogging them, and they are now in a renewed state of purity. Then they can with a good conscience receive Christ.

In this way and in others the ritual and experiential dimensions of Catholicism link up with ethics. Italians, it is true, often disregard the moral and social teachings of the Church: like many other Catholics they do not always follow it in matters related to divorce and abortion. But in general the Church is seen as the authority on morals, and so the person's daily life is integrated into religion.

Another way to get a feel for Roman Catholic values is through its symbols. The crucifix, showing the suffering Christ upon the Cross (often in realistic and bloody detail), tells the ordinary person that God can identify with his sufferings and the sufferings of his neighbors. Another crucial symbol is the Virgin Mary. How can we understand the Roman Catholic tradition, and Italian Catholicism in particular, without seeing the vibrant importance of the cult of the Blessed Virgin Mary? The story of Jesus's mother is given further definition by the Church—for instance, in the claim that she was taken bodily up into heaven at the time of her death. The Virgin is the representation, so important for Italians, of ideal womanhood and ideal motherhood. Mother and yet virgin, she is also inspiration for the priest who is a Father and yet is celibate.

The statues of the Virgin and the crucifixes of the suffering Christ are among the ways in which material things are used in the course of worship. The statues are more, and other than, art: they give a sense of the living presence of Christ and the saints. They are, in effect, acts of worship congealed into stone and plaster and metal. Much can be learned about religion from the way it expresses itself through such sculptures, paintings, and other objects. Also, as it happens, quite a lot can be learned from their absence. Many Protestant chapels and meeting houses are empty of any decoration or statues. Such artifacts are thought of as challenging the biblical command not to make graven (that is, sculptured) images. They are thought to encourage idolatry—idolatry being the worship of that which is not God. Similarly, Islam forbids the use of images of any kind. But the Roman Catholic tradition and the Eastern Orthodox wing of Christianity have, in their own ways, made use of visible representations of Christ, the Virgin, and the saints.

Both of these traditions venerate the saints. Here the observer needs to understand that although the Italian may call on St. Anthony, or San Pellegrino, or the Virgin Mary for help, he does not mean to worship them as gods: he calls on them because they, being close to God in heaven, can serve as helpers in petitioning God.

These, then, are some of the ways in which the observer begins to penetrate into the full meaning and context of the Mass. He or she thus begins to understand what it is like to be an Italian Catholic.

The ordinary Italian, even if a pious Catholic, includes more in his total worldview than the Catholic faith, it is true. There are, for instance, beliefs and values connected with the nation of Italy; and Christian faith has to be thought of in relation to other kinds of knowledge, such as that provided by science. So the whole comes to constitute a loosely-put-together patchwork. But for certain purposes we can see it as a version of the Catholic faith, which blends religious and secular values. The believer thinks of the faith as relating to the ultimate sense of the world, and thinks of God as the creator and guide—not just of the Church, but of the nation and the material cosmos as well, and of science as well as faith.

In such ways the observer builds up a picture of what it is like to be an Italian Catholic, ranging through the dimensions of the faith and so mapping its structures, and trying to get the feel of the believer's attitudes toward the various focuses of her religion—the Trinity, the Madonna, the Pope, and the local priest.

Exploring the Past and the Present

In conducting this exploration we are taking a slice in time: we are getting the feel of what the faith is like in the twentieth century. We could have tried to find what the faith was like in the fourth century, after the conversion of the emperor Constantine; or in the thirteenth century, at the time of the great saint and philosopher St. Thomas Aquinas; or in the sixteenth century, during the upheavals of the Protestant Reformation; or in the nineteenth century, during the fight for Italian independence and unity. Here we would be looking at other slices in time. Each slice represents a synchronic, or "same-time" picture.

It is not, of course, easy to find out what the faith was like in times gone by. Historical records are sometimes inadequate, and the nature of daily life was often not recorded since much of it would have been taken for granted and not referred to in documents. We cannot get into a time machine and glide back to Aquino in southern Italy to interview the young Aquinas, or speed silently back to the days after Constantine's legions were victorious at the Battle of the Milvian Bridge under the proud banner of Christ, or even make the shorter trip to see the world during the life of Verdi, when his operas thrilled all Italy and his name was a rallying cry for Italians against their oppressors.

Still, the past is not wholly hidden from us. The historian of religion looks to see how the present structures of religion have emerged from the deep and complex web of interactions of humans and events in times gone by. The historian can also, by seeing something of the religious heart of a tradition—the numinous experience, the piety of saints, the force of religious ideas, the lure of rituals, the dynamism of myth, the strength of the institutions of the faith— estimate how far religion has molded society and how far society by contrast has shaped religion. Usually it is a complex two-way interaction. Anyway, the historian can present not just a series of synchronic slices but also something of a moving picture. The historian deals with a "through-time," or *diachronic*, picture.

Methods of Exploration

The synchronic or "same-time," indeed contemporary, analysis through structured empathy of a particular faith in a given context is more or less the same as the methods of analysis used in anthropology. It is true that the social anthropologist tends to deal with small-scale cultures, often in the Third World, and it is true too that he or she will probably be interested in much else besides religion and worldviews—for example, the way kinship works; for the webs of family and clan life vary greatly among differing peoples and give different perspectives on a number of other things in their societies. But there is much that the worldview analyst can learn from anthropologists; the study of religion and anthropology are closely bound together. The same applies to sociology. The latter is deeply involved in the structures, including the belief-structures, of modern industrial societies. A joke has it that anthropology is about *them* and sociology is about *us*. But together, sociology and anthropology cover all cultures, and although their emphasis is on the social dimension of cultures (the way people act in and through the webs of social relations they are involved in), they nevertheless can throw much light on religion, too. Thus, the sub-disciplines of anthropology of religion and sociology of religion have come into being. Religion has its own social dimension; thus, we can ask the same question about today that the historian may have asked about the past: how do religious beliefs, feelings, values, experiences, rituals, and institutions interact with society as a whole, and with ideas and feelings other than those associated with a given religious tradition? To take a case from today: How does religion affect the media in the United States, and conversely, how do the media help to influence and shape religion? Is the television preacher the shaper of the system, the victim of the system, or both? Such questions are of profound interest for various reasons. To name but one: if religion still has a powerful function in society, we can infer something about religion's future.

If the explorer of religion needs to know something of the history of religions, it follows that he or she must come in contact with those people who, in one way or another, serve the historian in his probings: the archaeologist, who turns up old statues of the Buddha, or Dead Sea Scrolls, or ancient temples, or the models of soldiers buried in China's distant past; the language specialist, who has managed to decipher ancient languages and who supplies the key to understanding old scriptures; the art historian, who can trace developments in the way religion was understood visually; and so on.

The explorer of religion can learn much, too, from literature. Thus the novelists of modern times have often managed much more successfully than historians to create living pictures of religion in action. In his famous book *A Passage to India,* the English writer E. M. Forster (1879–1970) portrayed the subtle clashes between differing worldviews—Hindu, Muslim, Christian, Indian, British—in India under British rule in the early years of this century. In *The Brothers Karamazov* the great Russian writer Dostoyevsky (1821–1881) depicted in a most dramatic way some of the values and problems of Russian Christianity in the second half of the nineteenth century. In *Darkness at Noon* Arthur Koestler (b. 1905) gives an inside view of Marxist faith and its disintegration. Here and elsewhere there is a whole range of what may be called "worldview analysis in fictional form." The fact that it is fiction is one main reason why it goes beyond history. The historian has to write about what he or she can know. Sometimes in writing a biography—say, of Gandhi, or of John XXIII—a historian can flesh out a living figure. But for the most part the records are too sketchy to be able to give that full flow of a person's inner life which the novelist and the dramatist try to portray. They weave that flow from their own imaginations. Theirs is a creative structured empathy: they project their characters on a screen and then see how they move and feel. They are both inside and outside their characters.

Of course, we cannot just rely on fiction. Fiction has to be complemented by the realities of actual testimony and actual records. Religious writing often concerns the individual person, or at least the lone practitioner. We can see this in the guides to the art of meditation which have been written in differing religious traditions; and in the autobiographical poetry and prose of some of the great figures of the traditions, such as the monks and nuns of the *Elder's Verses* in Buddhism; and in the accounts by the Catholic mystic St. Theresa of Avila (1515–1582) of her inner life. Are there universal themes to be found in religious experience and feeling? This is one of the starting points for modern studies, most notably pioneered in *The Varieties of Religious Experience* by the American philosopher and psychologist William James (1842–1910). From his work and that of others, and from the speculations of Sigmund Freud (1856–1939), C. G. Jung (1875–1961), and other depth psychologists, the field known as the psychology of religion has arisen. Recent evidence suggests that religious experiences of quite a dramatic kind are much more widespread and varied than had previously been thought. What are we to make of them? Are they hints of heaven? Are they illusions?

We can begin to see why we refer to the modern study of religion as polymethodic—using the methods and ideas of many overlapping disciplines. This is not surprising, for the human being has varied relationships, and cannot be reduced to a single dimension of existence. Thus religion, pervading life in a strong or weak manner, has to be seen in many relationships. It has to be seen in relation to the past, so we need history to understand it; it needs to be seen socially, so we need sociology; it needs to be seen in relation to individual development, so we need psychology; it needs to be placed in religious context, so we need worldview analysis; it needs to be seen in relation to human consciousness, so we need literature and other ways into the feelings of others. And as a combination of all these things, it needs structured empathy.

There is a story of a man who felt ill, but in a vague way. He worried so much that a friend insisted on taking him to a clinic, where he saw all kinds of specialists: heart, lung, eye, brain, and so on. Each of them pronounced him healthy. At the end he said he still felt ill. "But," said his friend, "none of these specialists has found anything wrong with you." "But they haven't looked at *me*," the man said. Likewise it is important that even though we use many approaches to religion, we do not forget that in the last resort religion is people.

Exploring Symbolic Themes

Each person is unique; but even so, people think and feel according to patterns. The modern study of religion, in describing the forms which religion and symbolism express, gives shape to the language of life—the language of images and actions. If we can understand the themes that recur throughout religions, then we can more clearly decipher the meaning of life around us. This is where the typology of religion, as I have called it, is important. From another perspective we can call it the exploration of symbolic themes.

We have some such themes woven into the fabric of Italian Catholicism: in the Mass, for instance. The Mass is a sacred meal, although it is reduced to brief essentials as far as the actual eating and drinking go. But it does present to us anew the Last Supper when Jesus was with his close associates and friends. It should lead us to see something of the symbolic meaning of eating together. Consider how we often celebrate events through a banquet—a special meal expressing the togetherness of the group usually relating to some cause or some association—a school reunion, a political party, a retirement dinner, a wedding, and so on. We may be led to ask who we share food with: what people would we and what people would we not ask to our homes to share a meal? This question can lead to a consideration of matters of purity in food. Why do some religious traditions reject certain kinds of food? Even the most secular person in Western society rejects certain foods: dogmeat, for instance (though some other cultures eat dogmeat readily), and horsemeat (though in parts of Europe it is considered a delicacy). Is it that we feel that dogs and horses are too close to us because, as pets and in sports they enter into semi-personal relations with us? Once we begin to think about the meaning of food and drink we are given a marvelous opportunity to think again about what is, after all, so close to us that we fail to notice it; our whole way of living and acting is drenched in meanings.

Or consider the symbolism of cities. In religion there is the quest for the City of Zion; and indeed, in the last book of the New Testament, Revelation, heaven is depicted as a marvelous, jewel-spangled city. The destination of pilgrimage is often a city, for the holy city is seen somehow as being at the center. Here (in the center) is one of the great elementary symbols of human life. Jerusalem is at the center of the world, for the Christian, because it was the scene of the climax of the drama of Jesus's life. In the modern world the state capital is usually seen as the "center." It is from there that power radiates. Nations sometimes build new capitals to symbolize a fresh beginning, casting off old associations as the nation restores itself: thus Pakistan built its new capital Islamabad (City of Islam) partly to cast off the associations of the conquered past. The British built New Delhi (based on Old Delhi) to show off the new empire replacing the old Mughal Empire it had conquered. Australia, once it was freed from all but the most formal ties with the mother country (and consider the symbolism contained in ideas like "mother country" and "fatherland"), built its new federal capital in a stretch of bush at Canberra. A century and a half earlier the United States celebrated its status by creating a capital at Washington. These all are relatively new centers: but often it is the ancient centers that have the greatest magnetism—Banaras, Rome, Mecca, Athens, Istanbul.

But there is something about the traditional West European city that holds our attention. Coming toward Canterbury, or Salisbury, or Cologne from afar one sees at its heart, and rising above it, a great cathedral. The Gothic spire points to heaven: its whole message is one of straining upward. Inside, its pillars soar. They do not just bear a load. They are not squat. They yearn upward. So the cathedral is a stone act of prayer, of aspiration, of adoration. The traditional Western city had, at its heart, the symbolism of heaven. But nowadays, buildings in modern cities often climb higher. In New York, St. Patrick's Cathedral is dwarfed by the glittering rising columns of skyscrapers: buildings scraping heaven, now not so much pointing to heaven as symbolizing the height humans can attain. Wealth and dynamism here have their architectural language, and they dwarf the pointing fingers of St. Patrick's. Again, New York, like many other cities of the New World, is laid out in a grid: somehow this speaks to us of the rational mind, the conquest and control of the land. It foreshadows the rectangular landscapes of the American Midwest. The old European city tends to be more chaotic, with lines running hither and thither in bursts of design, such as the Mall in London (appropriately running from the Admiralty to the Palace, from one Britannia to another). Manhattan has its crookedness in Broadway: perhaps here there is a feeling for the arts and drama, which do not run along the right angles of the rational mind.

Once we look around us we find that our life is drenched in meanings, and everything has its symbolic sense, often changing, differing in one culture and time from others. The crosscultural exploration of religious and symbolic themes is a way we can understand this world of meanings. With worldview analysis comes symbolic analysis, for ideas need symbols to gain a grip on the world, and so stimulate action. It is no coincidence that between doctrine and ethical practice lies myth; for the stories which give us identity and a sense of direction also contain a strong infusion of symbolic elements. Thus Christ's sacrifice is like the breaking of bread; and just as in a family meal I commune with my fellow human beings, in the sacred meal I gain solidarity with the sufferings and glory of Christ.

We can see that an essential ingredient of the modern study of religion is *symbolic analysis,* which tries to throw light on the various themes which can be discovered crossculturally through the exploration of various worldviews. It is important that the universal and the particular be combined. Thus, the figure of Christ on the Cross is an instance of a more universal or general theme, the suffering hero; but it also has a very particular meaning in relation to the unique characteristics of Jesus's life, death, and resurrection.

Crosscultural exploration through symbolic analysis tries to make the strange familiar and the familiar strange. On the one hand, crosscultural exploration gives us a more familiar idea of what it is to be a Muslim in Iran or a Buddhist in Thailand. On the other hand, we begin to look afresh at many of the things we took for granted in our own lives and religious traditions. See them afresh and the familiar things seem strange.

This strangeness also leads us to ask questions anew. Not so long ago, I finished a course I had given on Christianity, in which I tried to describe it as one might any other faith, coolly but with structured empathy (or so I hoped). A student of mine said he had, as a result of the course, become a Christian. Previously, he had been so put off by preaching and slanted presentation that he had not realized that Christianity seen afresh was much more interesting and, for him, more compelling than he had ever imagined. In other words, he had been led to ask new questions. By contrast, those who have never questioned the values and beliefs they were brought up with may, through the realization of the plural richness of human religions, come to ask questions about their faith. So, although I have up to now stressed the descriptive and "bracketed" approach to world-views, there is no doubt that sooner or later questions of truth arise. What is the truth of religion?

Theology and the Philosophy of Religion

If these questions of truth arise from within the context of religious belief, they sometimes get worked out in terms of what in the West is called *theology*. Strictly speaking, the word ought to have an adjective in front of it—Christian, Jewish, Catholic, Protestant, Reform, Orthodox, and so on. For theology implies acceptance in broad terms of the truth of the tradition in which one is working. A Christian theologian accepts the Christian faith. This is the context in which many great Western theologians—Augustine, Aquinas, Luther, Karl Barth, to name but a handful—have worked. They have tried to present the religion of their tradition in a new way, in response to changes in the wider world. Thus, the modern Christian theologian has to see the doctrine that God created the universe in light of modern discoveries about the vast size of the cosmos and the long history of the planet Earth. How does he look on Genesis and its story of creation? The theologian has to see what the meaning of Christian love is in the context of a shifting modern society. How does he look upon divorce, or welfare? In all sorts of ways the theologian is interpreting the Bible and the tradition so that the meaning of the message is given an expression which makes sense today. In other words, Christian theology is a response from within the tradition to questions which are put to it by the changing world of knowledge and action.

But not all those who think about religion are committed to a particular faith. There are more general questions about the truth of religion which arise across the frontiers of any given faith. They are questions which crop up for anyone who takes religion and truth seriously. Usually such questions are thought of as "philosophical," and it has become common to think of philosophical thinking about religion as "the philosophy of religion."

The philosopher of religion asks questions about the validity of religious experiences. Do they tell us about the nature of life and the world around us, or are they just subjective feelings? If I feel vividly that I am one with nature and that all things in this wonderful universe are interconnected, does such a flash of insight really have any validity, or is it just me reacting, perhaps for some purely physical reasons—like taking a drug? Or are drugs, too, windows on reality?

Is there any good reason to believe that there is a God? People say that they have had experience of God; what does this actually mean? Although we think that the universe must have had some sort of beginning, does this mean that we have to suppose that there was a Creator who got it going? And when did He (or She) begin? And if He or She could be without a beginning, why shouldn't the universe also be beginningless?

Given that there are so many different faiths and ideologies in the world, how can we tell which is the truth? Are they all true up to a point? And if so, is one truer than the others? And how do we tell?

These thoughts are at first bewildering, and we seem to flounder. But they are questions which, in one way or another, each of us has to respond to, for we do in a sense live our lives according to the conclusions we reach. If I really think that religious experience has no validity, then there isn't much use bothering to live as if it had. In this case I still have to have a worldview, but it would not be one which would take too seriously the prescriptions of the Buddha, say, since he derived his teachings from his enlightenment experience. Nor would I take too seriously most of what Paul has to say in the New Testament, since again he derived his slant on practical things from his conversion experience and sense of unity with Christ. I might be a humanist, thinking that the highest value is reverence for one's fellow human beings. Or I might be a Marxist and work toward the revolution and what I thought to be a better world. Or I might be a hedonist, pursuing my own pleasures and satisfactions. But even here I have a worldview: "Eat, drink, and be merry, for tomorrow we die."

So in addition to questions about the nature and effects of worldviews, which we pursue through worldview analysis and symbolic analysis, there are also questions of evaluation. There are, that is, questions about the truth of worldviews, and about how we would set out to resolve such questions.

What the Christian or Jewish or Hindu thinker presents as the truth of his respective tradition has to appeal to experience, or to reasoning, or to revelation, or to two, or all three of these. And so we necessarily here are brought to think about what experience can show and what reasoning can demonstrate and what revelation can uncover. The general reflection about these issues goes, as I have said, under the name of "philosophy of religion."

These questions of truth are normative: they result in conclusions about what we ought to believe and what we ought to do—in brief, they result in conclusions about values. Whereas the descriptive or scientific study of worldviews puts "brackets" around values, but sees them as facts whether we approve of the values or not, the normative approach to religion, whether through theology or philosophy, is a more personal and social matter. A person or a society must decide which values are to be favored. Thus, too, the normative exploration of worldviews brings us to ethics, and to moral thinking as a means of trying to decide what should or should not be done.

The whole field of the modern study of religion is filled with many pathways, and many kinds of flowers and fruits and hedges. It has some ancient plants in it, but many others are quite young. It is a fascinating place to wander, and holds treasures for those who explore it. No one person can comprehend it all or travel through all of it. But the map I have just drawn may orient the visitor, and encourage further explorations.

The study of religion and worldviews is a study of the realities of human life. Let us therefore now draw another map, that of the individual religions and worldviews that inhabit, and have inhabited, our beautiful planet.

2 🌿

Worldviews:
An Inventory

THE WORLD can be divided up very roughly into six main blocs of belief. Among some there is acute tension, among others there are some affinities. The six are: the modern West, largely Christian in background, but plural in system; the Marxist countries from Eastern Europe to East Asia; the Islamic crescent, stretching from almost the shores of Australia through Indonesia, southern Asia, and the Middle East to West Africa; Old Asia, from India around to Japan, lying outside the Marxist orbit; the Latin South, from the Rio Grande down to Tierra del Fuego on the farthest point of South America; and the multitudinous smaller societies mainly of the South, especially throughout black Africa and the Pacific.

Each bloc has, so to speak, its outriders. The Marxist bloc has its outriders, such as Cuba and Angola. The West has its outriders, such as Australia and New Zealand; Islam has its outriders in Zanzibar and the Maldive Islands. The Old Asian bloc has its outriders in Guyana, in the Caribbean, and in Fiji, in the South Pacific. The smaller societies have northern outriders, among them Eskimos, Siberian tribes, and Native Americans.

If we can understand the main features of these blocs we can then go on to see some of the diverse structures which underlie

THE SIX MAIN BLOCS OF BELIEF

WEST	OLD ASIA
MARXISMS	LATIN SOUTH
ISLAMIC CRESCENT	BLACK AFRICA

39

them. For there are indeed differences underlying the apparently similar ideas and systems which go to make up each bloc. Let us then begin in order, starting from the West.

The Modern West

By the West I mean those countries which make up Western Europe, North America, and Australasia, and which share not only a Christian heritage but also a modern pluralism of belief. Such countries, by and large, make a distinction of some kind between Church and State, and are committed to allowing a great degree of religious and political liberty, and so diversity. Thus, though Protestant Christianity was a major formative influence on the United States, America is also a country with many other belief-systems. In addition to major forms of Protestantism, Roman Catholicism, and Judaism, there is a wide range of beliefs from other cultures (such as Buddhism and Islam), new religious movements (such as the Unification Church and Scientology), together with varieties of humanism and atheism which are either nonreligious or strongly antireligious. Nevertheless, the values of Christianity, and especially of Protestantism, have left their mark on America, while the political system can be described as pluralistic and democratic. By "pluralistic" I mean "allowing for many beliefs and lifestyles." The rest of the West, too, can be seen as partially Christian and plural in belief.

The Marxist Bloc

By contrast, in the Marxist countries, where religious practice is quite often tolerated up to a point, the system is one in which Party and State are closely allied. Being a leading functionary necessarily means being a loyal Party member, and this means in turn that members subscribe to the national variety of Marxism (as expanded by Lenin: hence it is often called Marxism-Leninism). Marxist orthodoxy includes belief that the primary causes of historical change are economic; that the class structure in a given society reflects various economic interests; that capitalism as the system of the West is inherently unstable; that revolution will bring about new socialist forms of government; and that ultimately there will exist a communist society in which all people are equal and live harmoniously together, possessing everything in common. Marxism is strongly atheist in character, since it regards religion as a projection (as we have seen) which helps to fool the lower classes with heavenly hopes, when the real task is to change the economic and social face of our world. Some countries have interpreted Marxism differently from the way it is officially laid down in Moscow. (The Russian Revolution in 1917 was the first successful Marxist revolution in history, and thus the Soviet Union claims leadership of the movement.) The Chinese version as elaborated by Mao Zedong adapted Marxist theory to the Chinese situation, chiefly by seeing the peasants, rather than the industrial working class, as the key to successful revolution and social reconstruction. Marxist governments, where they can get away with it, tend to try to crush religions and to insist on a rigid conformity of thought. They are not naturally pluralistic, but we might call them "monistic," for they stress one (mono) system of belief rather than many (plura). In this, Marxism is very like the system found in many countries after the Protestant Reformation in Europe, when citizens were required to conform to the religion of their particular country—so Protestantism was banned in Catholic Spain, and Catholicism in Protestant England. Only gradually was religious freedom won.

The Islamic Crescent

The Islamic crescent has its heart, of course, in Arabia—now called Saudi Arabia after the name of the ruling family, Saud. It was at Mecca that the Prophet Muhammad had his call, from which ultimately stemmed the religion of Islam, which means "submission"—to the one God, Allah. Islam spread rapidly, in the seventh and eighth centuries, across North Africa into Spain (from which it was finally expelled in 1492), and across the Middle East into Central Asia. Later, it also penetrated—by conquest, trade, and missionary endeavor—into northern and other parts of India, as well as Malaysia and Indonesia, island-hopping almost as far as Australia. Because it is based on an infallible Koran, daily acts of prayer, and other unifying practices such as the annual pilgrimage to Mecca, Islam has remained—despite some divisions—relatively homogeneous. The most important divergence inside it is between the orthodox or "traditionalist" Sunna and the Shi'a, strong in Iran and elsewhere. In the contemporary world, Islam is divided about how far it can adapt or make concessions to Western ideas and values, which have reached deep into Islamic countries because of earlier colonial conquest, international trade, and the great riches created by oil. The law derived from the Koran is often at odds with Western "modern" ideas.

Old Asia

Islam is virtually continuous from Indonesia to West Africa, but there is a wedge within this band constituted by Hindu India, which is part of the Old Asian bloc. While predominantly Hindu, India has also been mother of the amazingly successful missionary religion of Buddhism, which has spread through Southeast Asian countries, into China via Central Asia, into Korea and Japan, and into Tibet. There is no country to the east of India, apart from the Philippines, which has not been deeply affected by Buddhist culture and spiritual teachings. Even now Buddhism remains vital in countries where Marxism has not overrun it and closed down the monasteries. It continues to flourish in parts of Nepal and along the Himalayas, in Sri Lanka, in Burma, in Thailand, in South Korea and Japan, and still has a continuing presence among the Chinese in Singapore, Taiwan, and Hong Kong. Meanwhile, Hinduism retains a strong grip in the Republic of India, as well as among overseas Indians, from the Caribbean to South Africa and the South Pacific.

The Old Asian bloc (India, Sri Lanka, Burma, Thailand, Singapore, Taiwan, South Korea, and Japan) has adapted successfully, sometimes spectacularly, to capitalism. Asian culture tends to be rather plural in attitude, so that many differing beliefs and religious movements exist in Japan (such as Shinto and new faiths like Soka Gakkai), while Hinduism, it hardly needs saying, is a religion which contains a kaleidoscope of beliefs and practices: Hinduism is like a vast federation of mini-Hinduisms, and has also been influenced by Islam and Christianity.

Buddhism is different indeed from Islam. It does not subscribe to belief in a Creator such as Allah, and, while not excluding worship, it hardly makes this the center of the faith, as does Islam. Rather, it is a religion more intent upon meditation, and nourishes the life of the monastery. So it has a certain peaceful otherworldliness compared with the dynamic and politically oriented faith of Islam. The rather violent materialism of the Marxist tradition is also at odds with Buddhism, which thinks of the material world as dissolved into a whole swarm of short-lived and partly illusory events. Buddhism seeks nirvana and a kind of blissful emptiness, rather than an Islamic paradise made by God, with its beautifully described pleasures. Buddhism and Hinduism also incorporate the belief that all living beings are in a process of being born and dying and reborn and redying— the process of reincarnation, or rebirth, as it is variously called. The religions of Judaism, Christianity, and Islam, which all hark back to Abraham and the Prophets, do not accept reincarnation: our life is once and for all, and so much more dramatic. A person risks everlasting damnation if he does not conform to the will of God.

Buddhism has suffered greatly under the Marxist regimes of Asia, but it will no doubt see some revival, perhaps in a rather different form, if and as the Marxist regimes become more lenient with regard to religion. But there is no religion (other than Judaism in the Holocaust) which has experienced such losses and such traumas in the twentieth century. Confucianism also, which shaped the ethos of the old China, has been largely suppressed on the mainland, although its values still persist in Taiwan, Korea, and Japan, and somewhat too among the overseas Chinese. Likewise Taoism, the third religion of China—for it, Confucianism, and Buddhism together blended into the threefold practical worldview of the Chinese—has been sharply curtailed because of the Maoist revolution.

Chinese religious history has been remarkably fertile. The Confucian heritage gave rise to a remarkable systematization of its thought during the revival known as neo-Confucianism during the period from the eleventh to the sixteenth centuries. This worldview remains vital if we are to understand the values of traditional Chinese society. Taoism developed from its early beginnings as a worldview emphasizing non-action and harmonious simplicity of life into a hierarchical popular religion which reflected Chinese concerns about death and the possibility of immortality. Buddhism in

China grew new forms, some, like Hua-yen, emphasizing the way in which the whole universe is a complex unity made up of interconnecting parts, and others, notably Ch'ān Buddhism (Zen in Japanese) breathing new life into the practice of meditation and creating new styles of spirituality. There is also a substantial group of Muslims in China, going back to the eighth century C.E.,* and Christianity too has entered Chinese life both in early times and more recently through the work of Western missionaries.

A number of smaller faiths can be found in the Old Asian bloc. Thus, in India there are the Jains, austere followers of Mahavira, contemporary with the Buddha. Mahavira's rigid insistence upon not injuring living things (even insects and microbes) laid the foundation for much Indian thinking about nonviolence, and helped to shape the thought of the great peaceful nationalist hero Mahatma Gandhi (1869–1948) during his struggle for Indian rights and independence from the rule of the British. Small in numbers, the Jains are a prosperous and influential community. Another such group in India are the Parsees, descendants from Zoroastrians who fled Islamic rule and persecution in Persia (i.e., present-day Iran) and settled on the West coast of India, where they are now a strong element in the life of Bombay and other commercial centers. They keep alive the faith of Zoroaster, which once was the religion of the great Persian Empire. Zoroastrianism greatly influenced Jewish religion before the time of Jesus. It also affected the New Testament, especially in its picture of the Second Coming and final judgment of the living and the dead—which draws on Zoroastrian imagery. Important, too, in India are the Sikhs, another influential and dynamic minority. This religion originated in the attempt to combine the best and deepest forms of Muslim and Hindu devotion to God, but it emerged as a "third force"—leaning, however, in practice more to the Hindu than the Muslim side. Indeed, at the partition of India and Pakistan in 1947 most Sikhs fled Muslim regions and settled in the Republic of India.

At the other end of the Old Asian bloc, in Japan, there is the traditional "Way of the Gods," of Shinto, which lives side by side

*As this book is crosscultural, and is not just for Western Christians, I will be using the abbreviations B.C.E., Before the Common Era, and C.E., Common Era, instead of B.C. (Before Christ) and A.D. (Anno Domini).

with various forms of Buddhism. At one time it was mobilized as a militant national cult, to give meaning to Japan's adventurous conquests up to and during World War II. Its life centers on shrines where worshippers can gain rapport with the divine beings who dwell in, and express, the forces of nature surrounding Japanese life. In its myths it looks back to the glorious foundations of the world and of Japan as a favored land.

There are deep tensions between parts of this Old Asian bloc and Islam, especially in the Indian subcontinent. Although both Hindus and Muslims worship God, the strong Hindu emphasis on images of the gods (gods usually seen as so many differing reflections of the one divine Reality) leads Muslims to think that Hindus are idolatrous—and idolatry is the most serious offense in the Islamic book. So Muslim conquerors from the eleventh century C.E. onward destroyed many temples in North India. Muslims eat beef and pious Hindus, particularly Brahmins, do not; and Hindus sometimes do not respect Muslim customs. Poverty and political tensions have often given rise to murderous rioting between followers of the two faiths.

At the same time, the Old Asian religions have suffered, too, at the hands of Marxism. By contrast, the countries of this arc are, on the whole, integrated economically into Western capitalism, and there is a high degree of cultural exchange between the West and this Old Asia. Oriental religions have had a strong influence on the West, especially in the state of California, while Western "modernism" has a strong appeal in much of non-Marxist Asia. The most powerful synthesis between Asian ideals and Western values is found in Japan's economic miracle during the three or four decades after World War II.

The Latin World

The Latin South has its own characteristics. It has been strongly affected by Catholicism, which became the predominant and official religion of most of the region from the Rio Grande southward, in the wake of the sixteenth-century conquest of Central and South America by the Spaniards and (in Brazil) by the Portuguese. The islands of the Caribbean and some of the surrounding shore came to be colonized mainly by Britain, but also by France, Holland, and of course Spain. This rather special region also became, mainly because of sugar, an area of slavery, and an importer of other cheap labor, mainly from India. Likewise Brazil became a region of slavery and so today has a substantial black population. But the rest of Latin America is chiefly composed of two layers of society: the white or mixed layer inheriting the values of Spanish culture, and the lower stratum mainly of Indian stock, partially or wholly absorbed into the system, although some still exist in pockets of tribal and old indigenous life. This two-level society is most evident among the ruins of the old Aztec empire in Mexico and the Inca empire in Peru, while some countries such as Argentina and Uruguay are predominantly white nations of Latin stock. For various reasons, understandable through the general poverty of the lower stratum, the bloc has seen sporadic and increasingly frequent revolutionary movements: in Mexico, which has moved toward greater equality of the two strata; in Cuba, which has followed the Marxist path; and in Nicaragua and elsewhere. Moreover, the Catholic Church, since the Second Vatican Council (1962–1965), has become increasingly concerned with the problems of poverty, and has often taken a protesting and even revolutionary stance in contrast to its usual role as backer of the establishment and the rich ruling classes. In addition to the predominant Catholicism of the region, there are other religions, such as Voodoo in Haiti, which mingle African and Christian elements. Protestant missionary activity is quite strong in parts of the region, for instance, among the as yet unassimilated Indian tribes. Forms of Hinduism and Islam are also found in parts of the Caribbean. The Latin South differs from the northern West in not having, on the whole, achieved a pluralist approach to religion and politics, while it is in the process of developing the institutions of capitalism. But through the world Christian movement (the World Council of Churches, for instance) the problems of the Latin South are making an increasing impact upon the conscience of richer northern countries.

Black Africa and the Pacific

There are affinities between the Latin South and the other societies of the South. The most important component in the latter is black

Africa. Although in part Islamic, most of black Africa is a mosaic of small-scale ethnic groups which either continue with their indigenous traditions or embrace Christianity. The colonial period in the second half of the nineteenth century saw a scramble by European nations (Britain, France, Germany, Belgium, Italy) to carve up the "dark continent." At the same time extensive missionary endeavor, mostly Catholic in the French and Belgian regions and mostly Protestant elsewhere, succeeded in bringing a large number of Africans into the Christian fold. Now, in the twentieth century, a second wave of religious conversion is taking place. There are some ten thousand new African independent churches (independent, that is, of the control of the traditional missionary churches). These new churches for the most part deal with questions of ethnic and African identity in the face of the vast social and technical changes brought about by Western incursions into the region. Thus, independent churches are African in spirit, but deal with new problems. Another response to Western influence has been the creation of a type of Marxist regime in older Portuguese colonial territories, in Mozambique and Angola, and also in Ethiopia, which for most of its history was not conquered by the West. There is also at the foot of Africa the white-dominated nation of South Africa, which includes a strong element of Afrikaans-speaking folk who see their own destiny largely in biblical terms. They think of themselves as being like the people of Israel conquering Canaan; and they practice *apartheid*, a policy of "apartness" of races, which in effect means discrimination against non-whites.

Similar problems are to be found in the other great southern region, the South Pacific, where the peoples of Polynesian, Melanesian and other stock have largely converted to Christianity, while also trying to preserve their cultural identity in the face of Western influence (which was especially strong during World War II).

Because the multitudinous South and other regions where small-scale cultures try to preserve their identities have an interest in a pluralistic system, there are affinities between them and the West. But there are great tensions too; since Western commerce greatly exploits the South, there sometimes arises a strong Marxist strand in the revolutionary thinking among the people of those countries. For Marxism at the economic level tends to make sense of the experience of many of the poorer people of the South.

The Rise of Nationalism

We have now had a quick tour of the six blocs. But there is a pervasive feature of modern life which I have not yet directly com-
mented on. It is the growth of the nation-state and the ideal of
nationalism, namely that every people should in principle have its
own state. This ideal had its origins before the French Revolution,
but the revolution had an especially powerful impact on it. Later, in
the nineteenth century, some of the major European nations
achieved unification and independence—notably Germany and Italy,
but also Greece, Norway, Belgium, Holland, and Luxembourg. In
the twentieth century the movement grew, partly because of World
War I and the subsequent Treaty of Versailles which recognized the
ideal. As a result, Poland, Finland, Romania, Yugoslavia, Czechoslovakia, Albania, and Bulgaria achieved roughly their present form.
South Africa, Canada, Australia, and New Zealand had also become
independent states. After World War II the movement spread to the
rest of the world. The trouble spots of the latter part of the twentieth
century occur mostly where a national group—the Turks in Cyprus,
the Palestinians in Israel, the Catholic Irish in Ulster, the Basques in
Spain, the Muslims in the Philippines, for example—feels that it
does not have independence.

Nationalism is not quite a religion, but it has some of the same
characteristics. Thus there is a deep demand for patriotic loyalty to
the nation: citizens have to give money to the state to pay for arms
and for fellow citizens' welfare; they must, if necessary, be prepared
to die in combat; and if they betray the state, they are branded as
traitors and often shot. In the "monistic" states counter-revolution-
aries are imprisoned or killed, often for apparently mild offenses.

The ideology of the state is also clothed in religious garments:
there is a national anthem (solemn, it is hoped, and tear-jerking), a
national flag and other emblems, and pomp and circumstance surrounding state events. These national events often include marches
of ranked soldiers with formidable weaponry, for war is the great
sacrament of the modern state, cementing its loyalties with shed
blood, and weapons are a great symbol of collective machismo and
pride. The state has, to a great extent, replaced tribe, clan, and in
some ways even family, as the group with ultimate power over people's affections and loyalties. The educational system is one of the

great shapers of the nation, often imbuing the young with common values through nation-building myth (history textbooks) and sports which foster group identity. Education is also a channel for the national language. For instance, in place of the many dialects of Italy's regions, standard Italian became the nation's language; English is the common language which unifies the groups of different origins making up the United States. Problems have arisen among citizenry of nations which have inherited old colonial boundaries, as in much of Africa, where each country has within it a mosaic of ethnic groups and a diversity of languages. Often only the elite speak the official language (say, English or French) of the new national administration.

The national idea, then, has had a strong impact on the world. Virtually all the world is now covered by independent nation-states. Sometimes the national idea has also bred chauvinism, and the desire of one tribe to conquer others. Britain gained an empire. The Nazis ran riot through Europe. The Japanese tried to conquer most of East and Southeast Asia. The Soviet Union has in effect become an instrument for expressing Russian chauvinism, dominating the Islamic peoples of Soviet Central Asia, other related folk like the Ukrainians, and, by proxy through satellite Marxist parties, most of the countries of Eastern Europe. Hence there are from time to time outbursts of patriotic revolt against the Russians, as in Hungary in 1956, in Czechoslovakia a dozen years later, and most recently in Poland.

It is important to see how religion and worldviews are often deeply involved in the national idea; the advent of nationalism represents a new backdrop against which religious attitudes and worldviews are thrown.

The six blocs are themselves in interaction, an interaction which is only part of the wider global interplay which makes the present era such a creative and exciting one. Now virtually every culture is in contact with every other. There are Hindu swamis in San Francisco. There are Samoans in Auckland, New Zealand. There are Pakistanis in Bradford, England. There are Turks in Munich. The major cities of the world—London, Paris, Singapore, Hong Kong, New York, Los Angeles, Lagos, Buenos Aires, Colombo, for example—have populations which are mixed in ethnic stock, in religion, in custom. Such centers are new melting pots and each is a smaller version of the coming global city. We are all more and more tightly involved with one another. It is characteristic of culture-contact that new intermediate social forms are produced. The great religions are thus increasingly liable to influence one another, and to give birth to new varieties.

Such a state of affairs can also create a backlash. The Iranian Revolution is but one of a number of examples where a more conservative or "fundamentalist" interpretation of tradition evolves as a result of threats from various outside spiritual and material influences.

Because traditional religions often give the impression that nothing changes (it is often seen as the highest stamp of approval to say "This is how we have always done it," or "This is the same faith as that of our forefathers"), it is easy for us to underestimate changes which are taking place now and have in fact always done so. At the present time every society is experiencing the growth of new religious and ideological movements. Thus, there are new cults in America, independent churches in Africa, reform movements within Hinduism and Buddhism, and new varieties of Marxism. The process of religious and ideological change will likely accelerate as the world exchanges values in the marketplace of the global city.

Contributions of the Past

Any inventory of the major worldviews today ought not to neglect the formative traditions of the past—once great but perhaps now less evident. Looking back to the classical past of Western culture we find the religious thought which built upon Plato and which had such a large effect on Christianity in the early centuries—the worldview known as Neoplatonism (literally "new Platonism"). Its main focus, a reaching upward toward the experience of union with the One, the first principle from which the cosmos evolved, has likenesses to some Hindu thought.

A group of movements at the periphery of the early Christian faith drew inspiration both from the Hebrew past and other elements of Egyptian and other cultures of the Eastern Mediterranean. That group of movements is now known as Gnosticism, because the adherents sought to be Gnostics, or those who *know* (from the word *gnosis,* knowledge), that is, those who know through experience the true secret nature of the divine Being. Sometimes their ideas took root in Christianity; the Gnostics also helped to cause that faith to define itself, partly by reaction against some of their wilder and more heretical ideas. Some of the themes from Gnosticism were taken up into the religion of Manicheism, which had a wide currency in the Middle East at the time of Augustine (fourth and fifth centuries of the Common Era). Manicheism stressed the evil nature of the world and the need to strive for perfection in order to escape from the body. Echoes of Manicheism were found in later European movements in the twelfth and early thirteenth centuries, notably the Albigensian movement, which the Catholic Church crushed as heresy and which had its main base in southwest France.

Also of some later importance in the formation of modern Western culture were the old religions of Greece and Rome. Something of the atmosphere of Roman religion was absorbed into the Catholic tradition, while the mythology, philosophy, and art of Greece were major ingredients in the fifteenth- and sixteenth-century flowering of European culture known as the Renaissance. Important, too, were the ancient religions of Mesopotamia and Egypt which in one way or another left their stamp on ancient Judaism.

Many other religions which affected subsequent religious traditions have vanished: The great pre-Columbian religions of Central and South America, for example, and other mysterious civilizations such as that of the Indus Valley in northwest India. And even deeper back in the past are the marvelous cave paintings of southwest France and northern Spain: here and elsewhere we see enigmatic traces of old cults whose meaning had something to do with the hunting culture out of which they must have grown. Scattered in Europe and elsewhere are such megalithic or great stone monuments as Stonehenge on Salisbury Plain in the west of England—such artifacts are now intriguing clues for those who nurture theories of ancient gods. But without written records, or a way of deciphering some of the early records we have, it is hard to make sense of old religions, for we cannot through the written word voyage into the thoughts and feelings of these ancestors. It would be like trying to understand football by looking at dilapidated and overgrown stadiums.

Twentieth-Century Secular Humanism

Such, then, is a rough inventory of human beings' various religions. But there is more to be said about the present. We have seen that one major bloc is dominated by kinds of Marxism, which derive from modern antireligious theory of the nineteenth century. We have seen too how the backdrop against which the various beliefs move about among human societies has been altered by the forces and ideals of nationalism. But, at the same time, there is a strong thread in the Western bloc, not merely of Christianity and Judaism, but also of varieties of humanism. For many people today feel that the day of traditional religion is past: the scientific outlook has no place for God, or for reincarnation, or for other central traditional preoccupations.

At the same time there is a process taking place which some have called "secularization." That is to say, in modern societies people increasingly are moving away from traditional religious patterns. Thus, for instance, in Western societies many people are concentrated in cities and suburbs, and no longer in rural villages and small towns where society was more integrated and in which religion played a pervasive part. Greater mobility—with people moving from place to place in search of better work—has the effect of making us less traditional and more individualistic.

What a person believes becomes his own private concern. Moreover, for many people the choice is no longer in a traditional sense religious. There are more and more "religionless" people in modern society. Even in countries which have been thoroughly Catholic, such as Italy, there is some drift away from Church authority. Religion remains strong in such lands as Romania and Poland, under Marxist rule. But this is in part because when religion is oppressed it tends to rebound (the blood of martyrs, it is said, is the seed of the Church), and in part because religion—Orthodoxy in Romania, and Catholicism in Poland—is woven into the fabric of national feeling. Thus, at a time when these peoples wish to assert their identities against the Soviet Bear which looms above and beside them, the forces of patriotism and faith are blended together in a powerful mixture.

But if people sometimes discard the old religions, they still have some sort of view of the nature of life. At its most articulate level this worldview typically is scientific humanism. Let us try briefly to spell out what this means.

As *humanism,* it believes that the highest values are to be found in human beings and their creations. But it does not hold that humans survive death or have any kind of immortal nature; nor that they exist because they have been brought into being by a God. Traditional Western religious doctrines and myths are thus rejected. So the word "humanism" is used in rather a forceful and exclusive sense: it means that there is nothing higher than the human race. Of the two great commandments of the Jewish and Christian traditions, "Love God" and "Love thy neighbor," the first disappears, and morality flows from the second. But such humanism is also in an important way thought to be *scientific.* The person who holds to this worldview believes that all true knowledge about the world is ultimately to be found through science, or at least within the framework of a scientific outlook. We know about the universe by telescopes and space probes, by mathematical theories and physical principles. We know about living beings by beginning with biology. We are, admittedly, still very ignorant, but by experimenting, observing, probing, and theorizing we shall get to know more and more. There is no room in science for God or for nirvana. There is still less room to accept things merely on authority, whether of the Pope or the Buddha or the Koran or the Bible. Indeed, science flourishes best in a society which is open, where differing theories can compete and where people and education are not muzzled by ideological or religious orthodoxy. Scientific humanism favors liberty, a liberal outlook, and democratic institutions, and thus tends to be at odds with mainline Marxism. In some countries a form of social-democratic or liberal socialist outlook has been worked out which absorbs some of the thinking of Marx; but on the whole scientific humanism tends to be an ideology of the Western bloc, and has a strong influence side by side with varieties of Christianity and Judaism.

Humanism and Christianity have interacted in a number of ways. One strand in modern humanism, for instance, is the philosophy known as existentialism, expounded by such thinkers as Martin Heidegger (1889–1976) in Germany and Jean-Paul Sartre (1905–1979) in France. The movement owes much to the brilliant nineteenth-century Danish writer Søren Kierkegaard (1813–1855).

Existentialism has greatly influenced modern Christian theology, but at the same time it has been a vital force in rethinking humanism. Very briefly, it centers on the following idea: human existence cannot be defined or fixed—it is open to creative change, and this creative change depends on a new kind of freedom and authenticity of living in which the individual is not weighed down by the baggage of the past. Human beings have no essence; they do have, however, the possibilities of free existence. For the Christian thinker, truly authentic choice is found through Christ, seen as a person who, in his own day, broke through the baggage and entanglements of the past and of the ideas and legalisms of his time. For the atheistic existentialist, freedom is found in recognizing that there is no God who will help us gain freedom, and there is no sweet heaven after death: death has to be faced now, and life lived in creative awareness of it.

So in all kinds of ways we live, especially in the West, in an age of interplay, a flux of religions and worldviews, a new global city in which many differing ways converge. It is an exciting time. It is perhaps too a confusing one. But for all the novelties and the new philosophies we meet, many of the old traditions remain most vigorous. There is no way we can rightly understand our world unless we come to understand both those past great traditions and the new, emerging patterns of religion and humanism. Nor can we direct our own lives without giving some thought to the choices with which the world now presents us. We alone can choose, but we now find ourselves not in an orchard where there is only one kind of fruit to pick, but in a kind of arboretum where the trees and fruits are many and beautiful.

The Structure of Worldviews

The various belief-systems of the world have different pictures of the cosmos. We might think of the structures of these views as a triangle: at the apex is the cosmos, at one end of the base the self, at the other society.

Before we look at these different views I want to point out that I shall use the word "cosmos" (rather than "universe" or "world") to refer to the physical universe. "Cosmos" is derived from the

Greek word meaning "order," for ancient Greek thinkers were forc-
ibly struck by the orderly character of the world they found around
them—the sky, the stars, the earth, the oceans. "Universe" strictly
means "all that there is," so if there is a God the word should cover
both God and the cosmos he created. "Universe" often also more
narrowly refers to the physical universe and its living contents. I
think it will be less confusing to use "cosmos" when we mean the
physical universe only. The word "world" sometimes just refers to
the planet Earth, as when we say that the "world is round," and I
shall retain this usage.

For the person who believes in God (the theist), the cosmos is a
divine creation which reveals God's glory: I am a creature and I am
made in God's image, and others are too. For the self there is the
hope of salvation, a kind of blissful union with God, and for society
there is the hope of founding somehow a divine kingdom on earth,
a blessed society. I find my true self in worshipping God and in cher-
ishing others. Such, in brief, is the way the Christian theist tends to
look upon this triangle.

The cosmos is normally regarded by the theist, whether Christian or Jewish or Muslim, as having been created by God a finite
time ago. The cosmos is essentially good and glorious, however
much it may be marred by the work of hostile forces (traditionally
thought to be led by the Devil). The cosmos is full of signs of God's
goodness and of his purposes. This is so not merely because the stars
and the mountains produce in us a sense of God's majesty, but also
because God's purposes are to be found in the unwinding of events.
God as ruler of the cosmos was not just the creator of the world. He
is also the power who continuously guides it and keeps it going.
Those who think that God, having created the cosmos, is now
detached from it all, letting the universe run its own course, are
sometimes referred to as *deists:* a term for a type of Western thinker
in the seventeenth and eighteenth centuries. It represents a style of
thinking still found today.

For the theist, then, the cosmos is something which displays the
creative power of God. But in many societies the cosmos is not the
work of a single maker; rather, it has a more complex character: it
has in it many various powers and beings which animate different
parts of it. Thus, for example, the moon gleams at night as a sign of
the power of a female spirit controlling and animating the shape-

changing orb which we moderns know as a satellite of the Earth. The sun radiates heat because of the sun-god. In the streams there are haunting spirits, whose silent echoes are heard every time we go to bathe or let the cattle drink. The groves murmur too (maybe) with the shadows of our ancestors. The thunderstorm exhibits the dangerous power of the sky-god. So the cosmos is full of powers and gods, which are unseen but yet show themselves throughout nature. Such a belief-system, in which the cosmos is controlled by gods and other unseen forces, in the West is often referred to as *animism,* from a Latin word meaning "soul" or "spirit." Sometimes such systems are thought of as "polytheistic," that is, involving many (*poly*) gods (*theoi*)—as distinguished from monotheism. Very often such many-power systems also include belief in a High God, like the Roman Jupiter or the Greek Zeus, who is supreme, but who, for various reasons, may not be so easily approached or dealt with as the lesser gods nearer to human beings. In any case it seems absurd (to many people) to deal with an exalted God about the petty matters which cause us anxiety here on earth; so in some worldviews the High God is rather remote.

Important as animism is and has been, in many cultures it is fading for various reasons. For one thing, Christian and Muslim missions have made powerful inroads into much of Africa and the Pacific where such beliefs have been strong in the past. Although there are revival movements among such societies, the force of outside ideas is bound to modify them. Second, many of the older beliefs, long ago integrated into ways of life and methods of subsistence, are changing because of modern technology. The Eskimo settles into modern villages and uses new techniques of fishing. The nomadic herders of East Africa are often compelled to settle on limited territory. The Pacific Islanders turn crops to cash and benefit from tourism. The Australian aborigines work on cattle stations and accept social security payments. If there is an emerging ideology which seeks to refashion the old worldview in the light of modern knowledge, it is a kind of "environmental animism"—in which the cosmos is seen as containing powers and forces, including the human race, which need to live together in harmony. Such harmony is sometimes disrupted by the combination of the typically Christian idea that the human race has mastery over nature (as though we were not ourselves part of nature) with the modern methods of taming and exploiting nature. These methods are often short-sighted because, as we have already observed in our environment, such "mastery" can lead to the destruction of resources and the pollution of our surroundings. But important as "environmental animism" may be, the world of the small-scale societies is changing rapidly, and the belief in a many-power cosmos is fading from human imagination.

History has shown that the many-power cosmos has tended to be replaced by varieties of religion which transcend this idea or even replace it entirely with the image of a cosmos controlled by a single God. Thus, in Central and South America the old religions came to be largely replaced by Catholicism; earlier in northern Europe the old faiths of the Germanic and Celtic peoples and of the Slavs were replaced by Catholic and Eastern Orthodox Christianity. In India the various beliefs, myths, and practices have been progressively reshaped under the canopy of the Hindu worldview. In Southeast Asia Buddhism has found a place for the many powers, but strictly under the aegis and controlling surveillance of the higher doctrines of the religion. Through Indonesia and Malaysia, and in many other parts of the world, Islam has overtaken the older animisms, while in China a complex system of belief with Taoist, Buddhist, and Confucian elements has modified folk religion.

The world of many small-scale peoples has been one in which the cosmos is a jungle—the many trees representing the gods and spirits. When Islam or Christianity comes along the jungle is leveled, so that one Tree can be planted, that Tree which represents the One God. The old jungle may put forth shoots and seedlings, and these (the old gods a little revived) are the saints of Europe, Mexico, and elsewhere. Hinduism, however, does not remove the jungle: it treats the many plants as leading inward to the One Tree which is to be found at the Center. Buddhism, by contrast, though it does not remove the jungle, builds a road—the "eightfold path" which takes us to final liberation—around the jungle. Wander into the jungle if you wish, but that will not bring you further along the road.

If we turn to look at Hinduism we see a two-tiered view of the cosmos. On one level the cosmos is the body of the divine Being, and God, the second tier, is the soul which gives life to the whole cosmos. But whereas humans do not fully control their bodies (for what can I do consciously to alter the way my gallbladder functions or my liver secretes?), God controls everything. And while it appears that there are many gods in the imagination and the practical life of the ordinary Hindu, they are all seen as so many particular ways in which the one divine Being manifests her- or himself. But there is another level of Hindu thinking about the cosmos found in that system of belief and theology known as Advaita Vedānta—the non-dualistic (A-means "non" and *dvaita* means "dual" or "dualistic") Vedānta (the *anta,* or end of the *Veda;* that is to say, the final meaning of the Hindu scriptures).

According to this view the personal Creator who is the soul of the cosmos is not the highest reality. Beyond the Creator there is unity—the highest experience. The saintly searcher, the true yogi (or practitioner of self-control and meditation), is one who in his own soul realizes the highest knowledge: the self and the divine Being are one. In that state of unity and pure consciousness all differences between me and God disappear. The God who is "out there" and is creator of the cosmos, and the cosmos itself become for me in this higher state mere illusions. I have gone beyond the cosmos. From this angle, there is a view of the cosmos as a kind of mirage, a colossal conjuring trick, or—to use the Indian word—*māyā.*

In this system of belief the cosmos is illusory; but for ordinary purposes the cosmos can be seen as the product of the divine Being and as being God's body.

In the Western religions the cosmos is thought of as created once and for all. If you stick to a literal interpretation of the story of Genesis, and the calculations of the generations described in the Bible from the first man, Adam, down to later times, then we can date the creation of the cosmos at 4004 B.C.E. (according to one well-known calculation, at any rate). Many Christians and Jews do not now believe in that date, but would still think of the cosmos as having been created at a particular time, now believed to be some billions of years back. Many modern astronomers trace the creation of the cosmos back to a "big bang," when an explosion occurred, out of which the cosmos expanded into its present form. But for the Hindu imagination the cosmos has expanded and contracted repeatedly over vast periods of time, for God does not create once and for all, but rather, after periods of quiet and passivity He or She recreates the cosmos. Similarly, for Buddhism there is no ultimate beginning to things.

Nor, in Buddhism, is there a creator. There is no single all-powerful God. Buddhism does not, however, deny the gods, as we have
seen. They are reflections of popular ideas which are not to be dis-
missed out of hand, but they are not really relevant to the highest
aim of living beings. With Buddhism we have a rather different picture of the cosmos: it is not the creation of God nor is it the body
of God. It is a vast series of interconnected events, all of which are
short-lived. It is a huge cloud of processes. It is itself without permanent substance. Nothing in it is eternal or changeless; its heart is
empty. This "emptiness" is what the saint or the Buddha can see
when he or she gains enlightenment, or nirvana. For the Buddhist
the cosmos is a kind of mirage. Insofar as we think of it as solid, as
having permanence, we are deluded. It is not actually how it appears.
Everything is in flux, just as we are: I, however long I may wander
through life after life of reincarnation, have nothing permanent in
me, either. Only if I see the true nature of emptiness and impermanence, usually through a kind of inner vision brought about by following various practices of meditation, shall I gain liberation.

In China, Buddhism was affected by Taoism. In Taosim the true
nature of the cosmos was summed up as the Tao, a word which has
many meanings clinging to it—the Way, or Principle, or Method.
It was used in particular to mean the Way of the cosmos, the principle or spirit governing it. Buddhism identified this with the emptiness which lies beyond the impermanence of things. The two ways
of looking at the cosmos brought about that highly creative phase
of Buddhism known as Ch'ān in China and Zen in Japan, both of
which stressed the need for a kind of harmony with the true nature
of the cosmos.

These, then, are some of the pictures of the cosmos found among
traditional religions. In the case of theism, the cosmos is the creation
of a divine mind. In the Hindu tradition it is seen either as the body
of God or, alternatively, it is an illusion beyond which is ultimate
reality. In Buddhism, it is both uncreated and impermanent. In
Taoism, it is governed by a spiritual principle. In polytheism, many
divine beings are in interplay, often under the leadership of a High
God.

In all of these pictures there is some notion that by changing
one's orientation or by being in rapport with the divine Being
behind the cosmos, it is possible to gain mastery over it (in animism

that mastery is rather piecemeal). In short, all these views are in some degree or another mind-oriented. They see the cosmos as wholly or partly the product of a supreme mind, or of our own mind.

In contrast, materialism in its various forms sees the mind as just a byproduct of the cosmos. The world was not created by God; God was created by us and we are created out of matter. There have been materialist philosophies since ancient times—for example, in India at and even before the time of Buddha, and in ancient Greece. But in modern times there are two. One is Marxism which, in its understanding of human history, gives a special role to economics and theories of material production. Marx thought that life arises out of matter, and in due course society emerges in a form which contains within itself certain contradictions or tensions. These tensions bring about a struggle between economic classes which helps to fuel the onward drive of events. But culture and knowledge are essentially byproducts of material relations. For Marxists, religion is an illusion. There is no need to postulate a God to explain change and motion in matter: rather, the inner contradictions in matter supply the dynamics for such change.

The second form of materialism, "philosophical materialism," holds that conscious states—the center of what we call the mind— are nothing but specific kinds of physiological processes occurring in the brain and central nervous system. This doctrine produces a worldview which rejects claims that God exists in a purely nonmaterial state, or that the human soul has a real, but nonmaterial, substance. To put it crudely: if God existed he would have to be a material being like ourselves, and so could not be the creator of matter. Such materialism is, like Marxism, atheistic. But it differs from Marxism in not having the special theory of history and economics which has made Marxism such a telling force in the interpretation of historical experience.

These different pictures of the cosmos are affected partly by the human search for the truth about what surrounds us, and partly by the quest for meaning. The human being sees the cosmos as a kind of mirror: can she read in its strange and beautiful features a reflection of herself? What light can the sun and the stars throw upon the directions of life?

The varied worldviews as they come together in the global city pose vital questions about the future. Is human life to be exhausted in the struggle for material well-being? To what degree are we nourished by visions of the transcendent and of what lies somehow beyond the cosmos? What are the ways in which religion and science can live together, if in fact they can live together at all? How much will the traditional faiths change in their struggle to stay meaningful and believable to a world where human knowledge and technology are expanding so vastly?

From one perspective the different worldviews are maps of how to live. From another they themselves depict those powers in human experience and the cosmos which stir people to action. Figuring out their meaning is thus one way of coming to see what will happen in the complex emerging global civilization which is forming around us right now.

Central to the shape of traditional faiths, and central to the estimate of the spiritual power of human beings, are the patterns of religious experience which have irrupted into human life. To those let us now turn.

3 🌀

The Experiential Dimension

WHEN PEOPLE think of the cosmos as the work of a great God it is perhaps partly because they reason that the cosmos must have come from somewhere, and its beauties and design suggest a Creator of vast intelligence. Or it may be that they accept the word of others— as found, for instance, in such tremendous scriptures as the *Bhaga-vadgītā* or the Bible or the Koran. But it may also be because they have some feelings in their own experience of a majestic, terrifying, overwhelming, loving Being, a divine Reality. Indeed, if we look in the Song of the Lord (the *Gita*) we find there the most dramatic account of how the Arjuna, the hero of the narrative, is confronted by the Lord in all his many-formed glistening power, like a very personal nuclear explosion. And running like a thread through the Koran is the sense of the experiences of the mighty and compassionate Allah which came to Muhammad and set him on his amazing prophetic quest. The Bible, too, echoes with a sense of the mighty presence of the Lord—for Isaiah in the Temple, for Job in his complaining despair, for the apostle Paul as he plodded along the road to Damascus, ready to deal death to the disciples of that very Christ who now suddenly blinded him and crashed around his scared skull.

Not all religious people have such dramatic encounters. But people frequently do experience feelings which softly echo these great turning points in human history. Indeed, much of religious ritual is designed to express and to stimulate such feelings. The soaring columns of a great European cathedral, the dim religious light, the high-flying solemn choral music, the sanctity of slow procession, the clashing of the mysterious bells, the dark features of the great judge Christ depicted in the wondrous colored windows: all these things are meant to give us the feel of the Lord, the feel of the numinous God.

And in the humbler chapels of Protestantism, which are plain and without all the expensive and highly organized aids to experience, there is the intense feeling of the hymn, and the thundering voice of the preacher. It sometimes seems as if the preacher is possessed by some force outside of him and beyond him. That is as it ought to be, for he speaks and thunders not in his own name but in the name of the Lord to whom he has devoted his life, and it is this Lord whose majesty and mercy he seeks to express.

One can get a sense of the numinous God outside the cathedral, church, or temple—in nature. Religious thinkers and believers have long heard the "voice of God" in the wind of the tips of the soaring mountains, for instance, or in the churning of the ocean.

And sometimes the sense of presence comes to a person for no obvious outer reason at all. So we find many instances of people who are awed by an unseen force which seems wordlessly to approach them.

Numinous and Mystical Religious Experience

All this is one important strand of religious experience for which Rudolf Otto (1869–1937) in *The Idea of the Holy* coined the word "numinous." This he derived from the Latin word *numen*, a spirit—the sort of spirit that in Roman religion haunted the rivers and the copses and strange places and the threshold and the hearth: unseen forces sending a thrill of fear and power down one's back. For Otto the numinous experience is at the heart of religion. He defined it as the experience of something which is a *mysterium tremendum et fascinans*—a mystery which is fearful, awe-inspiring (*tremendum*, which literally means "to be trembled at"), and fascinating, and which, for all its fearfulness, draws you toward it. You get something of this feeling looking over a cliff: doesn't the great drop inspire fear, and yet aren't you also drawn toward it, so much so that sometimes you have to make a conscious effort to draw back? But above all, the sense of presence which confronts a person in the numinous experience is majestic: marvelous in power and glory. In their rather different ways the experiences of Arjuna, Isaiah, Job, Paul, and Muhammad are all numinous in character.

As I have said, for Rudolf Otto this kind of experience lay at the heart of religion. Through it he tried to explain the meaning of the Holy, and he saw holiness as the key category we use in defining religion. God is not just good: he is *holy,* and religion, for Otto, concerns that which is holy.

Otto also referred to the Holy as the Wholly Other—both because it was something completely other than the person encountering it, and because it was mysteriously other in quality from the things and people of this world. It is thus *different* and otherworldly, a description that fits in with many accounts of God in living religious contexts.

Otto was attempting to depict the central experience of religion. Since feelings were involved in the numinous experience he thought that the reader of his book would not understand it unless he too had had such an experience—and indeed, empathy would require at least some inkling of the nature of numinous feelings. But I think most people do understand: who has not felt awe before a storm; who has not had ghostly intimations of a strange presence; who has not felt dread? These may not amount to a full experience of the Holy but they are a step along the way.

Otto stressed feeling and the sense of the numinous because he wished to drive a path between physics and ethics, between the natural world and the world of value. If we go back to Immanuel Kant (1724–1804), chief figure of the European Enlightenment and the one who set the agenda for so much of Western philosophy since, we find a philosopher who wished to make sense of science—to try and see what the foundations of science are. But he wished to do this in a way which still left room for the moral agent; his philosophy recognized freedom of will outside the absolute constraints of the laws of physics. In so doing, however, it divided reality into two categories: science and ethics. Otto wanted to show how religion comes *in between:* it is in part about the cosmos, but it is not science; it is about action, but it is not just ethics—it is also worship. Worship comes in because the appropriate response to the Holy is indeed worship and adoration. Religion, in Otto's view, may also express itself as moral action, but at its heart worship is expression of a feeling of reverence for the numinous. Indeed, a typical characteristic of religion is that it involves the worship of God or gods. But is worship universal? And is it always of central importance? Are there religions, in other words, where worship is only secondary? The answer is yes.

There is another kind of religious experience—mystical experience—which has been very important for the history of humanity, and which does not seem to have the qualities Otto ascribes to the numinous. Thus, in the Indian tradition particularly and especially in Buddhism we find the practice of yogic meditation, aimed at purifying the consciousness of the individual to such a degree that all images and thoughts are left behind. It is as if the meditator is ascending a kind of inner ladder where at the highest rungs he or she gains a kind of pure bliss and insight, free from the distractions of ordinary experience. Very often this higher state is spoken of as being "non-dual," in other words, it is not like our usual experiences: in ordinary perception if I am looking at something, say a flower, then I am here and the flower is over there. I am the subject which sees: the flower is the object which is seen. But this distinction between subject and object seems to disappear in the higher mystical states, if we can judge from many reports. Also, such an ascent of stages of consciousness is usually said to involve the stilling of all feelings and the attainment of a perfect quietness. This is very different from the dynamic and shattering experience of the numinous.

As we shall see, there are some problems with the contrast which I am here trying to draw, but the contrast is nevertheless an important one. To sum it up: very often the mystical experience which arises in the process of contemplation or meditation is non-dual, but the numinous experience is very much dual; the mystical is quiet, but the numinous experience is powerful and turbulent; the mystical seems to be empty of images, while the numinous experience is typically clothed in ideas of encounter with a personal God; the mystical does not give rise to worship or reverence, in so far as there is nothing "other" to worship or revere.

This theory of mystical experience as "pure consciousness" helps to explain why we find systems of belief in the Indian tradition, most notably Buddhism, which do not give much importance to God or the gods, but put the highest value on personal liberation. The saintly yogi achieves the highest detachment and serenity, typically as a consequence of meditation which brings him to a state in which no distinctions can be made, in which the usual world of objects disappears. At the same time, however, this purity of consciousness usually is thought to bring about a kind of knowledge or insight: when a person sees the permanent, the impermanence of the world of objects is seen; when a person achieves the highest welfare, the truly unsatisfactory and suffering quality of ordinary life is known. Gaining true serenity, a person can reenter the ordinary world with equanimity, and know things and people in the new light shed by the higher state he or she has reached.

Thus it is that the central figure in the Buddhist faith, Gautama, left his wife, child, and luxurious life (according to the received story) to pursue the quest for the truth about the suffering of the world. After sitting at the feet of various teachers and practicing various kinds of self-control and fasting, he finally attained a state of enlightenment while sitting beneath a tree—the famous Bodhi, or Enlightenment Tree (an offshoot of which is still to be seen at Bodh-Gaya in northern India). He became thus the ideal expression of wisdom, who sought—and found—insight in the upper reaches of his consciousness, having tested in his mind various theories about the cosmos. As a result of his experience, he taught his new insight to a group of former associates, also yogis and seekers after truth, and spent more than forty years setting forth the doctrines and the path to liberation. Gautama did not teach worship. He did not speak of the Other. He did not prophesy in the name of the Lord. He did not put the mighty creator of the world at the center of his teaching and life. On the contrary: the creator god (Brahmā) of those who conserved the ancient tradition of the Vedas, the priestly caste known as Brahmins, he treated with irony. According to the Buddha Brahmā was merely under the illusion he had created the world—a mistake arising from the fact that after a period in which the cosmos lies dormant, asleep between two vast ages of dynamism, the first living being to arise in the new cosmic cycle is the god Brahmā, who ignorantly thinks that because he is the first being to emerge he caused what came after. But what came after was already programmed to emerge, independently of Brahmā's activity. This irony about the great god is an indication of how Buddhism, while not denying the gods outright, sought to put them down, to show that they were at best of secondary value. In fact, at the heart of the Buddha's message lies not the experience of gods or God but the non-dual experience of liberation. Virtually all the later teachings and variations of Buddhism can be seen as so many different ways of captivating human beings, through religious myths and practices, to set them forth on a path which will bring them freedom. This freedom consists of an experience of "emptiness," or purity of consciousness, together with the perception that this emptiness is the underlying nature of things, that they are without permanent substance.

But there is another strand in Indian thinking which is worth consideration and which helps to open up the debate about the contrast between the numinous and the mystical experiences. In those mysterious collections of writings known as the Upanishads, which came into being about the time of the Buddha, there are some famous so-called identity statements. These say "I am the divine Being," and "That art Thou" (usually interpreted to mean "Thou, as having within thee the eternal Self, art one with the divine Being"). The key words used in Sanskrit are *Brahman,* meaning the divine Being or Power, and *Ātman,* meaning "Self." The two are said to be the same. Now, if we spell this out in more concrete terms, what the Upanishads appear to be saying in such passages is as follows: "That divine Being which lies behind the whole cosmos, which creates it and sustains it and constitutes its inner nature, is the same as what you will discover in the depths of your own Self, if you will voyage inward through self-control and the methods of meditation and purification of your consciousness."

Here, in effect, the two strands of religious experience and thinking are being woven together. On the one hand, there is the numinous Brahman, seen as divine Power behind the cosmos and dimly visible through nature: this is the numinous Being who, in later Indian thought is portrayed in a more personal and dramatic way, as the great gods Shiva and Vishnu and as the divine female Kali, replete with power, terror, and love. On the other hand, there is the mystical search within. The Upanishads in a flash of insight bring the two together: the divine Being is found not only out there, but also within the heart. This is a theme of much mysticism elsewhere—among Christians, for instance, who adopt the path of con-templation in order to seek God at the depths of their souls.

But in doing this such Christians are seeing the inner path in the light of a previously accepted numinous God who is the object of worship and devotion. In the case of Buddhism there was no such prior assumption: Buddhism was interested more in pursuing the inner path without believing in the Creator and the Wholly Other.

Let us see how far we've come in setting out a theory about the types of religious experience. Some religious traditions or phases of traditions stress the powerful Other, the great Creator. Others stress more the inner quest, without reference to God. Others combine the two quests. Before going on to see the questions which stem from this theory, it may be useful to see whether there are other strands of religious experience to consider.

The British writer R. C. Zaehner (1919–1975) drew attention, as others have done, to the fact that in a number of cultural contexts people may have a very powerful sense of unity with nature—with the cosmos around them. This sense of being lost to oneself but yet united to the world around, this sense of being part of a whole, Zaehner referred to as the "panenhenic" experience. The word derived from Greek means "all (*pan*) in (*en*) one (*hen*) ish (*ic*)." This concept may have been important for teachers of early Taoism. It came to be important in the development of Chinese and Japanese Buddhism, for instance in Zen, where themes from Taoism were blended with the spirit of Buddhist meditation. Thus, often we find in Zen art the idea of the disappearance of all distinctions between oneself and the world around one. The Zen poem—haiku—attempts in brief compass to bring out something of this strange and yet also beautiful way of perceiving the world.

Another form of religious experience, prevalent among small-scale and hunting societies, is that of the shaman. The shaman is a person who, because of his special personality, can make contact with the supernatural world. He will go into a trance, and is thought to ascend to the heavenly world and to descend into the world of the dead. His ability to be in contact with spirits and his capacity to come back from the realm of death give him the power, it is thought, not only to tell where game can be found, but also to cure disease. Dramatically he can reenact the death and restoration to life of the sick person, and so restore him to health. Much attention has been given to shamanism by the modern historian of religions, Mircea Eliade (b. 1907), who sees it as a key phenomenon of archaic religion. This may be so because shamanism may have influenced early techniques of producing special states of consciousness such as methods of breathing and mind-control in the Indian and Chinese traditions—and out of this came the whole yoga tradition. On the other hand, a strand of the shamanistic experience is found in the phenomenon of being "possessed." In trance the shaman may be "occupied" by a god and so come to speak the words of the god. He thus becomes a crucial link between the world of spirits and the community to which he belongs. Out of this strand of shamanism there may have developed the tradition in which the prophet is not just confronted by God as the numinous Other, but also speaks in the name of the Lord as though he is, so to say, "possessed" by God. Thus God says to Jeremiah that he has "put words in his mouth" after mysteriously touching his lips.

So one model which we can propose about the way religious experience has developed is as follows: There are two developments of shamanism, which we might call the right wing and the left wing. The right wing focuses on the numinous experience of the Other, and the experience of the prophet is a special form of this. Institutionally, the successor to the prophet is the preacher, who tries to recapture something of the spirit of prophecy. The left wing focuses on the mystic or yogi, the one who practices the art of contemplation; institutionally, the successor of the mystical teachers of the past is the monk or nun.

This way of looking at religious experience, polarized into the numinous and mystical experiences, suggests that somehow mysticism is the same in differing religions, and that the difference between, say, the Christian and the Buddhist mystic is found in the kind of interpretation each places on her or his experience. Thus, the Christian finds in the light of the purity of her consciousness a sense of union with Christ, while the Buddhist sees the non-dual light as insight into the Emptiness, the Void, which lies in the midst of everything. But are the differences just a matter of interpretation? There has been much debate in recent times about this, for a number of reasons.

One is that, like Zaehner, some scholars think that there is a distinctive kind of mysticism which is different from the non-dual type (which he referred to as "monistic"). Zaehner thought that there is an inner experience the Christian and other God-oriented mystics undergo which involves the feeling of a loving relationship (he called this "theistic" mysticism). In this, Zaehner was defending belief in God, for he thought of the non-dual experience as being at a lower level and so not as important or revealing. But once we talk about levels we usually are talking about value judgments. Why is the loving experience better than the non-dual one? It depends on your point of view. For many modern Westerners the idea of a personal relationship with God is at the heart of religion, but for the Buddhist we have to get away from preoccupation with personhood, which is only a mask of the ego, of selfishness. Who is right?

Another consideration is this: How do we tell what belongs to the experience itself and what to the interpretation? If I see a rope on the ground and perceive it as a snake and so get a fright, is it not true to say that I experienced a snake? So, if a mystic sees the inner light of consciousness as manifesting the divine being, does he not then experience God?

It may be so. But still, the idea of the single type of mystical experience is useful, for it enables us to understand that there are recurrent patterns of inner consciousness into which, according to context, people of differing religious and cultural traditions read differing messages.

This idea also helps to explain some other things. It helps to explain why mysticism in the West and in Islam has helped to promote what has been called "negative theology," or the way of thinking about God which stresses what cannot be said: God is beyond language, beyond thought. This side of belief chimes in with the experience of pure consciousness: if indeed God is found within— in what contains no images or thoughts or distinctions, in this bright and purifying blank—then God cannot be spoken of as this or that. This "negative theology" is a counterweight to the positive, sometimes very human ways, in which God is spoken of, for instance, in the Bible. Many preachers talk of God as though he is a human being writ large, who tells us to do this or that, and worries about moral rules and whether there should be abortions or war. We should indeed see these important issues in the light of the highest values that we know, and for the Christian or Jew that means seeing them in the light of Eternity, of God. And since God is infinite, he has so much energy that it is not especially tiresome for him to worry about our minor human concerns. But even so there is often a need to counterbalance this human language about the divine Being with negativity: God may be like us but he is also very unlike us. He may be wise but it is not in the way in which a person would be wise. His goodness goes beyond all our ideas of goodness. And so on. So "negative" and mystical language helps to balance the other talk of God.

Also, our theory of two strands of experience helps to explain a tension which from time to time appears between mystics and orthodoxy in traditions which believe in God. The orthodox stress the holiness and otherness of God. The orthodox Muslim or Christian conceives of God as Other and of us merely as creatures. It is blasphemous to put ourselves on a par with God. But if the mystical experience is, as we have seen, non-dual, and if by contrast the numinous God is Other, different from us, then there is a problem about the mystic's non-dual experience of God. The mystic often is led by the experience to say that he becomes one with God. He loses his sense of otherness from God. And this may even lead to the paradox of saying that one becomes or is God (as the Upanishads indeed say). This happened in the case of al-Hallaj (ca. 858–922), a famous Sufi mystic within Islam. He thought that all duality between himself and Allah was washed away and so said "I am the Real," using here one of the titles of Allah himself. For his blasphemy, for that was how the orthodox saw it, he was put to death—crucified, in fact, for he was an admirer of Jesus and crucifixion seemed a suitably ironic punishment.

Our theory of types of experience is also useful in helping to explain differing patterns of doctrine. If you stress the numinous, you stress that our salvation or liberation (our becoming holy) must flow from God the Other. It is he who brings it to us through his grace. You also stress the supreme power and dynamism of God as creator of this cosmos. If, on the other hand, you stress the mystical and the non-dual, you tend to stress how we attain salvation or liberation through our own efforts at meditation, not by the intervention of the Other. You also tend to stress the emptiness of things, the idea of a liberation which takes us beyond this impermanent life. If we combine the two but accentuate the numinous, we see mystical union as a kind of close embrace with the other—like human love, where two are one and yet the two-ness remains. If the accent is on the mystical rather than the numinous, then God tends to be seen as a being whom we worship, but in such a way that we get beyond the duality, until even God disappears in the unspeakable non-dual higher consciousness. This is the position of Advaita Vedānta, as we have noted; it is also in rather a different way the position of Mahāyāna or Greater Vehicle Buddhism (which developed out of early Buddhism and became the dominant kind of Buddhism in China and Japan) in its mainstream.

There is another way in which we may look at the distinction between the numinous and the mystical. In the numinous, the Eternal lies, so to speak, beyond the cosmos and outside the human being. In the mystical, the Eternal somehow lies within us. In the first case we need to be dependent on the Other; in the second case we may rely upon our own powers, though the task of penetrating to the Eternal may be very hard. The numinous, in encouraging worship, encourages a loving dependence on the Other. The mystical, in encouraging meditation, encourages a sense of self-emptying. As we have seen, the two can go together. But there are differing accents.

In this discussion I have, of course, been oversimplifying. Because of the richness of ideas and myths in which experiences tend to be clothed, the feelings and insights people gain can vary subtly and widely in character. I have tried to combine Otto's theory with other theories which in modern times have emphasized the unity of mystical experiences across the religions. The famous writer Aldous Huxley (1894–1963) also emphasized such mystical unity. In his book *The Perennial Philosophy* he did much to influence Western thinking about the inner searches of Eastern religions, and so contributed to that flowering of mystical interests and gentleness which accompanied the otherwise turbulent 1960s.

Questions of Value and Truth

But a question is likely to remain in our minds. Is there after all any basis to these experiences? It is true that we may feel a sense of awe before the glories of the cosmos, or may from time to time experience a sense of the overpowering presence of God. It is true that yogis may purify their consciousness and feel thereby a sense of illumination and freedom. But so what? Aren't they perhaps delusions, these experiences? Is the mystical, non-dual experience not in the last analysis just a very interesting state of mind? And isn't the sense of presence of God just like a waking dream? We may feel that Someone confronts us: Arjuna in the Song of the Lord may think himself in front of Vishnu in all his dramatic and terrifying glory. But is this not something that can be explained by some theory of projection? Couldn't we say that Arjuna projected his vision outward onto the screen of the world and then took it to be something real?

From one point of view we should not be concerned about what the value of various religious experiences is or might be. They have the effects that they have quite independently of how we may view them. But many writers in one way or another have tried to argue that religion is indeed a projection; and if this is true, it would follow that key religious experiences are also projections. The projection theory is one explanation of how so pervasive a feature of human history arose and how it maintains itself.

Consider one way in which the numinous experience, or one of its offshoots, is quite common in modern life: the experience of being "born again." The person who feels this, in the Christian context, often has feelings not unlike those of the great reformer, Martin Luther (1483–1546)—a deep sense of sin and powerlessness. These are the mirror images, so to speak, of the power and holiness of God as the Other. In the face of the Holy the individual feels unholy. Christ comes to such a person, giving a marvelous reassurance. If he repents, then the Savior will overcome the sin and give the person new power in his life. Some would argue that it is the circumstances of the person's life and times that created in him the sense of sin, and that the threatening figure of God was something projected from his unconscious out of a sense of guilt, arising from infantile conflicts in the nuclear family. To say this is to echo the thinking of psychoanalysis, going back to Freud's influential book *Totem and Taboo* (1915). Freud gives a psychological interpretation to then current theories of totemism in archaic religion, in which each clan or group has a totem or sacred animal, which is normally forbidden or taboo. So wouldn't we, by Freud's explanation, be suggesting that his sense of the numinous (with the *tremendum*—"to be trembled at"—aspect being played by the Father and the *fascinans* by Christ) comes from his own psyche, triggered by the circumstances of his life? If we could manage such explanation consistently, it would no doubt be a great advance in trying to understand the power of religion and the ways in which it works.

But for the explanation to be valid certain conditions have to be met. For one thing, Freud's theory on the dynamics of the psyche would have to be confirmed in a variety of cultures. Here there is a problem with Freud's *Totem and Taboo* and his later ideas about religion. He did not have access to the wide knowledge of other religions which we now possess. The fact is that his stress upon the role of the Father figure in religion (which is, as it were, the heavenly image of the real-life father) is relevant only to some religions and not others. Moreover, the data which Freud drew on in late nineteenth- and early twentieth-century Vienna were largely related to a very special and not very typical society whose preoccupations were Christianity and Judaism.

For Freud himself religion was an illusion. His position has been influential not just because of the fruitful way in which he made use of the idea of the unconscious mind, but also because his picture of human nature and the path of self-understanding became itself an alternative to religion. The analyst was able to take over something of the priest's role: he was a new kind of pastor, very much in the modern idiom. The new teachings of psychoanalysis could deal with guilt and promise a new kind of spiritual health. The patient, in undergoing the process of analysis, went through a new form of religious initiation and renewal.

This leads us to see a problem about theories of the origins of religious experience. Such theories may, like Freud's, begin from the assumption that there is no ultimate religious reality—that there is no God. So they already begin from a particular worldview—a humanist one in the sense in which we used this term in the previous chapter. But what is the reason for starting with that worldview rather than with one which accepts the existence of something lying beyond the visible cosmos? Or is there perhaps some neutral standpoint between rejection of God and acceptance of him? (Or between acceptance of nirvana and rejection of it?)

To spell out further the problem about the Freudian position on traditional religion: isn't Freud using one worldview to judge another—like the Christian missionary we referred to earlier, who judges Hinduism from the assumptions of the Bible? Freud was—

with part of himself at any rate—claiming to be engaged in science. However, it is not scientific simply to begin with assumptions that would make a rival theory false before the evidence is properly examined. And once we begin to look at Freud's major writings on the origin of religion in the light of the evidence from the history of religions, we find that his theories break down. For instance, he thought totemism, or the worship of sacred animals, was a universal early phenomenon. He was relying on some contemporary anthropology that is now out of date. His idea that the leader of a primitive human horde had been killed by his sexually jealous sons was pure speculation derived in part from an aside in the writings of Charles Darwin. It is a remarkable thing that so speculative a theory should have won so much intelligent support in the 1920s. We can perhaps explain it the way many have chosen to explain the popularity of religion: it is a case of appeal, rather than truth.

I shall come back to the question of how we judge religious experiences, but first let us look at two further depth psychological approaches. One is that of Carl Gustav Jung, who broke with Freud in the early days of psychoanalysis, and took a positive view of the value of religion and of the symbols people use in myth and ritual, the symbols which, so to speak, well up from the human race's unconscious. Jung's attitude toward religious experience was ambiguous: although he did not affirm any particular religious doctrine, he nevertheless considered that religion could be useful in helping people reach balance and maturity, and achieve an integrated personality.

Erich Fromm (b. 1900), who belongs to the Freudian tradition, considered that religion could be a good force if it were humanistic. For him religion is unavoidable, for it represents for a group a common outlook and a common focus of devotion—and every group needs these. Fromm believed, however, that a religion which is authoritarian and rigid is bad for us. For one thing, all that is good and reasonable in ourselves is projected outward onto God, and we are left merely with a sense of sin and powerlessness. We are alienated from our own goodness.

It thus appears that from Fromm's perspective the numinous experience of the powerful Other is unhealthy. When he wrote about Luther (and Luther's religion was permeated with the sense of the numinous), he remarked:

Thus, while Luther freed people from the authority of the Church, he made them submit to a much more tyrannical authority, that of a God who insisted on complete submission of man and annihilation of the individual self as the essential condition of his salvation. *Luther's faith was the conviction of being loved upon the condition of surrender ...*

And this was because:

If you get rid of your individual self with all its shortcomings and doubts by utmost self-effacement, you free yourself from the feeling of your own nothingness and can participate in God's glory.*

There have been others who also looked at Luther from the perspective of psychoanalysis, and there seems to be some ground for thinking that the numinous awareness of God was able to play a key role in resolving conflicts arising acutely within Luther's soul. In other words, we have here a typical religious equation: a type of experience which had part of its dynamic from factors outside the individual, encountering the psychological condition inside the individual.

At any rate Luther's outlook, with its undue respect for power and authority and its sense of the complete sinfulness and evil in the human being when left alone and without the intervening power and grace of God, is, for Fromm, unhealthy. It is not humanistic, because it fails to mobilize what is good in human nature. By contrast, Fromm is more favorable toward the religion of the mystic and of Jesus as he, Fromm, interpreted it. For Fromm, the Oedipus complex which Freud saw as resulting from a child's sexual jealousy of the parent is not so much sexual as a craving for dependence on the parent. The adult, like the child, wishes to prolong childhood and to avoid freedom. But a truly humanistic approach is one which stresses freedom. When Jesus said "For I am come to set a man at variance against his father and the daughter against her mother," what he meant, according to Fromm, was that the individual must

---

*The quotations are from J. Milton Yinger, ed., *Religion, Society and the Individual* (New York: Macmillan, 1957), p. 392.

throw off the craving to be a child. Whether he is right in his feeling for what the Gospel means is another matter.

Fromm's way of looking at religion is quite openly judgmental. He distinguishes the good and valuable in religion from what he regards as dangerous and unhealthful. As I have said before with some force, it is important for us to look first not to questions of value but to questions of power and meaning—to see how world-views actually operate and what their significance is for human beings. But if I may comment on the question of evaluation, then I think we must look at religious experience in a wider context than the psychology of the individual, important though this is. We need to see the degree to which religion and its core experiences have been creative and destructive. Fromm, in writing the words quoted above, was trying to set the debate in a wider context, for he saw in Luther's attitudes some of the seeds of later Nazism. And it cannot be denied that sometimes the numinous and wrathful character of the experience of God can lean in the direction of hostility. Often the preacher "possessed" by the numinous also expresses hatreds. And, in particular, Luther was highly abusive of the Jews, and so contributed to that stream of anti-Semitism which was so destructive to Europe.

But on the other hand there are things to be said regarding the creativity of Luther the prophet. For one thing, Luther's revolution itself prepared the way for a critique of authority and for a new vision of the individual which has done much to shape Western culture. By a paradox, the human relationship with a powerful and merciful God can give the individual a source of independence against the powerful and often unmerciful pressures of the state, economic power, and prevailing values.

But perhaps the main thing we can learn from this brief look at some of the depth psychologists is that they too bring a worldview to bear in estimating religious experience. Their worldview is not that of any of the traditional religions. It tends to be humanist by denying the transcendent realm, that other depth which lies beyond the cosmos which the older religions see as the abode of the divine, or of nirvana. The depth psychologists tend to start from a picture of the human being trapped, as it were, within the material cosmos. In so doing, they beg the question of whether religious experience tells us anything about the way things are—the question of whether religious visions and insights "tell the truth." If there is only this cosmos, then nothing, however dramatic in experience, will make us aware of something outside the cosmos. The experience of what transcends or goes beyond the cosmos will always be interpreted as having its origins inside us. So the question of whether religious experience tells us the truth at all is a question that depends in part on the worldview with which we start. It looks like a circle. But it is not a circle to be trapped in, for what it shows is that questions of religious truth are a matter of the perspective with which they are viewed. And which perspective—the humanist or the religious—is more convincing depends on a whole array of details.

Initially, in worldview analysis, we are concerned with the power of religion and its varieties of experience. One of the things we can learn from psychology is that personal factors will be important in determining the degree to which a type of religion "catches on." And depth psychology helps to explore how symbolic patterns, of which we are at best only half aware, help shape our feelings and actions and thus prepare seed beds upon which the differing worldviews may grow.

4 ❧

The Mythic Dimension

WHEN THE Christian Church was making its way in the Roman Empire it had to struggle against the Greek, Roman, and other religions, all of which had complicated stories of the gods. The Christians often spoke of these stories rather disparagingly, because they were not based (said they) upon fact, as were the stories contained in the Bible—particularly the story of Christ and his resurrection. The Greek word for stories was *mythoi* from which we get "myths." As a result of this Christian campaign against myth we still tend to think of myths as "false stories." It is odd, incidentally, how even the word "stories" sometimes gets this sense, as when we say of someone that "she is only telling stories." But as we have seen, modern students of religion commonly use the word "myth" in a neutral sense to mean a story of divine or sacred significance, without implying that it is false or true.

For the fact is that the stories of the Bible, which are in many cases historically based, fulfill a function similar to some of the stories about the gods of Greece and Rome and elsewhere. The term "myth" is used to highlight this likeness of function among stories in different religions or cultures. Thus an Indian text says *Iti devā akurvata ity u vau manuṣyāḥ*: "Thus did the gods do, and thus too

79

human beings do." This briefly conveys the thought that the myth of divine action presents an example of how humans should act. The gods are thus seen as paradigms. Likewise, in the Christian tradition the stories of Christ and of some of the heroes of the Old Testament become patterns for the faithful to follow. Other religions have a story of how death came into the world, and we are reminded in this of the events in the Garden of Eden. So in this and other ways it is artificial to separate supposed false myths about the divine from "true" stories as found in the Bible or elsewhere. There are important questions to be asked about truth, but these come later.

But we are, of course, looking at these matters from the perspective of the second half of the twentieth century. We have our own way of looking at stories, and we should see what this is before we consider the nature of traditional myths. As we shall see, stories remain crucial to our world, though they now have evolved into different kinds and styles from those older myths.

The Power of History

Of those stories, narratives, and dramas with which we describe human and other actions and which have special meaning for us "moderns," history is probably the most important. We seem to have a powerful desire to discover what the past was really like, and to try to piece together a coherent story of events. Interestingly, part of that desire to know about the past involves understanding ourselves and who we are. Thus, in high school we learn about our history—going back to the events of 1776 and beyond, for the story of our group helps to give us a sense of cohesion, of belonging together. Think, too, how people like to trace their "roots."

In this we find two opposite tendencies tugging against one another. On the one hand there is the impulse to romanticize the past, to fashion heroes out of it (history as myth), because in a sense they make *us* greater. We draw substance from them. It is like ancestry: I think it is nice to be descended from somebody famous, for some of the fame then rubs off on me. But on the other hand, the dictates of truth and accuracy enter in. The modern historian goes on the evidence, as does the modern biographer. So sometimes our great heroes and great events suffer when the truth is revealed: it may turn out that our great leader in war was an alcoholic, or that some famous victory was the result of fortunate blunders rather than heroism and cunning. The fact that history is often about *us*, our nation or group, may encourage inflationary trends, boosting the "good" in it; while the more sober and scientific approach tries to be realistic, and may in fact seem deflationary.

Since the French Revolution, nationalism has helped to promote the writing of history as each national group tries to create, so to speak, its own past. It is now common to think of history in national terms—we talk of Italian history, American, Canadian, French, Indian, Cambodian, and so on—using modern political groupings in order to define the past. There was no consciousness as such of being Italian three hundred years ago: there were different regions of the peninsula under differing rules. The German statesman Bismarck was not altogether wrong in referring to Italy as merely a geographical expression. But Italy emerged as a self-conscious nation and it is from this standpoint that we look backward to the "Italian" past. Anyway, there is a strong trend in modern times to see history as a grouping of national histories, each of which illuminates the nature of the nation in question. In brief, the story of Italy or of the United States becomes a means of creating a consciousness of being Italian or being American.

So history is not just a matter of the scholarly investigation of the past: it also allows a people to form a national identity.

As for the tension, to which I referred, between history as myth and history as the result of critical inquiry, we might ask: "Why should we listen to historians who often puncture some of our cherished stories, and rewrite our past?" The answer is that scientific history has authority for us. The properly trained historian can tell us how things were. He or she is part of the fabric of modern scholarship and science which for us have an entirely convincing air. And this is where modern history is like traditional myth: myths too commanded that breathless authority, unquestioned reality.

The tension between history as myth and history as the result of critical inquiry is something which has become explosive in the religious context, where earlier histories tend to get rewritten. Nowhere is this more obvious than in the case of the Bible. Scientific and rather skeptical historians probe the documents which make up the Gospels or the books of Moses and cast doubt on some of the events there depicted. Did Jesus turn water into wine? Was he really born in Bethlehem? How did he relate to the people we know about from the Dead Sea Scrolls? We shall come back to these problems shortly.

Beyond the more particular historical narratives, there have grown up in modern times theories by which such narratives are interpreted. The philosopher Hegel (1770–1831) had an ambitious vision of the whole of human history as a process which he called "dialectic." This term could be translated as "argument," as though history constituted a complex debate or dialogue within culture, or within the human mind. He saw dialectic as a pattern in which one person affirms a position, called the *thesis*. Someone takes the opposite stance, known as the *antithesis*. Typically, truth lies between and beyond the two, and so a third position known as the *synthesis* emerges which takes up some of the points within both the thesis and the antithesis. This synthesis then becomes the thesis for the next phase of history, and so on. Thus, for Hegel, Jesus' religion was a thesis, Paul's the antithesis, and the two emerge as a synthesis, namely Catholic Christianity. This dialectical theory was an inspiration for Karl Marx, who translated it from cultural and intellectual terms into material and economic ones: so economic classes, for instance, came to be seen in dialectical struggle with one another. A middle point between Hegel's emphasis on the intellectual factors in human history and Marx's stress on the material factors is the sociologist Max Weber's theory of how religion affects economic development, which in turn affects the shape of those religious factors.

Also we find in modern times some people such as the noted English historian Arnold Toynbee (1899–1975) writing histories of the world. These are designed to let us see the whole sweep and meaning of the global past. These ambitious histories and theories do not please all modern historians, some of whom prefer to stick to the detailed examination of events rather than get caught up in speculation about great patterns of history. But the theories have had a great influence, nowhere more so than in the case of Marx's legacy. One reason for the influence of these theories is that we wish to "make sense of" the past, in a way that may guide us in the future. In a way these theories are the heirs of the traditional myths which recount the drama of the human race.

But as important as histories and biographies may be, there are other stories which modern people look to for illumination of the nature of human life—particularly literature and great novels such as those of Dostoyevsky, Balzac, or Hemingway, and dramas, whether on the stage or the screen. We have become used to the idea of finding truths about the world and about ourselves through what is for the most part *fiction*. Fiction is a category side by side with history, providing for us significant stories. In fiction and drama the events can become, by a kind of illusion, real to us. While we are in the theater we are gripped by what is going on. Within that framework of time and space, inside the theater during the performance, the story has authority and impact. Yet at the back of our minds we know that this is "only a play," "only a movie."

The Power of Myth

The myth is something which is told or enacted through a ritual like a kind of drama, and which exists in an unquestioned atmosphere. It is uttered with the implicit idea "This is how things are and this is how things have been." Unlike history, although not unlike some theories of history, myth can tell about the future—what the end of the world will be like, for instance. Very often the story of the human race and of the cosmos is depicted as framed by "first things"—the creation of the world, the making of the first humans, and so on—and by the "last things" at the end. Thus the Christian Bible begins with Creation and ends in Revelation, with the final summing up of things and the judgment by Christ.

Not only are myths "given," that is, they are told with authority—a breathless air of unquestionable truth—but they also often play strange tricks with things and people. In the Garden of Eden there are a mysterious tree and a speaking serpent, for instance. Myths often contain a set of symbols, that is to say beings and actions which have a meaning beyond themselves. So it is that Adam is not just a man, but stands for all men and women, and the action of eating the fruit has some half-known deep meaning which implies that by this act Adam and Eve are liable to experience death. Nothing here is quite what it seems to be: to decipher its meaning we need to look to what may be called "symbolic depth." In order to understand the mythic dimension we have to know something of the language of symbols in religion and human life. The work of Jung is fertile in this area, for he tries to give psychological insight into the kinds of symbols which he found to exist crossculturally, both in the East and the West.

Because symbols are important in traditional religion, as well as in literature, where they find a new life, it is not surprising that religious art, poetry, and music often convey aspects of the meaning of life. Thus, a branch of inquiry in the field of religion is "iconography," the study of the visual symbols of faith. And secular worldviews which most resemble traditional religions also express themselves through art, music, and poetry. Thus Marxism produces socialist realism, a particularly heroic style of art which invests matter with a kind of shining light and in fact brings out the symbolic importance of production, revolutionary war, and so forth in the furthering of socialism and the consummation of human history.

I have spoken so far mainly about the "telling" of myths. But often myths are not just told in a verbal transaction: they are acted out in ritual. Thus, in the Christian tradition the events of the Last Supper are acted out in the Mass (the Eucharist or Lord's Supper). The story is conveyed in action. The myth is the script for a sacred drama. Many ancient myths are scripts in this sense, and it is no coincidence that Greek drama emerged out of the sacred enactment of myths. The old stories were given a freer and more secular form in the tragedies of Aeschylus and his successors. Some scholars earlier in this century belonged to what was called the "myth and ritual school"; they argued that myth is always to be seen in a ritual context. Although this point of view is too sweeping, it has been illuminating to see how creation myths in the ancient Near East (for instance in Babylon), were reenacted annually at the great spring festivals (for the spring, too, is a miracle of re-creation).

Part of our life involves putting celebration and the meaningful events of the past together. People celebrate my birthday: they perform what, in a broad sense, are rituals, like wishing me many happy returns, buying me a drink, eating cake with me, giving me presents. What is it all about? What is so special about the day of the year in which my birth once happened? Although the idea of the birthday is simple on the surface, it pays to look deeper. First, my birth is important because it is the beginning of me as a person (at least traditionally we have thought that way, rather than thinking about conception, for it is obscure and invisible, while birth is a dramatic entry into the land of daylight). My birth then is my beginning; and beginnings, "firsts" of any kind, we tend to think of as being especially meaningful—the Wright brothers as the first people to fly; the first time Everest was climbed; the first person to run a four-minute mile, and so on. The first of anything comes to stand as the origin of its kind, and so symbolizes the whole kind. Thus my birth is the first of "me" events, and symbolizes them all. Through my birth my whole person is celebrated.

What does it mean to celebrate? Well, first of all it is a case of *doing* things. Even the words that others use are words that *do* rather than words that *state* or *describe* anything. They are utterances that modern philosophers, following J. L. Austin (1911–1960), call *performatives*. They perform something. When I say "I promise," I am doing something, namely promising, which is a kind of contract. If I say at my wedding "I do" (take this person to be my wedded spouse) then I have thereby entered into matrimony. My status is in this respect altered. When someone says "Many happy returns of the day," he is not describing things (as if he were saying "The sun is shining today"). It is not a statement which can be true or false, but it expresses a wish, and in a conventional way it congratulates me on my birthday. This is congratulating me on my existence, and expressing the fact that people cherish me.

Similar thoughts apply to the performances which occur on July 4, say, or on the anniversary of the Russian Revolution. Here a piece of history is made present and celebrated because it is the origin of the nation or of the state. Celebrating American independence is celebrating America. This ritual expresses and stimulates feelings of pride in the nation.

Thus, we can see traditional myths as often providing the scenario for performances designed to do things—bring about actual results in the world. For example, the celebration of God's creation of the world may help (so it is, or was, thought) to stimulate new growth and fruitfulness.

There is one other aspect of birthdays worth dwelling on. Theoretically, any day could do, if all people want to do is to express the fact that they cherish me. Why choose the actual day of my birth? Well, of course it is not quite the actual day: that happened many years ago and happened only once. But we look upon the "same day" each year as indeed being the same as the day in the past when I was born. It is the day that occurs at the same point within the yearly cycle, to which, for various reasons, we attach great significance. In terms of position in the relevant sequence, the day is identical in position to the date when I was actually born. So we have the idea of cycles in which the "same day" keeps coming around. Because of its resemblance to the original day it is thought to reflect that day, and so my birth becomes present again. What is past becomes present.

This is a crucial feature of much ritual. It makes possible a kind of time travel from the present to the past (and even sometimes from the present to the future, as when in Revelation the events of the last days are experienced by St. John here and now). Thus at Easter Christians are aware of the risen Christ as being present to them not as an event then but as an event now: "Jesus Christ is risen today" is what the faithful say at the climax of the Eastern Orthodox rituals. "He is risen," not "He was risen."

One feature of the mythic performance, then, is that the events described become present. *Then* becomes *now*. But when did the events occur? Sometimes they seem to have a rather vague location in time, like those stories which begin "Once upon a time." As the Gospel of John begins: "In the beginning was the Word and the Word was with God." But when was that beginning? Is it to be thought of as a date like 1776 or 1066, each of which is a "beginning," the one of the United States, the other of England?

The very influential historian of religions, Mircea Eliade, who was close in thought to Jung, has a special theory about the importance of the idea of "In the beginning." He considers that the prototype of myths is the myth of the formation or creation of the cosmos or of phenomena within it, such as death. The myth describes events occurring not in ordinary time, but in a kind of mythic time, or as Eliade puts it using a Latin phrase, *in illo tempore* ("in *that* time"). The Australian aborigines talk about a "dream time" in which sacred events occur. Eliade thinks that it was typical for early man to see things in his world as all the time reflecting that sacred reality "in the beginning." Jung would agree. For Jung the deep symbols or archetypes are present in the human race's unconscious, and they keep welling up into myths in differing cultures. Eliade makes the idea more specific in relation to the structure of myth. The myth describes the archetypes in motion: the ideas of new birth, of death, of wholeness spring to life in the myths of the first things. The telling of the myth recreates these realities and so it was that early man relived his deepest symbols. He overcame time and change by living in the light of that "time which is not time," *illo tempore*. By contrast, modern folk have cut themselves off from these sacred realities and live in the shadow of time and change, the terror of history, as Eliade calls it. We are governed by deadlines, clocks, schedules—the apparatus of the tyranny of time.

Similarly, in his studies of yoga and shamanism, Eliade sees the experiences a person attains through various techniques as taking her or him beyond ordinary time. Time is annihilated and so the person comes in contact with sacred reality.

There are actually many different kinds of sacred stories, and not all fit into the pattern of events in "dream time," "*that* time"—which is not quite historical or "our" time. For instance, the story of Exodus in which the people of Israel were saved from their oppressors through the guidance of their Lord—an event celebrated at Passover and at other times in the Jewish year—is meant to be about an actual time in the past. Another example is this: the story of Jesus' death and resurrection, which the Apostles' Creed of the Christian Church cites as being very dateable, "under Pontius Pilate." If we look East, to the story of the Buddha's enlightenment, again we see an event of sacred and liberating significance which took place at a particular time and in a special location.

It is perhaps wise to pause here to look at some of the most important kinds of traditional myths.

Some explain the origin of the cosmos as a creation, usually by the thought or the word of a divine Being. Some tell of the emergence of the cosmos out of some preexisting chaos or undifferentiated matter. For instance, in some ancient Indian myths the world is conceived of as an egg: the splitting apart of the egg gives rise to the cosmos. Others see the cosmic order as a result of the dismemberment of a primeval human being, or a sea monster (like Tiamat in ancient Near Eastern myth). Water often plays a vital part because, as many studies have shown and as we have seen, water in numerous cultures is the symbol of choas. Out of chaos comes order, the cosmos itself. Although the Genesis story, which is woven together out of various myths, has been put together in order to show in the most striking possible way the creation of the world out of nothing, and by the sovereign decision of God, here too we have reference to an earlier "something"—the waters over which the spirit of God brooded, and which symbolize a primeval chaos.

The stories of the beginning or emergence of the cosmos are one variety of a major and vital category of myths, namely those that tell about origins—for instance, how an institution (like keeping the Sabbath) arose, or how a particular kind of plant or animal came into being. Important in particular are those stories dealing with the origin of death. Here is a fine example of this type, which Mircea Eliade quotes in *From Primitives to Zen,* from Sulawesi in Indonesia: In the beginning the sky was close to the earth. One day the creator God let down a stone on the end of a rope, but the first man and woman refused it and wanted something else. So he let down a banana, which they eagerly accepted. Then God told them that because they had refused the stone and taken the banana they would be like the latter. Whereas the stone does not change, a banana plant dies while its offspring continue. This then is how death came into the world.

There are a large number of symbolic themes here. The idea that the sky, the divine home, is close to the earth, the human race's home, suggests that there is not, in the beginning, an alienation between humans and God, but they exist in a much closer relationship. The notion that the first man and woman's action affects the rest of their race ties in with a common theme that the symbolic first being not only represents, but somehow sums up in his or her own person the rest of the race. The fact that the first humans did not know what they were doing in choosing the attractive and edible banana suggests that God tricked them: this is in line with the belief that immortality is a divine thing and not for human beings to aspire to. The idea that what they choose is what they come to resemble (especially since in eating the banana they would somehow assimilate its essence) is a common one in mythic and symbolic thinking: like affects like.

The idea that the sky and earth were once close is linked to a common theme in which the High God withdraws upward, perhaps as a result of some stupidity or offense on the part of the first humans. After that the High God leaves the real work of shaping and guiding the affairs of the cosmos to lesser gods.

Themes of destruction are also important and thus in some

worldviews there are periodic creations and destructions of the world (this is most developed in the Indian tradition). Among cataclysms are great floods which are spoken of in a variety of cultures. Sometimes the theme of disaster ties in with the forecast of a period of peace and bliss to follow—hopes which, in a number of religions, have helped to inspire revival movements and sometimes rebellion.

There are all kinds of myths which tell of the exploits of the gods, heroes, and other supernatural beings who control and infest the cosmos and surround human life: these are often the material for great epics, as in the Indian and Greek traditions.

Although it is true that stories about origins are important in the field of myth, they are not the only type. In this respect Eliade exaggerates, and he also perhaps makes too much of the theme of "in that time." Not all myths stress that there is something timeless out of which time-bound things came.

Still, Eliade and Jung attempt to show how the world of archaic myth remains relevant to us today—that the symbolic themes which appear in myths are rooted deep in the human psyche and perception of the world. A major way in which Eliade has helped to illuminate myth is by making us take seriously the manner in which time and space symbolize so much in our world. Thus the whole pattern of our thought about height and depth, center and periphery, shows something of our almost instinctive orientation to the world. And it is no coincidence to find so many myths which portray a mountain, with the upper reaches the abode of the gods or God, as at the center of the world—Mount Olympus in ancient Greece, Mount Zion in Israel, Mount Meru in the Indian tradition.

But although we can recognize how myths have traditionally played a vital part in fashioning a worldview (in fact the worldviews of many small-scale societies are expressed predominantly through myths), there are now limits on their credibility. They no longer seem to speak with that breathless air of authority, and once they lose this they cease to be living myths and become curiosities, tales, plots for dramas and movies, perhaps, the raw material for speculation about human symbol-systems. Is it not the case that secular stories, such as the theories of history which we alluded to earlier, replace the traditional myths? And do not fiction and drama now offer an alternative to the older myth-telling?

Still, there is a place where the traditional mythic forms live on in a vigorous way: in the scriptures of the great living religions.

Once myths are taken out of the lips and hands of the storyteller and organized into scriptures, they have a new and different life. Thus, the Bible for the Jew or the Christian, the Koran for the Muslim, the Lotus Sutra for many Mahayanists, the Vedas and Gita for Hindus, the Book of Mormon for the Mormons—these and other sacred and revealed writings have a life of their own in inspiring those faithful who look to them for guidance. They are stories which are given the stamp of authority by God or the Buddha or another High God, and they are preserved in a form which invites interpretation and commentary. In fact, it is often through the commentaries that these works become significant to us. For one thing, commentaries often enable us to understand the doctrinal underpinnings of myth. Thus, if we look at a myth of creation by itself it may seem rather simple-minded: if God made the world, we ask, what out of? But doctrine helps to give sense to the idea that the world developed out of the divine Being himself, or that it was created out of nothing, since the divine Being experiences no limitations but can do anything. In effect what happens in the major religions is that the myth comes to exist alongside of and in interaction with the more abstract ideas of the doctrinal dimension.

For the most part, then, the dominant traditional myths now find their authority and their location in sacred books. New religious movements of the modern period accordingly create their own scriptures—such as the Book of Mormon, the Unification Church's Divine Principle, and so on. And it is precisely because these myths have been so recorded and preserved that they are open to the scrutiny of modern historical scholarship. When the myths themselves take the form of historical narratives, whether about Moses, Jesus, Muhammad, or other great founding figures, then the same tension which we spoke about earlier in relation to national histories should arise even more acutely here. Will modern history puncture some of our cherished beliefs? Once the critical historian looks on scriptures as mere documents, will their authority not come into question?

The Interpretation of Myth

There has come about, in the last hundred and fifty years or so, the modern study of the New Testament, where the problems of history and myth are most acute. The main documents of the early Church, and in particular the Gospels, were selected from a wide and growing range of writings which tried to interpret the life and message of Jesus. But they were selected not primarily as biographies or pieces of historical writing. The Gospels were meant to present the authentic Jesus of Christian experience, and were to be used in the course of worship, as they still are. Also, they were clothed in the language of the day (the Hellenistic Greek understood in much of the eastern part of the Roman Empire—maybe Jesus understood it, in addition to his native Aramaic) and in the metaphors of the age. Those who wish to stay loyal to the tradition may want to restate the message of the Gospel in different language for today.

Take two examples. When the New Testament says that Jesus ascended into heaven, do we think of him as literally going upward? Thanks to science and technology, we now have an idea about what "up there" is like which was not available to the original writers and hearers of the Scriptures. They thought of a three-decker universe— heaven above, the earth here, and the underworld below. Did Jesus go up like a modern rocket? Where is heaven—after you have gone up twenty or a hundred or a thousand or a million miles? In the older mythic sense, it was easy to think of the sky as being where God lives. Even if we think of heaven in terms of its being "the place where God is," our view of the cosmos, our cosmology, has altered. So how do we express what those writers and hearers were trying to say and think? Do we want to say that God exists, as it were, in a fourth or fifth dimension, outside space and time, yet always near us?

Let us consider another example. The Bible says that God is king, or like a king. The imagery of the kingdom of God is very strong. In those days kings had real power, but they do not today. At best they are constitutional monarchs, like the Queen of England—rich, full of prestige, a vibrant symbol, but without any genuine political power. The nearer equivalent to the old kingship is the U.S. Presidency. So do we now say: "God is our President"? If we simply use the actual language of the past, then, since meanings and circumstances have changed, the language now has a different force. So if you stick to the literal letter of the Bible you may be changing the meaning of what it was saying, is saying.

These problems of translating in order to reveal and express the original meaning are referred to as the study of *hermeneutics*. This derives from a Greek word for interpretation, and ultimately from the name *Hermes,* Greek god of messages. Hermeneutics is the theory of interpretation.

The modern probing of the New Testament as history has caused some arguments. Some feel that this secular approach to the text damages the authority of the Bible; they wish to reaffirm the unerring character of the text because it is inspired by God. Others feel that in order to be at home in the modern world we must arrive at a new understanding of the Bible which takes modern scholarship into account. The former are rather loosely called "fundamentalists"; the latter are often called "liberals." The fundamentalists too, of course, have a hermeneutical problem, for when they take the Bible at face value, aren't they reading the text with the eyes of twentieth-century people? And in doing so aren't they reading a lot of today's attitudes into the Bible?

Perhaps the most influential attempt to come to terms with the challenge of modern probings is that of Rudolf Bultmann (1884–1976). He introduced a program of what he called "demythologization." This means trying to see what the mythic and symbolic language of the Bible conveys, and then restating it without the mythological clothing of the original text. Thus, as we have noted, the Bible treats the universe as having three levels—heaven above, earth, and hell below. This picture is now at best just a metaphor, for how can we literally go "down" to hell? For Bultmann this three-decker universe no longer fits modern feeling or thought: we now see ourselves differently, on a blue- and white-clad sphere, the beautiful planet Earth, swimming in space around a star near the periphery of a galaxy in a huge and expanding cosmos which teems with galaxies. This picture is beyond anything the Jews of Jesus's day imagined. But it does not mean that we have to abandon the idea that Jesus brought something extraordinary into the world, and that he is the central figure in God's unfolding revelation of himself to human beings. These are the Christian claims. Here we must remember that Bultmann is not writing as a historian of religion, but more as a Christian theologian, that is, one who is trying to express and clarify in intellectual terms the Christian faith. But he has important things to say which are of great interest to the worldview analyst and student of religions.

Bultmann had to face the question of how we are to state the

Christian faith once we have gotten rid of those mythic elements he thought modern folk could not accept—miracles like turning water into wine, walking on the water, casting out devils, ascending into heaven, being born of a virgin through a miraculous conception, and so forth. In order to explain the true and inner meaning of these mythic representations of the truth about Jesus, he went to modern philosophy. Bultmann saw Christ's resurrection as enabling the Christian to participate in a new and authentic way of life. This new freedom cuts through the false values which stem from treating persons as objects and ourselves as members of the crowd. Although science can deal with the world of things and so can be objective, the personal dimension of existence has a different nature. When I truly talk to *you*, you are no longer a thing or a type, but a person who responds. Thus, too, with the human being's relationship to God: it is a relationship of love, and what the Jewish thinker Martin Buber (1878–1965) called the I-Thou encounter. Myths in part reveal the personal nature of God, for they deal with the material world as shot through with spiritual and miraculous powers; but they also can be taken "objectively," as though they are just about objects and events, and not about what they are pointing to. Faith is personal and is a relationship to a Person. It does not arise from belief in mere outer events, however objectively wonderful.

Whether it is possible to accept Bultmann's rather sharp differentiation between the objective and the subjective, and between science and faith, is open to debate. There is also some question as to whether his modern talk of living authentically really gets to the heart of what the Gospel writers meant. But his project of restating the Christian faith is interesting, for it poses questions of deep importance for us if we want to estimate correctly the power and future of traditional religious worldviews.

First, the rise of modern scientific and technical thought means that most of those who accept traditional myth are compelled, in one way or another, to make a distinction between the language of faith and that of science—between differing spheres of human experience and understanding. Bultmann does this in terms of the spheres of persons and of things. The Bible, in the last resort, is about persons and about God, the supreme Person: it is not a textbook of biology or of physics. So the myth of creation is about our relationship to God as our Father; it is not meant to be a material account of how the cosmos evolved.

But if we begin to make a sharp divide between myth and science, we already have a different frame of mind from that of the original myth-makers. The myths now have a new context, and so a new meaning. Our world has already been split up into differing compartments, and it needs some kind of theory to put the compartments together. In earlier days Christianity had a similar problem in the face of Greek philosophy. For Bultmann the theory is supplied by modern philosophy. So Christian faith has to be given a rather abstract framework, and explained through such terms as "authentic" and "personal existence."

Which brings us to a second thought about myth. If we are to follow Eliade and Jung, the ultimate meaning of myths has to do with deep impulses in our psyches. They have to do with how we can come to terms with our feelings, and how we can achieve personal integration and wholeness. For Bultmann, too, faith is a very personal and individual affair. But traditionally myth has a much more communal meaning. A myth is not just about me: it is about us. Thus in the Bible we have the story of how the children of Israel came to be and how they entered into a special relationship to God. Tribal myths deal not just with the creation of the cosmos, but with the creation or emergence of the tribe. This is where national histories resemble traditional myths. We should not, of course, underestimate the importance of the personal and individual side of religion. It is very relevant to the modern world. But it is also good to recognize that religion needs to make sense of the history of the human race: it needs to give an account of where we are and where we are going. The attraction of Marxism is that it provides such an account. For the most part, Christianity and other religions have tended not to interpret the times, and so have not seen the meaning of the human race's transition to modernity and the emergence of the global city. There are exceptions, however. The French Jesuit Teilhard de Chardin (1889–1955) created a picture of the evolutionary process leading up to the human race as we now know it, and beyond to a new and higher unity of the planet bound together by perfect love, which he saw in Christian terms as the coming of Christ. His vision was an attractive one to many traditional Christians because it brought science and faith together in a new way. Evolution was God's mechanism for spiritual progress. But the vision was also regarded as going beyond orthodox Catholic teaching, and his writings were for that reason condemned by the Church. He raised an important question, however: What accounts of the past and future are capable of gripping us in this modern and more skeptical period? What myths have that air of authority, that "reality" which makes us believe them, and not just treat them as interesting and perhaps insightful ways of conveying meanings in a poetic way?

For the fact is that human beings have the impulse to find out who they are by telling a story about how they came to be. Myth thus is the food which feeds our sense of identity. And when we see our identity and our destiny in relation to the unseen world—God or the dharma or the Tao or nirvana—then myth is given an added impulse, for we imagine the invisible through the visible and give life to our faith through symbols. They are thrown up at the point where our feelings and the cosmos intersect, just as myths which give us a past and a future arise at the point where I intersect with my fellow human beings.

5

The Doctrinal Dimension

RELIGIOUS and other worldviews nourish certain kinds of experience. They find part of their meaning in stories about the past and about the future, but because they are views about the world, and about the whole of life, they rapidly develop a strong doctrinal aspect. We have seen how Bultmann tried to make old Christian myth relevant by reinterpreting the Bible in light of modern German philosophy. If we look back in the Western tradition, we see how the Church tried to make sense of the varied ideas in Scripture and ceremony about God, Christ, and the Holy Spirit by formulating that central doctrine known as the Trinity doctrine, in which God is depicted as both three and one: one God but having three modes of being— Father, Son, and Holy Spirit. If we look toward Buddhism we see that the nature of existence is summed up by the three doctrines (the three marks of existence): everything in the world is impermanent; everything is without self; and everything is full of suffering, or more accurately, illfare. If we look to the Hindu tradition, we see a number of differing systems of thought about the true nature of the divine Being—systems known as Vedānta. In Marxism, the interpretation of the onward dialectical patterns of history depends upon a view of the cosmos as being made up just of matter (hence the name "dialectical materialism" for Marxist doctrine).

Functions of Doctrine

The doctrinal dimension has various functions. One is to try to bring order into what is given by revelation, and in story form, in the biblical narrative. This is true of the Trinity doctrine. The need for order, in this case, had to do with the tensions which existed in Christianity as a new religion arising out of a Jewish background. Early Christians found themselves worshipping Christ. They did not follow him merely because he had been an influential leader. He was not just a Socrates or a Plato, a great teacher. He was seen as the risen Lord; the central ritual of Christianity, the Lord's Supper, focused on him and on his capacity to save those who had faith in him. So he was seen in some sense as divine. Yet at the same time Christianity was firmly Jewish, believing in just one God. Christians, like Jews, refused to acknowledge the divinity of the Roman Emperor, and so were often persecuted as subversive. Their refusal was a sign of their strict belief in one God, in monotheism. But Christ too was God. How were these things—belief in the Creator God and belief in Jesus Christ—to be put together consistently? The Trinity doctrine tried to do this, and to present the plurality and the oneness of God. So one function of doctrines is to bring order into the material supplied by tradition.

Another function of doctrines is to safeguard the reference myths have to that which lies Beyond, to that which transcends the cosmos. It might be easy to think of the stories handed down in a tradition as being about supernatural beings who simply inhabit the world as if the God of the Old Testament dwelt in a whirlwind or a pillar or cloud, or Krishna were just a miraculous human figure who trod the streets and meadows of Brindaban in North India. Doctrines stress that there is something universal in and behind such figures: that God lies "behind" and "within" all events in the world, that he is somehow "beyond" the whole cosmos and is not bound to a single little part of it. These things are said through images and symbols in scripture, myth, and ritual; they are said more systematically in the form of doctrines.

Another reason why religions have doctrine is that they need, as we have seen, to relate their claims to the current knowledge of the age. Thus, in the early centuries the Christian Church found itself in a Roman world in which Greek culture and philosophy were the prevailing intellectual influences. If people wanted to understand reality they tended to go to Plato and Aristotle, as they might now go to science. But Plato and Aristotle were "pagans," or at any rate, pre-Christian. Somehow the Church had to come to terms with them. There were those who echoed the Christian writer Tertullian (?160–220) when he said, "What has Athens to do with Jerusalem?" (as if someone today were to say: "What has M.I.T. to do with Christianity?"). But it was not really possible to seal off the world of Christian faith from the wider world of human knowledge. And so, in evolving a philosophy which took some of the most creative ideas of the "pagan" tradition, Christianity developed its doctrinal dimension in a powerful way. Christian philosophy supplied the framework for the emerging civilization of Christian Europe.

Every worldview now has an even more exciting and difficult task than that experienced by Christianity as it emerged in the Greek and Roman world. Today there are great shifts and advances in knowledge. Our cosmos has been greatly expanded. Christianity and other religions and worldviews are meeting one another in a new global dialogue. So each worldview has to come to terms with the values and insights of the others. Daunting—but out of it creative new thinking about human life may come.

The doctrinal dimension is also important because it may help to reflect and stimulate a fresh vision of the world. Buddhism, for instance, is strongly doctrinal in many ways, and tends to play down myth. It pays a lot of attention to the analysis of things and persons. It argues that everything we encounter in the cosmos is short-lived, that the things which we see as being enduring and solid—like mountains and monuments—are really clouds or swarms of short-lived processes. This is very much in tune with the picture of the material world presented by modern physics: solid things are made up of atoms which themselves are bundles of particles, and consist mostly of empty space. The Buddhist picture of the cosmos and of ourselves (for we too, according to the Buddha, are swarms of short-lived events) is not just a piece of theory; it is meant to make you look at the world in a new way, to recognize its "emptiness," and to see that there is nothing solidly satisfying to be had by our grasping for things. It is meant to give you an insight into the way we can gain liberation. So the doctrines have a practical meaning, not just a theoretical one. They provide a kind of vision or way of looking at things, which itself can inspire us to act, and guide our minds in a certain way.

It is almost inevitable that a religion which develops doctrines should be involved in philosophical thinking and debate. Already I have referred more than once to philosophy. Since this word is one which has undergone various changes of meaning it is perhaps wise to reflect a little about what it means to us today.

It is, of course, a word of Western origin, and it reflects something of the ancient Greek world out of which it came. Other cultures do not have exactly the same concept; for instance, in India the term *darśana,* sometimes translated "philosophy," more literally means a viewpoint or worldview. It means more the *result* of philosophizing than the activity itself. The object of philosophy is to reflect broadly about human experience and knowledge in order to arrive at some overall conclusions about the world. But doesn't this view make philosophy the same as religion, for doesn't religion too end up presenting a view of the world? We ought to make three distinctions.

First, not all worldviews are religious. Some of them result from complex processes of reflection—from philosophy—rather than from the experiences or revealed myths at the heart of traditional religions. Second, the results of philosophy do not always add up to a system of belief which becomes embedded in a movement or institution. For instance, the ideas of the German philosopher Immanuel Kant (1724–1804) are of great significance for all modern thinking in the West. But there is no separate religion or worldview called Kantianism. When we use this word we mean the structure of doctrines Kant evolved about such matters as the relation of science and ethics and of mathematics and perceptual experience. Philosophy provides not so much a total worldview as an important set of ingredients which can be used in expounding, amending, or defending a worldview. Third, in recent times philosophy has taken on a rather technical role. As studied by scholars and students, it tends to give a central place to logic and to a range of problems arising out of modern science. It has also been, in the English-speaking world, much concerned with the analysis of language. Thus in the West philosophy now tends to mean something rather narrower than in the past, when it often aspired to construct worldviews, to comment more directly on human values, and to serve as a framework for evaluating moral questions.

Because the term "philosophy" implies the act of reasoning—trying to reflect rationally about experience and human knowledge—there are sometimes currents of feeling in religious traditions which hold that philosophy is misleading or positively dangerous. Many think that the highest truth is not discovered by reason, but by revelation. This debate has a special relevance to the question of whether it is possible to prove that there is a God. I shall return to this later on.

Aristotle remarked that you have to think philosophically because the question of whether you should or not is itself a philosophical question. If you conclude that religion is not a matter of reason, you have already been engaged in philosophy.

Not surprisingly, a general area of thinking called "the philosophy of religion" has evolved. It is concerned with reflections about how far reason can go in trying to arrive at religious truth. It can also, in a broader way, follow the logic of my argument in this book, and take in secular as well as religious worldviews. As such it becomes what may be called "the philosophy of worldviews."

Here, however, we get directly entangled in judgments about whether a given belief is true or false. We have crossed the line from description into the realm of evaluation. But first we must try to understand the structure of doctrines. Already we have done something in this direction by trying to see their various functions. I have already mentioned four. One is the function of bringing order into the material presented by tradition in the form of myth and religious experience. Another is to make clear the way in which religious symbols refer beyond themselves to what is ultimate and universal. A third is to relate the tradition to changes in knowledge. A fourth is to stimulate a vision of the world.

A fifth function, which has been of great importance especially in the West, is to define the community. Those who belong to the community have to accept a set of doctrines, and anything outside these may turn out to be heresy and warrant the expulsion of those who propound those ideas. This defining function of doctrines is less well marked in modern times, except in Marxist countries and in some parts of the Islamic world, because in Western countries

greater individual freedom of choice in religion has made it imprac-
tical to insist on rules of orthodoxy. Still, in each tradition there is
some scheme of belief which is typically accepted by its members,
and such a system gives shape to the world as perceived by the group.
In this sense there remains a definitional role which doctrine plays,
but we should note that it plays it in conjunction with other dimensions of religion, such as the style of ritual, and the mode of organization of the group. The doctrinal scheme is, in the case of Christianity, summed up in the Creed, an affirmation of belief in certain
things, events, and ideas which together define the Christian's faith.
In other words, when the Christian recites the Creed he is not just
repeating what he believes but is subscribing to beliefs which define
him as an orthodox member of the community. For what, after all,
is the community but the body of people who affirm these things?
Public affirmation is in itself an act in which the person reexpresses
solidarity with the rest of the community.

This is one reason why fierce controversy and persecution have
often sprung up over doctrines. If, in order to be saved, membership
in the community is necessary or at least highly desirable (for it is
through the community that the Christian is in solidarity with the
savior), and if faith defines the community and is summarized in doctrine, then the community must be clear as to what is true doctrine
and what is not. Those who deny true doctrine come to be seen as
threats to the community and to the assurance of salvation. They are
seen as subversive. It is easy in such a case to think that the Church
is justified in persecuting them. There is, of course, an underlying
question: How do we—how does anyone—know what the true doctrine is? We shall come back to this, as I have already said. But there
is something more to be said in trying to understand how doctrines
work.

More than once I have used the phrase "doctrinal scheme." I use
this to indicate that a religion or secular movement typically has a
set of doctrines which are, so to speak, woven into a scheme. I have
not used the word "system" here, as it is too rigid. The fact is that
religious doctrines are not quite as systematic, say, as Euclid's geom-
etry. You cannot begin from a few religious axioms and definitions
and deduce the rest of the system. Indeed, rarely can you talk about
proof. You can rarely say that one doctrine actually entails another;
that is, you can only rarely say that believing one doctrine means

that you absolutely *must* believe another, because the latter necessarily follows from the first one. Sometimes religious people think that it is part of the meaning or concept of "God" that he is good: so "X is God" would entail "X is good." But even here I have doubts, for two main reasons. First, it by no means follows that because X created the cosmos X is good (a creator might be malicious, or neither good nor bad, or beyond good and bad). If we spell out more fully what we mean by God, calling him "creator of the cosmos," it still does not follow that God is good. Second, when we say that God is good we may not mean "good" the way we mean it when we say a *person* is good. In order to understand what is meant we may have to spell out the whole context in which God operates. So we can't, simply by looking at the words themselves, be sure what we mean in saying that God is good.

All this is a roundabout way of coming to the point that the pictures doctrines paint are not rigidly systematic. They incorporate many pieces which are put together like a collage. They are more like schemes than systems.

It is the task of the intellectual in a religious movement—the theologian, in the Western tradition—to try to get as much "system" into the scheme as possible, and to present it all in an orderly fashion. This way the faith becomes more clearly articulated. But there is always quite a lot of flexibility—a certain degree of looseness—about the way doctrines fit together.

In spite of this looseness doctrines affect one another. They influence each other's meaning. Thus the nature of God in the Christian tradition differs from the nature of God in the Jewish tradition, because for Christians God the creator is seen in light of the doctrine that Christ is God. Thus at the start of St. John's Gospel there is a novel way of putting the creation story: "In the beginning was the Word, and the Word was with God. . . ." The passage goes on to identify the Word with Christ. Christ, though divine, is also human, and this human came into the world which in some sense he himself had created (but the world did not recognize its creator). This gives a whole new slant on the nature and purpose of God. So we can say that one major element in a scheme affects the other elements. A scheme is organic, a kind of loose organism, and to understand a scheme, it is important to see each part in the context of the whole. We can make a comparison with games. Every game has a scheme of rules. A goal in soccer differs from a goal in hockey, with each game having its own rules for scoring.

We might call this contextual element, then, the "organic" character of doctrinal schemes. Each scheme is unique. Christianity is unique because it has a scheme with a special shape, in part because the doctrines reflect the very particular mythic story of Jesus Christ. But Judaism is unique in a different way, for its scheme does not include doctrines about Jesus Christ, and evaluates the law quite differently. Although the two religions overlap and are alike in certain ways they each have their own special shapes.

While we can look at doctrines horizontally, so to speak, by seeing each in its own particular context, we can also consider them "vertically." That is, we can see how doctrines relate to other religious dimensions—experience and ritual, for example.

Let us illustrate this first by showing how the doctrine of God's omnipresence relates to experience and worship. "Omnipresence" is of course only a rather cumbrous expression for "being everywhere." According to classical ideas of God as creator of the cosmos, he is not just one who sets things in motion "in the beginning." Maybe (if Hindus are right) there is no beginning at all, only a cosmos in continuous change. God then becomes the continuous changer behind all the change—as though the cosmos is a tune and God the violinist who has always been playing. But whether or not we say the cosmos has a beginning, God is still "keeping things going." Thus he lies behind all the events that occur in the world. If the sun rises in the morning then God is behind that. If the flower grows then God is behind that. If the hail falls or the thunder growls, then God is behind that. If fire burns and flies bite, then God is behind that too. This, by the way, naturally poses what has been called "the problem of evil": for if bad and hurtful things happen, then God is behind them. How then can he be perfectly good? Maybe—and this is one way of trying to deal with the problem— bad things are the product of free human choices, like willful murders and cruelty. But there are bad and hurtful things caused naturally, by earthquakes and rabid dogs and viruses and storms at sea. Leaving this famous "problem of evil" to one side, the doctrine that God is present everywhere connects with the idea that he is "behind" everything that happens. His hand is everywhere—to use a metaphor (literally, of course, he has no hands).

I put "behind" in quotes above for good reason. It is not that God is quite literally *behind* what I see in front of me. I see a mountain from where I am writing this, but God is not the other side of the mountain (Milan, Italy, as it happens, is the other side of the mountain). God may be behind the wisteria leaves I see moving lightly in the breeze, but he is not literally behind them; an iron railing is literally behind them. So what does "behind" mean? It means something like this, that God exists in another, different dimension, energizing the cosmos. Maybe it is like me and my body. For I am, so to speak, "present" in my fingers: they respond to my directions and do what I want them to do. But you don't find me by cutting up my fingers and looking inside. God is working, as it were, within all things, but you don't find him by cutting them up and looking inside.

This doctrine that God as creative spirit is present within and behind all things has a strong significance in the dimension of experience. This is so in two ways. First, the doctrine means that the person with faith in God is always aware of God's presence: God is a friend and sustainer, and can always be turned to because he is never at any distance. His hand is seen in everything that happens. So a person of faith will have a strong sense of providence, of God's guidance over events. Even the bad things that happen may, in the long run, be good. Second, the idea that God is everywhere present corresponds to certain numinous experiences, when I may have a strong sense of God's powerful presence, or when, in the "panenhenic" feeling, I have a sense of communion with an unseen spirit pervading all that surrounds me.

So God is close by, and God surrounds me; but there is another way to explain my experience of him. The image that he is "behind" everything suggests a dualism; me here, God over there. This dualism derives from, and expresses, the spirit of the numinous and the sense of the "Wholly Other."

This is where the doctrine of God's omnipresence is relevant to ritual, too: to worship and prayer. For God can be worshipped anywhere if God is present everywhere. God may seem "more present" in some places and times (say, at the Eucharist or Mass, according to Catholics) than at others. But he is present everywhere and so can be everywhere contacted in worship and through prayer. There is no place where you cannot talk to God or feel his presence. These

are the implications, at any rate, of the Christian and other mono-
theistic doctrines of creation.

So the doctrines of omnipresence and creation are not to be seen
just as statements about how God relates to the cosmos: they are also
beliefs which are real in experience and in the practical life of religion. For those who have faith they are living, vibrant ideas, not just
theories. Let us now see how a rather different doctrine, that of the
Void in the Buddhist tradition, works both in context and in relation to other dimensions.

Buddhist Doctrines

The division of Buddhist thought into Greater Vehicle (Mahāyāna)
Buddhism and Lesser Vehicle Buddhism (of which Theravada is the
predominant school) was largely due to differing interpretations of
Buddha's teachings on attaining nirvana. Lesser Vehicle Buddhism
emphasized self-discipline and individual achievement. Greater Vehicle Buddhism developed the ideal of becoming a Bodhisattva—one
who concentrates on ridding the suffering of others—and a new
interpretation of the nature of the ultimate goal.

The doctrine I would like to discuss here—the doctrine that
everything is śūnya, or empty, or void, arose in Greater Vehicle Buddhism. This doctrine is a reaction against the more traditional idea
of nirvana found in Lesser Vehicle, and in particular Theravada,
Buddhism. This school saw nirvana as liberation from the cycle of
rebirth. It made a strong distinction between this world (that is, life
in the cosmos and the cycle of rebirth, or saṁsāra) on the one hand,
and the liberated state of nirvana on the other. Being a monk or nun
is the bridge toward nirvana. You need to withdraw from the world
to have a real chance of liberation. From the Greater Vehicle point
of view there was too rigid a contrast between the monastic community and the ordinary people, or laity. Also, it was easy to think
of the pursuit of nirvana as selfish—a higher selfishness, maybe, but
still selfishness. Is the monk who seeks liberation not just looking
after his own higher interests and trying thus to avoid future suffering? How does this square with the Buddha's continuous emphasis
on being selfless and having compassion for other living beings?

The doctrine of the Void ingeniously and illuminatingly dealt with all these questions. It begins from the premise that everything is impermanent. What we take to be fairly solid is just a swarm of events (as we have already seen). One event follows from a package of other events, each of which depends on a package of prior events. Nothing has its own independence. More than this: even the idea that an event is caused by a package of others is at best a provisional sketch. Reflection will show that the idea contains problems, indeed contradictions. If everything is truly impermanent, each event is instantaneous. So by the time an event occurs the package of events giving rise to it will have vanished. How can that which now does not exist cause anything to happen? Even the idea that everything depends on something else is just provisional: at a deeper level it is without substance. The world of causal relationships is empty. So nothing we see has any genuine reality. The world is, at bottom, empty. The bottom line is zero, as we might say.

But at the same time the Greater Vehicle does not throw away the Lesser Vehicle's stress on meditation. The purification of consciousness is still the central element of Buddhist practice. Such an inner state, bringing one toward liberation, is one of higher emptiness, beyond thoughts and images. In realizing complete freedom from the events and packages which make up the cosmos one experiences their inner nature—their Emptiness. So by a strange paradox the realm of nirvana or liberation is the same as that of *saṁsāra:* the emptiness of liberation is the same as the emptiness lying at the heart of the cosmos and at its every process. The real nature of things is empty: the true nature of liberation is empty. Consequently, one does not have to leave the world in order to gain the higher truth.

There is another consequence. The Empty, in addition to being the true nature of nirvana, and the cosmos, is also the true nature of Buddhahood. The Buddha achieved a mystical experience of the ultimate: it was a non-dual experience. The ultimate is Emptiness itself. The Buddha achieved a non-dual state of unity therefore with the Empty. He became the Empty. Emptiness is the essential nature of the Buddha. In aspiring, therefore, to achieve a similar non-dual experience of the Empty, I myself aspire to become a Buddha. In non-dual Emptiness there are no distinctions: we are all, so to speak, the Buddha. This idea that we all can gain Buddhahood was put in a picturesque way in the Greater Vehicle when it was said that Buddhas are as numerous as the grains of sand along the river Ganges.

One who is destined to become a Buddha is called a Bodhisattva; in the Buddhist tradition the Bodhisattva is one who sacrifices himself out of compassion for other living beings. Many stories of Gautama in a previous life testify to this idea: how as a hare he throws himself on a fire so that a hungry man should have food, for instance (folktales and the like were turned to good effect to illustrate the need for compassion). So the Greater Vehicle underlined the ideal of the Bodhisattva who, in his search for the ultimate, turns aside always to help others. Living in this world, he helps to spread the knowledge that at bottom liberation lies here—for Emptiness lies at the heart of everything around us, and in our selves.

Another term that is used is *Suchness:* the ultimate cannot be put into words, but only pointed at, as a finger points at the moon. The very word "Suchness" is meant to be like a finger: it points to what cannot be put into words. Here the doctrinal dimension shows how religious—and in particular, mystical—experience cannot be articulated in ordinary everyday language. Thus, a lot of philosophical thinking in the Greater Vehicle tries to illustrate the inadequacy of ordinary language by showing that all theories are true only at a surface level: at a deeper level truth is not to be spelled out—it is merely to be pointed to and experienced.

In short, the doctrinal dimension in this case ties in with the non-dual mystical experience and with the ethical demands of Buddhist compassion. The doctrines are a matter of experience and action as well as philosophy. Philosophy in this way becomes applied.

Whether we look East to Buddhist philosophy or West to reflection about God, there is great preoccupation with the nature of language. The Buddhist finds language misleading, for it assumes, wrongly, a solidity in the world, and assumes too that we have real selves—when the truth is that we too, seen in the light of the Buddha's insight, dissolve into swarms of events: we too are empty packages. For the Christian, Jewish, or Islamic theologian there is always the problem of how, or whether, the language used to talk about God really can be taken at face value. God is said to have hands, but does not. He is "behind," but not literally. And so theologians tend to come up with a theory of religious language—for instance, that everything we say positively about God has to be balanced by a negative, and that the only way we can speak of God is by *analogy.*

According to this view, God is wise in a manner which fits with his nature, and perfectly, rather than in the way we are wise, which is relative to our nature, and imperfect.

Doctrines and Truth

So far we have been looking chiefly at the nature and function of doctrines. What about questions of whether or not they are true?

Traditionally in India there have been discussions about the sources of human knowledge, and usually three have been seen as most important, although not all schools of thought have accepted them all as valid. They are *perception, inference,* and *testimony.* For example: I know that there is smoke on the mountain I see because of *perception.* I reason that there is a fire on the mountain by *inference* (because I see smoke, and make a deduction). If I heard on the radio that the fire had been started by an arsonist I would be accepting this information on *testimony.* The Indian tradition thought of religious experience as a kind of perception: for example, a mystic perceives the true nature of reality. Testimony was often thought of as being transcendental, that is, as having reference to that which lies "beyond" the cosmos. Thus, the Vedic scriptures were considered by orthodox Hindus to be testimony to the nature of the unseen divine reality. So we could recast the three sources as being *experience, reason* (which is the use of inferences), and *scripture.* In the West, too, there has been debate about the role of these three. For some, like Quakers, the most important source of spiritual truth is inner religious experience. For many evangelical Christians and for many Muslims the primary source of truth is scripture. For some thinkers it is possible to know that there is a Creator by reasoning (e.g., that the cosmos might not have existed, but does, so needs a Cause).

Traditionally in the West, this last idea has led to classifying knowledge of God under two headings—revealed theology and natural theology. "Natural" theology is knowledge which does not come through grace—that is, not through God's activity in revealing his will to us in the Scriptures and by revelation—but rather by the use of our natural endowments, in particular our reason. But it has been argued, chiefly by Protestant thinkers, that reason too is fallen. Because of the Fall of man humans can do no good without God (they argue), and this applies to all our natural capacities, including reason. Reason, being fallen, cannot give us knowledge of God.

At the same time, Kant and other more recent philosophers have criticized the traditional ways people have sought to "prove" God's existence. These traditional proofs found their classical form in the writings of Anselm (1033–1109), Aquinas (1224–1274), Descartes (1596–1650), and others. Basically they boil down to three main arguments.

The first, known as the Ontological Argument, was propounded by Anselm and Descartes, and rejected by Aquinas. It gets its name from "ontology" (reasoned inquiry, *logy,* into *onto,* being). It basically argues that God is to be defined as the most perfect possible being. But in order to be perfect, a being *must* exist (and a being who does not exist is less perfect). So, given the definition, God as the most perfect being must exist. Only if he exists is he absolutely perfect. If he had all other perfections but lacked existence, then he would be missing one perfection—existence.

For various reasons many philosophers have rejected the validity of this argument. Chiefly they object to the idea that existence is a kind of perfection. They think of the verb "to exist" as telling you whether what you have in mind is out there in the real world, or just in your mind. In other words, "exists" functions in language and in logic in a different way from "is wise," "is good," and so on, which express qualities that may or may not be perfectly manifested in God. To say "tigers exist" is not to claim that tigers have some quality, but to say that the cosmos contains tigers.

The second main argument is the Cosmological Argument (concerned with reasoning about the cosmos). Basically it argues that since the cosmos does exist (and it might not have existed), it needs an explanation—a cause "lying outside" itself. Opinion about the validity of such a piece of reasoning is mixed. Some feel that it still has force: we can still ask for an explanation of the cosmos, once all the scientific evidence is in, about the scale of the cosmos and (maybe) the Big Bang, which exploded outward in early moments of the present cosmic era. Others think that we can only talk seriously and meaningfully about cause and effect within the realm of events inside the cosmos, within the sphere of what can be observed and measured. Go outside the cosmos and you can no longer talk meaningfully about cause and effect. For one thing, if I say *this* causes *that* I am talking in the framework of time, for the cause comes before the effect. But we have no concept of time outside of the cosmos.

Already this argument raises an important issue about the relation of religion and science. Does religion have to be confined to what can be meaningfully dealt with by observation and measurement, and so by science? Much modern philosophy of religion has been concerned with this question. Is religious language (the language of myth, the language of mystical experience, the language of doctrines which point to the Beyond) the same as scientific language? Are there not different realms or levels of language, doing different things—science describing and explaining, religion expressing commitment and indicating meaning in life?

The belief that there are two realms of language, and that science and religion really have different roles and areas to which they apply, has two main forms. One is found in the existentialist writers, and we have already alluded to one example of this in the thought of Rudolf Bultmann. For him science consists of "objective" inquiry. But there is also the realm of personal (subjective) relationships, and this is the realm of religion. The second main version of this belief goes back to the philosopher Ludwig Wittgenstein (1889–1951). He saw language as having multiple forms and uses, among them the function of depicting the world in ways which helped to mobilize feeling and action—and herein lies the realm of religion. Although he wrote mostly inside the Western cultural tradition, his viewpoint can be applied—as I attempted to show in *Reasons and Faiths* (1958)—in a crosscultural way.

There are, of course, those who reject the idea of "two realms." The positivists, particularly in the work of the English philosopher A. J. Ayer (b. 1910), regard talk of anything that lies beyond what can be perceived directly or indirectly as being meaningless. Sentences which purport to talk of God are without meaning, for they can have no cash value in perception. For example: if I say there is life in other galaxies (even though none can now be observed), my statement is a meaningful claim, because I can imagine ways in which one could, through ordinary perception, find evidence to support it. We might, for instance, see evidence of it in some new measurements gained through observation by telescopes put into orbit around the earth. But if I talk of God, can there ever be any telescope which will reach him? The positivists, as their name hints, wish to stick to what *positively* can be found in science. No knowledge, they say, lies outside the scope of present or future science.

Marxists, too, if they are true to Marx's thought, reject religion not so much because it is meaningless, but because it is false. Again they see everything falling within the realm of science (as they define it). There is nothing Beyond this world.

But aren't these views in their own way dogmatic? Why should there not be two realms? And why shouldn't we follow the Indian writers and treat religious experience as a form of perception, and thus a valid source of knowledge?

The Cosmological Argument is important not because we think it proves anything, but because it raises the question of whether there is something Beyond the cosmos.

The third main traditional argument is the so-called Teleological Argument (from *teleo*, that which concerns the purposive). It typically argues that the things or processes in the cosmos display design or purpose. The planets go around the sun in an orderly manner, rather like the parts of a machine, and animals' eyes are well adapted to the tasks required. So there must be a Designer. On the whole modern opinion denies the validity of this argument. One reason is that scientific theory has shown how to explain astronomy, and animal adaptation without going back to the idea of a Designer. Another reason this idea has lost favor is that there is a lot of disorder in the cosmos too. The cosmos is not, after all, very much like a machine. If we find a wristwatch on the beach we can infer the existence of an intelligent being who made the watch. But can we do the same with a sea shell and a piece of slime?

It may be that the best the old arguments do is not to prove God's existence, but to raise the possibility of it. But even here we meet with a further question. Why talk only in terms of the Western God? What about Buddhist Emptiness, or the Tao of Taoism? There are many alternative religious traditions in this world to consider.

The existence of different religious traditions raises an issue about revelation or testimony as a source of knowledge. After all, many Christians or Hindus or Muslims may say that it does not matter about the traditional arguments: what is important is revelation (Bible, Veda, and Koran). Yet the conflicts among the scriptures themselves lead us to ask questions: for example, how do we know one book of revelation is true rather than another?

In recent times particularly, we have been led to ask some vital new questions about the relationship of the great faiths. Why follow one rather than any of the others? So a new branch of the philosophy of religion may be called the "philosophy of religions" in the plural, or more broadly the "philosophy of worldviews." It would deal with the nature of religious truth and concepts in a crosscultural way.

In this context we are moved to think about religious experience as a source of knowledge of what lies Beyond. If we ask why we should take the Veda seriously, one main answer is, "These works are founded ultimately on the visions of early seers and sages." If we ask about the Bible, leaving aside its historical narratives, we might say "Its ideas are founded on the visions of the great prophets and on the experiences of the risen Christ." If we ask about the Koran, we are led to the revelatory experiences of the Prophet Muhammad. If we look toward Buddhism, at the heart of its message lies the enlightenment of the Buddha. So in all these cases we appeal to religious experience, and especially that of the great persons of faith, as the basis for our commitment to their way of seeing the world.

It is possible here to open up only briefly these deeper questions of philosophy. But we can sketch two positions, one skeptical of religion, the other positive. The second is (roughly) my own view.

The first is this: modern folk can do without religion. There is no sense in speaking of a Beyond, for our only access to it would be by revelation or religious experience. But knowledge does not rest on old books; science advances and revises all that we once thought we knew. As for religious experiences, skeptics would move that those who have them—prophets and mystics—often conflict and this fact throws doubt on their validity. Skeptics hold too that we can explain religious experiences as the product of illusions born of our wish to find meaning outside of ourselves. They contend that it is better to change the world to alleviate suffering and improve human existence than to waste effort on dreaming of heaven. We need a secular worldview, not a traditional one.

The second position is this: Why is there a cosmos? What is the inner nature of things? We seem always to be driven by our questions beyond the realm of pure science. And similarly with our pursuit of worldly goals. Should we alleviate suffering and increase happiness? Of course, if we can, but what is true happiness, and what is the deeper nature of suffering? Religions contain spiritual experiences and symbols which give us a deeper view of these questions. We can see patterns of religious experience which suggest that there are different models of the Ultimate as Beyond the cosmos and yet somehow deep within our own consciousness. This is not surprising, since the whole of our experience revolves around the mystery of blind and mute nature evolving into conscious beings like ourselves, so that nature's colors and shapes themselves are in part a product of our consciousness. She makes us and we make her. Religion can throw light on this mysterious middle role of consciousness in our cosmos.

All this leads to the question: which religion? One test, in my view, is whether a religion can make some constructive sense of other faiths; dismissing them as false and idolatrous is not making sense of them. Another test is whether a faith can live in harmony and creative interaction with science, and that means that, like science, it has to be critical of itself. In light of such tests, it seems to me that some phases of religion are better than others. I leave it, though, to you to pursue this line of exploration; for in our world, ultimately it is for me to decide for myself and you for yourself. And this too limits (I think) the authority of tradition. Even if I accept authority from outside of myself it is I and no one else who does this. So the drift of reasoning about religion is toward you and toward your reflections and decisions.

Whatever we say about the truth of religion and personal decisions about it, the importance of doctrines as a dimension of human worldviews cannot be denied. Doctrines are organically related, as we have seen, to other dimensions of religion, among them ritual, through which we mobilize feelings and act out our symbols. Doctrines are also closely related to the value judgments we make, and among these are the moral values we bring to bear on life. We have noted that there is a question of what true happiness is, and the answer depends upon our view of the world. The question of happiness is closely related to moral action, much of which is concerned with trying to seek the welfare, and happiness, of others. This leads us into the realm of ethics, in a cosmic as well as a personal context. To that let us now turn.

6

The Ethical Dimension

THE ETHICAL dimension of a religion or worldview is shaped by the other dimensions, but *it* also helps to shape *them*. If the numinous experience revealed to early Israel and to the prophets a mysterious and dynamic deity, their moral insights suggested that this God was a good God. He demanded not just sacrifices but also contrition, not just observance of the Sabbath but also uprightness in conduct. If the mystical experience revealed to early Buddhism a realm of peace and pure consciousness, moral insight also showed that this peace was to be shared with others, and that ultimately no inner illumination not accompanied by compassion for the suffering of other living beings was worth having.

Buddhists, Hindus, and Jains have a special attitude toward moral action because they believe in reincarnation. Since one may be reborn in animal or insect form, one must have a sense of solidarity with other living beings. In the religions of the West, however, the dominant view has been that human beings have souls but animals do not. In theory, at any rate, there is a greater moral obligation felt in the Indian traditions toward animals and other living forms than has been the case in the West. But in recent times in the West a greater concern with our living environment, together with the influence of the East on our culture, has led to changes in attitudes. We see campaigns to save whales and leopards, for example. Whatever our specific attitudes, there is no doubt that the scope of morality is affected by our general worldview.

Morality is affected also by our picture of the ideal human being. The Christian looks to Christ and to the saints and heroes of the tradition. The Buddhist looks to the Buddha, the Muslim to Muhammad, the Hindu to Rama and Krishna and others, the Taoist to Lao-tse, and the Confucianist to Confucius.

So we can already see that there are ways in which the ethical dimension relates to religious experience, to doctrines about the cosmos and to the mythic and historical heroes of the traditions.

In modern times an attempt has been made to try in one way or another to set up ethics on an independent basis—that is, independent of traditional religious belief. But as we shall see such an attempt cannot be completely successful, because every ethical system seems to raise questions about the worldview behind it.

Thus, probably the most powerful and influential ethical system—or set of systems—in modern times has been utilitarianism, which had its chief expression in the nineteenth century through the writings of John Stuart Mill (1806–1873). Its importance lies in trying to see moral action in terms of its utility, and utility in terms of whether something helps to produce human happiness or to reduce human suffering. It thus shapes much of modern politics and economics in the democratic West. In the West we tend to think in utilitarian terms: to think of whether a given aspect of our institutions, such as divorce law, will bring the greatest happiness to the greatest number and the least suffering to the least number. We conduct economic policy on the basis that we should prosper—in such a way so that everyone can realize a reasonable degree of happiness and freedom from poverty. The American constitution speaks of the pursuit of happiness, and socialism is often based on the idea that it will banish poverty and free people for better things. In such ways our whole Western culture is drenched with utilitarian thoughts.

This utilitarianism is often coupled with the idea, celebrated by the scientific humanist, that the basis of all values in the individual human being, and that what is most important is how individuals relate to one another. In his book *I and Thou*, the Jewish writer Martin Buber looks, as we have seen, to the deeper human relationships as the center of the meaning of life.

Somewhat opposed to the individualism of much of the West's thinking is the collectivism of the Marxist tradition. Here human behavior and economics are so closely woven together that ethics too is seen as collective: actions are good insofar as they bring about a revolution which will consolidate socialism, or insofar as they preserve the revolution and help in the march toward an ideal society in which human beings live in harmony.

The study of religious ethics can deal either with the facts about morality and structures of moral thinking, or else it can reflect on what is right and wrong from a normative stance. Our prime concern here is with the former approach, but I shall say something briefly about the normative questions in due course, that is, about what ethical values we might adopt.

Comparative Religious Ethics

The crosscultural study of religious ethics is sometimes called "comparative religious ethics." This is quite a recent coinage, and only in the last few years has a really systematic attempt been made to open up the field. However, there were some notable previous enterprises which dealt with ethics in a comparative way. Perhaps most important among these was the *Encyclopedia of Religion and Ethics,* edited by James Hastings before, during, and just after World War I. The *Encyclopedia,* in many enormous volumes, gave liberal and learned treatment to a host of vital themes in the study of religion and, as its title implies, included much on moral views and practices everywhere in the world.

At one level, comparative religious ethics is aimed simply at delineating the various moral systems found in societies all over the world. Sometimes it is necessary to distinguish between what are called the great and the little traditions. For instance, one can view the ethical beliefs of the Sri Lankans from the angle of the great tradition, namely, official Buddhist belief as expressed through the scriptures and the preaching of the monks. But one can also see what the actual beliefs are in the villages of the highlands (for example), where elements other than "official Buddhism" come into play. Or, one could look to what the actual moral outlook is, say, of the average Italian as compared with the official teachings of the Catholic Church. Probably it is enough for us to say that just as there are many Buddhisms and many Christianities, so there are many Buddhist moralities and many Christian moralities.

When we find that there are in fact likenesses and differences among cultures in regard to right and wrong, we begin to ask wider questions. What accounts for these likenesses and differences? One thing we might begin to do is to correlate moral values with kinds of doctrines, myths, and experiences.

But the major faiths have much in common as far as moral conduct goes. Not to steal, not to lie, not to kill, not to have certain kinds of sexual relations—such prescriptions are found across the world because such rules are necessary if there is to be a society at all. The widespread breaking of these rules would lead to chaos. Society can exist only where such wrong acts are in the minority.

But what they mean in greater detail may vary quite a lot. In matters of sex, for example, there are varying systems. The Christian generally has only one wife, divorce notwithstanding—and for a long time in much of the Christian tradition even divorce was ruled out. The Muslim male, in contrast, may have up to four wives at one time, and divorce is built into the original legal system. As for killing, some societies allow the right of self-defense, and in war the killing of the enemy may be deemed a duty. But some religions are chary of war or exclude it altogether, as do the Quakers; for others war is a natural means of spreading the domain in which the faith is exercised. This is notably so in the Islamic idea of the *jihād*, or holy war.

The way in which the rules themselves are viewed often differs, and this means that there are different models of virtue. For the Jew and Muslim, for instance, the rules are part of the fabric of divinely instituted law—Torah and Shari'a, respectively. Obedience to the rules is obedience to God. In Judaism, obedience is qualified by the belief that the commandments are part of a contract or covenant between God and his people. In Buddhism the rules of morality are part of the "eightfold path" which leads to ultimate liberation. It is not that God has to be obeyed, but rather that, as part of the general effort at self-purification, it is wise to be good. The model for the monotheist is the obedient person of faith, such as Abraham. The model Buddhist is the person of superior insight.

Although Hinduism often involves belief in one divine Being, it shares with Buddhism a sense that the law or dharma is not so much something which is commanded by God, but rather that it is part of the nature of the world. The law is part of the fabric of the cosmos, so that to follow it is to follow the natural bent of things. Thus Hinduism makes the caste system (itself controlled by dharma) an aspect of cosmic order. Moreover, the order of the world includes the way the moral fabric of things is expressed through karma. My moral acts will bear fruits both in this life and in subsequent existences. So even if ultimately—as some believe—karma is controlled by God, there is still a natural mechanism which rewards good and punishes evil. This comes to be tied in with the idea of merit: the wise person acquires merit through his good deeds so that he may be reborn in more propitious circumstances.

In order to see in more detail how belief and spiritual practice affect ethics, it may be useful to sketch the dynamics of a number of systems.

I have already alluded to the way in which in the Buddhism of the Theravada, ethical conduct is woven into the eightfold path and so becomes part of the means of attaining liberation. This helps to explain why one of the five precepts of Buddhism forbids taking "drugs and intoxicants" (the word covers liquor and other things) because liquor clouds the mind and also arouses anger. The clouding of the mind must be avoided because the task of the saintly person is to cultivate clarity of consciousness and self-awareness. It is through this clarity that detached insight can be gained; such insight is liberating and can bring about ultimate decease and escape from the round of rebirth. Further, anger and allied emotions are the opposite of the peace which liberation should bring. So far, then, we can see the ban on drugs and liquor as fitting into the way a person should train herself. But not everyone is at all close to gaining nirvana. Monks and nuns are sometimes thought to be closer to attaining nirvana, but the ordinary lay people may have their chance in some future life. The teaching of karma and rebirth binds together the differing layers of Buddhist society by projecting a person's career into the future beyond the grave. The ordinary person gains merit by virtuous acts in this life and hopes for some better state in the next. Indeed, the person who gives generously to the Order and follows the moral path may be reborn in a heaven. This heaven, though, is not everlasting. It is not the final goal. Here is a major difference between Buddhism and traditional Christianity. In Christianity the final judgment consigns people to heaven or hell. But in Buddhism, a person's merit is in due course exhausted, and she is obliged to disappear from paradise and be reborn in some other state—perhaps as a nun close to gaining nirvana. This is in accord with the Buddhist idea that all existence, including heavenly (and for that matter hellish) existence is impermanent: only nirvana is the Permanent, and it lies beyond existence, beyond this world and the next.

In brief, Theravada Buddhism has traditionally seen morality as part of the path which leads to nirvana, and as something which operates within a universe controlled by karma. Karma is the law of reward and penalty within the framework of rebirth, in which my status as human or animal or whatever results from my acts in previous lives. In Theravada Buddhism, morality is seen as partly a matter of being prudent—either because it helps achieve the state of final freedom and true happiness, or because at least it helps to give you a better life next time around. Morality also involves peace and, in some degree, withdrawal from the bustle of the world. This Buddhist moral code has two tiers: there is a higher, more severe, level of personal conduct for monks and nuns, a less rigorous ethic for the laity and the mass of the people.

The ethic of Islam, in contrast, has quite a different atmosphere. For one thing, it does not (until we get to the mystical movement of inner quest known as Sufism) have two levels. It is a religion which applies equally to all men under Allah. The duality between the numinous Allah and his humble worshippers gives the latter a sense of equality and humility. Thus, in Islam (the word literally means "submission to God"), there is a strong sense of brotherhood. It is true that, from a modern Western point of view, there is inequality for women. Islamic law and custom, stemming from the Koran and from the developing tradition, impose restrictions on women. Men can have up to four wives at once, but polyandry (that is, a woman having several husbands) is ruled out. Although it is not laid down in revelation, the custom of wearing the veil is widespread for women in Muslim countries. Even if women have property rights, and are protected by what in the time of the Prophet was an enlightened system of divorce, the modern Westerner and quite a few reforming Muslims might think women's status inferior. But this is not the way orthodox Muslims view things. For them, Islamic law treats women and men as being separate and equal, because they have separate natures and functions.

The Otherness of Allah, which flows from the numinous character of the Prophet's revelations, means that all that is created is seen as coming from him: the laws by which people are supposed to live flow from him too. Thus the pattern of religious experience which was so central in the rise of Islam is consistent with, and indeed favors, the belief that there is a divinely instituted law. It happened also that early Islam saw itself as related to other revelations as given to such prophets as Noah and Jesus. In Judaism the Law is a crucial element: so, too, in Islam there was Law, but Law with its own special features, for this was a new revelation to Muhammad which would set its seal upon the other traditions.

The emphasis on law also sprang from the strong sense of community in early Islam. Not only are all men under Allah brothers, but there is a particular community which has his blessing. This community was brought into being under the leadership of the Prophet, and before his death had succeeded in uniting a large part of the Arabs of his immediate region. The Islamic community was just embarking on those spectacular victories which stretched the new imperial power from Afghanistan to Morocco and from Spain to Iran. So the Law became the way the details of community life were defined. It covers much more than morals in the narrow sense: it embraces questions of finance, slavery, ritual, and so on.

Along with their moral teachings, religions tend to demand certain religious duties, such as keeping the Sabbath, going on pilgrimage, giving alms to the monastic order, and so on. They are religious duties rather than ethical ones in the sense that the latter directly concern people's dealings with other people: religious duties deal especially with duties to God or duties to those who in some special way manifest religious truth. The idea behind such duties is often that they simply arise from the nature of faith: the person who loves God worships him, and this is a religious duty as well as being a result of such love. Sometimes they are seen as duties because they help to bring about that kind of feeling which makes them a joy as well as an obligation. Sometimes they can be seen as a kind of exchange: the Buddhist who gives food to monks or nuns gets from them teachings which help her on the path toward perfection.

The importance of brotherhood and the community in Islam is

seen in the requirement to give alms. The poor brother or sister is helped. The duty when called on to fight a *jihād,* or holy war, on behalf of Islam reflects the fact that Islam does not make a sharp division between Church and State. The aim is to build a society which is Islamic, and this may mean using all the levers of power, including war against the enemies of Islam. Since Allah is, in essence, power—however much Allah may also be compassionate and merciful—it is not surprising that earthly power should be seen as a way of expressing and strengthening Allah's dominion. By contrast, Buddhism centers not on power but peace, even emptiness, and tends to have an "otherworldly" outlook. The problem of Buddhist kingship is the issue of how power can be used at all, for power may mean trampling on the lives of people, thus corrupting our consciousness, and storing up bad forces of karma.

The contrast between the Islamic and Buddhist traditions comes out also in the figures of the great founders. Muhammad was not just a man of God: he was the skillful diplomat, statesman, and general. The Buddha, according to predictions at his birth, was either to become a political world-conqueror or a spiritual one. In leaving his princely palace and setting out on the quest for truth through poverty and homelessness he gave up all worldly power. In return he gained enlightenment, and in fact helped to shape the world that came after him. But there he was: the lone sage, lean from fasts, his eyes unmoving beneath the tree as he attained purity of consciousness and that inner light which for him lit up the nature of all the world and became the source of his teaching. He was diplomatic in his preaching skills, and kingly in his noble demeanor. But he was not literally either a diplomat or a politician, still less a general. Three centuries or so afterward, the Indian emperor Ashoka destroyed a neighboring people in his pursuit of wider imperial power; but he was so tormented by his aggressive actions that henceforth he tried to rule as a king of peace. At the heart of Buddhism there is a dilemma about power.

Christianity presents a third face. (And Buddhism, too, evolved a somewhat different emphasis in its later forms.) Christianity's face is that of Christ's, and he unites in himself motifs that help to shape Christian ethics. Through much of Christian history Christ basically has come in two guises: as the God who, becoming man, met death upon the Cross, and as the God who, risen into the heavens, comes to judge the living and the dead, at the dreadful and glorious end of human history. The first Christ is empty of power, in the worldly sense: the second is the essence of majesty. The one is the suffering Servant, the other the fearful Judge. All of this reflects the fact that Christians have seen Christ as both human and divine. He lives in two worlds: in our earthly world he bears the marks of humility and love, and in the other, the numinous power which belongs to the divine Being.

To some extent this ambiguity is found in the way the New and Old Testaments relate to each other. Christianity inherited much of the early Jewish tradition, but looked at it in a different way. It kept some of the old Law, notably the Ten Commandments, but it thought that Christ himself was now the pattern for living, and so his life, death, and resurrection brought in a new covenant. Although Christians thought of the old covenant as part of the way God revealed himself to people—and to the people of Israel in particular—there was no need to follow the Law in the old way.

The two faces of Christ have given Christian morality a tendency toward inner struggle. Thus, for the early Church, participation in warfare was wrong, as Christians sought to live a harmless and upright life. Yet the Church was the extension of God's power and had responsibility to the world God had created. When the Church came to dominate the Roman Empire, emphasis began to be shifted to the theory of the "just" war. A war might justly be fought in self-defense; later also religious wars, known as the Crusades, became duties. Christ as judge came to be seen as the embodiment of power in the service of justice.

But at the heart of Christian morality is the ideal of *agapē,* or reverential love: the love of God and neighbor. This love for other human beings extended to one's enemies, following the example of Christ, who had said "Father, forgive them" from his Cross. This reverential love stemmed partly from the perception that every person is made in the image of the Creator and thus in the image of Christ himself.

Christian views of ethics are also much affected by the doctrine of the Fall. Judaism has not made of Genesis what the Christian tradition has. For Christianity Adam's acts implicate the whole human race in a disaster, as a result of which human nature is corrupted. Humans are not able to be virtuous by themselves but need the help of God, through grace. The great emphasis on original sin arises from the conviction that Christ's death made a critical difference to the relationship between God and the human race. So it was clear that the greatness of Christ as "second Adam" must be reflected in the vast significance of the first Adam's act, whereby he and Eve and all of us became separated from God. The salvation in Christ presupposed the Adamic disaster. Thus, Christianity has seen human nature as being unable to perfect itself by human action—only by tapping the power or grace of Christ can the Christian grow in moral stature. A major thought of the early reformers, Luther in particular, was that the Roman Catholic Church suggested that people could (and should) improve their spiritual status by going on pilgrimages, giving to the Church and the poor, attending Mass, and so on. All of this suggested that people could gain something by performing good works, when it is only through God's grace (said Luther) that we can do anything good.

This position holds that much depends on the means of grace, that is, the way through which the Christian is supposed to receive the power of Christ. In much of mainstream Christianity, Catholic and Orthodox, that power comes primarily through the sacraments, above all the Mass or divine Liturgy. For much of later Protestantism, the chief sacrament is the Word—Christ as found in the Bible and in preaching, stirring people to holy living. The sacraments stress the divine side of Christ; preaching often brings out the human side. In the one case we receive power through the action of God in ritual; in the other case we gain power through inspiration and the example of the man Jesus.

Many of the later disputes about details of morality spring from some of these ideas and practices. The Catholic Church's defense of marriage as a lifelong union and its opposition to divorce owe a lot to the notion that marriage is a divinely created sacrament. The sacrament of marriage confers God's inner grace and power on a couple and a family through the physical and social acts of living together. The Christian debate with others over abortion stems from the question of the sanctity of human life, which in turn has to do with the doctrine that the individual is made in the image of God. And Christian social action, such as that of Mother Teresa of Calcutta, stems from this same sense of reverence for others, which is part of true love, following Jesus's example.

If Christian attitudes demonstrate a tension between this world and the other, so there is a tension in Buddhism between liberation and compassion. As we have seen, there is a certain prudence about right behavior: being good helps toward the attainment of final release, or at least in getting a better life next time around. But compassion for the suffering of others should mean sacrificing oneself, even one's own welfare. Even nirvana may have to be put off if I am to serve my suffering fellow beings. Out of this self-sacrifice there came to be—as we have seen—a strong emphasis in Greater Vehicle Buddhism on the figure of the Bodhisattva, the being destined for Buddhahood who nevertheless puts off his own salvation in order to stay in the world to help others. There were various figures of Bodhisattvas who came to be revered and worshipped, such as the great Bodhisattva Avalokiteśvara who, as his name implies, "looks down" with compassion upon those who suffer in the world. The Bodhisattva was thought to have attained such a vast store of merit through his many lives of self-sacrifice (given that he had gained enough already to be "due" for nirvana) that he could distribute this immense surplus to others to help them on their way. Thus, the otherwise unworthy faithful person could, by calling on the Bodhisattva, gain extra merit, bringing her closer to final release from suffering. So in many ways the Greater Vehicle idea runs parallel to Christianity. But instead of the idea of love or *agapē,* in Buddhism compassion is central.

Just as in Christianity "living in the world," rather than withdrawal from the world, was emphasized, so in the Greater Vehicle the sharp cleft between nirvana over there (so to speak) and worldly life here, was called into question. It is possible for the Buddhist to pursue his ideal of imitating the Bodhisattva (indeed of *becoming* a Buddha-to-be) through living the good life in this world. Sometimes this had strange results. In medieval Japan the warrior class came to see techniques like archery and swordplay as methods which, if suitably adapted, could teach selflessness. In this manner even warfare would be a means of gaining higher insight. On the whole, however, Buddhist ethics have been eager to minimize violence.

The Nature of Morality

In all these examples we can see that ethics is not treated in isolation, and what is right and wrong is seen in the light of a wider cosmic vision. Yet in modern philosophy, especially since Kant in the late eighteenth century, there has been a quest to establish what Kant called the "autonomy," or independence, of morals. Philosophers have tried to show that right and wrong can be defined independently of some wider superstructure of belief. What is right and wrong is right and wrong not because God or the Buddha says so: God or the Buddha says so because he sees what is right and wrong. What is right is right because it is right on its own account, not because God says so. Kant thought the test of what is right and wrong is the so-called categorical imperative, to which he gave various formulations. In essence it amounted to a two-sided demand. One side holds that anything which moral beings will must, to be right, be capable of being a universal law, that is, a law which all can follow. The other side holds that I should treat another human being always as an end in himself and never merely as a means. Kant thought these principles were categorical, not hypothetical. A categorical imperative is absolute; it applies unconditionally. A hypothetical imperative is, by contrast, one which applies only if some condition is met. For instance, the imperative, "If you want to avoid lung cancer, give up smoking" is hypothetical, because it depends on a condition, namely that you want to avoid lung cancer. You might not care. But (according to Kant), "Do not steal" is unconditional. It applies whatever your desires are. Indeed, typically, moral imperatives run contrary to what you want. A moral demand is one which I can will to become a universal law. Thus, stealing cannot become universal without a contradiction. If people did not refrain from stealing there would be, could be, no private property; without property there would be nothing to steal. Likewise it would be self-contradictory to imagine universal lying. If everyone lied there could be no orderly system of communication, and language would collapse. So the very use of language presupposes truth-telling.

Kant thought also that the categorical imperative as a test of what is right and wrong is not something imposed on the individual from outside. To act morally she has to revere the moral law and apply it to herself. So each moral person is a legislator and, in a sense, the source of morality. It is presupposed that all people, as the source of morality, are to be given reverence. Hence the second formulation of the categorical imperative, requiring us to treat another person never merely as a means but also always as an end in herself. So treating a person, say a prostitute, merely as a means for producing pleasure, is an offense against the moral law.

All this implies that we can by reason establish what is right and wrong; morality does not have any external source, not even God. It derives, as I have said, from each person as his or her own moral legislator.

But although Kant argued for the independence of morality, and so was the forerunner of many other Western thinkers who believe that you can have "morals without religion," he thought that from a practical perspective God was presupposed by the moral law. It seems incongruous that virtue should not be matched by happiness. But in this world it is not possible for the virtuous person to gain the bliss that he or she deserves. Moreover, it is not even possible in our brief lives to achieve absolute goodness or moral perfection. We can only attain an approximation. Yet, in principle, the moral law makes absolute demands on us. Kant thought that the demands of the moral law in practice indicate that we should live on after death, and that God should in the end match our virtue with full happiness. So God and immortality are practical outcomes of the demands of the moral law. Although morality does not derive from God, we can infer a God from the moral law.

Instead of immortality, Kant could no doubt have thought of reincarnation as an alternative model of the upward striving for ulti- mate perfection. Had he been an Indian he might have come to very different conclusions about the presuppositions of the moral law, and karma might have taken the place of God. What appear to us as reasonable conclusions from within the perspective of our own cul- ture may in fact look different from another cultural perspective.

There are other problems with Kant's position. Not all moral rules conform to his test. Although he may be right in thinking that stealing and lying contain, if universalized, an inner contradiction, this does not so obviously apply (for example) to incest. We could imagine a society which does not have a strict rule against incest. Perhaps it would not break down, although it might be inferior to ours. There are also problems with the exceptions that inevitably seem to have to be made to any rule. Wouldn't stealing bread to feed a starving child be justified if there were no other way to get food? Kant's doctrines have been subject to much debate. Refinements of his approach—what might be called the logical approach—to morality have been made in modern times. But partly because of dif- ficulties in his position, many modern philosophers have looked to consequences as holding the key to right and wrong.

In this view, known as utilitarianism, the test of a rule or an institution or an action is whether it brings the greatest happiness to the greatest number of people and/or the least suffering to the least number. Stealing becomes wrong not only because it harms individuals, but also because it encourages people who militate against society. There are problems with the utilitarian view as well. What if sacrificing a small minority led to greater happiness for the majority? We might justify treating people merely as means if all we were interested in was worldwide happiness or suffering. Kill a person for some crime, in order to keep society orderly and make people safer and happier: is this not treating the criminal just as a means? The next thing we know, we might treat noncriminals in the same way.

A Normative View

Already we are sliding into questions of what is normative. What is actually right or wrong? Up to now we have been trying to look at patterns of ethical thought in relation to the religious ideas and practices that shape them. What I now venture to say on what I think to be right and wrong is only one opinion (I have no special authority), and there can be many others. But it might be interesting for you to think about some of the ideas which occur to someone, like myself, who has immersed himself in the comparative study of religion and of comparative religious ethics.

The first thing to see is that we live in a global city in which different cultures and worldviews interact. When one group seeks to impose its standards on a group that does not share the same values, conflict arises. So it seems to me that there is a great case for religious toleration, and for a form of society in which there can be genuine plurality of beliefs and values. This toleration should breed an ethic of what might be called social personalism: I respect the social values of the other person because I respect the person in question—what another loves I love (in a way) because I love her.

But second, it seems to me that the purport of religion is to stress the spiritual life—worship of God, a vision of the goodness of the world, the practice of meditation, a perception of the impermanence of things, and so on. Morality has to be related to such spiritual vision and life. It is true that the religions do not agree by any means and their atmospheres often greatly differ. But they still are like fingers pointing at the moon; they point to what lies Beyond. This pointing to what lies beyond challenges the "worldly" notions of happiness and welfare which often enter into the calculations of modern folk, in the utilitarian tradition. True peace of spirit can (I would suggest, from a religious angle) be achieved only if one is in relationship to what lies Beyond. What is needed is *transcendental humanism*: prizing human welfare but seeing it in the light of a vision of what is eternal.

We can learn something from the tension in religion, between the dynamic power of the numinous experience and the tranquility of the mystical. There is a tension, too, between the divine and human sides of Christ, and between the otherworldly and this-worldly side of insight and compassion in Buddhism. The religious person should not shrink from action in the world, and we should welcome the turbulence of human creativity and drive. But it has to have a balancing sense of peace. Thus it would seem to me that at times we cannot shrink from the use of force: society needs it to maintain order, and nations and classes may need protection from genocide and slavery. But the true aim should always be to minimize violence. As we sometimes cause pain to minimize pain, as in surgery, so we may use force to minimize violence. This attitude is often not reflected in the machismo of police forces or the nationalist hatreds of the military, although they often say that their true aim is order and peace. Force and violence are distasteful, and because they are minimally needed their excessive and common use should not be condoned.

Ultimately we need the sense of the Beyond in order to see anew the sacredness of the person. In a sense, each person is a world, a cosmos in herself. The world is alive when the cosmos and human consciousness interact, and the fields are lit up with green, the sky with blue, the birds with fluttering motion, the rain with wetness, and the sun with warmth. From my cosmos I should revere the world of others: persons are in this way like gods, and should be treated with reverence in their creativity and joy, and with compassion in their lonely suffering. Religions give differing expressions to the overarching meaning attached to each individual. Faith helps us to see the immortal dignity of each person.

Well, religions have often used force on people and have often been intolerant. In our own day, secular worldviews have engaged in force and practiced intolerance of human values. But perhaps because of this, the religious and secular worldviews can learn from mutual criticism.

7 ❧

The Ritual Dimension

In LOOKING at the ethical dimension we have seen something of the values, and of the actions controlled by values, that enter into our lives. But equally central to religion, and vital for living worldviews, is the dimension of ritual. We may talk about belief in God as though it is just a matter of thinking that some statements are true— that a creator of the world exists, that he or she is good, and so on; but more deeply and more directly God is the being who is to be worshipped.

What is worship? Well, I can worship God in my heart and you cannot in any obvious way see what is going on. But it is also typical and somehow more basic for worship to take a partly outward form. Worshippers bow down, or kneel, or stand up and sing. More elaborately they may pay their reverence to God or a god by making a sacrifice or going on a pilgrimage. Ritual is often assisted by various external visible means, such as the use of candles, flags, chapels, temples, statues, ikons, and so on. Look at a cathedral and you are, so to speak, looking at an act of worship frozen into stone. Look at a crucifix and you are looking at a feeling of faith congealed into wood and metal. And music, that wonderful and wordless way of expressing feelings, can be audible adoration, a flow of sound dedi-

130

cated to sacred things. So there is basically a strong outer aspect to ritual in general and to worship in particular. Typically ritual has a bodily basis, so that worship is a bodily reaction to something unseen.

We saw earlier that language is often used performatively. We do things with words, as when with "I promise" I promise, and with "Thanks" I thank. Performative acts also consist of bodily gestures, as when I agree by nodding, or I greet by smiling, or I mourn by weeping. In ritual both words and bodily gestures typically are used, and ritual acts thus are a special class of performative acts. They range from highly formal acts (or at least those given precise form), like the Mass in the Catholic tradition, to less formal and more flexible acts—for instance, personal prayer does not have any fixed form and I could pray while walking along, kneeling, or sitting.

The importance of ritual in religion is like the importance of performative acts in social life. If I am walking along the street and see a friend, I wave. I do this out of friendship, so my act helps both to express my warm friendly feelings, and to reinforce the bond between the other person and myself. It is an act of communication, but I am not communicating information. Rather I impart a feeling and reinforce a relationship. Religious ritual also conveys feelings and relationships, and indeed often transfers an unseen reality from one sphere to another. For instance, the Catholic Mass conveys something of Christ to the participant: the body and blood of Christ—his essence—are conveyed to the person taking communion. The bread and wine *become*, in the rite, his body and blood, so there is a double transformation: the material things are first transformed, and in being consumed by the participant they enter into her and change her.

The modern study of religion has made much progress in analyzing and understanding the ritual process. Let us look at two examples, namely sacrifice and so-called rites of initiation.

Rituals of Sacrifice

In one kind of sacrifice the first-born of a flock is sacrificed to a god or to God. The logic of the operation is complex. First, the first-born is the ideal representative of the flock: being the first stands for the whole, and as we have seen we often celebrate the class or whole of something by celebrating the first (the first persons to fly, the first to stand on the moon, the first human being, etc.). Second, the rite of sacrifice involves making the victim sacred. This indeed is the literal meaning of the term in the Latin word *sacrificium* from which the English is derived. Why does the thing sacrificed have to be made sacred? Because it is to be transferred to the Beyond, to the sacred god; and sacredness attracts the sacred and repels the profane (what is not sacred). So if the sacrificial offering is, so to speak, to make the journey from the seen to the unseen world it must be "attractive" to the god. Thus, the ritual includes selecting a perfect specimen if not the first born, and conferring purity on it. The specimen reflects the nature of the god who has an ideal, pure nature. But at the same time the god has power. For example, in ancient Greece people made sacrifices to Poseidon, the god of the sea (originally a god associated with horses—as if the Greeks graduated from wild chariots on the plains of their early native lands in southern Russia to the carriages of the sea). The idea was to be on good terms so that the god might be appeased, grateful for the solemn sacrifice. The god was an unseen Being whose face, as it were, was the sea and whose body was the ocean; whose facial expression could be stormy and whose frown was like a hurricane; whose smile could be limpid and sparkling; and whose laughter was the chuckling waves under the boat's prow.

Some have thought of sacrifice as a case of (to use a Latin phrase) *do ut des:* "I give in order that you will give." It seems almost as though religion here is a matter of bribery. But it is probably truer to most sacrifice to characterize it as *do et das:* "I give and you give," or, to spell it out a bit more, "I give to you and hope that you as a kind being, well-disposed toward me, will grant me what I want." So the sacrifice opens up communication with the god in a benign manner, establishing good relations.

When I give a present to a friend it is a concrete sign of my friendship; it is a gift between equals. If a true friend, she will doubtless reciprocate. But the relation of human and god is not equal, so the human being has to make his sacrifice into an act of praise. Praise or worship acknowledges the god's might as well as the inferiority of the worshipper. Greek myths are littered with stories of those who wrongly try to be equal to the gods and neglect such an acknowledgment of our lower nature. Disaster overtakes them for their *hybris* (as the Greek has it), their grasping pride, their undue ambitiousness. It is also said that those whom the gods love die young. The person of fortune and talent is like the gods, and as if in fear of such a person's rivalry the gods, jealously, cause his early death. There is a hint of this attitude in the story of Adam and Eve: having eaten of the tree of the knowledge of good and evil they become like gods, threatening the creator. Such are mythic ways of indicating the gulf between the ideal and powerful beings of the Beyond, and us mortals. So, in brief, the sacrifice involves praise and the acknowledgment of divine superiority. A sacrifice occurs in the context of worship.

If we follow the logic of sacrifice further, we can ask why the sacrificial being is killed. And why is it sometimes burnt? The victim is killed because it is taken out of the visible world and sent to the unseen world. The essence of the being—its soul—migrates to the Beyond. Burning a sacrifice is a particularly meaningful transformation: it transforms the victim into sky-going smoke, and the essence of the sacrifice rises upward and disappears in the direction of the abode of the gods.

Incidentally, and to amplify what we have earlier noted, consider the symbolic web of ideas surrounding the very notion of *upward*. The gods are superior: but "superior" literally means "above" or "higher up," while "inferior" means "lower down." We talk of high quality, lofty ideals, promotion, a top executive, a towering personality, top-level decisions, and so on. Height symbolizes goodness, power, and perfection. Lowness symbolizes humility, powerlessness, poor quality. So in the mythic schemes of the cosmos there is glorious heaven above beyond the sky, purgatorial and gloomy regions below in the underworld, and the middle earth, the intermediate mixed realm where we have our life.

In short, the sacrifice, although it involves an unequal relationship, creates a path of communication between humans and the god. Because the human beings give what is theirs, they give "part" of themselves, and thus express their solidarity with the god.

The performance of sacrifices in the past was often aimed at influencing a god's behavior in some material way. It was thought that different parts and aspects of nature were controlled by divine forces, and were, so to speak, animated matter. The sea or the wind or the sky or a river or fire could be separate expressions of different gods. A god would relate to the material expression as a soul to a body. Sacrifices were like gifts which established good relations with such forces and aspects of nature. But sacrificial ritual could have a more obviously ethical and spiritual meaning. The sacrifices offered to Yahweh in the Temple at Jerusalem could be seen as ways of giving honor and dominion to the one God, or as being ways of expiating bad behavior and sin. This is natural enough, too, in human relations: the husband who "makes up" to his wife after a quarrel by bringing flowers is acting like a sacrificer, for the flowers, if accepted, create or recreate a bond, and the breach is healed.

The gods of mountain and stream and sun and fire have faded over much of the world, and the sacrifices of the God of Israel have long since been discontinued, however much their meaning may be pondered by modern students of the Torah. Sacrifice no longer has the power it once had. But the principles it exhibits are still vital, for sacrifice shows something about the essential transactions involved in human–God relationships. If blood sacrifices have faded, offerings of other sorts still are made, as ways of opening up communication with what lies Beyond.

At one time in the history of the modern study of religion there was great debate about the relation between religion and magic. The debate carries on to some degree among anthropologists. Doesn't sacrifice sometimes look rather like magic? Magical rituals, however, are those which use formulas and performative acts to influence events more or less independently of the gods—like sticking pins in a wax image to bring trouble and pain upon my enemy, or uttering an incantation as I sow a crop to ensure its fertility. Such uses of ritual techniques have often been entangled in religion. Very often they are a testimony to our "trying anything": in matters where we have little control, it is at least no loss to try to bend things by words and gestures. If they do not work we are no worse off. Moreover, there is a gray area where we are not sure whether what we call "magic" does or does not work—in matters of illness, for example. Magic words may indeed have a healing effect, and a doctor's bedside manner is a distant relative of the witch doctor's healing formulae. But it is surely true that improvements in technology, for instance in agriculture, modify the use of such ritual techniques, and they begin to lose their prestige. Technology then itself becomes a new kind of magic.

The individual and personal counterpart to sacrifice is prayer, for this too is considered a way of opening up a path of communication with what lies Beyond. A good example of the logic of prayer is found in Islam. The Muslim who unrolls his prayer mat and bows down in the direction of Mecca is expressing quite a number of things. Have you noticed how Persian and other rugs from the Islamic world often have flowers and birds in their design? The reason is that a prayer rug is like a garden. Paradise is a garden too (the garden of Eden was Adam's paradise). Much of the Muslim world has sought to create a paradise on earth in gardens and courtyards. As the little poem has it, "You are closer to God in a garden/Than anywhere else on earth." So symbolically the Muslim makes a little oasis, a little heavenly place where he can pray. He unrolls his rug, marking off his sacred space from the profane space around him—be it street, field, or office floor. The pious Muslim gives himself a certain sacredness: he is slightly purified (at the mosque his preparations are more elaborate, and he washes himself to get himself in the proper state for communicating with Allah). He makes himself attractive to Allah, so as not to be repelled. When he bows down and touches his forehead on the ground he expresses in this bodily action his profound humility or "lowness" before God, thereby indicating Allah's vast, infinite superiority. Bowing in the direction of Mecca, he is directing himself in thought and by orientation toward the sacred stone there, which is the holiest place of contact between Allah and this earth. For him Mecca is the center of the cosmos and the place most charged with power and holiness. The city of Mecca is where Allah revealed himself primarily to the Prophet, so the contact between heaven and earth had its most dynamic expression there.

Also, in bowing toward Mecca the Muslim aligns himself with more than the place of revelation: he affirms his solidarity with all those others who face Mecca—with all his Islamic brothers, in other words. His prayer opens up a path to heaven—but by way of the community as well as the Prophet's message.

In essence, this account I have given so far of sacrifice and prayer follows the thinking of the French scholars Hubert and Mauss—who in 1898 published a famous essay on sacrifice—and to some degree that of Eliade. I have also incorporated some of my observations from my book, *The Concept of Worship* (1973).

In many cultures the formality with which sacrifice needs to be conducted (if it is to be properly acceptable) gives rise to a class of sacred specialists: priests. The person who offers a sacrifice may hire a priest to perform the task (a common feature of the Hindu tradition, which has given the priestly or Brahmin class the highest social and sacred status). But where the ritual is simpler and less formal, the individual can perform it effectively. An extreme form of informality is to be found among the Quakers, whose meetings have a spontaneous character: the group waits in silence for the Spirit to move one of its members to speak or lead a prayer.

In addition to sacrifices of the more literal kind in which an animal or other offering is made, the Catholic tradition has made use of the idea that the Mass is a kind of sacrifice. In commemorating the death and resurrection of Christ it relives the self-sacrifice which brought about a new relationship between God and the human race. Christ's death on the Cross is seen as a sacrifice (a kind of human sacrifice, we might say). The Mass re-presents this sacrifice. It makes it real here and now to the believer.

This points to another important aspect of ritual: A celebration of a rite is the re-creation of an event which myth describes, making it real now. It is as we have already seen, like time travel. The far-off past event becomes real to me *now*. The replay of the ancient drama is a contemporary event happening to me here and now. In Christianity, Jesus's death is seen not just as an historical event which happened quite a long time ago in Palestine, but as something present to the believer through ritual and inner experience here and now, in New York City or in Manchester, England, in the late part of the twentieth century.

Religions, as I have suggested, vary in the importance they attach to the formal and external aspects of ritual. There is a tug of war here. Consider a gift: I give something to a dear friend. It is a token of my friendship. But clearly the thought is important, the feeling behind the gift. On the one hand, the important thing is the inner feeling I have for my friend. On the other hand, the gift makes that feeling manifest. One reason for this is, in giving the other something I prize—suppose it is one of my favorite books—I give the other "a piece of myself," a little bit of me. Why? Because we think in a special way when it comes to possessions and people: we think according to the notions of "mystical participation," to use the phrase coined by the influential French anthropologist Lucien Lévy-

Bruhl (1857–1939). (Strictly, it is the translation of his French phrase *participation mystique.*) My possessions are not quite separate things: they are part of a wider me. Try a little experiment. Leave a cheap ballpoint pen on a table, and watch your reactions if someone else picks it up. *My* pen, you think: how dare she take it! It is like an invasion of my space, or as if she had snipped off a bit of my hair. So the pen, trivial as it is, "mystically participates" in you, and you in the pen. Our truly valued possessions illustrate a much stronger bond, of course. A sacrifice, too, is "part of me," which I dedicate to a God or gods. It happens with groups as well, not just things. I am a Scotsman: in some way I mystically participate in Scottishness. If I hear other people insulting Scotsmen or Scotland I get upset. They are taking something of me and from me. Christ, in being human, participates in the human race, and the human race in him (thus goes the thought of much early Christian writing). In sacrificing himself he gives an offering on behalf of the human race which expiates the evil in which human beings are involved, through Adam and later generations.

So there is a way in which the concrete outer thing—the lamb sacrificed or the book I give to a friend—is a vital aspect of conveying feeling and opening communication. It is a symbol. It needs, however, to be accompanied (most of us tend to think) by sincere feelings. If I make no concrete gesture of contrition for some misdeed, then repentance is cheap. If all I have to do is make some external mechanical gesture, it may not be true contrition. So there is a tug of war between outer and inner: a gesture must be made, but that in itself is not enough, the gesture made must be sincere.

In Protestant Christianity and in Buddhism the emphasis, historically, was on inner feeling rather than outer formality. In the case of Reformation Protestantism salvation was thought to come from God and his grace alone. Attending Mass or performing pilgrimage could not in itself gain anyone spiritual advantages, and was, in fact, considered untrue to the Gospel and to the sense of the numinous. The Protestant tradition has often stressed not outer ritual, but inner experience modeled on ritual: reliving the drama of baptism, for instance, by having the inner experience of being "born again." In the case of Buddhism, the rejection of sacrifices was in part due to the refusal to think in terms of mystical participation, which Buddhists thought leads to attachment to the world. If I get rid of "mystical participation" I am no longer attached to my book or my pen. Only by the purification of consciousness, and by the stilling of personal desire, do we attain liberation—not by any external acts.

This is not to say that there is no ritual in Buddhism. In later Buddhism there is a return to some of the Brahmin style of ritual thinking. At the time of the Buddha's death (ca. 483 B.C.E.) there was already the beginning of a cult around his ashes. They were distributed to *stūpas* or shrines, the predecessors of the modern temple and pagoda. The pious Buddhist pays reverence to the relic of a Buddha, or of some saint of times gone by. But on the whole, the Buddhist attitudes toward ritual are utilitarian. Ritual helps people to gain a better frame of mind. It does not bring about results in and of itself. In Sri Lanka, for instance, there is no question (at least in theory) of communicating with the Buddha as though he is a god who can be talked to in prayer, or acknowledged through sacrifices. At nirvana his individuality disappeared. There is no question of thinking of him as a continuing being. It is neither correct to say that he does exist nor that he does not. So ritual is not worship, but rather a skillful means of helping Buddhists on their upward and inward path.

Some of the logic of sacrifice carries over into modern secular ritual, particularly in regard to the nation and the state. Typically, a modern Western nation sets aside a day to commemorate those who have fallen in battle—Memorial Day in the United States, Armistice Day in the United Kingdom, and so on. Often, commemorating the dead by laying wreaths on some representative tomb or tombs, say, of the Unknown Soldier, is a means of paying homage to those who died for us. In doing so we renew our bonds with them. They in turn gain sacred stature from our reverence. We acknowledge the meaning of their sacrifice in battle. Dying for a nation enhances the substance of that nation. War itself, in causing people to die for the group, enhances the group. Similar thoughts apply to heroic, living achievements: men on the moon enhance the prestige and substance of the nation that put them there. Much of the secular or "civil religion" (to use contemporary sociologist Robert Bellah's phrase) is a matter of performative acts which enhance the collective substance of society.

To sum up so far: sacrificial and other rituals are performative acts in which communication is established with the Beyond, or in the case of secular ritual, with the nation or group. In expressing ritual feelings, such as awe, something is conveyed—reverence for the divine Being, as in the Mass; or homage to the national spirit, as in a military parade. Rituals can be formal or informal. The emphasis in some religions is inner experience rather than outward acts or gestures.

Rites of Passage

Another important class of rituals is what have come to be known as rites of passage, following the work of the Belgian anthropologist Arnold van Gennep (1873–1957). These are rites which accompany vital transitions in life, as in puberty rites when young folk make the transition to adults; or as in baptism, when a person makes the transition from being outside to being inside the Christian community; or as in marriage, when two people move from one relationship to another. The rite is ceremony, or ritual, which marks a person's passage from one category to another.

Consider for a moment the difference between being a child and being an adult. Being a child means, among other things, that people *treat* you like a child: they may, for instance, "talk down" to you. Being an adult means that people usually treat you like an adult—it means that they have certain expectations of you. An adult is someone who can take a job, be married, and so on. The category "child" and the category "adult" are both charged with meanings that relate to the performative acts of, and for, children and adults. They are "performative categories." That is, they are categories that define behavior in a given context. Virtually all our social categories, and many others, are performative. So if a person makes the transition from one category to another it is important to mark the transition in some way. In many societies this is done very clearly and decisively through ritual. Thus, in many smaller societies, boys at puberty undergo various ordeals which do two things—they destroy their old identity as children and prepare them for their new responsibilities as adults. Such a ritual typically involves three stages: first, separation from the old; second, a limbo stage, called "liminal" (after the Latin word *limen,* a threshold, for the person is, as it were, crossing the threshold); and third, the stage of being incorporated into the new identity.

We can see something of this in the rituals associated with marriage. The night before the wedding, the bridegroom has a party with his men friends. Such a stag party is a farewell to the unmarried, bachelor state, a final "night out with the boys." The bride, when she comes to the church, is "given away" by her father, signaling that she is leaving the pure daughterly state and becoming something else. In the ceremony itself the performative utterance "I promise" seals the bond. The feast after the ceremony is itself a kind of limbo. It is secular, and yet the bride stays in her ceremonial dress. Then the pair leave for the honeymoon. This is a kind of sacred interlude, the truly liminal phase, when the pair are out of sight in some unusual place which is neither their old home nor their new dwelling. The end of this liminal phase occurs when the bridegroom, now the husband, carries his wife over the threshold and they set up home together. Now, because they are husband and wife, they are treated differently by the rest of the community. The new spouses are now the married couple. In modern society, with people living together before marriage, or without being married, the categories get blurred, and this very blurring sometimes creates performative awkwardness.

It is interesting too how a new category can be formed out of what before might have been thought of as betwixt-and-between. Thus, in traditional society hostility to homosexuals can occur because people wish to work with two clearly defined categories, male and female. The adult who has some male properties and also some female ones becomes a threat to the two-category system. So he is rejected, or she is, by performative acts designed to exclude or humiliate her or him. However, such ritual rejections can be met by a counterattack. This is what has occurred in recent times by Gay Liberation tactics, which essentially are ritual tactics—first the use of positive performative words such as "gay" rather than "queer," second by demonstrations expressing gay solidarity and defying older conventions. The result is to begin to establish along with male and female heterosexuality a third, intermediate category, namely "gay."

The extension of childhood and of education has also led to some blurring of the child versus adult distinction, and slowly we have developed a third and intermediate category, the "teenager." But it remains an awkward age, for the social roles of the teenager are often conflicting. Which is he (or she)—child, or adult? How is he or she to be treated? Many older societies seem to have ignored this category altogether. In India, for instance, child marriage was the norm; if marriage was arranged before puberty, the intermediate stage, with all of its conflicting social roles, was abolished.

In religious rites of passage the symbolism is often complex. Thus, the rite of baptism in the Christian tradition signals, in essence, the transition from solidarity with the old Adam to solidarity with the new Adam, Christ. In baptism by immersion, a person goes down into the water, the symbol of chaos and death—although it is also the symbol of purification because by water we become clean. The person thus dies with Christ, crosses a threshold, and rises again to life with Christ through his resurrection. She thus becomes part of the new community which is linked in substance with the Lord. Christ is seen as the vine and the individual Christians are the branches, so that the Church is, in a sense, part of Christ. Typical of such ideas of "mystical participation" is the thought that the Church both is and is not Christ, as my pen (in the earlier example) is and is not part of me. At any rate baptism brings on new life within the community, and death to the old self. It also gives the person access to the sacramental life of the Church.

The betwixt-and-between, or liminal state, is regarded as full of power, but it may be holy power that is manifested there, or something unpleasantly dangerous. So it is with people who fall between categories: Jesus, for instance, who is both God and human being, whose mysterious words and actions were regarded by some as full of holiness and by others as dangerous.

As we have seen in the case of Buddhism, rituals can be used to bring about certain states of mind. They are important more for their results than for their inner meaning, in such a case. For instance: if I lay flowers before a statue of the Buddha, I feel serene, and gain merit, and my action is important for its effect on me. There is a difference here between religious practices related to the experience of the numinous, and those with a more mystical, inner direction. For the religion of the numinous, worship is a response (to the overwhelming Other) which is in itself appropriate. It is the proper response to the sacred and powerful, much as we might think that an exclamation of admiration is the proper response to a beautiful sunset. The admiration does not bring the sunset about. It reflects it, tries to give it its due, so to speak. But often in Buddhism and elsewhere, things are the other way around: the doctrines and the practices are the proper ones because they help to bring about the purified and luminous consciousness which induces peace and insight. They are proper teachings and methods of mind-control and physical technique, such as breathing in a certain way, because they engineer the experience of the Void.

In Islamic and Christian mysticism matters are more complex, for the acts of prayer and the ascetic practices which stem from extreme piety and devotion to God turn, little by little, into techniques of contemplation. When this happens, worship and mysticism blend, and the numinous response mingles with the mystical method.

At a less dramatic level, ritual such as solemn worship helps to engender as well as to express feelings of the awesome majesty of God. Hymns help to heighten people's sense of the unseen. Icons and other kinds of art become pointers to the Beyond. Art itself is brought into the service of religious practice. This indeed may go a long way back in human history. There are, on either side of the Pyrenees and elsewhere in Europe, those famous caves where old paintings of magnificent animals and strange human figures could be seen by the flickering light of ancient hunters' torches. What do these mysterious drawings, with animals and other outlined figures sometimes imposed one on top of the other, really mean? We may never find out for sure: but the evidence suggests that the very act of making these pictures was itself sacred. Art was seen as a way of creating a response to the strange forces surrounding the human race.

Increasingly, modern religion has come to give weight to inner experience, whether it is the sense of being born again, or the sense of gaining illumination and vision. The popularity of forms of Zen Buddhism and other Eastern mysticism in the 1960s and 1970s was a reflection of the fact that Western people more and more felt a need for authenticity, to cut through the formal ritual of much organized religion, and to find the meaning of faith vividly in personal experience. This personal side to religion is likely to lead more and more to the feeling that rituals really have their ultimate meaning in experience. They gain their validity from the feelings they evoke and the visions they help create.

The "sanctity" of the ritual dimension of existence seems to apply in even the most secular contexts. For, as we have seen, rituals help to create and preserve categories. One category of the most fundamental importance in the world is the category of *person*. But what, in the last resort, is a person? A person is a living being of a certain kind, but more than that she is a living being who is to be treated in a certain way. She is to be treated with dignity and as a being whose feelings matter. There are, as we saw earlier, performative acts which are proper responses to her as a person: she is not to be humiliated through acts of discourtesy and disdain, but rather, she is to be given the sense that others prize her. Ultimately that is how we all would wish to be treated. As it is, much in modern life denies such treatment—huge economic forces can bear impersonally upon us; many governments practice torture, imprisonment, and other kinds of humiliation in a reckless and widespread way; and some political philosophies deal in the abstractions of revolution as if human beings can be discarded when necessary. All such assaults on persons are, among other things, ritual assaults, or failures to give due ritual recognition to the individual. They are failures in courtesy, gentleness, and the assigning of respect and dignity to human beings. In short, the very idea of a person is itself a performative concept. We gain our substance from the courtesies and loving gestures we extend to one another.

Thus it is that the ritual and ethical dimensions of life go together. Kant's notion that we should treat others never merely as means, but always as ends in themselves, is a call for us to show others, through personal acts, that they have dignity and are worthy of our personal concern. In Christian and Jewish terms we can say that every person is made in the image of God, and that as we worship the Creator we venerate the reflection of the divine in one another. And what does it mean to venerate? It is implicitly to show, in gesture, our sense of the sacred character of that which we venerate. Veneration belongs to the ritual dimension of religion.

The ritual and ethical dimensions cannot exist except in the social context, as we have suggested. So let us now move on to sketch that social dimension of religion and existence.

8

The Social Dimension

In a small-scale society—the sort of ethnic group anthropologists have most liked to study—there is typically a single over-arching worldview. Individuals may have variations in belief, and some may have their skeptical impulses, but on the whole such a society has a single system of religious beliefs. Most larger societies are different, for various reasons. For one thing, as we have seen, nation-states increasingly display great internal pluralism—that is, they include a variety of minorities, often from afar. Such a society has within it a mosaic of worldviews.

Second, the increase in division between Church—or mosque, or temple—and State (true in the modern west and some Eastern and other countries) means that citizens can, both inwardly and outwardly, affirm different beliefs, including the rejection of all formal systems of belief.

Third, many modern industrial societies have undergone much secularization, in the sense that many people are alienated, or at least distanced, from formal religion or ideology. In many societies, then, a division exists between those who are "committed" to a religious or other belief-system, and those who are not. Not surprisingly, in modern times Western religion has stressed faith and commitment.

144

For a person must have faith and commitment if he is to be distinctly religious. In many a traditional society, including the small-scale ones of the past (for things are changing there too), a person was brought up with a set of values, including religious ones. For traditional Italy it was quite "natural" to be Catholic. Catholicism was assumed, as it was assumed that a Romanian would be Orthodox or an Iraqi Muslim. But, in modern societies this is not always the case.

Modern Social Theories

Anthropologists have been good at seeing the way the different parts of society fit together, and how the whole works. Religion often has been explained as having a vital social function. One theory, called *functionalism,* has it that society and its many diverse components, among them religion, can be understood according to the functions, or needs, they fulfill, and thereby help to maintain social equilibrium. Functionalism's most important founding father was the French Jewish social theorist Emile Durkheim (1858–1917). He had trained to become a rabbi. Seeing belief in supernatural beings as something with no clear basis in reason, he sought to explain religion as a reflection of social values. He was thus a prime exponent of projectionism which, as we have seen, has played so strong a part in the development of psychological and sociological approaches to religion in modern times. In a way, Durkheim was drawing a picture of society which was a secularized version of the Jewish community. But now the giver of the law is not Yahweh, but society itself, which secretly disguises the origin of its values. They might appear to come from on high but actually, argued Durkheim, they come from within.

Modern structuralism, too, has come out of the anthropological tradition. Structuralism attempts to see the structures which underlie myths and other aspects of a given culture, as well as the ways in which they are integrated together. Claude Lévi-Strauss (b. 1908) in a number of highly potent writings described how we can see various polarities in myth and in society as reflecting a deep-seated mode of thinking. Structuralism is a way of trying to piece together the logic of stories which otherwise seem mysterious and chaotic, by bringing various symmetries and problems to the surface. This method, although useful in interpreting myths, is not a way of explaining myth and religion as a reflection of their social function. Rather, it is a way of showing how the various parts of a culture hang together. It is easier to work out structural patterns in a single integrated culture, and so structuralism is a method peculiarly relevant to the anthropologist.

But although the work of anthropologists has deeply affected the study of religion, the great religions have had a different shape from that of religions in small-scale societies. While in small-scale societies religion is part of the fabric of society, the great religions often started within societies as novel forces, challenging the assumptions of the rest of society. When religions start—early Christianity, Buddhism, and Islam for instance—they have not been concerned so much with maintaining equilibrium as with providing—in a revolutionary way—a new way of looking at the world and at society. For another thing such religions typically migrate from one society to another: they have a missionary outreach. Again, they have tended to create a deeper sense of their own distinct history than is usual in the functional religions of smaller ethnic groups. In a word, they have a more plural and a more dynamic context. So sociologists have become more and more interested in the way religions and worldviews create, or inhibit, change. This was true already in the writings of Marx, for although religion might often have a conservative role, ideas themselves were one ingredient in those changes by which a new phase of the historical process unfolds.

This interest in the creative role of religion is evident in the ample writings of Max Weber (1864–1920). As we saw earlier, he questioned why the rise of capitalism happened in the West, and how much the Reformation had influenced it. He saw Luther's work as helping to clear away the old order. On the one hand, Luther's stress on faith directly suggested that salvation is an individual matter. The individual is thus a key element in a society. The rise of individualism meant many things, among them modernization, and flexibility in the use of human resources. We can see how Luther's teachings thus favored the rise of the urban middle class which was so vital a factor in the creation of capital.

Luther's rebellion against the Papacy, the support he received from German princes, together with his own contributions to the modern German language, particularly through his translation of the Bible—all helped the development of national consciousness. Nationalism was to play a strong role in modernization. In some of the new nationalisms of northern Europe—in Holland and England, for example—mercantile activity and Protestant religion interacted powerfully. Beyond Lutheranism, the new Calvinism provided an even more complete worldview which could favor capitalism. No longer was the ascetic life something which was lived in monasteries. The Christian lived vigorously in the world, and at the same time was not "of it." The sobriety of the citizen of the new community helped the accumulation of savings and capital. The Protestant community was not lavish with display and ceremony and spending great wealth on cathedrals and festivals. But having individual wealth might be a sign of God's favor.

Conversely, Weber was intent on showing that the forces which brought about capitalism in the West were not present in India or China, but that there were other, countervailing forces. Confucianism, though rational and this-worldly, was at the same time deeply wedded to a classical order in which the gentleman scholar, well-versed in ancient writings, was the key figure. Hinduism's caste system gave restrictive roles to the various strata of society, keeping artisans to traditional tasks and merchants to a particular status.

More recently, the economic miracle of Japan has spurred questions of how far its Buddhist, Confucian, and Shinto heritages have helped to account for this success. Was Buddhism's special development in Japan toward a "this-worldly" Zen a factor? Does the idea that Buddhism uses "skill in means" to achieve its message give Japanese society a pragmatic slant? Does Confucianism, once released from the inhibitions imposed by the old educational system, encourage a new sense of hard work and order? There is a growing interest among economists in those deep cultural factors which may lie behind economic development.

This discussion of the relationship between economics, society, and religion shows us that the essential question regarding the social dimension of religion is this: To what extent is religion a reflection of what goes on in the structures of society, and to what extent does it bring these structures about? Or to put it more directly: What effects does religion have? Or is it itself just an effect?

Naturally, these questions are put too simply. We are always concerned not with religion as such, but with a particular religion, a particular society or group of societies. And we may not be dealing even with a particular religion but, more accurately, with a particular movement, sect, or denomination. It may even be that we are not so much dealing with an institutionalized form of religion, but rather with a kind of religious experience or a particular symbol or an idea. There is no doubt, for instance, that the writer Alan Watts (1915–1973), who was a guru of Eastern spirituality (which he blended with his own values and Anglo-American background), had an influence on the counterculture and the turbulent events of the late 1960s and early 1970s in America. He established no denomination, no church, but rather articulated and promoted some ideas, an atmosphere, a slant on life, a worldview. None of it constituted an institution, yet all of it had an effect. And at the same time, Alan Watts's own experience was conditioned by his times—the times he himself helped create.

Social Theories of Religion

The social exploration of religion often has to be very particular and limited. Yet by examining specific events, ideas, and expressions we may, perhaps, venture on some more general reflections and theories.

The American sociologist Peter Berger (b. 1929) in his book *The Sacred Canopy* and elsewhere has written of the "methodological atheism" of the sociologist. It is better to use the expression "methodological agnosticism." The point Berger wished to make is that the sociologist does not bring God into his account of how things happen. He does not assume the existence of God in order to explain events. It is one thing not to assume that God does exist; it is another thing to assume that he does not. If we assume, more generally, that there is no Ultimate, no Beyond, then we assume that religion is false. Religion, then, is a finger that points, but at nothing. There is no moon for it to point to. It does not seem especially scientific to begin with the assumption that religion is false, nor need we begin with the assumption that it is true. What we are concerned with is not the truth of religion, but its power. If we are adhering to a scientific stance or methodology, we should be neutral regarding the truth or falsity of religion; we should be neutral as to whether the finger points at the moon Beyond or at nothing. This is why it is better to speak of "methodological agnosticism": the agnostic has not decided whether God exists; the theist and the atheist have.

The chief object of the social-scientific study of religion is to see how the social dimension relates in influence and power to the other dimensions. There is, however, an ambiguity in the idea of the social dimension.

Religion can be so deeply integrated into social life, as in many small-scale societies, that it is impossible to isolate and study as a distinct phenomenon: it is an aspect of the life of the group. But it is sometimes the case that religion exists as a separate institution, part of, and yet independent of the rest of society. Thus in Western countries there are separate religious organizations, old and new—here we mean everything from the Catholic Church, to many small denominations and sects, to new religious movements, to religions coming from foreign cultures. When I talk about the social dimension of religion I may be referring to religion in a broad social context; or I may be referring to the actual institutions themselves.

Thus, American religion—say American Catholicism—is not merely institutionalized in a certain way: there is a broader significance that religion has in American society. American Catholicism contributes to American social processes and at the same time is affected by them. For instance, it affects attitudes on issues of abortion, and it has contributed many notable figures to American political and cultural life. Conversely, American democratic ideals and American culture have influenced American Catholicism—consider how American education, armed with American football and Notre Dame, reflects a blend between American and Catholic values. If we are thinking of societies which are not integral, like small-scale societies of the past, then the social dimension is, more narrowly considered, the way in which a religion is institutionalized. More widely considered, the social dimension is the social role in the wider society which the religion plays. A major part of the sociology of religion is devoted to the question: How far does the institutional dimension of a religion affect the wider society and how far does the wider society affect it?

We have been looking at worldviews in general, not just confining our attention to traditional religions or religion in the traditional sense. A similar approach to that taken above can be taken in looking at institutionalized worldviews of a secular kind. Thus, we may consider how successful the Chinese Communist Party has been in reshaping the values of Chinese society, and how far the cult of Chairman Mao was able to maintain some of the initial élan and drive of the revolution. In short, are some of the same things happening in China as are happening in the evolution of a church or religious movement? We have the founding charismatic hero (St. Francis or Mao); the charisma becomes something not personal but is "routinized" through the ongoing institution; and there arises a division of followers into those who pragmatically adhere the routines, and others, more radical, who try to recapture the spirit of the "early days."

This idea of charisma (a word derived from the New Testament and referring there to what is given through God's grace) was first elaborated in a systematic way by Max Weber in his account of the evolution of religious institutions. For religions, with all their appeal to the past, actually tend to run in cycles, in which first a key role is played by the prophet or mystic as blazer of a new trail. In the ensuing period the preservation of his insight, and the evolving pattern of religion, can lead to a traditionalism which does not quite match the breathless novelty of the original message. So the tradition prepares for polarity and a possible struggle: in preserving the founder's message it preserves a memory of revolution, but in being faithful and conservative it creates a layer of traditionalism. The time bomb ticks away until a new prophet or mystic arises who may latch on to the quiet forces of revolution.

For a new revolution to be effective one needs the right conditions. It is said, "Cometh the hour, cometh the man." It is equally so the other way around: "Cometh the man, cometh the hour." Thus we can point to forerunners of the Protestant Reformation, but various sorts of kindling were required in order for Luther's spark to create the blaze. So far as we can figure out from the ancient records, the period of the Buddha was "right" for him: there were cities expanding along the banks of the Ganges and nearby which contained a growing new mercantile class to whom the Buddhist teaching appealed. For one thing, Buddhism made much of giving, but little of sacrificial ritual. The "new men" of the emerging culture along the Ganges could free themselves from the entangling tabus of the Brahmins and, in acquiring merit by supporting the Buddhist

Order, assure themselves of a better life. When we see the rise of a new religion we are wise to look to the social conditions which favored it. In modern times we can likewise ask: What are the appealing factors in the cults or new religious movements? How do they match certain social needs?

We can see various ways in which religion is relatively dependent and relatively dynamic. Is it importing its values from society, or is it, on balance, exporting them?

In more detail, of course, one can see how religion works in a particular region or for particular social groups. After all, if a religious movement attracts people it may be because it is responsive to their needs and slant on life. It is interesting to investigate the social and psychological background of those who join a particular group, such as the Unification Church, or Zen Centers, or Orthodox Judaism.

Sometimes such affinity is a matter of personality type. But it can also and more frequently be seen in social terms. Thus studies at various times have shown that, in American society, there is more interest in religious questions among women than among men. This fact was brought out clearly by Gerhard Lenski (b. 1924) in a study conducted in 1953. There may be two explanations, given the position of women at that time. First, women have a greater part to play in bringing up children, and the question of how to prepare the young for life tends to raise questions about religious tradition and the ultimate. Second, women—having less power—are from one perspective a minority group, and religion is often a means of expressing the predicament of those who feel themselves "underdogs." A study of whether women's liberation has made substantial differences to the position of women would tell us if these hypotheses about the function of religion are valid.

Religion, Society, and the Secular State

The connection of religion and oppression is strong in Marx. This has led to some embarrassing questions about the survival of religion in supposed Marxist societies. In theory, since religion represents the sign of the oppressed creature and the opium of the people, the need for it should wither away in a socialist context. But in fact some paradoxes exist in the actual development of religion under socialist regimes.

If we look to Poland and Romania, the one Catholic and the other Eastern Orthodox, there can be little doubt that the great piety and solidarity of the people of these countries in the practice of their faith owes much to nationalism. But the survival of religion in these countries also perhaps reflects the fact that there are aspects of life which the state belief-system cannot easily cope with. Each individual, for example, has to come to terms with death, whatever the social system. The rituals and traditions of the Church can seem rich and illuminating in comparison with the drab life socialist methods bring, at least in Eastern Europe. Alienation may actually be greater under totalitarian socialism than under older, less rigid political and economic systems. Socialism may actually intensify the disease it claims to cure. For at least a part of alienation is a sense that one lacks power over one's work and environment. A system so highly centralized and enforced by a pervasive police gives much less power to the individual than most consumerist societies.

There is an ambiguity in the notion of "secular" society. Often when we think about the secularization of life, we think of ways in which traditional religious values and practices no longer have the same power. The older peasant culture of Europe, for instance, was soaked in the rhythms of religious life, but with the Industrial Revolution, and before that the Reformation, much of that older religious life began to wane. For one thing, the rhythms of the city were different from those of the countryside. For another, the older, extended family ties, which themselves had religious roots and expression, began to weaken with the new mobility of the industrial society. Then again, the new forms of social and economic organization promised a richer life here and now. By the early twentieth century, in America and elsewhere, the dream of "a chicken in every pot" and a car in every garage came to be a way of making the pursuit of happiness—the creed of the new society—more concrete. Thus, from one angle secularization means a drift from traditional religious customs and ideas: instead of feast-days, football games; instead of pilgrimages, tourism; instead of cathedrals, movie theaters; instead of penances, diets; instead of hymns, the Beatles; instead of God, love; instead of crusades, war; instead of Christendom, the nation; instead of the Bible, the newspaper; instead of prayer, television; instead of salvation, happiness; instead of peace of mind, fun;

instead of confession, psychoanalysis; instead of sin, problems; instead of the Second Coming, progress.

But there is another meaning of the term "secular" that is different, though connected. A secular state is one with no official religion. There was a time when, to be a citizen in good standing in Sweden, you had to be a Lutheran, in Spain a Catholic, in Egypt a Muslim. The assumption was that a regime required religious sanction and that sanction should be recognized by all those loyal to the regime. So Catholics were often expelled from England, Jews from Spain, and so on. But toleration, pioneered in England from 1688 onward, in America from its beginnings, and in France after the revolution, came to be the hallmark of the modern liberal state. Such a state might retain some acknowledgment of the primacy of some religious denomination, but in practice allows for a variety of beliefs, including atheism. Thus, in an American state university, for example, though there may be Religious Studies as a wide and impartial department exploring religion and religions, there cannot be denominational teaching. You cannot preach Judaism or Christianity as if this were the religion of the state. If you want to be confessional in education you have to "go private." This system, with the state being neutral and "above" religions is what we refer to as the "secular state."

In this second sense you may have a secular state with a very nonsecular population, as in the Republic of India which is more or less neutral in matters of religion, unlike Pakistan, which is a religiously defined nation with an Islamic constitution. India is overwhelmingly religious, mainly Hindu, but with a vast Muslim minority and groups such as Sikhs, Parsees, and Christians as well.

Whereas the secular state occurs chiefly in the West, with variations in Africa and elsewhere, the most important type of rule matching the older religious states is the modern Marxist regime. There the citizen is expected to conform to the official worldview. If a person is a pious Christian or Buddhist he may be thwarted in his career. A friend of mine was imprisoned in a European Communist state for being an active Buddhist. The situation is like that of England, Spain, or Egypt, once upon a time. In fact, it may be a more intense version of the old system because authoritative control—spying on citizens, for example—is now more efficient than it was.

Such a system may be called "monistic" (i.e., unitary in belief) in contrast to the pluralism of the secular state. So one meaning of "secular" is roughly "nontraditionally religious." The other meaning is "nonmonistic." In a "monistic" State (which is not secular in the sense in which the Western democracy is) the ideals may be secular in the sense of being modern, nontraditional, and antireligious. The ideal Soviet man is pictured with a tool or a gun ready to work or do battle for the revolution, armed with new technology, turning his back heroically upon the oppressive and pious past, no longer in need of the "opium" of the people, with no interest in the Beyond, only in the shining future in which a new world is being fashioned. Similar things can be said concerning the new ideals of China, both under and beyond Mao.

But the two senses of secularization are connected, for the effect of toleration and other forces in the modern secular state tends to make traditional religion an *option*. There are many choices within it, for there are many varieties of religion to choose from. Faith becomes increasingly a private affair, and this tends to erode traditionalism. Older religions become denominations within a wider whole. Making religion a private matter can also lead to religion's becoming just a minor element in a total fabric of living. Just as a person belongs to the golf club, so he may join a church.

A major task of the sociology of religion is to plot the kinds of changes affecting religion in the modern world. Among these secularization, as in the growth of nontraditional attitudes, is obviously important in the Western world. Moreover, it is not a matter just of seeing how far traditional attitudes persist. They change under the impact of new forces. This is evident in the way new religious movements have arisen in Africa and other southern regions of the world. It is evident too in the way in which older religions, such as Hinduism, have adapted to the challenge of the West and to the impact of modern science and technology. Hinduism has fashioned for itself a new philosophy based on old sources in which religion and science are seen as differing responses to the same cosmos, which to the eye of the mystic and the devotee is divine—and to the eye of the scientist is a material order to be understood and controlled.

Those who hold that religion can be explained by its social function like to think of the new religious movements of the small-scale societies as responses to dislocations: they spring in a sense from the fact that a society is threatened from outside, fails to function properly, and needs some new solution. This new solution is often a fantasy solution (according to this view), but it is in a sense an expression and projection of the sense of struggle which the society is facing. Thus many movements combine magic and the idea of a millennium, a new social order of prosperity and peace. In New Guinea and other parts of Melanesia in the South Pacific in this century there have been a number of so-called cargo cults, in which the hope of magical access to the White Man's goods (often thought to have been stolen from the ancestors of the natives) arises, leading to a new social order in which the natives live at ease and in harmony. We might see such cults as using elements from the natives' understanding of life in order to deal with the dislocations caused by the incoming White Man.

The hope of a new social order coming through divine action is not something new. It was part of the hope of the early Christians and of various sections within the contemporary Jewish community. It is a way in which people draw substance and power from the future. The Melanesian who constructs a "magical" airfield in the hope that planes will land there with goods that until now only the whites have had access to may seem naive; but we should not forget that the ideal of a New Jerusalem built in our own country is one of the potent dreams which has drawn Western civilization forward. The question, though, is how such dreams can be used creatively. The cargo cults are doomed to disappointment when interpreted just in terms of commodities. But the dream of a new community was used creatively by the Mormons—and without that dream there would have been no Utah as we know it today.

Because the peoples of the world are in close interaction, with new forces continuously being brought to bear on every society (with smaller societies particularly feeling the strain), there is a wide spectrum of new religious movements. This suggests new ways in which the social sciences may be illuminating. For we may learn lessons from the way some of these movements develop and apply this knowledge to the historical understanding of older faiths in their early days. We may have a better understanding, for instance, of Christianity when it was a "new religious movement."

Indeed, we can apply various categories to such movements. It is useful at this point to go back to a distinction between the Church and the sect made by Ernst Troeltsch (1865–1923), a Christian theologian who took sociology seriously. The distinction between these two types of religious organization, together with the related notions of the denomination and the cult, have been prominent in sociological study. The sociology of religion, however, remains over-committed to Western language, reflecting the special experience of the Christian tradition, and the terminology does not fit at all well in Eastern and other non-Christian contexts. However, Troeltsch's distinctions represent a beginning of classification. One point has to be made before we proceed: Weber, Troeltsch, and others used what can be called "ideal types" to classify and illuminate data. The ideal type is a model which may not be a full portrait—indeed, it cannot be a full portrait—of the complexities of actual institutions. But the model serves as a useful simplification to help us understand the data more broadly than would otherwise be possible. "Church" and "sect" are ideal types in this sense.

The Church as an institution both dominates and is dominated by the social structure in which it finds itself. It dominates because it seeks to permeate the whole of a society and to use its influence to make society more Christian (or more Buddhist, for example, if we are thinking of the Sangha in Sri Lanka or Thailand). It is dominated by society in the sense that it necessarily takes on some of society's characteristics. Thus, the early Christians did not have a church in this sense: their movement was akin to today's sects. But Christianity came to be the religion of the Roman Empire, and in so doing the Roman world became Catholic and Catholicism itself became Roman. By contrast, the sect is more in the nature of a counterculture. It tends to reject a church's compromise with the world. It stresses ideal behavior and a closed circle, to which admittance is by conversion (while, by contrast, one tends to be "born into" a church).

Sometimes sects accept society and affirm its goals, but see their own prescriptions as better ways to achieve them. Christian Science and Transcendental Meditation, for example, believe that they have certain special ways of enhancing health and life in society. Sometimes they substitute for worldliness a superior ethic in which a community, more or less uncontaminated by the world, seeks salvation—this is a common feature of communal groups. The commune is often seen as the ideal society within society. The sect, then, is very much an in-group. A good instance are the Jehovah's Witnesses, with their predictions of the end of history and the taking up of those who are saved (the rest of the world perishing without trace). There are also sects which are, in principle or in practice, at loggerheads with society, and which seek to change it radically, possibly by rebellion and upheaval. A secular variety of this type is found among the Italian Red Brigades and other leftist terrorist groups in Europe—revolutionary sects who suppose that through chaos they will bring about the collapse of the existing order and the coming into being of a new, more just society. Sects of this type often aggressively seek conversion, in their hope to radically change society.

Between the sect and the Church there lies the denomination. This is, so to speak, an organizationally separate branch of the Church. Unlike the sect, the denomination has a certain degree of integration into the wider society. What in one country may be a church can, in a more plural setting, become a denomination. In America, for example, Catholicism is a denomination somewhat on a par with other Christian denominations, although other parts of the Roman Catholic Church (in Spain and Italy, for example) are in the relevant sense *churches*.

More recently it has been fashionable in Western contexts to add the category "cult"—a sect in the making, such as the Moonies, the Hare Krishna, and the Scientologists. Most have charismatic leaders. There does not seem any great reason to treat them differently from sects (they may in time become "normalized" within society and become denominations.) Some of these movements need to be understood in a wider context than a single society or nation. They are transnational. They are attempts to weave together elements from differing social and cultural backgrounds. The Moonies (followers of the Reverend Sun Myung Moon) incorporate ideas from the Confucian tradition as well as evangelical Christianity into a new mixture with its own particular dynamic. The Hare Krishna movement takes on more than Indian qualities in the context of New York and San Francisco.

We live at a time when the opportunities are unique for seeing the way religions and worldviews change through their interaction and migration. Already the study is beginning of how religions react when they have an extensive diaspora, that is, where adherents live scattered in foreign places and cities; for example, Hinduism in Fiji and Guyana, Buddhism among Vietnamese in Los Angeles, Chinese worldviews in Singapore and San Francisco, Islam in Britain and Germany, Zulu religion in the cities of South Africa, and so on. Moreover, we have unfolding before us many movements in which elements from different traditions are put together as ways of reacting, sometimes creatively, to the problems raised by the collision of differing cultures and lifestyles.

Clearly, religion itself is deeply affected by social change, and new movements arise and grow from the challenges of change and interaction. But these new movements have their own dynamic, in tapping reserves of myth and symbolism and creating new combinations of values. Often the charismatic leader is a person who somehow experiences in his own life some of the tensions which he seeks to express and to cope with, on a larger scale, as a religious leader; in this way he often unknowingly prepares the way for a new social pattern.

We have here sketched briefly some of the ways in which the social sciences can approach the religious factor in human life. The social approach to religion can help us to reflect upon the future of religion and some of the larger issues raised by its study.

For the fact is that religion is itself affected by the new perspectives we are continually gaining by studying it. We are in this as in other areas of human life coming to a new kind of self-consciousness. To some thoughts about the future of religious and other worldviews I now turn.

9

Reflections on the Future of Religion and Ideology

MANY EDUCATED people in the West, impressed by the increasing secularization of society and by their own view that religious tradition no longer has much intellectual power, have tended to think that the study of religion is rather old-fashioned. It might be able to tell us some fascinating things about the human past, but it does not promise to unlock many secrets of the future. Even now throughout the world of English-speaking philosophy there is a wide dismissal of religion as irrational, and many of those affected by the tradition of Marx and Freud think that traditional religion is bound to fade. Yet there are, as we have seen, forces—both rational and emotional—which suggest otherwise.

For one thing, some of the secular gods have shown clay feet. Consider the dreadful fate of Kampuchea (or Cambodia, as it used to be called) after the success of the Khmer Rouge takeover in 1975. Here was a social revolution guided by a new secular ideology based on principles worked out by the French-educated leader Khieu Sampan. It was not orthodox Marxism. Rather it was an antitraditional attempt to produce a rural-based communist society totally cut off from the outside world—particularly from the capitalist system which was seen as part of that colonial past, and which had led to

159

the bleeding of Cambodia and its corruption by French and other cultural influences. The 1970s' revolution produced untold misery. Its end came with an invasion by Moscow-allied Communists from Vietnam who practiced a secular ideology of such harshness that hundreds of thousands of people from Vietnam took to perilous boats across the South China Sea in order to escape. The initial success of the Khmer Rouge had partly to do with American bombing and other incursions, which prevented Cambodia's survival as a neutral nation. Such intervention, under the orders of President Nixon and Secretary of State Kissinger, could in a sense have been well-meaning. It was all done in defense of the Western democratic ideals of freedom, and it was done with the careless and cruel confidence of those who think that military-technological power can solve most problems. Kampuchea is a tragic example of the effects of secular ideologies when they are launched without regard for the people who must then live with them. The Khmer Rouge had a creed that was mad and unrealistic; the Vietnamese creed was cruel; the Buddhists' was too passive; and the Americans' too technocratic.

The environmentalist movement, from the late 1960s onward, has also been a sign of the crumbling of older kinds of materialism and of the easy dismissal of religion. The view that nature is just material, waiting to be shaped and exploited on behalf of the human race, has given way to a new vision of the webs which bind together the different forms of life in their environment, and which thus bind together both organic and inorganic nature. This perception of the flow back and forth between us and nature owes something to Eastern religious influence. Schumacher's pioneering book *Small is Beautiful* was greatly influenced by Buddhism; other authors have been influenced by Taoism and Native American and other traditions. Thus it is incorrect to assume that it is more "rational" to adopt a materialist worldview which dismisses traditional religious values.

The fact that religion persists and has frequent revivals, even in areas such as the Soviet Union, where the context is not at all favorable, suggests that some of the emotional and ritual needs of human beings are not well addressed by secular ideologies. Western liberal democracy can produce "the lonely crowd" and the sense of loss of identity, while Marxist totalitarianism can fail to respond to the creative visions of human beings and their need to deal with suffering and death. Secular worldviews too easily ignore the visions and intuitions of something Beyond.

At the same time, nationalism remains a force of great emotional power. For many people "freedom" and "liberation" refer not to personal freedom or individual liberation, but rather to the liberation of the national group. Every self-respecting oppressed ethnic group has a "national liberation front." Nor should we underestimate, especially in the southern hemisphere the continued appeal of Marxism as a way of solving social and economic problems in emerging countries—especially those which link their oppression to the colonial past and to the Western countries, and therefore to capitalism. We shall continue to live in a world where traditional religion and the secular ideologies will be in powerful interplay.

Does our study of religion and worldviews suggest how human beliefs will develop? And in what sort of world?

It seems clear from past and present developments that the unfolding of future religion will occur within a new wider community—the totality of the globe, what I have called the "global city." Religion and the secular ideologies find themselves more and more in a state of self-consciousness. They look at themselves in a mirror. The very attempt to explore religions and to analyze worldviews produces images which in turn affect those religions and worldviews. The maturing disciplines of the social and human sciences have done much, in the last century and in this one, to influence such attitudes. We know more about our own history than any previous generation. We know more about populations, shifts in economic behavior, changes in marriage customs—more, in short, about the varieties of society in the world than was ever possible in the past. We know more about the religions of the world, and we know more about revolutions, governments, bureaucracies, voting preferences, political attitudes, than ever before. We know more about patterns of human belief and action than was possible in premodern times. We see ourselves—sometimes clearly, sometimes not so clearly—in the new intellectual mirrors we have made.

There are two sides to this tremendous explosion of knowledge, one connected with the global city, the other connected to the questions of truth and analysis. On the one side, the very knowledge we have becomes a mode of introducing cultures to one another, and so of opening these cultures to influences which themselves bring changes. I was involved in being general adviser to the BBC television series *The Long Search:* this series itself reached millions of people in and beyond the English-speaking world. It affected, among others, an aunt of mine, the widow of a Scottish Presbyterian minister, and a fine person. She said she had not known how much good there was in Buddhism and other religions of the East. Already her attitude toward Christianity was being slightly modified. Such communication systems as television and books, and the migrations of individuals and groups, have the effect of opening up paths between faiths which affect those faiths. They will never again simply be able to ignore one another naturally, and cutting a faith off from the rest of the world will result in a new kind of global sectarianism. (The Ayatollah's Iran is in danger thus of becoming, as it were, a global sect.)

On the other side, there are questions about the rationality of religion and about the validity of religious experiences and symbols. For, in a world in which more and more people are experiencing the effects of science and are being introduced to a scientific education, issues of religious belief, and the relation between belief and science, are bound to come up. Some arise directly from the modern study of religion: how far can we account for religious ideas by saying that they are projections whose origins lie in ourselves and in human society? To what extent can we think of religion as being an area of experience, like music or morality, with its own principles and its own inner dynamic? What difference do our theories about religions and ideologies make to the way we are to see the future of human beliefs?

The Future of Belief

I want to explore the answers to these questions in light of the writers and theories we have already alluded to. My argument is itself a brief kind of speculation—some suggestions about ways we might look at religion and the secular worldviews. I shall do so by looking at the three points of the triangle that worldviews refer to: the cosmos, the self, and society.

First, the cosmos. We may draw a line between those who adopt a humanist view and those who, as in traditional religions, have a belief in some ultimate Being "beyond" the cosmos. For the so-called scientific humanist there is nothing to know which lies outside of this universe of ours. But for the traditional believer the cosmos wears another face: for the theist it is the creation of a good God; for the Buddhist it is the cycle of rebirth beyond which lie ultimate liberation and Emptiness; for the Taoist its inner unseen nature is the Way. We have already seen how, according to one form of modern existentialist philosophy (in the writings of Bultmann and Buber), we should see personal relations as lying outside the area of scientific inquiry. These relations, in their most authentic form, are the province of religion.

A similar view of different origins comes from the later writings of the philosopher Ludwig Wittgenstein and others influenced by him. In this view, religious language has its own inner logic, and the religious believer does not differ from others concerning facts about the world but rather brings her own set of pictures to bear in interpreting those facts. She "sees the world as" having been created by a God, for instance, or lives in light of the picture of the Second Coming. Such "seeing as" or "picturing" does not exist in the same dimension as science. It is an alternative way of seeing and experiencing the same cosmos that science tries to understand—though with very different motives and tools.

The existentialist and the Wittgensteinian approaches can be called "two-aspect," in the sense that scientific knowledge and religious perception see the same thing (the cosmos) under two aspects, as on the one hand open to scientific exploration and on the other hand as conveying religious meaning.

It seems to me that a two-aspect theory like this provides a way for many scientifically educated people to begin to harmonize science and religion. But more has to be said, because the idea that we see the cosmos as this or that stresses content—the results of scientific inquiry or of religious faith—but it does not say anything about method. After all, science is not so much a set of results (although it produces many results) as a way of unlocking the secrets of the cosmos, a method by which we enter into dialogue with nature. This method is a matter of observation, and measurement. But you cannot say the same of religion, which is not a way of observing, per se, although it does include a way in which a person lays himself open to experience.

Thus, if there is a method in religion, it is not the same as the so-called scientific method. It is rather a method of prayer, of contemplation, of exposing the self to the ultimate. One might say that religion opens one up to the numinous and to the mystical. If there is a method it is a kind of self-preparation for experience of the Beyond.

Religion in this view is a way of coming to experience (among other things) the cosmos. It is seeing the things in this world around us as having a special set of meanings. It is not so much trying to understand how they work, but rather seeing them in the light of eternity. There is here a likeness between religion and painting. The painting gives us new eyes to see sunflowers or canals or people or fruit. A painting does not theorize about these things; it sees them both in new ways and "as they are." The painter gives an immediate force to what he paints. And the person who has a religious view of things sees them as having a special, "immediate" force and meaning. The sun becomes a sign of God's power, and benevolence, and sometimes wrath; the morning mist gives a sense of immediacy and impermanence.

Religion, however, cannot be untouched by the unspoken thoughts of a scientific culture. Science is always revising itself. Today's theories may be scrapped tomorrow, and nature has many surprises in store for us. So there is an element in science which is *critical*—a point much emphasized in the writings of Karl Popper (b. 1902). Science advances through the criticism and testing of theories. Good theories are those which survive such criticism. In a modern society a degree of openness in which our theories can be fully criticized is essential, if science and technology are to flourish. Such a society cannot be an authoritarian one, obviously. So how can authoritarian *religion* blend with such an open and scientific culture?

If symbols of authority—the Pope, the Bible, the guru, the charismatic leader—persists in religion, it is probably because they are being seen increasingly as ways and means of discipline. They are themselves symbols and persons who help us in the pursuit of that opening up to God or ultimate freedom. Just as Buddhism, in its seeking for a glimpse of that enlightenment which suffused the Buddha's consciousness, has created the society of the sangha, or monastic order, with its rules and rather strict discipline, so too other religions have used authority as a means toward a higher experience. But such authority is bound to be modified in the context of the open society. And increasingly, men and women who accept the discipline of an authority do so because they have chosen to do so. There is, in a plural and open world, no compulsion to accept this or that. So in its own way religion is likely to become more and more "empirical": that is, it is likely to be seen as testable in experience, a matter of "come and see."

Yet such openness creates its own backlashes. The freedom and ability to choose, which are characteristics of a plural society, often create their own problems. People often feel a need to go back to a purer authority—a kind of fundamentalism, a literalness, a faithful acceptance of what one is told. So, side by side in the emerging global culture with a new free and easy individual kind of religion, there is likely to be a whole array of backlashes, of rather harsh reaffirmations of older moral, social, and doctrinal stances.

We can distinguish two main forms which the religious "vision" of the cosmos can take. One sees the cosmos as having "behind" it a personal Being. The other sees it as having "behind" or "within" it something eternal and yet indescribable—a Way, Emptiness, nirvana. The one vision is nourished by devotion and the experience of the numinous, the other by the practice of self-control and the inner mystical experience.

The two visions sometimes blend, so that the Beyond is also "within" and the personal has an unspoken depth. This type of vision is important if we are trying to estimate how in the modern world the religious understanding of the self may fare. There remains in each human being a feeling that we find meaning both outwardly, in relation to the people we know and love and the things we do and possess, and inwardly, in relation to what lies in back of all our experiences. Each of us is a center of consciousness. We often feel that the world would not exist without our own individual consciousnesses. For aren't we the ones who somehow impose on the great flux out there the shapes, smells, sounds, and sensations that arise from our consciousness? The cosmos as we know it is the result of an interaction between what is mysteriously out there and what lies within. It is as if the atoms and molecules and particles whose swarms make up the world around us are nothing at all in themselves, until they spring into life when lit up by the multicolored light of our consciousness. One of the quests of the yogi and the mystic has been to search out that ego—that pure consciousness which lies in back of all our experiences, to find, as it were, the true essence of ourselves, and so the pure essence of the light which lights up the world.

The outer sense of the personal behind the cosmos and the inner quest for pure consciousness are both reflections of the fact that the universe has to be interpreted in the light of our existence. However small and insignificant this planet may be against the great face of the galaxy-sprinkled cosmos, it is nevertheless inhabited by conscious human beings. The materialist begins with matter and sees consciousness just as a special species of matter—matter in its most refined form. But we can look at things the other way around: matter is seen in quite a new light when we see that out of it emerges consciousness. Why not see matter as oriented toward consciousness? And could it not be that there is a divine consciousness which lies behind the material cosmos? These are options of belief and interpretation which remain open to us. And because the mystery of our self-consciousness remains great, religious traditions will still represent to us possible experiments in living.

Moreover, the patterns of religious experience will still continue to bubble up in the human soul, whatever their ultimate origins and whether or not they give us an insight into something Beyond. From this point of view religious experience is likely to remain a thread in human culture and life. It will continue to breed for us its own special ways of seeing, and feeling about, the world. How to interpret it is another matter. It might even be that a kind of religious humanism could emerge in which the numinous character of the cosmos is recognized, not one showing that there is a God, but one offering a way of responding to the wonders of life. In this way religion would take its place alongside art and music as a form of response and creativity.

Such a "religious humanism" is already prefigured in the writing of Jung. His idea is that in the unconscious there are certain deep patterns of symbolism which are manifested in myth and art and which help to express and to solve problems of living—problems such as how to understand and face evil. Jung's theory suggests that traditional religion supplies ways of bringing about wholeness in our personal lives. Such a humanism is richer than the usual Western variety, which simply stresses the need to value and revere human beings without recourse to God. Jungian humanism, however, makes some use of the resources of religious myth. And here the comparative study of religion has a vital task to perform, for now there lie before us the myths of all the world which can be explored for their capacity to bring to the surface those symbols of male and female, of wholeness and disintegration, of good and evil, of creation and destruction—all the myths which have arisen in the human race's long experience of the mysterious give-and-take with a delightful but threatening cosmos.

So we can say that a variety of religious options and possibilities continues to open up, even in the more unified world of the global city.

As we have seen, myth is not just a matter of a symbolic way of looking at the world. It is a way of coming to an understanding of one's own identity. The modern counterpart of this is history: it is through the rediscovery of the past that we know who "we" are. We have been passing through, and still are passing through, a period in which the primary political force has been nationalism. Thus, the nation or ethnic group must, so to speak, fashion its own history and its own roots. But there are signs that broader forms of history are becoming more meaningful. For instance, black Africa is evolving its own consciousness of what it is to be African. This new sense of the African past is a guide to the special role blacks can play in the evolving culture of the globe: Africa can revitalize music and art and expressions of joy and responses to suffering. In the Pacific there are attempts to express the "Pacific way"—the style of living and culture characteristic of the South Pacific as a whole, in the light of a shared ancestry and history. Already there is a sense of the history and destiny of the West—that is, primarily Europe and America—as creating a scientific and individualistic civilization.

Among these patterns, the great religious traditions will more and more ask themselves what the meaning of their past is in view of the present unification of the globe. There may still be dreams in some religions of becoming, so to say, the church for the whole globe, as Christianity did for the "known world" of the Roman Empire. But it seems more plausible that religions will function more as denominations and sometimes as sects. They will be denominations in the sense that they will live together with a certain mutual recognition, each perhaps feeling that it has the right slant on life, but not altogether excluding the visions and values of the other traditions. Each will strive to bear witness to its own true self, and to spread such light as it possesses, but without the real hope of becoming the exclusive faith of all the world. Because such a tolerant attitude is in some degree threatening to the authority and certainty of the past, the backlashes in each faith will take the form of a global sectarianism. The conservative and traditionalist response to pluralism is to reaffirm the exclusive rightness of one's tradition and one's revelation. This will involve a degree of inner withdrawal from the concerns of the wider world. It will involve a kind of isolationism. We can see this happening in areas of the Islamic and Christian worlds, among Hindu militants, and occasionally in the new religions of Japan.

All these various changes and responses are relevant to the way in which we may come to understand society—to understand one another. There is here a certain tug of war. In a new and often disturbing interaction between cultures and ideologies, it is natural for different groups to try to affirm their own special identities. Sometimes traditional religion will be an important ingredient—Buddhism as shaping Sinhalese identity, Orthodoxy as shaping Romanian identity, Zulu Zionism as giving new meaning to Zulu identity, and so on. But at the same time we are shaping a global society. How is the identity of that society to be understood? As the identity of the human race, no less. But this itself implies that we should see human history as a whole in a new light. Those who see it just as exhibiting the rhythms of the Marxist dialectic, or the unfolding guidance of Allah, may have to come to terms with a more plural approach. For if, as I have suggested, there is likely to be a denominational trend in the great religions, there is also likely to be what might be described as a "federalist" trend in world history. The global society will be looking back to a variety of histories—Russian, Chinese, American, African, Pacific, and so on. From the insights into and experiences of these various civilizations the tapestry of a new world civilization will be woven. Even if each tradition stays true to its own message, it will have to operate in a context of this federal world civilization.

Such a development will give the history of religions an interesting role to play in education. It is a role foreshadowed by Eliade, who suggests that the history of religions interprets for the modern world the world of archaic men. I would put it differently: in addition to trying to describe as accurately as possible, and with structured empathy, the meaning of past forms of religion, we may also wish to see what those forms still contain in the way of creative messages for our own global civilization. We thus have a modern form of the cult of ancestors. In traditional societies there is communication with the ancestral dead; now we, too, can achieve contact with Zarathustra, the Buddha, Christ, Maimonides, Ghazali, Mencius, and Marx through the medium of history.

Worldview analysis enables us to communicate not just with our spiritual ancestors, but with one another. In that goal we find the creative task of making ourselves mutually intelligible. Here too it may be possible to reflect upon the lessons offered by different cultures and belief-systems. I am not, of course, presupposing here that everything is good in other cultures, or in our own. We need to be critical as well as appreciative. But by what criteria? That, of course, is the crucial question. At the very least we can agree that each culture has some distinctive contribution to make to our understanding of the world.

Moreover, the very "federalism" of the emerging global civilization and the study of religions and worldviews may themselves offer clues about how to evaluate the creative uses of the past.

First: it seems to me that the very process of establishing a federal approach to cultures implies an attempt to combine loyalty to one's tradition with respect, and so toleration, for the traditions of others. It is worth noting here that the candid exploration of religions and worldviews, now so vividly a part of the Western intellectual scene (not just through the study of religion but also through the human and social sciences), is not possible in monistic societies as I defined them earlier. The open exploration of different commitments does not flourish where the distinction between Party (or Church, or mosque) and State is not clearly and appropriately made. But part of toleration and empathy is the ability to understand some of the insecurities which breed intolerance; so, up to a point (indeed, as far as possible), the intolerant can be tolerated in a tolerant society—and the intolerant in a tolerant globe.

Second: a critical approach to religions and worldviews has to look to what the main point, or objective, of a system of belief is.

We can evaluate Christianity by its capacity for love, and its commitment to live a spiritual life close to God. We can judge Buddhism by its insight and compassion. We can judge Marxism by its actual social reforms and efforts toward a better life for ordinary people. It will probably turn out that the various goals and central objectives of the differing faiths are not all that incompatible. Such compatibility already suggests ways of cooperation.

Third: because it seems that there are no proofs for or against the validity of any worldview, people should accept that different ways of life are, so to speak, different experiments in living. None can lay claim to an absoluteness. Such absoluteness is not available until the end of time when all perhaps will be revealed. (But even then the belief that there is an end to time is itself one of the things which may be disputed and argued about in that soft and hazy way which is demanded by the actual situation.)

But—it may be answered—many people believe in faith, and in one faith alone: some take the Bible as absolute; others the Koran; others the Vedas; others the Marxist tradition. People do, in fact, lay claim to an absoluteness, and it is not for me to look down on those of fervent commitment. But it must be said that the certitude of those who have such faith is not a public certitude. The faithful often think that what they see so clearly is obvious to others. It is not so. If it were, there would be no great divergences between worldviews. So while certitude must be respected, it is not something which rests on outer proof. It may be that the search for proofs is a snare which the religious and others would do well to avoid.

Fourth: the impulse to walk in others' moccasins already implies respect for others. Such respect is heightened, perhaps, by the thought that human beings have that consciousness which is the silent turning point of the whole world—or perhaps by the belief that they reflect something from the Beyond. But respect is not, of course, just a matter of understanding the others' point of view. Respect implies that one acknowledge the dignity of the other. So it seems to me that one test of a religion or worldview is the degree to which it is actually able to help those whose dignity is threatened by poverty or humiliation, by cruelty or callousness. Religion can never seal itself off from the cry of those who are in distress, and retain its integrity.

As a result of this test it may turn out that "true" religion is not to be identified with any tradition as a whole, but rather with individual movements and people within it. There are, after all, both callous Christianities and compassionate ones. This is another lesson we can draw from the study of worldviews: there are many more varieties than at first meet the eye; and our broad categories of "-isms" are often misleading, for they simplify a human world of great complexity. But maybe that is good. It is as though we see a hillside full of flowers, some yellow, some purple, some red, some white, some blue, and think that there are five sorts of flowers. But when we come among them we find each color covers a swarm of differing kinds of flowers, so many that the true classifications cross the boundaries of color: white and purple clover at first belonged apart, but upon a closer look are seen to be close sisters.

The kind of federalism I have been advocating may also be useful as a banner for the smaller cultures on our planet. I think we can safely say that the old world of the anthropologist is fading away very rapidly. Indian villages in the highlands of Guatemala, once a world of their own, now receive on cheap transistors the insistent messages of a global world, while guerrillas and government officials suck them into wider political struggles than they have ever known. Remote African nomadic tribes are now visited by experts in cattle-raising, and they too are beginning to tap the silent waves of the air. Those in remote New Guinea valleys are now asked to vote and to sell their pigs for market. Coral islands see the cruise ships and the frigates of great white powers circling like predators. There is hardly a tribe or small people left untouched by huge and accelerating waves of outside influence. The disturbance can be both entrancing and threatening. If small-scale societies embrace new religions, it may be one sign that they wish to cope with change by somehow reaffirming their own identity. And ultimately, although they need to live in a wider world, they need also to see their own place in it. This is hard to do: but it is a social and psychological project which breathes, perhaps quite unknowingly, the spirit of federalism, the federalism of the spirit that seems to be one major trend in a shrinking but divergent world.

There will be many surprises in the ferment. We are drawing to the end of an epoch in which older philosophies had great dynamism—the utilitarianism of the West, Marxisms, existentialism—and older religions still have great self-confidence. We are entering a new phase of human history, and in that phase the study of religions and analysis of worldviews have a great part to play.

These chapters have been an invitation to the field of religious study. Finally and briefly I shall suggest ways in which it is possible for you to travel further.

Further Explorations in Religion and Worldview Analysis

USUALLY a book like this lists books for further reading, and indeed here I too make some suggestions. But it is worth remembering that books are only one means toward understanding the world. In the case of religions and worldviews it is useful, I think, to use the six dimensions—experiential, mythic, doctrinal, ethical, ritual, and social—as a kind of checklist, so that you can approach any religious movement or tradition in a reasonably rounded way. Once you look to those dimensions you will see very quickly that the world beyond books holds many other keys to understanding. For instance, if you are exploring the Roman Catholic tradition you will need most of all to get a feel for the Mass. One of the best ways, indeed an essential way, is to attend the Mass if you are not already familiar with it. You will then be a "participant observer." In that way you will be taking part in fieldwork, much as an anthropologist might in some culture which he or she seeks to understand.

If you are already familiar with the Mass, it is probably because you are a Roman Catholic or have been brought up in that tradition. There are pitfalls here. You may think you understand it better than you do. Familiarity may lead to the dulling of questions. The person to whom the Mass is strange will sometimes have a fresher grasp of some of its outstanding features. Moreover, there is always more to learn about any tradition even if you know a lot about it already: the structure of the contemporary Mass, for instance, has to be understood against the background of what happened at and after Vatican II. That again presupposes some idea of the period before, when the structure of the Mass was dictated by the tradition of the Council of Trent—in an era when the architecture and painting of churches tended to have a certain baroque style, rich and dark and heavily adorned. As for the other religious dimensions, you need to understand many things, such as what is distinctive about Catholic ethics; what the shape of Catholic doctrine is; the story of the Church as seen through Catholic eyes; the nature of Catholic mysticism and the particular style of the Catholic sense of the numinous; the shape of Catholic institutions; and above all, the Papacy. In addition you have to realize that although Catholicism is worldwide it exists in many varieties. The darker and more austere forms of Irish Catholicism differ from the more exuberant and carefree Italian Catholicism, and both differ from the activist Catholicism of the United States. Happily, ours is an age when travel is easy. If you have eyes to see there is much to find out about forms of faith in foreign lands.

It is easy, if you live in Madison, Wisconsin, or in Edinburgh, Scotland, to do your "fieldwork" next door, by going around to the nearest Presbyterian or Catholic Church. It might seem more difficult to do fieldwork on, say, Buddhism. But still, the same six-dimensional checklist can be used, and although the fuller fieldwork—seeing Buddhism in some of its typical Eastern environments—may be something that has to be postponed until you can travel, there are in our Western societies many minorities from Eastern cultures; there are also many people who have joined Eastern religions. You do not, after all, have to go to India to see Buddhist meditation in action. It is true that a religion outside its original cultural context will have changed. Some who know Buddhism from New York become disappointed in Sri Lanka, just as Christians from Nigeria are often disappointed with the faith they find (or do not find) in England, whence came the missionaries.

But if travel in the flesh is not always possible, you can travel in the mind. Not only can books take you richly into other minds, but there are many films which can give an insight into other faiths: for instance, the BBC television series *The Long Search,* shown widely from time to time in the United States, Britain, and elsewhere. Other films such as Renoir's *The River* give a feel of other cultures and other climes.

We often underestimate, in the formal study of religion, the insights that literature can provide. E. M. Forster's *A Passage to India,* for example, gives a marvelous picture of some of the religious and cultural divergences in British India. There are, of course, many other major literary works of great religious depth, from Aeschylus and Shakespeare to Sartre and Solzhenitsyn.

Literature is, in part, just a portrayal of people, but people seen through the lens of art. One can also, of course, see religions and worldviews through the eyes of people themselves. I earlier put great emphasis on structured empathy. This "entering into" other people's thought- and feeling-worlds is essential to the central descriptive task in the study of religion. But a major part of this "entering in" can be achieved by talking with people. What does the Christian faith mean to this person or another? What does Buddhism mean? Entering into a dialogue with someone is an important ingredient of further understanding. But we need to know how to ask and how to frame the right questions.

This is one of the jobs of the teacher of religious studies: to help people to frame the right questions. A good introductory book in the field of religion and worldview analysis can give people that initial understanding which steers them away from foolish and blinding questions. It is not much good charging into the mind of a Buddhist with such a question as "Do you believe in God?", for, as we have seen, the worldview of Buddhism is completely different from the worldviews of the ancient Near East and modern West (the worldviews which helped you frame that question).

Part of the problem of cultural and religious diversity is language. The person who wishes to explore the New Testament ought to realize that it was initially written in Greek, and that some of the translations we use are questionable. Thus *agapē* is translated as "charity" or as "love," words which in modern English usage have a different flavor from the Greek (the one veering toward alms-giving, and the other toward sex and romance). It is not possible for you to learn a whole language, perhaps, although it is surprising how many people manage to get caught up with the spell of such languages as Hebrew, Sanskrit, Pali, or Greek. But it is good to be aware of the problem, and often possible to learn at least some of the key ideas and the key features of a language. For instance, knowing about the way vowels were treated in writing Hebrew helps us to understand why there are often ambiguities of meaning in the original, and the fact that Chinese is monosyllabic, and not given to abstract nouns, tells us why there is a certain style of concreteness about classical Chinese texts. The myriad translations of the *Tao Te Ching,* the classic of Tao, become understandable when we notice the epigrammatic and laconic nature of much Chinese poetry. So even if we do not learn a language we can learn something about languages.

In talking of structured empathy I have in effect sketched a mode of travel into other minds, but usually we think of this in terms of my traveling here and now into the minds of others here and now. Religious traditions and secular worldviews require some time travel, however. The world of Paul is not our world, nor is the world of Karl Marx. We need imagination to feel what the Roman Empire and Palestine were like in the days of Paul, or what European capitalism and London life were like in the days of Marx. So part of our inquiry into worldviews must be historical. Here it is useful to read not just a history of religions, such as my own *The Religious Experience of Mankind* or Trevor Ling's *History of Religions East and West.* It is also important to read some wider account of the relevant culture: a history of the Roman Empire, or of ancient India, or of China.

The judicious use of encyclopedias is often useful, especially the so-called Macropedia section of the *Encyclopedia Britannica.* This has many excellent articles on the great religions and the religions of Africa and elsewhere. (It is rather weak, from our point of view as explorers of religion and culture, in its country-by-country accounts. Thus, if you look up a country such as Romania, you'll find little on the spiritual and intellectual side of Romanian history and culture, but more on the religious traditions as a whole.) The *Encyclopedia of Philosophy* contains a great deal on religious doctrines.

It is also a good idea, in developing a feel for religions and worldviews, to think about symbolism. This can often be done in the environment around us.

Symbols help to bring us to an understanding of the rituals of the social context in which we find ourselves: the whole body of lore which centers around the meal, for instance. Thinking about the rituals attached to eating will help us understand communion, fasting, and other sacred approaches to food and drink.

The symbols of everyday life are also a bridge to understanding the visual language of sculpture and painting. Sit before a fine Buddha statue from India in one of our major galleries, or look at its photo in a fine art book, and ask yourself what messages it conveys. First of all you can do so without reference to the conventional parts of the iconography, like the arrangement of fingers and hands, which constitute a separate language which you need later to learn. You can start by thinking about the *spirit* of the sculpture. What does it communicate? Likewise with the Crucifix or an icon of the Virgin Mary. Or go into a church or temple and think about the meaning of its space. What do Gothic arches mean? What does the shape of a Buddhist temple complex convey?

There is a great deal in which we can immerse ourselves if we are going forward in the everyday exploration of religious and other values. But what (you might say) about inward practice? What about prayer? What about meditation? I think it is important to have at least a preliminary experience of the spiritual life. I do not mean by this that we necessarily should get converted, or be "born again" (but maybe you already are). I mean that because prayer and meditation have meant, and continue to mean, so much to so many, it is important for us to have an inkling of what it is like, if we do not have this knowledge already. Even if we have been brought up to say the Lord's Prayer or to go to synagogue, it does not follow that we know what the self-training of the mystic is like, or what the sense of the presence of God is. Why not try to imagine what the religious life is like? Collections of mystical and devotional writings can tell you a lot. And why not try meditation, for that matter? Why not stay in a monastery? Even if you do not believe in God, why not act *as if* the world around us is continually speaking messages to us from the Creator?

None of this will mean that you will brainwash yourself somehow into adopting beliefs you do not truly hold. For religious experience needs to be interpreted, and it is you who will be supplying that framework. Perhaps inevitably you will be drawn into some reflections about the truth of religion and the truth of secular world-views (the truths are two sides of the same coin).

In order to do this, it is important to get some orientation in the philosophy of religion; there are a number of good modern writings which arise out of the debate about empiricism. They arise, that is, out of the debate about whether all knowledge has to be empirical—a matter of seeing, hearing, smelling. This debate is, in effect, the debate about scientific humanism: is it necessary for all knowledge ultimately to be scientific (that is, knowledge based upon seeing, hearing, and so on, but expressed through mathematics and theories about what patterns lie behind what we see)?

It is also wise to ponder some of the best doctrinal writings of the modern age—ones which take Christian or Buddhist or whatever doctrine seriously and try to present them systematically. How does a person who has thought about his or her tradition come to give it meaningful shape in today's world?

It is wise, too, always to see religion in its interplay with the changes now going on in our world. In trying to understand secular ideologies such as Marxism, it is necessary to look to political theory and economics. We cannot see what faiths and philosophies mean until we see them within the world of suffering, of poverty, of upheaval. For a great engine of faith, whether secular or traditional, is hope: hope is something which the poor and the oppressed, indeed all of us, need to feel and which all perhaps pray and work for.

I think a sensitive understanding of worldviews is a marvelous preparation for life in our world, and it is a substantial ingredient in proper reflection upon the ways to move our societies forward. So a wish to explore the field more, to voyage inwardly and outwardly through the symbols, experiences, and thoughts of human beings, is not a luxury. It is an exciting quest and there are many valuable things to discover. But it is also a crucial part of any person's self-education. *Bon voyage.*

Further Reading

Some useful general introductions to the history of religions are:

TREVOR LING. *History of Religions: East and West.* New York: Harper and Row, 1970.

NINIAN SMART. *The Religious Experience of Mankind,* 2d. ed. New York: Charles Scribner's Sons, 1976.

R.C. ZAEHNER, ed. *The Concise Encyclopedia of Living Faiths.* Boston: Beacon Press, 1967.

Also helpful are the articles on religious and other philosophies in the *Encyclopedia Britannica,* Macropedia section; PAUL EDWARDS, ed., *The Encyclopedia of Philosophy* (New York: Macmillan, 1967); and JAMES HASTINGS, ed. *Encyclopedia of Religion and Ethics* (New York: Charles Scribner's Sons, 1961).

On the history of the field and some of the major contributions:

MICHAEL BANTON, ed. *Anthropological Approaches to the Study of Religion.* New York: Methuen, 1968.

RUDOLF BULTMANN. *Jesus Christ and Mythology.* New York: Charles Scribner's Sons, 1958.

MARY DOUGLAS. *Purity and Danger.* Boston: Routledge and Kegan Paul, 1978.

EMILE DURKHEIM. *The Elementary Forms of the Religious Life.* Winchester, Ma.: Allen Unwin, 1976.

MURRAY EDELMAN. *The Symbolic Uses of Politics.* Champaign: University of Illinois Press, 1967.

MIRCEA ELIADE. *The Quest.* Chicago: University of Chicago Press, 1975.

E. EVANS-PRITCHARD. *Theories of Primitive Religion.* New York: Oxford University Press, 1968.

SIGMUND FREUD. *The Future of an Illusion.* New York: Norton, 1976.

JOHN HICK. *The Philosophy of Religion.* Englewood Cliffs, N.J.: Prentice-Hall, 1973.

WILLIAM JAMES. *The Varieties of Religious Experience.* New York: Macmillian, 1961.

C.G. JUNG. *Symbols of Transformation,* 5 vols. Princeton, N.J.: Princeton University Press, 1976.

HANS KÜNG. *Does God Exist?* New York: Doubleday, 1980.

CLAUDE LÉVI-STRAUSS. *The Savage Mind.* Chicago: University of Chicago Press, 1966.

TREVOR LING. *Karl Marx and Religion.* Totowa, N.J.: Barnes and Noble Books, 1980.

W.J.M. MACKENZIE. *Political Identity.* New York: St. Martin's, 1978.

JOHN MACQUARRIE. *Twentieth Century Religious Thought,* Revised ed. New York: Charles Scribner's Sons, 1981.

DAVID MARTIN. *A General Theory of Secularization.* New York: Harper and Row, 1979.

ALBERT MOORE. *Introduction to Religious Iconography.* Philadelphia, Pa.: Fortress, 1977.

RUDOLF OTTO. *The Idea of the Holy.* New York: Oxford University Press, 1958.

JOHN PASSMORE. *A Hundred Years of Philosophy.* New York: Penguin, 1978.

DAVID ROBERTS. *Existentialism and Religious Belief.* New York: Oxford University Press, 1959.

ERIC J. SHARPE. *Comparative Religion—A History.* New York: Charles Scribner's Sons, 1975.

NINIAN SMART. *Philosophers and Religious Truth.* New York: Macmillan, 1970.

———. *Beyond Ideology: Religion and the Future of Western Civilization.* New York: Harper and Row, 1981.

WILFRED CANTWELL SMITH. *The Meaning and End of Religion.* New York: Harper and Row, 1978.

FRITS STAAL. *Exploring Mysticism*. Berkeley: University of California Press, 1975.

W.T. STACE. *Religion and the Modern Mind*. New York: Lippincott, 1960.

ERNST TROELTSCH. *The Absoluteness of Christianity and the History of Religions*. Atlanta, Ga.: John Knox, 1971.

VICTOR TURNER. *The Ritual Process*. Ithaca, N.Y.: Cornell University Press, 1977.

GERARDUS VAN DER LEEUW. *Religion in Essence and Manifestation*. Magnolia, Ma.: Peter Smith, 1967.

ARNOLD VAN GENNEP. *The Rites of Passage*. Chicago: University of Chicago Press, 1960.

JACQUES WAARDENBURG. *Classical Approaches to the Study of Religion*, vols. 1 and 2. Hawthorne, N.Y.: Mouton, 1974.

JOACHIM WACH. *The Comparative Study of Religions*. New York: Columbia University Press, 1958.

MAX WEBER. *The Protestant Ethic and the Spirit of Capitalism*. New York: Charles Scribner's Sons, 1977.

BRYAN WILSON. *Magic and the Millennium*. Brooklyn Heights, N.Y.: Beekman Publishers, 1978.

J. M. YINGER. *The Scientific Study of Religion*. New York: Macmillian, 1961.

INDEX

Index

188   Index